The Politics
of Victimization

The Politics
of Victimization

Victims, Victimology,
and Human Rights

ROBERT ELIAS
Tufts University

New York   Oxford
Oxford University Press
1986

Oxford University Press

Oxford   New York   Toronto
Delhi   Bombay   Calcutta   Madras   Karachi
Petaling Jaya   Singapore   Hong Kong   Tokyo
Nairobi   Dar es Salaam   Cape Town
Melbourne   Auckland

and associated companies in
Beirut   Berlin   Ibadan   Nicosia

Copyright © 1986 by Oxford University Press, Inc.

Published by Oxford University Press, Inc.
200 Madison Avenue, New York, New York 10016

Oxford is a registered trademark of Oxford University Press

Library of Congress Cataloging-in-Publication Data
Elias, Robert, 1950–
The politics of victimization.
Includes index.
1. Victims of crimes—United States
2. Criminal justice, Administration of—United States. I. Title.
HV6250.3.U5E44   1986   362.8'8'0973   85-21746
ISBN 0-19-503980-7
ISBN 0-19-503981-5 (pbk.)

2 4 6 8 9 7 5 3

Printed in the United States of America

To my son, André

*You were born, my son, just when I was about to blow your
planet up. It was only your arrival that saved me. At least,
it was you who stopped me from killing mankind in my heart.
You reconciled me to the human race and bound me irrevocably
to the history, the crimes and hopes, despairs and disasters
of all men (sic). I tremble for their fate . . . and for yours.*

EUGENE IONESCO, *Victims of Duty*

I have finally begun to see this.

*   *   *

To S.

*Who taught me a new sensitivity to violence and oppression,
and who gave me compassion and direction.*

*   *   *

And to the late Graham Wootton

Who inspired me, and who helped affirm the path I have taken.

Preface

Someone once warned me that to write properly about crime and victimization, one can hardly help examining the society generally. This has been undeniably true. By necessity, I have been unable to consider victimization as a disembodied slice of the American system. Understanding victims and victimization has required more than merely analyzing criminal justice, but rather much wider social, political, and economic relations. Ultimately, I argue that we cannot understand victims apart from the American political economy.

As its title suggests, this book analyzes victims politically, an approach pursued by design, yet unavoidable (to really understand victims) regardless of my intentions. Beginning there, this work has several purposes: First, its political analysis of victims and victimization fills an obvious gap in the victimology literature. Victimology provides a valuable interdisciplinary focus, yet while many sociologists, lawyers, psychologists, and other professionals have been well represented, few political scientists have worked in the field. Consequently, victims and victimization have received little political inquiry.

Second, the book provides an introductory overview of the study of crime victims and victimization; that is, a review of victimology. We have accumulated over forty years of victimological writing and research, most of it emerging in the last twenty years. It has appeared in journals, edited volumes, conference papers, and specialized empirical studies, yet we have done little to comprehensively examine the findings and integrate them into a single analysis. This book provides that synthesis and summary for teachers and researchers. It also acts as a supplementary, introductory textbook for courses on subjects such as victimology, criminology, and legal process, criminal justice, law enforcement, civil liberties, urban studies, political economy, public policy, and human rights. Students will acquire both an overview of the field, and a perspective that will likely challenge conventional beliefs. Ideally, the book will generate valuable discussion and debate, and be inspirational as well as educational.

Third, this book proposes a broader victimology that transcends officially defined *criminal* victimization. In particular, it traces the relationship between victimology and human rights, and advocates a "new" victimology of human rights, including victims of both crime and oppression. A society unconcerned with human rights violations, and their victims, can likewise provide little help for crime victims nor any significant reduction of criminal victimization since most crime arises in response to various forms of oppression.

This book derives from my previous work in victimology, criminal justice, and human rights. Working as a researcher with the Vera Institute of Justice's Victim/Witness Assistance Project in New York City several years ago, and then on a book about victim compensation, I began recognizing the political uses of victims, beyond the humanitarian rhetoric, and how victim initiatives very often reflect "symbolic" politics with little tangible improvement of victim rights or assistance. I have been particularly influenced here by non-Americans (not to be confused with un-Americans) with whom I have interacted in various settings. Also, from my human rights work at home and abroad, I began seeing the rights of crime victims as intimately connected to broader human rights concerns, rather than to the American law-and-order initiatives which seek to promote victim rights by restricting the rights of defendants and the general public. In examining victimology's origins, I discovered that as first conceptualized, it too stressed human rights, and not merely criminal victimization. This book strives to recapture those early conceptions.

Since I have been inspired by many people's work, and since this book overlaps at least political science, political economy, human rights, and criminal justice, as well as victimology, I have many people to thank. I do so gladly.

I owe an enormous intellectual debt to many people for their influential ideas: C. Wright Mills, Jeffrey Reiman, Philip Slater, Erich Fromm, Christian Bay, Theodore Roszak, Bertrand Russell, William Ryan, Frances Fox Piven, Richard Cloward, Richard Falk, John Berger, George Orwell, June Jordan, Sheila Rowbotham, Murray Edelman, Howard Zinn, Alan Wolfe, Noam Chomsky, Aldous Huxley, Edward Herman, Murray Bookchin, Albert Camus, Richard Sennett, Ralph Miliband, Hugo Bedau, Ira Shor, Charles Beitz, Chadwick Alger, Isaac Balbus, Frances Moore Lappe, Alice Walker, Joseph Collins, Paulo Freire, Bertram Gross, Barbara Ehrenreich, Milan Kundera, Pablo Neruda, Manning Marable, Cosmas Desmond, James Petras, Herbert Gans, Michael Harrington, Teresa Hayter, Laurie

Wiseberg, Herbert Marcuse, Barrington Moore, E. P. Thompson, George Lakey, Mark Gerzon, Robert Johansen, Laura Nader, Andre Gorz, Eric Hobsbawm, C. B. MacPherson, Alvin Gouldner, Stanley Aronowitz, Irving Louis Horowitz, Jacques Ellul, Harry Boyte, Herbert Schiller, Angela Davis, Brian Wren, Eric Olin Wright, Eduardo Galeano, Michael Klare, Gene Sharp, Malcolm Feeley, Michael Lipsky, Stuart Scheingold, and Jerold Auerbach.

In victimology and criminal justice in particular, I have been very influenced by Emilio Viano, Kurt Weis, Wesley Skogan, John Conklin, LeRoy Lamborn, Stanley Johnston, Jan van Dijk, Alan Harland, Joanna Shapland, David Miers, Lynn Curtis, Gary Marx, Gilbert Geis, James Brady, William Chambliss, Charles Silberman, David Friedrichs, Edwin Schur, Julia Schwendinger, Herman Schwendinger, David Greenberg, Elliott Currie, Barry Krisberg, Duncan Chappell, Stephen Schafer, Benjamin Mendelsohn, Ezzat Fattah, Stephen Spitzer, Richard Quinney, Nadine Taub, Shoshana Berman, Jacqueline Scherer, Tony Platt, Paul Takagi, and Nils Christie.

I also have been greatly affected by the work of Michael Parenti and Eduard Ziegenhagen. I particularly appreciate their pre-publication reviews of this book, and their helpful suggestions, many of which I have taken.

I have benefitted immeasurably from my work in the last several years with the Vera Institute of Justice in New York City, with the courts in Washington, Brooklyn, Newark and Boston, with crime victims in Brooklyn and Newark, with human rights groups in Boston and New York, with the Tufts University Center for European Studies in Talloires, France, with the International Institute of Human Rights in Strasbourg, and with human rights organizations in Geneva, where I wrote a portion of this book.

On a more personal level, I gratefully acknowledge two political scientists who have, unwittingly or not, provided me indelible (and I fear unreachable) models of scholarly work and achievement: James Eisenstein and the late Graham Wootton. I likewise appreciate the support given by many colleagues at Tufts University and the intellectual and moral stimulation provided by many of my undergraduate and graduate students. At Oxford University Press, my editor, Susan Rabiner, her assistant, Rachel Toor, and my copyeditor, Rosemary Wellner, have been very patient and helpful as well.

Most of all, I owe a great personal debt and much gratitude to several others for their support, inspiration, patience, and encouragement, given either directly or indirectly: Shyami de Silva, Maryanne Wolf, Barbara Wien, Paul Joseph, Daniel Poor, Rebecca Linsner, Bill Hoynes, Richard Tobin, Laurie Poore, Angelica Pinochet, and my family.

Looking back at all these influences, I wonder whether readers will see any of my own ideas. I am tempted to take full and exclusive credit only for any good ideas herein, but I assume that readers know better.

I complete this preface, considerably disheartened as the predictable results of the current American administration become all too readily apparent. I shudder thinking about the new victims it creates both at home and abroad, yet stand convinced that better days lie ahead. Like the writer Bruce Franklin, I console myself by looking "toward a future in which the victims become the force destined to destroy empires and build new nations."

Cambridge, Mass.   R. E.
January 1986

Contents

9. The Politics of Victimization / 229

The Politics
of Victimization

1

The Hidden Dimensions of Victimization: Victims, Victimology, and Human Rights

One of the first goals of any society is to make its inhabitants feel safe. More of our collective resources are devoted to national security and local safety than to any other need. Yet Americans feel far less safe, both at home and abroad, than they did fifty years ago. Our nuclear arsenal, the guns under pillows, and the multiple locks on city doors betray our fears without easing them.

PHILIP SLATER, *The Pursuit of Loneliness*

POLITICAL INQUIRIES

Americans are a frightened people. We anticipate victimization even more than we experience it, although much actual victimization does occur. We mostly fear being robbed, raped, or otherwise assaulted, or even killed. Yet, while these crimes have captured our imaginations, they comprise only part of the victimization we suffer. We face not only the danger of other crimes, but also countless other actions that we often have not defined or perceived as criminal, despite their undeniable harm. We may have a limited social reality of crime and victimization that excludes harms such as consumer fraud, pollution, unnecessary drugs and surgery, food additives, workplace hazards and diseases, police violence, censorship, discrimination, poverty, exploitation, and war. We suffer victimization not only by other individuals, but also by governments and other social institutions, not to mention the psychological victimization bred by our own insecurities.

Yet, for all our fears and suffering, we often understand victimization only very narrowly. We accept superficial explanations and solutions that perpetuate standard clichés and ignore the political roots of victimization. Instead, suppose we learned that historically many groups have been accepted as legitimate (i.e., acceptable) victims, and that such groups exist among us today? What if crime victims have been backed by interests that may care less about victims and more about other goals, and promote policies that may create more victims not fewer?

Suppose we discovered that how we define crime and victimization may have little to do with objective harms, causing us to overcriminalize lesser harms and undercriminalize, if not ignore, greater harms? What if we learned that law enforcement sought to maintain or manage crime, not to prevent or reduce it, or sought social control of certain population groups, not crime control? What if crime waves, media coverage, and official crime statistics had little to do with the real victimization level? What if we found our fears and insecurities about crime artificially manipulated for political purposes? Suppose we discovered that most people commit crime, not just certain groups? What if the real career criminals were corporate offenders, not common criminals? What if we found that victims have often been offenders before, and vice versa? What if we discovered that we were as likely to be victimized by a friend or relative as by a stranger? And suppose we learned that victims served important political and symbolic functions in criminal justice which better explain official concerns for victims than humanitarian impulses?

What if we knew the major sources of victimization, but claimed we had little knowledge and therefore refused to act? Suppose we discovered that the United States had the highest imprisonment rate in the world? What if we learned that victims often support anticrime policies that will not reduce crime, and may increase it? And what if we discovered that we blame much crime and victimization on victims themselves?

Suppose we found that those who most feared crime have the least chance of victimization? What if we learned that victimization increases as law enforcement spending increases, and that we bear the expense unequally? Suppose we discovered that those least able to bear crime's burden suffer the greatest victimization? What if we found that crime provides big business for people we consider legitimate entrepreneurs?

What if we learned that despite official calls for victim participation, judicial personnel rarely require substantive victim involvement, and usually consider it an intolerable burden on their work?

What if victims' most frequent involvement in law enforcement amounted to agreeing to dismiss their case? Suppose we found that court officials did not practice or seek an adversarial contest, but rather cooperated in producing rapid dispositions? In other words, what if we learned that the legal process was much more an administrative proceeding than a judicial one?

Suppose we discovered that defendant's rights received as little protection as victim rights and, in any case, had little to do with victim prospects in criminal justice? What if we discovered that victims suffer a second victimization in the criminal process? What if victims practically never attended trials because practically no trials ever occur, and suppose that at those few that do, victims found themselves on trial as much as the defendants? Suppose we found that officials regard crime and victimization as an attack on society, and not on individual victims? And what if we discovered that the best participation for victims in law enforcement may be no participation at all?

Suppose we discovered that some forms of victim advocacy had numerous ulterior motives, goals and functions that rendered tangible assistance either secondary or irrelevant? And, what if we learned that some forms of victim assistance, such as victim compensation, might make victims more dissatisfied with government and criminal justice than if no program had existed at all?

Finally, what if we learned that victim rights could be best pursued through human rights initiatives? What if we discovered that rights may depend more on political and economic power than on universal standards and formal constitutional protections? And suppose we found that crime and oppression have common sources, and that oppression may cause crime, and vice versa?

If we learned all these things, then we might seriously question our criminal justice system, and perhaps other institutions as well. Asking some serious political questions will be one of our primary objectives.

A POLITICAL ANALYSIS

This book examines victims, victimology, and human rights. It provides an introductory review of conventional victimology, which studies criminal victimization. Thus, it will stress the experience of crime victims, largely within the American context, but informed also by comparative perspectives. It will examine criminal victimization, its sources, its impact, and our official, public, and private responses. It tries to better understand crime and criminal justice, through the victim's perspective, which also provides a much starker and more poignant picture of crime and victimization.

We respond here to the crime victim's new resurgence during the last two decades, yet our analysis will differ significantly from standard victimological works. Much victimological literature pits the offender against the victim, emphasizes the criminal's supposed "paradise" of rights, protections and programs, and bemoans the victim's fate by comparison. Much other victimological writing does quite the opposite, emphasizing victim precipitation and implicating victims in their own victimization. Despite victims' rising (if ever so slowly) star, we still often regard the victim ambivalently, almost as if "victimization" implied "loser" in our strongly success-oriented society. If we do not actually implicate victims for their victimization, then we at least often scorn them for their bad luck.

We will examine the great amount we have learned about crime victims, but we will not blame victims, nor will we blame offenders. In fact, the greatest evidence may support the view that *both* are victims. In any case, we will argue for a victimological analysis that rejects stereotypes and questions conventional wisdom about crime, victimization, and criminal justice, and which analyzes victims in a broader, more political context.

We emphasize a political approach not merely because victimology, as an interdisciplinary science, has perhaps been overly dominated by legal, sociological, or psychological perspectives, and not a political one, although that is undoubtedly true. Rather, a political perspective represents not merely another approach, but one uniquely equipped to understand victims, victimization and even victimology in a much broader and perhaps more comprehensive context. A political approach may shed valuable new light on what we know about victims, and on what directions we should pursue in the future.

Some have suggested what political science might offer the study of criminal justice: It might help us measure the impact and consequences of government programs on serving their formal objectives. It might measure their impact on informal objectives, as well. And it might bare the competing mind sets of researchers and practitioners.[1] Yet this may represent only a very limited political science agenda, doomed to asking only very restricted questions, to accumulating only very limited knowledge, and to proposing few or no solutions for public problems. It may represent, in other words, an unnecessary, political science of helplessness and hopelessness.

Political science and political analysis can offer much more. They could, among other things, investigate the fundamental sources of laws and policies. They could investigate the relationship between political power and crime control. They could examine justice's impact on different groups, races, sexes, and classes. They could help discover victimization's sources. And they could create alternative policy and structural models to reduce victimization and strategies to achieve them.

The more one examines criminal justice, the more one discovers how it cannot be understood, either as micro or macro policy, outside a broader political analysis. In many ways, to study criminal justice is to study the broader society, and a political analysis will shed much light on that inquiry. Thus, we will analyze criminal justice politically, emphasizing political economy and organizational behavior as two important explanatory variables. By approaching criminal justice from the victim's perspective, we will also provide a politics of victimology, which attempts to develop, among other things, a political theory of victims and victimization.

While we will review the standard victimological literature, emphasizing a political perspective, we will also explore a "new" victimology that examines victims and victimization much more broadly than most researchers have thus far. We seek a more encompassing and imaginative victimology. As Emilio Viano has argued:

> It is important for victimologists not to repeat the same errors of atomized thinking, researching, and theorizing that have characterized quite a portion of criminological research, nor should they overlook the real causes of victimization, as criminology did with crime.[2]

Thus, we will try to dissolve the "mental prison"[3] that often characterizes how we think about victimization, and substitute a new, broader conception that considers not only common crime but also corporate and state crime, that examines not only individual criminals but also institutional wrongdoing, and that encompasses not merely traditional crime but all crimes against humanity. In sum, we will wed victimology to human rights.

A "new" victimology would, ironically, only return us back to our original conception of victimology, established over forty years ago. Back then, we defined victimology as the study of *all* victims, not merely *crime* victims. We should recapture that focus.

Our analysis will review the victimological literature, and use it to help pose controversial questions, frequently political ones, concerning our conventional wisdom about crime, criminals, victims, victimization, and criminal justice.

OVERVIEW

In the chapters ahead, we will consider the crime victim's evolving, historical role, as well as "cultural" victims, as found in our literature and social perceptions. We will analyze victimology's scientific and political development, and its scope, considered both within and beyond its relationship with criminology. We will examine the politics of how we define and convey popular conceptions of victimization, and consider the extensive victimological findings on the kinds of victimization, who victimizes, who suffers victimization, and where victimization occurs. We will contrast our "social reality" of crime and victimization with objective circumstances.

We will consider what we know about crime's sources, and what or who we usually blame, contrasting conventional explanations with controversial alternatives, stressing the political implications of each theory and their implications for victims. We will examine who suffers financially, physically, and psychologically from victimization, and who may profit. We will examine victim motives for participating in the criminal process, and the victim's impact throughout the system, emphasizing the clash of victim goals and official objectives. We will also assess law enforcement's impact on victims, and examine the special case of female sexual assault victims.

We will summarize victim needs and problems, examine the various approaches to victim assistance, assess their impact, and note their other functions beyond serving victims. We will also consider victims of oppression, examining the evolution of human rights, the social reality, sources and impact of oppression, and human rights enforcement and advocacy as they relate to victimology.

Finally, we will review the major implications of our political analysis and end by exploring a prospective, politically sensitive, "new" victimology of human rights.

2

Rising Stars: Victims and Victimology

History is just one damn thing after another.

HENRY MILLER

We must understand our newfound concern for the victim in its historical context. While we have recently isolated crime victims for special attention, we have really only rejuvenated their much more prominent past from a relatively long dormancy. Understanding victims' evolution will help us evaluate their contemporary role, their cultural significance, and how it shapes our perceptions and attitudes toward victims today.

We cannot fully understand the victim's recent reemergence without also examining the scientific field that helped pave its way. We must also examine victimology's scope, to reveal its methods, approaches, and perspectives. And we will consider how public policy has shaped victimological perspectives, and vice versa.

The developments we trace here reveal how the public, the state, and a discipline have treated victims, which may show the victim's future role or suggest new directions beyond our past efforts, for significantly improving the victim's lot. We may best do this by considering crime victims within a broader human rights context. By applying human rights standards both to states and to victimology, we can elevate victims and their rights to their next stage of development.

THE EVOLVING VICTIM

Early History

The crime victim's role has changed dramatically since primitive times.[1] Prior to social organization, people merely took the law into their own hands and avenged their victimization unconstrained by outside interferences.[2] Victims extracted personal reparation if they had the strength. Victim retaliation served as the earliest form of social control,[3] albeit an unorganized one.

With increasing social differentiation, social groupings began to emerge as clans or tribes[4] and responding to victimization became a collective responsibility.[5] Rather than a completely disorganized system of personal revenge, reparations began to center around kinship groups. Within clans, damages were allocated among family members. Between clans, a victimization might begin a "blood feud" of endless attack and retaliation where any member of each clan became fair game for the other. Entire clans became "victim surrogates."[6] Vendettas characterized personal disputes, and mass vendettas sometimes became genocide.[7]

Besides retaliation, clans might launch "pre-emptive raids," thus victimizing to prevent their own victimization.[8] Disputes violated "tribal international law," requiring the balance of power to be regularly restored.[9] Although violence often characterized these disputes, exchanges or even sorcery might be used instead. "Voodoo spells" against offenders were often taken quite seriously, forcing assailants to settle disputes to break the spell. Some victims even resorted to a highly ritualized suicide to convince their clans they had been wronged.[10]

Gradually, alternatives to perpetual retribution arose, largely to reduce violence and feuding. When surplus wealth emerged, offenders began offering it to victims to repair offenses. Soon, this became more formalized and began involving third parties, as, for example, with the Code of Hammurabi which required restitution for wrongs done. Although victims retained their prominent role under this system, notions of deterrence already began competing with victim interests.[11]

Many societies and civilizations used restitution to settle disputes and repair victimizations, including the "death fine" of the Greeks, the early Hebrews, the Indian Hindus, and the Turkish Empire. Restitution also appeared in the law of Moses and in the Roman Law of the Twelve Tables.[12] Restitution first came as property, yet it increasingly changed to money payments as the bartering system began to decline.[13] Monetary reparations were based primarily on the crime, the class position of the victim and offender, and the solidarity of kinship groups. Soon, monetary values were attached to all offenses.

By the Middle Ages, resolving offenses by compensation had become formalized and further developed into the "composition" procedure.[14] In Germany, for example, both punishment and compensation were imposed on offenders, as third-party mediators played an increasing role. Disputes between victims and offenders changed into "judicial duels."[15] Before this, disputes were neither defined nor perceived as "crimes," but rather as torts, even when violent. A retreat from collective responsibility toward individual responsibility began as far back as classical Greece and Rome.[16] Coupled with the emerging state and church, "crime" (or "sin") became an attack on society, not merely on separate victims, and offenders became individually accountable for their actions.[17] If they did not repay, they became outlaws, either ostracized from their communities or subject to physical retribution, including murder.[18]

Medieval revenge sought to protect threatened social interests and ideals, increasingly defined as commerce.[19] State power was used to promote dominant interests. Upper classes began using the law both to control lower classes and to avenge their wrongs, yet disadvantaged people could not do the same. If lower classes received any compensation, it was devalued proportional to the victim's status. Later, the rise of monarchs further bolstered the state's role in "criminal justice." Kings, anxious to replenish depleted coffers or merely to gain new revenue, began taking part of the victim's compensation as a fine. By the mid-thirteenth century, for example, English kings were receiving about one-sixth of their income from the criminal process.[20] The fine gradually gained importance equal to restitution, and finally replaced it altogether.[21] While state control theoretically represented all public interests, in practice it was dominated by only a few.[22]

Eventually, we viewed crime as an offense against the state, not the victim. The previously united civil/criminal procedure split into two parts, allowing victims to bring actions against their offenders only in civil proceedings.[23] Except for the "adhesive" procedure, used selectively during the sixteenth and seventeenth centuries to allow victims to pursue restitution at criminal trial,[24] victims had substantially lost their criminal justice role by the end of the Middle Ages.

American Role

In some systems, the victim role survived longer than in others. In the American colonial period, for example, the victim made key decisions and received direct benefits. Victims either acted as police and prosecutors themselves or paid others to do so. The victim or a watchman might make an arrest, or victims might pay sheriffs or private individuals to apprehend the offender. Victims would pay the justice of the peace for a warrant, would investigate the case themselves, and would pay informers and a private attorney to prosecute the case. Colonial law allowed victims to collect multiple damages from offenders, and even authorized offenders to be bound into servitude. Wealthier victims could pay the state to incarcerate criminals.[25]

This non-state approach avoided the government tyranny some colonists feared along with the costs of maintaining a law enforcement system. Yet, as community responsibility and control began declining, new laws and a greater state role emerged. Laws created bounties for finding offenders, and then rewards for convictions, which lead to a prosperous "information" trade. As in earlier societies, crime control became more and more a governmental activity, and restitution was abandoned by the early 1800s.[26]

Meanwhile, Europe had, for several centuries, relied not only on state fines, but on increasingly barbaric ordeals or punishments against offenders. By the nineteenth century, criminal justice systems had become a part of the "social contract" designed to promote social order, and punishment was calculated by the harm done to society, not to private victims.[27] These developments significantly influenced early America. Yet, by the mid-1800s, American reformers had successfully protested torture as a punishment, and substituted a more "humane," penitentiary system for deterrence and reform. Although this apparently humanitarian impulse soon gave way to equally punitive and torturous prisons, the penitentiary system had further limited the victim's access to redress. While some suggested that prisoners earn restitution money in prison, low wages and business opposition effectively blocked this alternative.[28]

After the American Revolution, the criminal law was used to maintain order against any organized opposition, and especially to protect property.[29] As state power increased, the victim role declined, not only because victims could no longer expect benefits from their participation, but because involvement now would likely impose new costs. The private prosecutor declined as the state's interest in punishments and fines increased. Victims were barred from bringing criminal fraud prosecutions and relegated to civil proceedings. The decline in community responsibility and the increasing corruption of private police helped develop an institutionalized, public police force, which further limited the victim's role, particularly when police became immune from suits for false arrest while victims were still liable for improper civilian arrests. The police have increasingly viewed their role as protecting society, not individual victims, which may sometimes cause victims to take the law into their own hands.[30] Sporadic efforts arose throughout the nineteenth century to revive the concept of offender reparation. In 1847, Bonneville de Marsangy outlined a plan of reparation in France, as did criminology conferences in 1878 in Stockholm, 1885 in Rome, 1890 in St. Petersburg, 1891 in Christiana, 1895 in Paris, and 1900 in Brussels.[31] These proposals made no headway, however, and restitution was ignored for another half century thereafter.[32]

By the modern era, victims had lost virtually their entire role in criminal justice. From the time when they completely controlled such conflicts, their role diminished as third-party intermediaries, and especially when the state emerged, until finally offenders lost all responsibility to victims, and victims lost most of their usefulness to officials. The victim was ignored because crime became a social offense, and by the twentieth century the offender's motivation (including any possible victim participation) became irrelevant. Definitions of crime and responsibility emerged to protect a given social order, its conditions, values and interests, and thus state control relied on excluding the victim.[33]

Yet, doing so did not necessarily enhance actual social control. The individualized focus on offenders ignored both the impact of victim-offender relationships and the effects of social ills on producing crime.[34] The steadily expanding criminal law did not completely impose social control or reduce crime. And its expansion has helped undercut the social control functions of less formal mechanisms, such as communities and victims themselves.[35] Regaining the victim role in criminal justice may benefit not only victims, but also help restore our declining social balance.

THE CULTURAL VICTIM

Part of contemporary crime victims' tenuous status may come from their cultural role, which has evolved and been inculcated historically, beginning undoubtedly with victims' connection to sacrifice and religious rituals.[36] As the religious example suggests, victimizations may not always be deplored; they may fulfill certain functions. Thus, we should not expect that victims will be universally pitied, or even recognized as victims.

In the modern era, we have good examples of our ambivalence toward victims, which may help explain their long exclusion, and their difficult road back into importance. We must examine the cultural sources of that ambivalence. For now, we can consider the victim's relationship to literature, social perceptions, and social functions.

Literature

> *Western man in the last century has suffered the loss of that luxurious illusion of personal control over his own affairs, and has instead become the victim of the very complexity that has defined his recent achievements over matter.*   PAUL BRUSS, *Victims*

Literature can help us see how victims can transcend their victimization by affirming their individuality and importance. Yet in much literature, victims figure very prominently, but often unsympathetically. While Chaucer stressed the hapless victim of fortune as "naive," more modern writing portrays victims as "losers."[37] In a literature significantly divorced from any diety, the victimization becomes increasingly meaningless and irrational. While some victims, such as those in Bertold Brecht's plays,[38] understand their victimization and resist, others, like the characters of Eugene Ionesco, William Faulkner, and Franz Kafka, find it absurd.[39] Some writers, like Albert Camus,[40] have portrayed people who suffer from this sense of absurdity or hopelessness, as victims of nihilism.[41] As Saul Bellow tells us, literature "pits any ordinary individual against the external world and the external world conquers him, of course."[42] In Bellow's novel, *The Victim*, for example, the average, respectable protagonist becomes a victim of circumstance and of his fellow humans; he confronts crisis and watches his world and himself deteriorate.[43] Modern literature portrays victims, but less to sympathize with them and more to force us to reevaluate our world. For example, authors such as Ralph Ellison, F. Scott Fitzgerald, Arthur Miller, Allen Ginsberg, and Richard Brautigan present characters as the victims of the American dream.[44]

When victims suffer directly from individual attackers, instead of from broader social forces, they fare little better in our literature. As in Fyodor Dostoyevsky's *Crime and Punishment*,[45] these works orient us much more strongly toward offenders, sometimes sympathetically.[46] Truman Capote's *In Cold Blood*, the story of a Kansas family's brutal murder, directs the reader toward the criminals as victims since it carefully distances us from the family, and we learn little things about the family that further alienate us.[47] This effect is no accident. As Capote has said:

> It's what I really think about America. Desperate, savage, violent America in collision with sane, safe, insular, even smug America—people who have every chance against people who have none.[48]

Other literature finds the victimization's sources in social conditions, thus rendering offenders less culpable. While this view bears some considerable truth, such treatment still deemphasizes its effects on victims. In Anthony Burgess' *A Clockwork Orange*,[49] for example, young delinquents terrorize the persons and property of haphazardly chosen victims, and yet we see Alex, the ringleader, as a victim of the modern age.[50] In *The Executioner's Song*, Norman Mailer portrays Gary Gilmore, the multiple murderer who helped restore the American death penalty, as the product of a sick society.[51]

Sometimes literature not only identifies with offenders and deemphasizes victims, it also blames victims for their own victimization. As the title of Franz Werfel's novel *The Murdered One Is Guilty* suggests,[52] some writing portrays the victim as precipitating crime. Even literature that focuses almost entirely on the victim can leave a negative effect. In *Looking for Mr. Goodbar*, Judith Rossner constantly undermines our feelings for the female victim raped and murdered after being "picked up" at a single's bar.[53] We learn early about her inevitable attack and, as we follow her from bar to bar toward this end, we begin to believe she has asked for her fate, that she wants to be a victim. "Even her murderer must be, we are persuaded, a victim of her barely suppressed need for extinction."[54]

Other crime literature, including that portrayed on television, similarly downplays the victim. Typically, "cops and robbers" stories emphasize precisely those actors, with law-enforcement officials inevitably winning the day. These images undoubtedly dominate our culture, even more than the "criminal as hero" theme. When victims receive attention in literature outside the "blaming the victim" theme, the other extreme often emerges. In Gary Kinder's *Victim*, for example, the imbalance tilts overwhelmingly toward the victims of a brutal crime whose perpetrators have been imprisoned, but who "still remain alive."[55] The book ignores the social sources of violence and appeals to the public's bloodthirstiness for revenge. As a recent work, it may be the unfortunate symbol of the crime victim's new reemergence.

In sum, contemporary literature conveys several themes about crime and victimization. While some have captured public attention and official interest more than others, only recently have more (if not excessively) sympathetic treatments of victims emerged. We can gauge the victim in relation to social perceptions and functions even more specifically than through literature. Examining people's attitudes toward victims and their responsibility, through surveys and experimental situations, helps us identify specific cultural beliefs and recognize their political and behavioral impact.

Social Perceptions and Functions

Several themes emerge from public, and even official, attitudes. Many beliefs stereotype particular victims, while others help observers evaluate and assess victim behavior. We tend to assess victimizations strongly by whether the victim has sufficiently, if not vigorously, resisted the crime, for example.[56] This seems to reflect our strong cultural attachment to "rugged individualism." We tend to much more strongly accept victimization the less we have to see it or its effects,[57] or the more it involves people in personal relationships. Here, our cultural preference for privacy emerges. We have traditionally tolerated abuse in relationships or in isolated locales such as the home, reasoning that they represent private domains, and that a man is the "king of his castle."[58]

Many cultural attitudes about victims attach to specific groups, such as women. Often they perpetuate myths that help justify the victimization; sometimes they can provide some advantage. In rape cases, for example, a beautiful female victim will often win our sympathies more easily than others.[59] On the other hand, we often blame female victims for being revengeful, emotional, provocative, and promiscuous.[60] We frequently believe that spiteful women cannot be trusted. Emotional women cannot really remember what happened during the incident. Women who claim they have been sexually assaulted have probably invited it, or desired it. Our "puritan" values hold women to amazingly spartan standards, yet we believe that women all secretly long to be promiscuous. By and large, although we show some ambivalence, our reaction (or inaction) to female victimization, especially to sexual assault and family violence, suggests that women represent "culturally legitimate" victims,[61] along with several other groups.

Our tendency to blame victims for their fate comes from several cultural attitudes. American culture, and also our political philosophy, tend to posit a "just world" view of life.[62] We conclude that even if victims do not precipitate their crime, they nevertheless must deserve their fate because good people manage to escape harms and live the good life. This attitude emerges not only from lingering religious teachings, but also from our strong attachment to the tenets of "social Darwinism." If people get victimized, it only shows their unfitness. As a result, many totally innocent victims tend to blame themselves for their fate.[63] Although we have softened our rhetoric, we seem to practice an only slightly more subtle social Darwinism today, which may be why we react to victims so inadequately. The oft-repeated view that America is the most difficult nation in which to be poor (as one kind of victimization)[64] exemplifies this cultural attitude.

Taken together, these cultural beliefs affect not only public, but also official and offender attitudes. Offenders sometimes legitimize their crimes by characterizing their victims as deserving.[65] They need not look far for cultural support: they can choose from many ready-made indicators of victim blame. Many cultural beliefs surface in the language and discourse of both offenders and officials. The language that offenders select to describe the incident and the victim can often excuse the offense.[66] Likewise, officials such as police officers attach social labels to victims through language that often implicitly attributes blame or responsibility.[67] We will later examine the mechanisms, such as the media, that help transmit these cultural beliefs, and that thereby shape our social reality of victimization.

While some cultural attitudes toward victims may be universal, many seem to arise particularly from certain societies. For example, in comparative studies of reactions to rape victims in the United States and West Germany, American men were much more inclined to blame women for their fate.[68] America, in particular, seems to have comparatively harsh attitudes toward all but officially useful victims.

Finally, we can begin suggesting the social functions of our cultural attitudes toward victims. These beliefs not only reflect our political ideology of rugged individualism and the survival of the fittest, they seem to substantially enhance it. They more than simply identify our cultural traits. Instead, they may inculcate a particular ideology about how the world must work, which may legitimate, justify, and solidify existing social relations and structures. They tell us which victims will receive official recognition, and which among them will be treated as truly blameless. The "cultural victim" tells us more than merely how we regard victims generally. It reveals American political theory; that is, the ideology of liberal capitalism.[69]

AN EMERGING VICTIMOLOGY

Scientific Developments

While crime victims entered this century with virtually no formal law enforcement role, some new support for victims emerged from the professional and scholarly community as early as the late 1930s. A considerable boon to the victim's revival by mid-century came from the development of "victimology," or the science of studying victims.[70]

We can trace victimology as far back as 1937, when Beniamin Mendelsohn began gathering information about victims for his law practice.[71] He did further research on victims, including a rape study in 1940. Mendelsohn not only coined the term "victimology," but also several related concepts such as "victimity" to suggest the converse of criminality.

This work received its first big boost from the post-World War II humanitarianism that emerged in the late 1940s.[72] By forming organizations such as the United Nations, many dreamed of a world free from war, violence, ignorance, poverty, and disease. The international community began creating covenants that would protect and advance people's rights and shield them from victimization. These impulses helped stimulate victimology's development. They helped establish the international exchange of ideas and information that has always characterized the field. Mendolsohn and others formulated a broad-based victimology that considered not merely crime victims, but all victims.[73] It encompassed victims produced by politics, by technology, by accidents, as well as by crime. Yet the struggle to maintain this broader perspective (beyond crime victims) has been a difficult one.

In 1948, Hans von Hentig provided the first landmark victimological study: *The Criminal and His Victim.*[74] This was soon followed by Henri Ellenberger's "Relations psychologiques entre le criminel et sa victime."[75] Beyond other more superficial treatments, von Hentig and Ellenberger went to the heart of the "victimal" experience. Yet both restricted their studies to "crime" victims, and emphasized the victim-offender relationship, thus not only constricting the field but, ironically, also providing early evidence that might as easily blame victims as support them.

The field's focus on criminal victimization and victim precipitation intensified through the 1950s. Following von Hentig's and Ellenberger's lead, various "victim typologies" emerged to describe the kinds of people victimized and their relationship to offenders. In 1957, Margery Fry detailed the victim's suffering and proposed a new victim compensation program.[76] In 1958, Marvin Wolfgang finished a large homicide study, which included extensive information on victims and how they may have contributed to their victimization.[77] That same year, major breakthroughs and papers appeared in the Netherlands, France, Japan, and Argentina.[78] In 1959, the *Journal of Public Law*[79] ran the first of several symposia and special issues on victimology that would appear in various journals during the next twenty-five years.[80]

In 1963, New Zealand created the first compensation scheme, followed by programs in Great Britain and California the following year. Within a few years, a great many plans emerged in the American states and around the world. In 1966, the first American national victimization survey was conducted. In 1968, Stephen Schafer published the second landmark victimological study, merely reversing von Hentig's title: *The Victim and His Criminal,*[81] and LeRoy Lamborn published his lengthy, groundbreaking article, "Toward a Victim Orientation in Criminological Theory."[82] In 1972, Minnesota created one of the first, formal restitution programs to allow offenders to repay their victims. Several more would follow in the next decade.

In 1973, Israel Drapkin organized the first of many international conferences on victimology in Jerusalem.[83] Subsequent meetings would be organized by Edith Flynn in Boston in 1976,[84] by Hans Schneider in Muenster in 1979,[85] by Koichi Miyazawa in Tokyo in 1982, by Ezzat Fattah in Vancouver in 1983,[86] by Paul Separovic in Zagreb in 1984 and 1985,[87] and by Emilio Viano in Bellagio in 1975[88] and 1982,[89] in Washington in 1980,[90] in Siracusa in 1982,[91] and Lisbon in 1984.[92] In the early 1970s, Koichi Miyazawa founded the first Institute for Victimology in Tokyo,[92] and the first American victim/witness assistance programs emerged. In 1975, the National Organization of Victim Assistance was formed.[93]

In 1976, Emilio Viano founded *Victimology: An International Journal* in Washington, and became its editor. In 1977, Eduard Ziegenhagen published the third landmark, general study of victims, *Victims, Crime and Social Control.*[93] In 1979, the World Society of Victimology was created under Hans Schneider's direction in Muenster. In 1981, the National Victims Organization was founded. In 1984, Andrew Karmen published the first general victimology textbook: *Crime Victims,*[95] and members of the World Society of Victimology met to push the United Nations to create an international covenant to protect crime victims.

Political Developments

While victimology progressed professionally and academically, and while it helped promote victim interests scientifically, the victim's status reflected various political developments as well. Unfortunately, the post-World War II euphoria about human progress lost considerable momentum because of the Cold War and the Korean War.[96] International concerns about promoting rights proceeded only very slowly during the 1950s, and victimology, with its increasingly "criminal" preoccupation, made only slow strides until the 1960s. Although the civil rights and anti-war movements in the United States, and comparable movements elsewhere, helped promote a climate for considering victims generally, not until compensation programs arose in the late 1960s did crime victims really begin to emerge.[97] We can speculate about the deeper political origins.

In the late 1960s, many conservatives (followed by public opinion) strongly rejected the recent Warren Court decisions promoting defendant's rights. This backlash against what some people viewed as "handcuffing the police" helped promote a new concern for the other party in the criminal process: the victim. A law-and-order, "get tough" stance on criminals emerged as a major plank of the Nixon campaign in 1968. Simultaneously, with escalating crime and increasing demonstrations and disruptions in the nation's cities, politicians began to doubt whether the country would weather the storm.[98] Some felt our police forces were relatively unprepared to deal with major protest movements.[99] Finally, many became disenchanted (despite our minimal efforts) with rehabilitation as a correctional goal.[100]

Some believe that officials reacted by looking for better social control mechanisms. A few advocated restitution to rehabilitate both offenders and victims. But most others responded in two other directions. One was to significantly liberalize welfare eligibility and benefits to appease rising demands.[101] The other was to significantly intensify police forces and law enforcement, beginning in 1969 with the huge funding programs of the Law Enforcement Assistance Administration of the U.S. Department of Justice. A concern for victims, and the rise of compensation programs, were part of these responses. Serving as typically both welfare and criminal justice programs, compensation plans provided a new technique for social control.[102]

While victimology may have escaped its ideological clutches,[103] the victim's rise seems most related to a new conservative surge in American politics, which increased in the early 1970s, receded briefly, and then reemerged with new force in 1980.[104] Yet, despite the conservative, national politics of the early 1970s, local, grassroots movements continued to develop.[105] One of those, which gained national prominence during the Equal Rights Amendment debates of the Carter years, was the women's movement. Aside from the conservative, law-and-order movement of the 1970s, the women's movement has undoubtedly provided victims the most gains, at least for female victims.[106] Other movements may have contributed as well, including those for children, consumers, homosexuals, and the elderly.[107] Even the civil rights movement, often associated with defendant's rights, helped victims by promoting police professionalism, equal protection of the laws, and some inroads into checking victimization's sources.[108]

By 1978, the Carter Administration, while paying no particular attention to crime victims, helped revitalize a global human rights movement that had faded from prominence since the early 1950s. This new international concern for victims may have stimulated victimology toward a new focus. The victimologist Stanley Johnston, for example, had been arguing at least since 1973 for a "supra-national criminology," and began connecting victimology to human rights thereafter.[109] And in 1979, the World Society of Victimology emerged with some new international concerns that would later culminate in accepting Mendelsohn's broad definition of victimology,[110] and with efforts to seek an international covenant on crime victims at the United Nations.[111]

The current Reagan Administration has also made a strong pitch to capture the victim issue. It created the President's Task Force on Victims of Crime in 1982, and backed the 1982 Omnibus Victims of Crime Act and 1984 Crime Victim Assistance Act. It ignores human rights victims (at least in the American sphere), instead championing crime victims with a new dose of conservative, law-and-order rhetoric.[112] Victimology's ideological and scientific future may depend on whether it responds to conservative, parochial interests or progressive, international forces.

THE SCOPE OF VICTIMOLOGY

Methods and Directions

Victimology provides much more than merely a random collection of victim studies. It has sought to build a scientific discipline[113] by substantially defining and framing the aspect of society it wishes to study, by devising a set of specific questions, and some guiding theories and by developing scientific methodologies for collecting information. We should examine these developments as well as victimology's current shortcomings.

CONTRIBUTIONS. Although victimology began by studying all victims, most of its output and history has stressed crime victims. Thus, it has mostly defined itself scientifically as the study of *crime* victims. Despite those boundaries, it has still considered many issues that criminology has traditionally ignored.

Victimology has contributed victim typologies that describe victims and their relative risks, their culpability, and their relationship with offenders. It has identified our relative vulnerability to crime, the ways victims may precipitate their victimization, and the victim-offender dynamic. Victimology has helped us view the criminal episode through the victim's perspective. By promoting victimization surveys, it has helped reveal the actual victimization level, explain non-reporting, and clarify the "dark figure" of crime existing between official statistics and victim experiences.

Victimology has allowed us to consider crime's impact on victims, including its costs and its effects on our fears and attitudes. It has allowed us to understand the victim's role in law enforcement and its impact. It has focused on kinds of crime we had previously ignored, such as sexual assault and family violence. It has explored new victim services and assistance and methods of preventing victimization. It has helped inject some sense of community into how we react to the crime problem.[114] And it has promoted international comparisons and exchanges of victimological information.

Victimology has provided groundbreaking new concepts, such as the victim's functional responsibility for victimization,[115] the victim's role in social control,[116] the notion of conflicts (between victims and offenders) as "property" (which courts should not take from victims),[117] the offender's "self-legitimation" of victim attacks,[118] and the "culturally legitimate" victim.[119] The discipline has taken us beyond criminology's individualized focus on offenders to a more universalistic orientation to victimization.[120] It has allowed us to transcend the "victorology" criminology has largely practiced, which has shown a greater interest in the winners than in the losers of criminal activity, stressed the criminal as an individual, mobilized public and police forces to fight criminals rather than crime, and lost sight of victims and of sociological findings about the social conditions from which crime arises.[121]

In sum, victimology has provided new methods for understanding not only victims (who had long been ignored), but also crime generally. It has allowed us to view crime as a totality, and to fill criminology's many gaps. Beyond its scientific achievements, it has also made a normative contribution. From being a victimology of the "act" (of crime), it has increasingly become a victimology of "action,"[122] which promotes, and not merely studies, victims. Aside from being at the forefront of developing new victim services and assistance, it has helped spearhead a new political movement for victims.

DRAWBACKS. Despite these accomplishments, victimology has been variously faulted: Methodologically, it has gathered data from very varied sources. Information culled from official statistics, victimization and self-report surveys, case studies, archives, experimental and quasi-experimental studies, anecdotal reports, and participant observation has vastly enriched our victimological data.[123] Yet, while some claim that we have not collected enough data,[124] the more frequent (and truer) complaint suggests that our data far outstrip our theories. Our excessive empiricism without theoretical foundations has brought a flood of data with which we often can make little sense.[125] We often find ourselves only repeating criminological inquiries, this time on victims.[126]

Some suggest that we must break the shackles of criminological methodology by devising new theories and by applying an open systems approach to our inquiries.[127] Others question the research methods used for certain kinds of victimization, such as rape.[128] Some regard "victim precipitation" as an exaggerated and contradictory concept[129] that favors the offender's perspective no less than criminology.[130] Others suggest that by emphasizing victim culpability, we blame victims, and particularly groups such as sexual assault victims, thereby helping transform rape into a victimless crime.[131]

A much deeper critique of victimology challenges its scientific boundaries. It suggests that victimology has unnecessarily constrained itself within traditional criminology's boundaries, adopting its same, conservative mentality.[132] We will examine the major arguments for remaining within criminology, and then those for a broader vision.

Victimology in Criminology

Most victimological research either implicitly or explicitly accepts a role within criminology,[133] partly because most victimologists began in criminology, which still provides a convenient framework. Others have remained for some more conscious and specific reasons. For example, some have apparently rejected a broader victimology for ideological reasons. One writer suggests that having victimology embrace the broader scope of "critical" or "radical" criminology would negate its concerns for victims, yet this ignores critical criminology's emphasis both on social victims *and* crime victims.[134]

Likewise, some writers have so strongly embraced conservative, hardline criminal justice policies that a broader victimology would be a contradiction in terms.[135] Ironically, on the opposite end of the ideological spectrum, Soviet researchers, perhaps fearing their accountability under a broader victimological definition, have also pursued their victimology well within criminology.[137] While we American researchers often avoid a broader victimology because we deny our "class struggle," Soviet researchers avoid a broader victimology because they claim their "class struggle" has ended.

Finally, several writers have suggested that victimology fills important gaps, which now allows criminology to finally establish itself as a science,[137] and, without it, criminology would lose half its subject matter: victims.[138] That is, victimology has not only brought victims into criminology, it has also exposed the victim-offender relationship without which criminology could not claim to be a complete science.[139] Others fear that once expanded beyond criminal definitions, we would have no firm boundaries, or would define everyone and everything as victims.[140]

Victimology Beyond Criminology

> [We should avoid being] the intellectual who can make the most
> atrocious act of murder seem natural and just, while arguing that a
> spontaneous act of self-defense is violence demanding the most severe
> punishment, the bland advocate whose hands remain spotlessly white
> while he sanctions the killing of the most innocent among the
> oppressed.   H. BRUCE FRANKLIN, *The Victim as Criminal and Artist*

While the overwhelming victimological consensus accepts its criminological boundaries, various writers have argued or implied that we must move beyond criminology.[141] Hans Schneider, for example, has recently supported Beniamin Mendelsohn's broader, pioneering definition of victimology on the World Society of Victimology's behalf.[142] Beginning with Mendelsohn's vision, let's explore victimology's possible new directions.

Mendelsohn began by defining "victimity" as the whole of the socio-bio-psychological traits common to all victims, which society wishes to prevent and fight, no matter what their determinants are.[143] He argued that we must consider how victimization relates to living conditions and a society's overall needs. We must examine not merely victimization's immediate causes, but its underlying roots as well. We should consider how the social structure may be criminogenic. Victimology should be an autonomous science that deals with all victims, and with all sources and kinds of victimization. Finally, victimology should respond to the "danger complex":

> In advanced countries people live in a consuming society where the amount and quality of goods are constantly increasing. These same goods, if used wrongly, produce victims such as the dead, the wounded, invalids, victims of professional diseases, of environmental pollution, of malnutrition, and of genocide, etc. All this is a threat to the very existence of humanity. Thus, we have arrived at the heart of the problems to be solved by victimology.[144]

Others have recently echoed these or similar themes. Some say that we must question the official definitions that victimology seems so ready to accept.[145] Another suggests that we attribute some victimization to entire systems.[146] Some complain that victimologists have preferred the most common, least controversial, most easily applicable definitions of victims. Instead, we must broaden our definitions, and enter on-going debates about victims of consumer fraud, pollution, poverty, malnutrition, inequality, racism, sexism and ageism, mental health, and legal injustices.[147]

Feminist victimologists have invoked international human rights standards in examining female victims, such as victims of sexual slavery.[148] Others argue that we must study victimization caused by the state and its power structure, looking not merely at individuals, but at relationships of power and oppression, and considering victimization such as genocide, displacement, persecution, colonialism, psychological labelling and conditioning, repression, and discrimination.[149] Another proposes a wider victimology of "social vulnerability" guided by its traditional quest for justice.[150]

Some suggest that we relate victimization to class conflict, modes of production, and dominant interests, and seek social, not official, definitions of victimization.[151] Others argue that certain cultures, such as the capitalist culture, may impose a structure of victimization.[152] By promoting an applied victimological research, we might practice a "victimology of action" that opens new frontiers.[153] We could emphasize victims of "criminal events" that transcend strictly official definitions of crime.[154] Just as the "new" criminology has overcome traditional boundaries,[155] a "new" victimology could raise victim consciousness and pursue new, social justice concerns.[156]

Some writers believe that a broader victimology can overcome individualized approaches and thereby help examine victimization's social sources.[157] Others see traditional criminology's emphasis on the state as victim as diverting attention not only from individual victims, but from the victimization the state itself produces.[158] Some view victimization broadly as an "enforcement mechanism for an achievement society," and thus seek a victimology that encompasses the victimization such societies generate.[159] Victimology could become the science not only of *studying* victims, but also of *reducing* victims.[160]

A global victimology could help institutionalize an international criminal law and crime rate.[161] It could consider governments as well as individuals as victimizers, and examine broader categories of victims, such as those victimized by repression, alienation, or the Cold War. Some suggest, for example, that we recognize how nationalism, abetted (if not "precipitated") by blind patriotism, causes victimization. Failing to oppose government victimization might be considered part of victims' "functional responsibility" for their own victimization.[162]

The 1980 Caracas Declaration of the United Nations, the International Association of Penal Law, and the Commission on International Criminal Law of the International Law Association have proposed international criminal law mechanisms that show new concern for victims, and that examine crime within broader social contexts and structures. The 1984 Draft Resolution on Victims of Crime and Abuses of Power of the Seventh United Nations Congress on Crime Prevention and the Treatment of Offenders stresses the victimological effects of international crimes, defined by human rights standards beyond narrow, national crime definitions.[163] Other signs of a more global approach have emerged from those who seek United Nations protections for victim rights,[164] and who see victimology as ultimately pursuing human rights.[165]

CONCLUSION

At one time, crime victims virtually monopolized criminal justice. Over time, law enforcement became a shared activity, and finally victims lost their role almost completely. By the mid-1900s, victims had been formally excluded from criminal justice for several centuries.

Cultural beliefs have often either deemphasized victimization or blamed victims, thus further excluding victims. We have reinforced these beliefs by how we treat victims in modern literature and media, where offenders and officials seem to receive considerably more attention. The resulting popular attitudes have deemphasized victimization and enhanced values of "rugged individualism" and the "survival of the fittest," which have helped legitimize social conditions and structures and served ideological functions. Thus, the "cultural victim" seems to suffer a social as well as a criminal victimization.

An interplay of scientific and political forces has helped revive the victim. Beginning in the 1940s, and particularly by the late 1960s, an emerging science of victimology significantly boosted the victim's role and status. At the same time, political developments, such as the civil disturbances of the 1960s, the law-and-order backlash of the late 1960s and 1970s, the women's movement in the mid-1970s, the human rights movement in the late 1970s, and the new reactionary politics of the early 1980s have also apparently promoted victim interests. The victim has emerged from both conservative and progressive impulses.

As a science, victimology has achieved a great deal. Not only has it addressed long unanswered questions in criminology, it has allowed us to understand crime or victimization as a totality emerging from the dynamics of victim-offender interactions. Yet, despite its advances, victimology has been faulted for both methodological and theoretical shortcomings. Its excessive empiricism and preoccupation with victim precipitation have drawn particular fire.

Victimology's most significant drawback might lie in confining itself almost exclusively to criminological boundaries. Despite its broader origins, the discipline has rarely considered anything but crime victims and criminal victimizations. A few critics see a broader role for victimology, which would fulfill not only victimology's now traditional tasks, but also consider broader criminal definitions, the victimization's social and governmental sources, and victim-producing cultures. This would allow us to consider other kinds of victims, victimizers, and victimizations. It would promote a wider and more international victimology. It would be a "new" victimology of human rights.

We will explore these possibilities in subsequent chapters. For now, we must recognize that victims have progressed considerably, at least symbolically, in the last twenty-five years. The victim's rise has closely paralleled the development of scientific victimology. And the victim's future may depend on the interplay of that science with politics. We now turn to examining our first substantive victimological issue: the level of victimization, in fact and fiction.

3

False Images: The Social Reality of Victimization

The law is used to impose a given mind set on all participants. The resulting content of the law embodies the ideologies of lawmakers and judges. How they experience the ideology inherent in a culture becomes established mythology in the laws they make and apply.

IVAN ILLYCH, *Tools for Conviviality*

We are humble subordinates who can scarcely find our way through a legal document and have nothing to do with your case except to stand guard over you for ten hours a day and draw our pay for it. That's all we are, but we are quite capable of grasping the fact that the high authorities we serve, before they would order such an arrest as this, must be quite well informed about the reasons for the arrest and the person of the prisoner. There can be no mistake about that. Our officials . . . never go hunting for crime in the populace, but, as the Law decrees, are drawn to the guilty and must then send out us warders. That is the law. How could there be a mistake in that? FRANZ KAFKA, *The Trial*

What determines our consciousness of victimization? Our standard and immediate understanding usually suggests images of "criminal" victimization. To assess victimization, we would typically consider the level and nature of crime, where and by whom it was committed, who was victimized, and under what circumstances. Yet these standard images of victimization may be limited and misleading.

Most of us share a selective perception of victimization, as we react to its symbolic representation[1] through cues provided by our laws, our education, our media, our politics, our political socialization, and our culture. These forces create a "social reality" of victimization[2] that only partially defines the victimization actually suffered. Our "real" world of victimization represents a social construct. We react to social meanings conveyed to us by preformulated ideas and definitions.[3] What appears or what has been conceptualized as victimization may depend on influences beyond actual conditions.[4]

While we might reasonably exclude some kinds of victimization from our understanding of "criminal" victimization, we may have excluded many "crimes" from our consciousness as well. By using human rights standards of "crimes against humanity," for example, or perhaps even less encompassing criteria, we could vastly enlarge our conception of "criminal" victimization.

To understand both the reality and the "social reality" of victimization, we must examine the victimization level, the kinds of victimizations and their sources, where and by whom they are committed, who gets victimized, and under what circumstances. But first we must consider what limits our perceptions of victimization, including the forces that help define, measure, and interpret victimization and what functions they might perform. This might allow us to begin imagining broader, alternative concepts of victimization that we might adopt and start understanding victimization not as a series of discrete events, but as a social phenomenon with social sources. We might view victimization as indicating social integration or disintegration, and reflecting broader social forces with a wider historical context than we have thus far considered. In other words, we cannot separate victimization from its social roots or functions.[5]

VICTIMIZATION LEVEL

Defining Victimization

> *Who makes the laws for that hangknot?*
> *Who says who will go to the calaboose?*
>
>   WOODIE GUTHRIE

Everyone readily recognizes the difference between criminal and legitimate behavior, or at least we tend to view the distinction as fairly obvious. Yet it may not be so self-evident. Our definitions of crime do not reflect merely commonsense notions, since they exclude many serious harms and yet also include many other acts whose seriousness or criminality we might seriously question.[6] Formally acknowledging victimization depends on complex determinants, such as the perpetrator, the victim, the harm, and the circumstances. The criminal law recognizes some victimizations and not others. Yet decisions about what we label and treat as crime may not reflect objective harms, and thus to understand criminal definitions we must examine the interests of those who shape those decisions.[7]

PUBLIC INTERESTS.   The democratic pluralist view claims that legislation and policy reflect public preferences, at least indirectly. While every interest cannot always be represented or always win policy contests, it will never be totally excluded and, in the end, majority rule will reign. Thus, the criminal law should also correspond to public choices. Therefore, if we selectively define crime, it does not indicate the influence of special interests, but only of selective preferences. Accordingly, public interest groups and public officials can also successfully promote our interests in lawmaking since we cannot do so more directly ourselves.

SPECIAL INTERESTS.   Yet many dispute the pluralist view. They find public preferences and public opinion largely ineffective, especially for important policymaking. They see public interest groups as routinely unable to outweigh special interests. For all their negative publicity for defending "criminals," the American Civil Liberties Union, for example, has rarely affected the legislative process, even if it has won some important court cases.[8] And while public officials such as law enforcement bureaucrats may influence lawmaking, as in their significant impact on drug laws and enforcement,[9] critics find even them overshadowed by more powerful interests.

Despite formal democratic procedures, special interests may largely dominate lawmaking, policymaking, and public opinion, marshalling the resources necessary to wield the most effective political power.[10] Criminal definitions help set social boundaries in any society,[11] but many believe that those dominating the society's political economy will most likely determine where those boundaries fall.[12] Dominant interests may shape policy to achieve certain objectives and perform certain social functions. And they may shape public opinion, through various means, to rally support for their world view, even if it serves public interests much less than their own.

SHAPING PUBLIC PREFERENCES.   Thus, even if the public more significantly influenced lawmaking and policymaking, we would have to consider the forces determining its preferences.[13] Does public opinion reflect the public's real interests or what it has been convinced will serve them, but which objectively may not? For example, why does the public consistently believe that increasingly stronger police forces will reduce crime, when we have already strengthened them persistently with no apparent effect? The public may act with something less than free will and objectivity even when it has some minor influence on policymaking.

Public opinion can hardly be shaped monolithically, however. We do not entirely support current criminal definitions. Public preferences, for example, could not have caused us to exclude corporate wrongdoing from the criminal law since we sometimes do regard these acts as criminal, even beyond the few that have actually been criminalized.[14] Nevertheless, the public still predominantly accepts the conventional wisdom about the *most threatening* crime and criminals: the criminal law, reflecting dominant interests and perceptions, may help promote a certain consciousness and even ideology about crime.[15]

IDEOLOGICAL FUNCTIONS.   Aside from serving special interests directly, the criminal law may also perform social or ideological functions. It formally creates victims by defining the criminal threat. Yet, since we largely downplay individual victims, we view the state or society as the effective crime victim instead, as if we really constitute a united national or local community of interests, and as if we all jointly determined the threats we should most worry about. Having helped define (and create) the crime problem (or, some would say "scapegoat"), some believe we ritually protect the state and society from this threat by punishing "offenders" whom we have often discriminantly defined and apprehended.[16] Thus, the state defines the threat, inculcates a public perception about offenders and social harms, and then rescues the society from that threat, consoling the public and reinforcing state neutrality and legitimacy. Instead of orienting the criminal law to perceptions emerging from popular experience, discussion, and preferences, those controlling the criminal law may institutionalize crime definitions that preempt and condition popular conceptions.[17]

EVOLVING NEEDS.   Some believe that official definitions of victimization emerge from power and struggle, which powerful economic interests may dominate. Definitions will change historically, according to this view, not because substantially different interests emerge to dominate, but because persistently dominant interests change definitions to suit changing economic conditions and political needs.[18] For example, some argue that historically the poor have increasingly threatened upper classes politically and physically, and thus the criminal law has stressed the social control of lower-class behavior, such as by selectively defining lower class, but not upper-class, property violations as criminal.[19] The meager control of white-collar activities the criminal law provides may be largely symbolic regulations passed to bolster state legitimacy in the public's eyes, but not for serious enforcement.[20] Law enforcement agencies generally ignore corporate crime, but, when pursued, its perpetrators have little chance of punishment. When punished, they rarely go to prison (and even then for time best measured in days), and at most usually receive token fines.[21] Our society seems to allow victimization through the silence of the law.[22]

As this argument suggests, we may have defined crime, and victimization, selectively. From having previously used theft and vagrancy laws to enforce low-wage labor[23] to our current, selective prohibitions on drug use,[25] we may have aimed the law primarily against certain harms and against certain people while immunizing other interests. Yet we have not discriminated according to what acts and actors produce the most harm. On the contrary, some of our most serious harms and threats come from those people whom we most exclude from the criminal law.

Excluding Harms. We seem to have excluded, for example, many corporate, and white-collar harms, and much state wrongdoing, including harms produced while ostensibly "enforcing" the law.[26] We have largely excluded family violence from formal consideration,[27] ignoring victims of endangerment (if not outright harmful acts), and the victimization of social, individual, or group "interests."[28] We have assessed blame and defined victimization through mechanisms designed to prove "intent," when they might as easily be assessed by the "predictable consequences" of our acts. We do ostensibly regulate some harms excluded from the criminal law through the civil law. Yet actual regulation seems well within narrow limits of what the state and dominant interests deem socially injurious and "punishable."[29]

Real Threats. To understand this selection process, we can compare the human and financial costs produced by homicides to that produced by acts largely ignored by the criminal law. In 1974, for example, our 20,000 homicides contrasted quite favorably with the 14,200 deaths from workplace accidents, 100,000 deaths from workplace diseases, 219,000 to 328,500 pollution deaths, 16,000 deaths from unnecessary surgery, over 20,000 deaths from improper emergency care, 2000 to 10,000 deaths from unnecessary prescriptions, and untold tens of thousands of deaths from symptoms of poverty such as malnutrition and poor health care. Each year, as many as 25,000 people lose their lives, and 130,000 get injured, due to product defects, with 900 deaths from the infamous Ford Pinto gas tank alone. While we deplore our homicide rate, which kills one person every 26 minutes, we virtually ignore our loss of one person every 4 1/2 minutes from a workplace disease or accident.[30] Not only do these acts produce much more social harm than conventional crimes, but since they produce preventable and predictable fatalities, they do no worse in satisfying the norms of responsibility we enforce, for other activities, under our criminal law.

Suppose we take the mine owner who persistently exposes his workers (most of whom have no alternative employment) to working conditions he knows to be unsafe (and which could be made practically risk free as other nations have done), and which will predictably kill a certain number of his workers each year. Should we regard him as any less criminal than the addict who robs a grocery store to pay for his habit, and who unintentionally kills the clerk who tries to prevent the robbery? Suppose we also consider the car manufacturer (as in the recent Ford Motor Company case) who knowingly refuses to prevent or fix a safety defect that will predictably kill a certain number of drivers annually, but who completes a cost/benefit analysis showing that paying off possible legal suits will be more economical than altering the car's design or making repairs. Should we consider him to be any less criminal than the unemployed person who believes it will be more economical to kidnap and perhaps kill the son of a wealthy entrepreneur than to seek and work a typical, unskilled job? Should we consider the victims produced by these events as different either?

UNDERVALUING VICTIMIZATION. Criminal laws not only define victims and victimization, they also determine how seriously we treat them. The law may define circumstances or characteristics that officially "reduce" the victimization, if it has not been excluded entirely. For example, we recognized rape as a crime, but rape laws have delegitimized victims' claims almost by definition. By requiring special corroboration of the rape and by extracting the victim's sexual history, the law helps lessen the victimization officially, perhaps disqualifying it altogether from recognition.[31] Aside from sexism,[32] racism or classism may also influence the criminal law, effectively excluding (or lessening) some legitimate victims (by refusing to recognize them), and even creating victims itself.[33] Historically, people have resisted racism, classism, and sexism, yet their resistance frequently ends up defined as crime, which makes the state the victim, instead of those oppressed.[34]

SUMMARY. The criminal law may provide the first narrowing of our consciousness of both crime and victimization, a process that continues in enforcement and subsequent stages of the criminal process.[35] It may create an "official" or "social" reality of victimization which, among those harms it defines as criminal, stresses acts mostly committed by less privileged people, deemphasizes and softens the acts committed by more privileged people (such as so-called white-collar crime), and then excludes from its definition other, extensive, and (usually more) harmful acts altogether, such as corporate crimes, state crimes, and what human rights advocates would call "crimes against humanity."[36] The criminal law may convey the values and symbols of a prevailing ideology, internalized by officials, the public, and even by those whose interests it does not serve.

It may also help determine the enforcement level against those acts and actors defined as criminal, and legitimize state violence for implementing such laws.[37] Despite evidence that no significant differences exist in criminality (as now defined) across classes,[38] and that upper-class wrongdoing may considerably exceed all others,[39] enforcement stresses lower-class wrongdoing much more than other groups.

IMPLICATIONS. We need not accept the most critical assessments to suspect that we have selectively defined crime and that it has important implications, particularly for victims. First, we must recognize the politics of defining the criminal law and how what we consider criminal might not be so self-evident or neutral after all. We might begin considering the foundations and premises upon which we create the law and who has the power to create victims and for what purposes? Second, our definitions may exclude from sanctions many people whose wrongdoing rivals or surpasses those we do emphasize.[40] It may distort objective threats and harms and divert us from recognizing serious private wrongdoing, as well as from structural crimes and injustices.[41] Third, the law's influence transcends its formal representation in criminal codes;[42] its presumptions enter our moral structures, administrative rules, institutional values, public beliefs, and everyday behavior. Laws create norms that provide the ideological underpinnings of all social relations.[43] We often accept the law as neutral when instead it might express class and group interests, and not majority interests.[44]

Next, such definitions profoundly affect victims. We do not consider as victims those people who have been victimized by wrongdoing which we have not labeled as criminal, despite their losses and suffering. How we define crime and victimization also affects how we treat them even when their suffering does fall within the criminal law's purview.[45] Within our legal definitions, victims lose their victimized status if, in any way, they "precipitate" the crime against them. Yet we may not apply unbiased concepts of victim provocation: Consider that most rape laws, for example, strongly presume that the rapist was lured into committing his act. For some relationships, the potential rapist receives immunity by definition, such as the effective spousal immunity often extended for assault and battery,[46] or the husband's immunity when he rapes his wife.[47] The law has traditionally treated women as men's property.[48] Women and other designated social groups may become culturally legitimated victims.[49]

Some believe we cannot legitimately define victims or victimology without evaluating the legal system by which we label events as criminal. If it legalizes unjust rules and institutions, we may well question criminal definitions, and even whether the law itself may be criminal.[50] Others argue that victimologists have uncritically accepted official definitions of victimization; they could instead begin defining victims and victimization using broader criteria, perhaps from some general theory of the state or from universal human rights standards.[51] As an alternative, we might define social injury according to people's rights, not according to the functional requirements of our social institutions.

Overcriminalization

The major cause of crime is law.

EDWIN SCHUR, *Our Criminal Society*

While the criminal law undercriminalizes many harmful acts, or at least significantly discriminates against whom it applies the criminal label, it also suffers a contrary problem. Increasingly, our "overcriminalization" of the laws has produced its own biases and problems.[52]

LEGALISTIC SOCIETY.   As far back as the 1830s, deTocqueville characterized America as the most legalistic society he could ever imagine. In his view, practically every problem transformed itself into some legal issue or action. Yet, in the 150 years since, we have vastly intensified that tendency.[53] Steadily, we have politicized and legalized previously private issues into public issues. Sadly, we have individualized our resort to the government process by promoting lawsuits rather than socializing private problems into general public issues.[54] Nevertheless, the law has vastly expanded, as well as our unflaging faith in law as logically and capably solving our problems.

Yet, beginning in the 1960s, and particularly with the widespread and visible official lawbreaking of the following decade, we have increasingly questioned law as a panacea for social ills. Law now frequently symbolizes the "unfulfilled promises" of American society.[55] In particular, some have questioned our strong tendency to legislate morals and to enforce them with criminal penalties.

Many have been particularly skeptical of so-called victimless crimes. These offenses, consisting mostly of "vice" crimes such as drug use, gambling, prostitution, pornography, and vagrancy, have no conventional victims.[56] While some suggest that such acts victimize the perpetrators and the society,[57] they generally fail to satisfy the standard criminal definition: harm to others. We might also question, both morally and pragmatically, the use of criminal sanctions to protect people from themselves.[58] In any case, while we have also undercriminalized many actions having real victims, we have also overcriminalized many other actions having no traditional victims at all.[59] Even more tragically, overcriminalization may provide more than merely unnecessary protection: it may produce conditions that significantly enhance other conventional crimes and, thus, conventional victimizations.[60]

Overcriminalizing the laws may generate significant new, and often violent, crimes against others. Drug and prostitution laws provide two examples. Besides discriminating,[61] unrelated to the harm produced, between upper- and lower-class drugs and drug users, and between "call girls" and "street walkers," and customers and prostitutes, respectively, these laws also generate new crime.[62]

DRUG LAWS.   Drug laws, for example, artificially raise drug prices beyond the few cents each dose really costs, thus promoting crime in at least two ways: First, they create an underworld of drug use and distribution that provides organized crime with an opportunity it can hardly refuse. Second, they require addicts and other users to raise considerable money to afford their drugs, which creates new (and often violent) crimes.[63]

Recent reports show inordinate violent and property crime related to drug use and addiction. Yet, despite the high level of drug-related crime, users have actually been remarkably self-restrained in committing crime compared to the resources (over twice what they now steal) they would seem to need to support their habits, given current prices.[64] A recent program in Amsterdam, which distributes free heroin to addicts, responds specifically to the link between drug use and new crimes.[65] Other nations, such as Britain, have already decriminalized most drug use, and related crime has plummeted.

PROSTITUTION LAWS.   Likewise, prostitution laws unnecessarily envelop "working girls" in an atmosphere of crime and violence.[66] Instead of receiving police protection against violent customers, prostitutes "buy" pimps for safety (against both the police and customers), and for generating business. Yet frequently, and predictably, prostitutes suffer violence from those same "benefactors." When arrested, they often get involved (if they have not been already) in drug crime by acting as police informers or customers in exchange for more lenient treatment.[67] Although prostitutes actually represent both victims and offenders, officially we treat them only as criminals. Yet this need not be the case. West Germany and the Netherlands, for example, have legalized prostitution and provided government protection. Altogether, 100 members of the United Nations have deregulated prostitution,[68] and only the United States (among all nations) continues to define it as a crime.[69] Better yet would be to eliminate the reasons, emanating from patriarchial societies, why most prostitutes are forced into solicitation in the first place.

In sum, those committing victimless crimes have every incentive to commit further crimes producing real victims, and then, in turn, are much more susceptible to becoming (often violent) crime victims themselves, from being embroiled in the criminal atmosphere that morals legislation helps create. Yet the victimization and other adverse effects of overcriminalization do not end here.

POLICE CRIMES.   Overcriminalizing the law hampers law enforcement in several ways. Vice enforcement often dominates police work. A recent study, for example, shows that Philadelphia's police department spends over one-half its time on vice work.[70] Public drunkenness constitutes one-third of all American arrests.[71] This diverts considerable time and resources from more serious crimes with actual victims. As suggested earlier, overcriminalization generates new crimes, which makes enforcement even more difficult. Besides sustaining a lucrative organized crime, others resort to crime to cope with an artificially created criminal environment.[72]

Vice work also embroils police officers in a criminal atmosphere they may find impossible to resist.[73] At the very least, they must enforce laws against activities they may not personally oppose and they may themselves practice. They must also use tricks and deceptions, such as entrapment, to enforce these laws, which not only violate constitutional prohibitions, but blur the distinction between the lawbreakers and the law enforcers. This escalates when police officers actually do violate the law, either to enforce vice laws, or to commit vice crimes themselves. As the movie *Serpico* vividly dramatized a few years ago, it takes remarkable self-restraint to avoid being "on the pad" or other police illegality related to vice enforcement. Perhaps the problem emerged most succinctly in the Knapp Commission report on the New York Police in the mid-1970s, which found that the city's largest drug dealer was the police department itself![74] The recent Huang case in Boston's Chinatown, where a man soliciting a prostitute was apparently beaten by a police officer during the arrest, suggests that vice enforcement might also contribute to police brutality against minority races. Overcriminalization, beyond everything else, can stimulate new crimes by law enforcers, and when we learn about such wrongdoing, it promotes an increasing disrespect for the law generally.

Finally, overcriminalizing the law involves the police excessively in social control, and illegitimately in private behavior. By defining many "normal" activities as criminal, the state legitimizes police surveillance and population control, unrelated to any harm their acts may produce. Many believe that by selectively enforcing such laws, or by having excluded some people's behavior by definition, overcriminalization focuses extensive, even repressive, control predominantly on the lives of the powerless and the lower classes. Some even argue that defining (as much vice law does) the erotic as criminal serves to suppress a crucial, and potentially explosive, creative potential that would otherwise challenge the established order.[75]

Measuring Victimization

> *You could look it up.*   CASEY STENGEL

Having suggested the definitional problems of measuring victimization, we can now consider the specific instruments that measure the crime rate. They can tell us many things about victimization, but, most frequently, we use them simply to show how much victimization we suffer. These figures significantly affect public policy and perceptions, and thus we must closely analyze how they are derived. Our so-called "crime waves" may reflect the ebb and flow of politics and organizational imperatives much more than actual crime.[76] Crime waves may be generated, for example, to fuel political campaigns or to justify new police spending or crackdowns.[77]

OFFICIAL STATISTICS. The Uniform Crime Reports (UCR) compiled by the FBI provide the most visible measure of crime and victimization. These official statistics show a sharp increase in both violent and property crimes since World War II and especially since the 1960s. In the last twenty years, they show that crime has risen by an average of 350% in each category,[78] although we may have reached a peak sometime in the mid-1970s. Between 1964 and 1977, for example, violent crimes rose from 190 to 482 per 100,000 people, and property crimes rose from 2150 to 4800.[79]

Apparent increases such as these, however, may not result merely from escalating crime. A higher reporting rate explains at least some of the increase.[80] In fact, some argue that instead of a "crime wave,"[81] we may be experiencing a "crime reporting wave."[82] Yet even if statistics reflected real crime increases, historians suggest that we have only begun to approach comparable crime levels in our past.[83] This hardly dispels our high crime rates, but only suggests our long history of extensive violence and crime.

VICTIMIZATION SURVEYS. Official statistics in the UCR, and comparable measures in other nations,[84] apparently indicate only part of
the crime problem, however.[85] Beginning in the late 1960s, researchers, and later the government, began assessing crime through victimization surveys. These surveys, which cover all the UCR crimes
except homicide, have shown that official statistics have underes-
timated actual victimization by from 300 to 500%.[86]

Many writers have compared official statistics to the victimization
surveys to account for the large discrepancy.[87] They find that it comes
mostly from victims' reluctance to report crimes to the police. This
may result partly from personal reasons, but also from organizational incentives in criminal justice.[88] Victims fail to report crimes
for many reasons, but most often they feel that nothing can be done.
Usually they are right.

Police resources might be insufficient to handle many minor offences. Promoting too many prosecutions for trivial offenses might
also alienate citizens from the police. Inconsistencies can result from
arbitrary recording practices and political and budgetary considerations, which bias each department's reporting.[89] Since increasing
crime reports may either help or harm the police, manipulating statistics might be inevitable.[90] Finally, police officers might record crimes
discriminantly because of personal biases and preferences, situational factors such as the offender's or victim's behavior, and pressures for productivity.[91]

The so-called "dark figure" of crime between official statistics and
victim surveys might come partly from methodological errors or
techniques.[92] For some crimes, such as commercial robberies, the
differences might be rather small in the first place.[93] Also, the surveys may measure not merely more crimes, but different crimes.[94]
And victims might be inclined to overstate[95] or understate[96] their
victimization.

Despite these reservations,[97] most researchers place much more
confidence in victim surveys than in official statistics, even though
the public seems primarily influenced by the latter.[98] The first scat-
tered and sporadic surveys were supplanted by the National Crime
Survey,[99] and much has been made of its many potential uses, ranging from assessing victimological risks,[100] victim characteristics, resistance strategies, victim-offender interaction, and police responsiveness,[101] to criminal justice planning and evaluation,[102] analyzing
victim recidivism,[103] understanding (and perhaps quelling) fear and
other reactions,[104] examining crime's impact,[105] focusing on a single
crime type,[106] analyzing a single city or state,[107] and comparing our
victimization levels to those of other nations.[108] Despite these uses,
plans were made to discontinue the victimization surveys, perhaps
because of the embarrassingly high level of victimization they revealed.

Researchers in many other nations have also conducted their own victim surveys and studies, including Australia,[109] Britain,[110] Holland,[111] Germany,[112] Japan,[113] Switzerland,[114] Finland,[115] South Africa,[116] Scandinavia,[117] Italy,[118] Canada,[119] Belgium,[120] Sweden,[121] Israel,[122] and the Soviet Union.[123] Some less developed nations have followed suit, including India,[124] Nigeria,[125] Ethiopia,[126] Zambia,[127] Egypt,[128] Panama,[129] Brazil,[130] Colombia,[131] Mexico,[132] and other countries in Africa and Latin America.[133] While American crime rates usually far exceed those of other nations (murder, for example, is 9 times more likely than in other industrialized nations),[138] some of the same patterns of victimization are present.

OTHER MEASURES. We have also measured victimization and its characteristics by other indicators.[135] The recent computerization of some big city prosecutors' offices has provided a rich and expanding collection of prosecutorial data on crime.[136] Numerous researchers have also measured crime through longitudinal studies of so-called "birth cohorts," which follow the lives (and potentially the "crimes") of selected groups over long periods of time.[137] Other sources include self-report surveys,[138] archival data (from hospital, police, court, and insurance records), experimental (laboratory and field) and case studies, anecdotal stories, and participant observations.[139]

Our various indicators of victimization may overstate the amount of people involved, since they ignore those victims and offenders involved in crime more than once, and those victims who also double as criminals, and vice versa.[140] Nevertheless, indicators of victimization measure only some crimes and some victimizations. Beginning with how we define crimes in the first place, we only selectively measure victimization. Among those acts formally defined as crime, our official statistics only measure crimes duly reported and recorded. Victimization surveys reveal many more crimes. Yet, even by official measures, we must be greatly alarmed by our crime level. We must be concerned, too, about the political manipulation of crime rates, which not only may distort the real crime level, but as "crime" rates, and not "victimization" rates, they may also distract attention from those victims who bear most of that crime and violence.

Ideology, Victimization, and Public Opinion

*Well, my dear, you know the law **is** necessary, and what's necessary and indispensable is **good**, and everything that's good is nice. And it really is very nice indeed to be a good, law-abiding citizen and do one's duty and have a clear conscience.*

EUGENE IONESCO, *Victims of Duty*

Could there be any police so vigilant and effective for the protection of all the rights of persons, property and character as such a sound and comprehensive education and training as our system of common schools could be made to impart?   HORACE MANN

Our perception of crime and victimization derives presumably from how we define crime, how we measure it, and how we enforce it. Yet as we have seen, these indicators, and their social meaning,[141] may distort the real victimization level. The objective reality of crime and victimization might be considerably different. Yet only the "social reality" of victimization will likely be reflected in public opinion.

SHAPING PUBLIC OPINION.   What forces shape that opinion? While we might expect actual victimization to strongly influence it, the evidence suggests otherwise.[142] Neighborhood networks and word-of-mouth communications may help determine attitudes,[143] but the fundamental sources might lie considerably deeper in the American consciousness. We may absorb, unwittingly, an ideology of victimization and insecurity.

In fact, as Russell Baker has suggested, we may have developed "an almost hysterical preoccupation with security":

For five weeks I traveled across beautiful autumnal America. It was like a booby hatch for the criminally insane. . . . At various stops along the route there were campaigning politicians clamoring for use of the electric chair, the gallows or the gas chamber as devices for restoring public civility. Everywhere one was confronted with . . . a national obsession for more . . . security. . . . [I]n Beverly Hills . . . [e]very other house, it seemed, bore a large placard announcing . . . its private security guard service, and most . . . said "Armed Response." . . . Very little of this "security" existed 20 years ago, but now it is a national passion. The irony is that the more "security" we buy, the less secure we are.[144]

It would be even more ironic if we discovered that our insecurities reflected our socialization more than objective dangers. Insecurity helps bolster public support for strong authority, but it also may cause us to project our fears outward. We may support quick, forceful solutions, and may even respond to our *perceptions* of a threat with violence of our own.[145] In fact, it may not be too much to wonder whether in addition to crime causing an obsession with security, an obsession with security might also cause crime.

In any case, besides the influence of the law, victimization, and interpersonal communications, we might well examine the effects of other socialization forces. Our officials, educators, professionals, researchers, commissioners, and others may shape our attitudes toward victimization (and other public issues). Despite their apparent diversity, in what we often view as our pluralist society, their views might actually be remarkably similar and reinforcing.[146] Perhaps the greatest influence—partly because it substantially (and selectively) conveys and translates these other sources for the public—comes from the mass media. As a mediator between government and the public, how have the media translated official statistics and statements into public perceptions?

Media Influence

> *The bias of the headlines, the systematic onesidedness of the reporting and the commentaries, the catchwords and slogans instead of argument. No serious appeal to reason. Instead a systematic effort to install conditioned reflexes in the minds of the voters—and for the rest, crime, divorce, anecdotes, twaddle, anything to keep them distracted, anything to prevent them from thinking.*
>
> ALDOUS HUXLEY, *Island*

Despite some inconsistencies, we can hardly view the evidence as encouraging. Sensationalized, misleading, and often inaccurate cover stories like *Time*'s "The Curse of Violent Crime," *Newsweek*'s "The Epidemic of Violent Crime," *U.S. News and World Report*'s "Street Crime: People Fight Back," the *New York Times Magazine*'s "Crime: How It Destroys, What Can Be Done," and ABC television's series on "Crime in America" typify the coverage. The problems are many.

OFFICIAL PERSPECTIVES. The media convey information about specific crimes and about crime trends almost entirely through official law enforcement statements and perceptions—not necessarily an unbiased source.[147] They portray the seven "index" crimes as the society's most serious victimizations. They never question how we define crime, and subsequently measure it, thus conveying a highly selective version of the problem and its perpetrators.

SENSATIONALISM. The media often sensationalize crime, pandering more to unique angles than to reality. Stories about bailed or paroled prisoners who commit murders, for example, provide "good copy" yet these situations rarely happen. We learn that the "curse of violent crime is rampant," that we live in a "reign of terror," that our attackers are "increasingly brutal marauders," "mean, antisocial people with macho complexes," that we have been "held hostage to the irrational acts of a relatively small cadre of career criminals," and that we have been dealing inefficiently with "a handful of savages." We see crime charts dripping with blood, and read false statements or innuendos portraying juvenile justice as a free ride, criminal justice as scrupulously fair to minorities, Cuban exiles as Miami's crime problem, a small core of hardened criminals as committing most crime, bailed defendants as rampant offenders, and plea bargaining as threatening justice for the victim.[148] Such stories undoubtedly shape our consciousness and convince us that we do not deal harshly enough with our criminals. Sensationalism and media competition reinforce a false sense of victimization that frequently emerges as "crime waves" that bear no relation to actual crime levels.

Our nonfiction literature does no better. Consider the synopsis that appeared on one recent book, advertised as the first to concern itself with victims:

> It is still one of the most shockingly brutal crimes on record. On April 22, 1974, five innocent people interrupted a robbery in an Ogden, Utah, hi-fi shop. Senselessly terrorized, they were tortured without mercy, forced to drink hydrochloric acid and shot in the head. Sixteen year old Cortney Nesbitt miraculously survived . . . he remains disabled but alive today. *So are the men responsible.*[149]

This describes an undoubtedly horrendous crime, with whose victims we should surely sympathize. But, in its context, it says much more. It panders to our bloodthirstiness. As the first sympathetic treatment of victims, the book portrays this kind of terror as being the norm, a crime, that while "perhaps" extreme, could happen to any of us. It also places the crime's entire onus on the offenders without considering the society in which such an offense could happen. Both the book's text and its synopsis inculcate further brutality—the death penalty—as the only solution. Popular books such as these convey powerful messages.

SUPERFICIALITY.   The media almost always view crime superficially, not only closely reproducing official explanations, but virtually ignoring the underlying sources of crime and victimization (such as social values and conditions),[150] and promoting a superficial view of appropriate responses. *Time* either suggests or implies that we have crime because of blacks or other minorities, because of a "lost, counterculture generation," because we ignore a handful of hardened, recidivist, career criminals, because we have too many drugs and (alas, a germ of truth) guns, because we do not have enough prison space, and most of all, because we have an inefficient criminal justice system.[151] Nothing appears about crime's structural characteristics, and only a passing reference to social ills such as poverty renders them irrelevant or inevitable.

ENTERTAINMENT STEREOTYPES. Finally, the media, in both the news, and especially in their "entertainment" programs, convey distorted images of crime, criminals, victims, and police work, which, constantly reiterated, cannot help profoundly affecting public perceptions, not to mention its values and quite likely its behavior. Some describe television in particular as "propaganda for the status quo."[152] About law enforcers, the media promote a "Dick Tracy mentality"[153] that falsely separates police and criminals, or law-abiding citizens and lawbreakers, into "good" guys and "bad" guys; falsely portrays businesses, and middle and upper, instead of lower, classes as bearing most victimization;[154] and falsely overstates the violent crime level.[155] They also falsely show police rigorously fighting white-collar, organized, and upper-class crime,[156] falsely exaggerate the threat of terrorists and revolutionaries[157] and falsely portray police officers respecting suspects' rights when they routinely do not, or, alternatively, violating rights without the slightest questioning of police behavior.[158]

The media further mislead when they portray blacks as naturally violent, lower classes and minorities as naturally criminal, men as heroes when they dispense lethal violence,[159] women and blacks as deserving their fate,[160] offenders as isolated individuals separated from social forces, privileged victims as innocent and underprivileged victims as culpable.[161] They present the exotic and peculiar as commonplace, and a worldview featuring an "abnormally high proportion of sexy women, violent acts and extra-legal solutions to legal problems."[162] The media also exploit victims with splashy headlines and riveting dramas, either exaggerating the victimization experienced or underestimating the victim's reaction.[163]

VIOLENCE. Quantitatively, the media present extraordinary violence, occupying three-quarters of all television time. Over one-half the characters commit violence, and one-tenth kill. On average, each prime-time television program contains two crimes, usually violent.[164] In childrens' television, 92% of the programs show violence. Three-quarters of the characters commit violence, with 17 cases occurring each hour.[166] Such a bombardment of violence artificially reinforces an aura of crime, yet may well desensitize us to its effects. Moreover, the net effect may be a "demonstration of power and an instrument of social serving, on the whole, to reinforce and preserve the existing social order."[167] It generates fear, anxiety, and an identification with the unconstrained and violent forces of the law.[168]

MEDIA IMPACT. Yet some have questioned the media's actual impact. While some groups in the population might suffer a kind of "vicarious victimization"[169] from media reports about crime, the media may be too remote and vague to affect attitudes and behavior. People may use social networks, more than the media, to assess their victimization risks.[170] People's psychosocial orientation toward punishment, already deeply ingrained, may affect their attitudes toward the death penalty, for example, more than media coverage.[171]

Many others disagree. As an important socialization force over time (the average American will spend 7 years watching television, for example), the media may considerably affect our attitudes toward punishment, including the death penalty, yet seem less influential when measured as discrete news or drama coverage. The media may affect our fear of crime in particular.[172] Their influence may be hidden since we have few population groups that they ignore, with which to make fair comparisons.[173] While the public fairly accurately estimates neighborhood victimization, the media induce them to vastly exaggerate national levels.[174] Those reading newspapers with the greatest crime coverage show the highest levels of fear and those watching television the most have the most distorted view about crime and its victims.[175]

Public opinion about crime and punishment (including the death penalty) exhibits considerable volatility, unrelated to changes in official crime rates or actual crime,[176] suggesting the media's possible influence. Many people believe the common crime rate exceeds what the media portrays.[177] This might mean that opinions develop independently from the media, but more likely that the media set a base perception level, which the public believes does not reveal enough. Abroad, we find exaggerated fears (compared to actual crime) attributed to sensationalist media coverage as well.[178]

We have mixed evidence about the media's impact on actually inducing crime or violence. Some suggest its effect might be exaggerated, yet we cannot easily ignore other studies to the contrary, including those showing how the media may create its own victims.[179] Even if not affecting actual behavior, it may increase people's tolerance for crime and violence, which may impede a sense of revulsion on which we could work to reduce victimization.[180]

PSYCHOLOGICAL SYMBOLS.   According to some, the media imposes or reinforces simplistic notions through superficial psychological appeals. They may mystify instead of clarify, especially in a society generally adverse to critical thought. They may shape people's views, and yet claim to be merely responsive.[181] As Harold Lasswell has suggested, the media may be imposing itself on comparatively virgin ground:

> The environment of the infant and child is teeming with words of
> ambiguous reference, which take on positive or negative significance long

before there is enough contact with reality either to define their frame of reference, or to distinguish those whose frames of reference are wholly indeterminate. As an "adult" the individual continues to respond to those articulations in many childish and juvenile ways very often imputing some special significance to them. Such words are "law and order" [and] "patriotism."[182]

People may simply accept the first credible guidance they receive and ignore any subsequent cues. Or, if confronted, more or less simultaneously, with conflicting information, they may accept views that support the most easily digestible symbols.[183] This probably explains much of the popular reaction supporting "the police" and their efforts to maintain "law and order,"[184] even through questionable uses of force. Some argue that the "law-and-order" outcry may be a crime in itself: the "theft of reality," or the stealing of real pain and fear from real victims, and attributing it to middle and upper classes and to the government.[185]

While we cannot call the evidence on the media's effect totally conclusive, we have strong reasons to believe that it substantially shapes the public's perspectives about crime and criminals. Yet the picture it conveys may significantly distort reality or, at best, only suggest a selective reality of victimization. To what extent do media outcomes reflect government preferences and motives?

GOVERNMENT MOTIVES. We cannot assume that the government wants to convey an objective account of crime and victimization.[186] As H. L. Mencken once suggested: "The whole aim of practical politics is to keep the population alarmed (and hence clamorous to be led to safety) by menacing it with an endless series of hobgoblins." If nothing else, state officials seem caught between wanting to portray crime as a minor problem to reinforce their legitimacy[187] and effectiveness and wanting to portray a major crime problem to justify various enforcement measures and an aura of restricted freedoms and state power in exchange for greater security.[188] Yet the state, with media assistance, may have reconciled this conflict quite nicely, although never permanently.

The distorted concept of victimization conveyed by the media may perform many valuable functions, intentionally or not. According to many researchers, it helps generate a certain level of fear and insecurity,[189] deflects attention from official actions and alternative forms of wrongdoing,[190] maintains and promotes social control,[191] and perpetuates existing social, economic, and political arrangements.[192] Others argue that the distortions perpetuate myths that criminal justice serves general, and not merely special, interests,[193] develops false racial stereotypes,[194] poses offenders as scapegoats for social problems,[195] ingrains ideologies stressing the poor as criminal threats to other classes,[196] and promotes partisan political goals.[197] They may also promote unrestrained police measures and get-tough punishments, which can create incredibly harsh beliefs. Take, for example, the mother of two Ohio college students who advocated police firing on students even for minor acts such as going barefoot and wearing long hair.[198]

MEDIA COLLUSION.   Conventionally, we believe the media vigorously scrutinize state activities. Yet the media may not effectively check state actions and statements.[199] While debates about media-government collusion have been treated extensively elsewhere, we must at least wonder about whether we can rely on the media to objectively portray crime and victimization to the public. As we have begun to suggest, we might well expect the opposite.[200]

While the media pursue their own separate agenda, largely related to making profits, we cannot discount their relationship with government, and the symbiotic interactions they routinely pursue for mutual purposes. Some argue that what promotes state power and legitimacy will often simultaneously sell newspapers. Others suggest that intentional or not, we can hardly discount the "social production" of the news and the orchestrating of public opinion through official statements and dutiful media acquiescence, if not encouragement.[201] Some believe the media readily allow officials to manipulate the news through symbolic appeals, often lacking in substance, yet free of critical media review.[202] Without prompting, the news and entertainment media might promote law-and-order values for market reasons,[203] yet their motives might lie deeper than immediate profit. Given the structure of media control and ownership, the media may have as much at stake in preserving the current social order as do officials and other elites.

We need not accept the most extreme views, nor certainly assume any sort of conscious and overt conspiracy between the media and government, to wonder whether a certain ideology of crime and victimization may nevertheless pervade public opinion. If so, certain popular views about criminal justice policy may have less to do with people having objectively assessed their real interests and the best route to achieving them, and more with having absorbed attitudes and preferences externally imposed for quite different reasons. Taken together, the way we selectively define, measure, and convey conceptions of victimization suggests that crime victims represent "political victims," or victims officially recognized, through a highly political process. Later, we will suggest that even more so, "political victims" might designate those who suffer victimization by the state yet receive no recognition at all.

VICTIMIZATION: WHAT, WHO, AND WHERE

I was hit with a bat on my head and right arm. He knocked on my door and said "Here's your birthday present," and then hit me with a baseball bat wrapped in Christmas paper.

A BROOKLYN CRIME VICTIM

Kinds of Victimization

What we acknowledge as victimization depends on political definitions of crime that exclude some considerable loss and suffering. With that caveat, we can at least examine the victimization we do recognize.

Even as limited by definition, the United States has the highest crime rate in the world.[204] Criminal victimization may result from violent, personal, property, organized, professional, white-collar, corporate, juvenile, sexual, and family crime, from political crime such as terrorism and rebellion, or from state crime such as corruption, structural violence, and repression. Some offenses, like "victimless" crimes, may produce no direct victims at all. Officially, we do not treat these crimes equally, either in our enforcement or punishment. Some have barely been defined as criminal in the first place. The variation may depend more on who commits each crime than on the crime's inherent threat or damage. Understandably, violent crime creates the strongest public reaction and considerable human damage.[205] Beyond contemporary personal violence, the United States has had a very violent history,[206] and we have well deserved the label "violent society."[207] Nevertheless, we may feel much less revulsion to such crimes than other nations would since our society's high violence level, and our media's preoccupation with portraying it as news and fiction, may desensitize us to its effects. Somehow, we also allow violent crime to be relatively ignored by the police, despite its apparent seriousness.

MURDER. Violent, personal crimes include robbery,[208] assault,[209] suicide,[210] kidnapping,[211] and lethal threats, but we tend to stress murder and rape most of all. In 1980, there were 548,809 robberies and 654,957 assaults, yet we have been most concerned about the more than 20,000 homicides that occur annually in the United States— about one every 26 minutes. Some happen accidentally, others inadvertently, but less than 5% are planned and premeditated.[212] Some see mass or serial murders escalating, such as those committed by the infamous "Son of Sam," or those during the recent "Mc-

Donald's Massacre," or those at Jonestown.[213] The homicide rate steadily increases, reflecting only part of the increasing viciousness[214] and prevalence of violent crime.[215] About one-half of the increasing death rate comes from escalating murders. People living in major American cities have a greater chance of death by murder than American soldiers had of death in combat in World War II,[215] including a significant rise in firearms murders. Yet, although very high, the homicide rate is lower than the death rate from pneumonia, cancer, heart disease, household fires, auto crashes, and suicide.[217] Most of these actions, or their sources, have not been defined as crime, yet they could be.

SEXUAL ASSAULT

> Even tonight and I need to take a walk and clear
> my head about this poem about why I can't
> go out without changing my clothes my shoes
> my body posture my gender identity my age
> my status as a woman alone in the evening/
> alone on the streets/alone not being the point/
> the point being that I can't do what I want
> to do with my own body because I am the wrong
> sex the wrong age the wrong skin . . .
>
>   JUNE JORDAN, *A Poem About My Rights*

Although rape was long considered a sexual crime, the women's movement has helped us recognize it as actually a violent crime.[218] As Barbara Starrett has suggested:

> The male society has made rape the prototypical expression of its patterns. Domination of the other by force: of nature and land and resources, of "inferior" nations and groups of women, of money and markets and material goods. . . . Victim . . . is the most descriptive noun we have to designate the role women . . . must play. . . . [In] male institutions, [y]ou are either the victim or the oppressor.[219]

Over 60,000 female rapes are reported each year, 5 to 10 times as many as in Europe,[220] yet that underestimates the actual amount by at least four times,[221] and perhaps by as much as twenty-five times. What we do count shows that a rape occurs at least once each 6 minutes.[222] Male rapes, often in prisons[223] or among homosexuals,[224] apparently constitute only a fraction of the female total.[225]

Many women refuse to report this crime because of its stigma or their likely treatment in the criminal process.[226] While we have increasingly recognized rape's seriousness and prevalence, we have made little headway in reducing it or in promoting the victim's role in prosecuting the offender. Although rape is the leading crime against women and the fastest growing index crime,[227] prosecutions have not increased.[228] The dramatic increase in rape may partially reflect a new willingness to report the crime, as women have gained new support and independence in recent years. Yet officials seem little more willing to act.

Other personal, and often violent, victimizations include sexual and family crimes, many of which overlap. Besides rape, sexual crimes might range from the less serious adultery and bigamy to the more serious, forceful sodomy, pedophilia, and child incest.[229] All of these either can or do affect the family as well. Rape may also occur in marriage and the family, yet the law rarely defines it officially so. Child stealing may also be a family crime since although many children get kidnapped by strangers, many others get abducted by one of their parents, often when custody has been lost due to divorce.[230]

BATTERING

> *How'd you like to go to the moon, Alice? Boom . . . zing!*
>
> RALPH KRAMDEN, *The Honeymooners*

The most frequent and perhaps most serious family crime is battering. We might view this as a sexual crime, since although a sexual act need not be committed, the crime emerges from sexual relations. Sexist attitudes and male superiority have helped produce and rationalize this crime, which normally involves men beating women. Along with childbeating and "granny" beating, wife battering has become a crime of enormous dimensions.[231]

One estimate puts the number of wife batterings at 3,759,193 in 1980, and yet, as with rape, many more occur than women have actually reported. Another estimate shows wife battering occurring ten times more than rape.[232] Often beatings are not isolated events in a given household; most police calls go to homes where violence has occurred before, usually many times.[233] The battering cycle often ends in homicide, sometimes committed by the woman victim, in revenge or desperation.[234] Yet between 2000 to 4000 women also get beaten to death annually, and overall beatings constitute the largest single cause of female injuries.[235]

The home and the family have become the most violent places in society.[236] One of every ten married women has probably been beaten,[237] about 282,000 men get beaten by their wives annually,[238] and violence of all forms probably occurs in at least 60% of all households.[239] When women get battered, it dramatically increases their tendency to beat their children.[240] Yet, for all this violence, we treat the family and the home as sacrosanct.[241] Either we ignore the violence as a private matter, or take it as culturally acceptable, or both. Some believe that a nation's aggressiveness can be measured by its family violence,[242] and its civility by its willingness to consider it a public problem, yet we have been very slow to do so.

PROPERTY CRIMES. These crimes involve the largest number of victimizations.[243] Although violent crime has been extensive and serious, about 85% of all reported crime is nonviolent. Thefts, for example, were reported 1,073,998 times in 1981, constituting about two-thirds of the reported index crimes. Much property crime occurs directly through robberies,[244] burglaries,[245] thefts,[246] and arson.[247] Whether as little as shoplifting, pickpocketing, or minor bunko crime, or as much as mugging, purse snatching, and bank robbery, these crimes predominantly shape our concept of property loss.[248] But property loss resulting from various other offenses, such as fraud and embezzlement, far exceeds that produced by the acts we emphasize or even criminalize, yet we enforce and punish them much less.[249]

WHITE-COLLAR AND CORPORATE CRIMES

> *Now as through this world I ramble*
> *I see lots of funny men*
> *Some will rob you with a sixgun*
> *Some with a fountain pen*
>
> WOODIE GUTHRIE

We can best identify some kinds of victimization by their perpetrators. Thus, victimization results from the activities of white-collar, corporate, and professional offenders, organized crime figures, juvenile delinquents, terrorists and dissidents, and government officials. While we deal severely with terrorists and dissidents,[250] we treat many of the rest as if they were not criminals at all. We have largely ignored white-collar, corporate, and government wrongdoing, for example, except for the most blatant actions, either by excluding their harmful acts from the criminal law or by nonenforcement. Although official statements and popular culture picture law enforcement working vigorously against organized crime,[251] most police work actually emphasizes small-time gamblers, drug dealers, and drug users. And, ironically, our juvenile justice system emerged ostensibly to immunize delinquents from the adult criminal law, and yet by doing so has often exposed them to more severe treatment.[252]

More specifically white-collar crime includes various offenses committed by white-collar workers and managers, usually for personal reasons, against employers, the government, and individuals. It might emerge as embezzlement or consumer fraud by small businesses, or employee pilfering, credit card fraud, and so forth.[253] Corporate crime includes offenses committed by corporate managers, or by corporate institutions, for corporate benefit, although some individuals may gain simultaneously. It might affect administration, the environment, finance, labor, manufacturing, and trade. Its victims might include consumers, the economic system, the environment, labor, government, and the public.[254]

Corporate "crime" might include deceptive practices and packaging, worthless or unsafe products (like the recent Eli Lily arthritis drug case), corporate propaganda, check kiting (such as the recent E. F. Hutton case), false accounting, built-in obsolescence, unethical government influence, unethical competitive practices, excessive profits, trade interference, secret warranties, contrived shortages, improper inspection and testing, excessive mark-up, money laundering (like the recent Bank of Boston case), excessive promotion, fraudulent billing (like recent General Electric practices with the Pentagon), bankruptcy fraud, consumer fraud (such as the recent Exxon overcharging case), deceptive advertising, pollution, workplace hazards, and diseases. Or it could involve union busting, tainted food and drugs, kickbacks, payoffs, bribes, insurance fraud, receiving stolen property, securities fraud, tax evasion (like the recent Cartier jewelry case), negligence, computer fraud, price fixing and monopolization, confidence games, improper campaign contributions, unjust wages, collusion, stockholder fraud, and blockbusting.[255] More broadly, some consider the corporate system itself as criminal for how it helps create and maintain poverty, hunger, unemployment, homelessness, repression, and war.[256]

The above list provides only some of the kinds of corporate wrongdoing that actually occur. Yet we have defined few of these offenses as criminal even though they produce far more property and personal damage and loss (including death) than common crimes. Many of these actions generate no regulation or control whatsoever, and most of those that do emerge only from civil or administrative law. When attempted at all, enforcement largely defers to the offenders, and penalties tend to be either token or nonexistent. Various studies show corporate crime to be extensive (60 to 90% of the top 500 corporations), occurring over long periods, and repeatedly (2.1 times annually for each corporation in one study).[257] By those relatively few actions labeled criminal, virtually every person in society has probably been regularly and routinely deprived of their physical and fiscal assets.[258]

ORGANIZED AND PROFESSIONAL CRIME

Organized crime is a blight on our nation. While many young
Americans are lured into a career of crime by its promise of an easy

> *life, most criminals actually must work long hours, frequently in*
> *buildings without air conditioning.*   WOODY ALLEN, *Getting Even*

Two kinds of crime seem to fall somewhere between typical common crimes and classic white-collar offenses, with some overlap. Organized and professional crime create victims in ways similar to other crimes, yet they have uncommon perpetrators and effects.

Organized crime, or the orgainzed pursuit of illegal activities as a business enterprise, provides considerable crime, yet involves relatively few offenders.[259] By its tight-knit, hierarchical, specialized, and monopolistic structure, it has dominated several areas of crime.[260] Our overcriminalized laws have helped it control vice crimes such as narcotics, gambling, prostitution, and pornography.[261] Its more white-collar crimes include loansharking; labor racketeering; coercive and protection contracts; extortion, manipulation, and embezzlement of stocks, bonds, and credit cards; securities manipulation and theft; improper political contributions; welfare swindles; oil pricing fraud; and computer crime.[262] It apparently also "owns" some political and law enforcement officials.[263] In fact, much organized crime may occur with the specific approval or at least acquiescence of state officials.[264]

Although involved in some "predatory" crime, organized criminals view themselves primarily as businessmen providing desired goods and services.[265] They also have substantial holdings in "legitimate" business enterprise.[266] Organized crime offers members an alternative, business career, particularly tempting for those blocked from legitimate opportunities.[267] By some accounts, "organized crime pursues the American dream, at any cost and by any means."[268] In any case, organized crime has a significant effect on producing both blue-collar and white-collar crimes.

Professional crime may occur through skillfully pursued, strong-armed, and even violent crimes, like robbery, yet most often it describes thefts through well-planned, nonviolent acts. It might include pickpocketing, institutional thieving, auto theft, shoplifting, forgery and counterfeiting, confidence games, extortion and miscellaneous rackets such as using illegal checks, credit cards, and money orders.[269] Professional crime overlaps organized, common, and white-collar crimes, yet it differs from each. Unlike organized crime, which purports to provide a service, professional crime tends to be more predatory and parasitic.[270] And, unlike common and white-collar crimes, professional crime involves the skillful pursuit of illegal acts, on a persistent and regularized basis, instead of only sporadically and amateurishly. Crimes committed professionally occur relatively infrequently since few make crime a career. Nevertheless, professionals may victimize people more extensively and efficiently than most other criminals.

STATE AND POLITICAL CRIME

> *Of what use is it for the shopkeeper to raise the alarm when the*
> *criminals and the civil guard are the same people?*
>
> J.M. COETZEE, *Waiting for the Barbarians*

> *Bring back the life*
> *of Claude Reece Jr.*
> *I want the bullet from his head*
> *to make a Benin bronze*
> *to make an explosion of thunder*
> *to make a cyclone*
> *I want the 14 years of Claude Reece Jr.*
> *shot on the 15th day of september*
> *shot in the back of the head*
> *shot by a police officer*
> *shot for being black*
>
> JAYNE CORTEZ, *Coagulations*

> *Tell me something*
> *what you think would happen if*
> *everytime they kill a black boy*
> *then we kill a cop*
> *you think the accident rate would be lower*
> *subsequently?*
>
> JUNE JORDAN, *"Poem About Police Violence"*

These crimes describe illegality by and against the state, respectively. We normally reserve the label political crime to offenses occurring during or for the purpose of protesting or altering existing social, economic, and political structures.[271] Political crime may violate routine or specialized laws designed specifically to curb political opposition. It might include treason, sedition, espionage, sabotage, assassination, war collaboration, draft and civil rights violations, student protests, and advocating radical beliefs. It might involve various kinds of terrorist acts. It might also violate legislation limiting free expression, as with demonstrations, picketing, and marching laws. And it might involve common crimes committed for political ends. Normally, we would consider the state and the society as the chief victims of political crime, including government officials who might suffer attacks. Yet, some innocent bystanders may also be victimized in the process.[272]

Some question how we label political crime, complaining that we encompass all perceived threats, widely defined, instead of merely those acts directly designed to violently subvert the state or society. Political crime should also include state crimes to preserve social order, such as police brutality and rights violations. Some view these crimes as a kind of repression that violates laws, abridges rights, denies liberty, and administers violence for political and economic purposes, and which might even involve genocide, torture, imprisonment, domestic and foreign intervention, surveillance, evasion and collusion, war, and murder.[273] In this sense, protestors may become victims of political crime committed by the state.[274]

Three other kinds of state crime also occur: corruption, misfeasance, and structural violence. Corruption misuses governmental processes for personal gain, and might include bribery, kickbacks, and payoffs.[275] Misfeasance includes illegal or improper behavior committed while performing official duties, such as brutality, lawbreaking, or lethal force while enforcing the criminal law.[276] Structural violence results form institutionalizing injustices such as racism, sexism, classism, inequality, and militarism.[277] Much of this behavior also escapes criminal law definitions. Moreover, we seem to legitimate much government wrongdoing, or questionable behavior, by assuming such actions promote goals such as national and domestic security and law and order.[278] When we do act against government abuses, we focus almost exclusively on individual wrongdoing. In cases such as ABSCAM, we might even create criminal situations to tempt the "bad apples" holding high elective office.

On the other hand, we rarely seem to question the apparently much more widespread, fundamental, and damaging structural abuses committed by government. Even Watergate, which probably revealed only fragments of state wrongdoing,[279] was not used to challenge our politico-economic system. By selectively purging only the most blatant wrongdoers, it further legitimized state activities: "the system worked!" Did it really?

VICTIMLESS CRIMES.   Finally, so-called "victimless" crimes, such as drug use, gambling, prostitution, drunkenness, homosexuality, pornography, fornication, and vagrancy, seem by definition to produce no conventional victims or victimization.[280] Yet some argue that even if they do not directly injure other individuals, they may nevertheless victimize the perpetrator and the society.[281] This reinforces crime as an offense against the society generally instead of against specific victims, contradicts the victim's interests, and acquiesces to an unnecessary overcriminalization of the laws.

Overcriminalization also produces more victims than would otherwise exist because of the secondary crimes it generates. As suggested earlier, criminalizing drugs, for example, artificially raises their value, requiring all but the richest users to commit other crimes to support their habit.[282] Criminalizing prostitution subjects "street walkers" to violence from pimps and customers, and pushes them into other crimes to help make a living. Vice enforcement preoccupies police work,[283] strongly tempting officers to commit these and other crimes themselves, and, at the very least, diverts valuable time away from preventing other victimizations. So-called "victimless" crimes produce extensive victimization after all, yet ironically, they result primarily because they have been defined as criminal.

Who Victimizes

> *You felons on trial in courts*
> *You convicts in prison cells*
> *You sentenced assassins*
> *Chain'd and handcuffed with iron*
> *Who am I that I am not on trial or in prison?*
>
> WALT WHITMAN

> *We have met the enemy and he is us.*
>
> POGO

Our concept of criminals begins with how we define, and even how we enforce, crime. Under current definitions, we have excluded considerable (although not all) "white-collar" and government wrongdoing and wrongdoers. Having done so, we tend to emphasize lower and working classes as our major criminals, since we view them as responsible for most crimes, particularly as portrayed in the crime index.

CLASS.   Considerably more uniformity of wrongdoing across classes and other backgrounds exists than we might imagine.[284] Obviously, the kind of offender might vary significantly for some crimes, such as for corporate kickbacks or welfare fraud, but predicting the perpetrators of most other crimes is much more difficult. While we cannot review offender characteristics for all offenses, we can at least identify some trends and provide some examples.

Self-report and other studies show no significant differences among classes in the amount of crime (even as now defined) committed.[285] One study, for example, showed 91% of the respondents (in a sample dominated by upper classes) admitting to at least one offense for which they could have received a prison sentence.[286] Middle-class thefts cost far more than lower-class thefts.[287] Three-quarters of all employees steal from their own companies[288] and corporate criminals steal the most. The cost of only one of many large corporate abuses each year often matches the losses from all common thefts combined.[289] We have both upper- and lower-class shoplifters and juvenile delinquents. While classes may differ in some of their crimes, the overall amount is similar. In fact, for some crimes that we largely associate with lower classes, such as juvenile delinquency, black lower classes and white upper classes do not differ,[290] and the latter may actually even excel.[291] Also, the so-called "dark figure" of unreported or undetected corporate crime (which some estimate as 100 times greater than known offenses) vastly exceeds the figure for common crimes.[292]

Moreover, lower-class wrongdoing does not wreak more damage than upper-class crime, as we normally assume. White-collar and corporate property crime, for example, vastly exceed lower-class property crime.[293] Corporate criminals commit crimes repeatedly, as well: one study showed 90% were recidivist offenders.[294] Although lower classes do seem to contribute greater violent crime, upper classes may contribute as much or more overall violence, such as through workplace hazards,[295] which have simply not been defined as crime, but should be. Lower classes do commit much crime, yet our view of them as the predominant criminals may have less to do with their relative tendency to commit crime and more with selective perceptions and enforcement.

Poverty and unemployment may provide powerful incentives and frustrations for crime. Yet the wealthier may have their own motivations for crime, including economic competition, the drive for profits and personal advancement, and the frustrations of a dog-eat-dog society. Many business executives, for example, find it very difficult to even locate the fine line between legitimate and criminal business behavior, much less avoid crossing it.[296] All classes seem to have motives for committing crime, some related to material or status needs, others to psychological alienation. More important, not only does crime occur across classes, but one's class, and the very existence of classes, may constitute a major crime source as well.

RACE.   We view our stereotypical criminals as poor, young, non-white males. This does describe those most embroiled in the criminal process, but largely only because of the racial biases of law enforcement. Racially, for example, blacks, hispanics, and native Americans all enter the criminal process in numbers significantly exceeding their proportion of the population.[297] Blacks constitute 11% of the population, but 26% of all arrests, and 51% of all violent crime arrests.[298] An estimated 90% of all black Americans will be arrested at some time in their lives.[299] They will be eight and a half times more likely than whites to go to prison as well.[300] One study shows that proportional to their population, native Americans get arrested three times more than blacks and eight times more than whites,[301] while another report indicates arrest rates eight times as high as blacks and twenty times more than whites.[302]

GENDER AND AGE.   Sexually and chronologically, young men break the law much more than older men, and all women, in virtually every setting,[303] including both violent and property crimes.[304] While women have shown increasingly criminal patterns,[305] men, including many juveniles, commit the most serious crimes. They also seem more capable of committing some of our more atrocious crimes, such as mass murders.[306]

Men mostly victimize men (among the crime reported), but also violate women extensively. While nonwhite men seem more inclined toward street violence, white men, from all classes, seem equally inclined toward violence toward women, particularly in the home. Rape studies, for example, have shown that this violence emerges rather uniformly throughout the population, and does not confine itself to "subcultures" of violence, or to psychotic minds.[307] Rapists share the same sexist beliefs prevailing throughout the population; they differ only in how they act out their attitudes.[308]

While spouse abusers' other characteristics often include alcoholic parents and their own alcohol problem, their own prior abuse, and feelings of oppression, the underlying force of such violence seems to have more to do with culturally legitimated male dominance than particular offender traits.[309] Having baseball bats for sale inscribed with the words "wife beater" provides only one small example.[310] Things like this might also make women, usually less inclined toward violence, change their behavior for the worse, such as in child abuse where the women who commit such violence have usually been battered by their husbands.[311]

CAREER CRIMINALS.   Already, we should have some doubts about the supposed "career criminals" who terrorize the rest of us.[312] Relatively few offenders make crime a career, despite media portrayals to the contrary,[313] although many of us might use crime to supplement lagging careers or to overcome barriers to developing them. Given their recidivism rates (as high as 90%), corporate criminals might make crime a career more than common offenders, especially given the paucity of law and enforcement governing this behavior.[314] Nevertheless, few criminals qualify as professional in their skills. Recidivism, often taken as indicating criminal expertise, in fact reveals the opposite. We know about recidivists because they number among the very few offenders we catch—hardly a sign of expertise. Some victimization results from professionals, such as contract killers,[315] but it contributes relatively little to the common crimes we most often fear. We might find considerably greater professionalism in the white-collar, corporate, and government wrongdoing to which we pay considerably less attention.

VICTIMS VS. OFFENDERS.   Furthermore, we typically exaggerate the distinctions between victims and offenders, treating them as two completely separate groups, and labelling the former as "innocent" and the latter as "guilty." Yet, this seriously underestimates their shared characteristics. Aside from the burgeoning literature implicating victims, to varying degrees, in their own victimization, we have considerable evidence that victims and offenders overlap.[316] Some offenders have been victimized previously, and react with new crimes when nothing happens to their attackers.[317] Various reports show that many violent crime victims have committed violent crimes before, and vice versa.[318]

One study shows 36% of victims as prior defendants and another 16% as both defendants and victims before.[319] Two studies of murder victims show that 50% and 62% of the victims, respectively, had criminal records.[320] Another lists 27% of the victims as defendants before.[321] A report on aggravated assault victims shows that three-quarters had a prior record.[322] In fact, being a victim or an offender might contribute toward one's assuming dual roles. Offenders, interacting in a criminal atmosphere, often find themselves victimized eventually, and victims might commit their own crimes out of frustration or revenge for their past victimization, sometimes reacting excessively.[323]

VICTIM-OFFENDER RELATIONSHIPS.   We also seriously misrepresent the relationships between victims and offenders. Although we might better emphasize race, class, and national relationships in understanding victimization,[324] we have also explored the personal relationships involved in crime and found them extensive.[325] We picture strangers as committing most crimes, yet in fact we will more likely be victimized by an acquaintance, friend, or relative.

Particularly with violent crimes, victims and offenders often have had some past or present relationship of some sort. Two-thirds of all rape victims, for example, know their offenders, as do three-quarters of all aggravated assault victims.[326] A prior or continuing relationship occurs in one-half of all felony arrests, and in one-third of all property arrests.[327] Many apparent arson victims end up being the criminals responsible for setting the fires, to collect insurance or to expel tenants. Many other crimes emerge from a "subculture of violence" in which it may often be almost a matter of chance who becomes the victim and who becomes the offender for any given criminal event.[328]

IMPLICATIONS.   According to conventional wisdom, those who victimize include a relatively small number of hardened, career, and often "savage" criminals,[329] predominantly young, lower-class non-white males. Beyond these stereotypes, however, we find many contradictions: Recidivism has been considerably exaggerated,[330] few offenders have criminal careers, most offenders are white and spread rather evenly across classes. Most criminals are not strangers; more often they have present or past relationships with victims. Victims and offenders often come from similar backgrounds and have past experiences as both victims and offenders. Who victimizes? To a substantial extent, we all do. What appears to be greater criminality by some people stems substantially from who attracts the greatest enforcement, prosecutions, convictions, and punishments. Some people do commit common crimes more than others, but they may be precisely those who have the greatest, and maybe even the most justifiable, reasons for doing so.

Who Suffers Victimization

> *Murderer and victim both shout 'Aaah' to get our attention.*
>
> EUGENE IONESCO

Our understanding of victims bears misconceptions as well. Restricted criminal definitions reduce the range of harms we classify as criminal victimizations, and thus also limit those we recognize as victims. Beyond that, we also often attribute the greatest victimization to the wrong groups.

VICTIM TYPOLOGIES. Since the earliest days of victimology, various typologies have been devised to classify victims. Mendelsohn typed victims according to their culpability, including completely innocent, minor guilt, ignorant guilt, voluntary, greater (than offender) guilt, complete guilt, and false victimization.[331] Hentig classified victims using psychological, social, and biological factors. Besides distinguishing born victims and social victims, he included the young, females, the old, the mentally defective, immigrants, minorities, dull normals, the depressed, the acquisitive, the wanton, the lonesome, fomenters, and the excluded.[332] Barnes and Teeter added the negligent victim, while Reckless and the President's Commission on Law Enforcement and the Administration of Justice distinguished the reporting and nonreporting victim.[333]

More recently, Fattah has identified nonparticipating, latent, provocative, participating, and false victims.[334] Sellin and Wolfgang have defined primary, secondary, tertiary, mutual, and no victimization. Landy and Aronson have emphasized attractive and unattractive victims, while Geis has stressed victim responsiveness. Lamborn has designated initiators, facilitators, provocateurs, perpetrators, cooperators, and instigators.[335] Finally, Schafer has suggested a typology based on victim responsibility, including unrelated, provocative, precipitative, biologically weak, socially weak, self-victimizing, and political victims.[336]

Researchers believe these typologies have some important uses, such as to explain victim-offender relationships, assess victim risks and responsibilities, clarify victims' biological, social, and psychological characteristics, and devise prevention strategies. While each typology offers something toward these goals, many imply the victim's guilt and none seems to provide a comprehensive classification.[337] They also largely promote a very individualistic view of victimization that examines victims and their relation to offenders, but ignores crime's social context.

We can measure people's risk or likelihood of victimization by their desirability, vulnerability, availability, susceptibility, resilience, and provocativeness.[338] Provocativeness implies that victims might help induce crime: their own behavior may increase their risks. Desirability denotes one's relative attractiveness as a target. Susceptibility indicates one's inclination or frequency of victimization. Vulnerability designates a person's relative strength for resisting victimization. Availability describes one's accessibility for victimization. Resilience measures a person's ability to absorb crime when victimized. Who gets victimized the most thus depends on which concept we use.

VICTIM STEREOTYPES.   Conventionally, we stereotype certain people as the most likely victims and pay them the most attention. We emphasize the victimization of women, children, and the elderly (outside the home); of the police, society, and government; and of middle and upper classes. Yet these may actually be atypical victims. Some of them do bear risks, yet their actual victimization rate either is low or misleading. Women, children, and the elderly seem relatively vulnerable and may have less resilience than others when crime strikes. White, middle- and upper-class communities may appear most desirable, at least for property crime. In our crime-ridden nation, the society by definition seems susceptibile to victimization. And by virtue of their work, the police seem relatively available for victimization as well.

Yet women, children, and the elderly suffer victimization by common crimes (as compared to the family crimes we largely ignore) relatively little compared to young men. Nonwhite, lower-class people get victimized more extensively for most common crimes, particularly by violence, as compared to white, middle-, and upper-class people. Also, we might well view the crime committed against businesses, government, social institutions, and the police within the context of the legitimate resistance they might create. Businesses, particularly small businesses,[339] do bear considerable victimization, yet they may create precisely the conditions and incentives conducive to crime, committed both by insiders (such as employees)[340] and outsiders (such as community members).[341] The crime emerging during the New York City blackout several years ago, for example, did not strike randomly, but rather against specific business targets, which served as either the symbolic or actual object of ghetto frustrations.[342]

In fact, organizations seem susceptible to victimization by all classes when viewed as too big, wealthy, impersonal, or bureaucratic,[343] or when invisible, impersonal, or anonymous.[344] Moreover, our conception of the society and state as the crime victim may be true theoretically, yet it robs individual victims of the attention they deserve. Also, while government portrays itself as the constant victim of terrorism,[345] some believe that state terrorism far exceeds individual terrorism.[346]

Finally, contrary to conventional wisdom, police officers do not suffer excessive victimization compared to many other professions and many other kinds of crime victims to whom we pay only minor attention. Furthermore, the lethal force they wield, and the role they play, might induce victimization much more than the victim precipitation we sometimes attribute to others.[347] Ironically, much police victimization comes from people we rarely consider their enemies:[348] 40% of police injuries and 20% of police homicides come from people involved in family disputes.[349]

THE REAL VICTIMS. Overall, the greatest victims of common crime, when we combine the various measures of risk and likelihood, are precisely the most likely offenders, or at least those most likely apprehended: poor, young, nonwhite males.[350] Earlier, we showed that many offenders also suffer criminal victimization and often include people who have some relationship with offenders. These people have the least opportunities or resources to avoid crime, and even minor victimizations affect them considerably. For this and other reasons, these victims find themselves not only most likely to be victimized, but to be victimized repeatedly.[351]

They, and some other groups, appear particularly susceptible to a victimization cycle. One of every five violent crime victims, for example, experiences a similar crime again within six months.[352] Only 1% of the population bears one-quarter of all multiple victimization from violent crime, 2% absorb one-third, and 5% suffer one-half.[353] Almost one-quarter of all sexual assault victims have suffered that crime more than once.[354] Very many blacks, native Americans, the unemployed, and welfare recipients suffer repeated victimizations as well. These people become "recidivist" victims, not because they ignore available precautions or because they precipitate crime, but because they live in the circumstances most conducive to victimization, with the least defenses available.[355] Public policy contributes considerably to this maldistribution of victimization.[356]

More specifically, who gets victimized the most and what are their characteristics? Most victimologists have examined only those officially victimized the most; that is, the victims of officially defined crimes. We have treated victims of white-collar and corporate crimes very ambivalently, often considering them more as dupes or losers than victims.[357] For now, we will look exclusively at conventional crime victims, and postpone examining other victims to our subsequent discussion of human rights. There we will consider, among others, victims of government repression; of political, economic, and social institutions; and of corporate and other organizational abuses.

As for official crime victims, we could compile a long, and rather obvious, list of those victimized by all the kinds of crimes and offenders we have already identified. Rather than belabor that commonsense notion, we will stress instead the characteristics mostly associated with victimization, remembering that these traits will vary with the specific crime.

RACE AND CLASS.   Many of the same characteristics that dispose people toward social, political, and economic victimization also incline them toward criminal victimization. A few have suggested that some people are "born victims."[358] Those physically, politically, and economically weak and unpopular bear some of the greatest burdens.[359] Race and class, often acting together, help determine one's victimization, for example. Blacks,[360] hispanics,[361] native Americans,[362] and the poor[363] bear a very disproportionate victimization, especially from violent crimes. People we have labeled as "deviants," such as mental patients, prostitutes, alcoholics, drug addicts, homosexuals, religious cultists, and prisoners, also suffer a disproportionate level of victimization, compounded by our general tendency to ignore it.[364] Harvey Milk, for example, the gay San Francisco supervisor, was murdered substantially because of what his victimizer viewed as his aberrant behavior.

One study shows victimization for blacks and the poor three to five times higher for robberies, two times higher for assaults, and four times higher for rape[365] than whites. A more startling report shows black victimization seven times higher for assaults and twenty-five times higher for robberies with assaults than for whites.[366] Blacks suffer 89% of all violent crimes, 80% of all personal robberies, and six to eight times the total victimization of whites, according to another study.[367] Blacks get victimized more violently by whites than vice versa, black women suffer more than white women, black men most often get assaulted and robbed, and black women most often get raped.[368] Blacks get hurt disproportionately by property crime as well.[369] And the unemployed (mostly poor and disproportionately minorities) suffer victimization two to three times more than the employed.[370]

Homicide kills black men more than any other cause,[371] and is the fourth leading source of death for all blacks combined.[372] The risks of homicide measure 9.3 per 100,000 people for whites, and 77.9 per 100,000 for blacks.[373] Ninety-five percent of all black homicide victims get killed by fellow blacks.[374] In sum, to be poor and a minority substantially increases one's risks of victimization.[375] Victimization also correlates highly with using public transit, poorly policed streets, fixed incomes, physical vulnerability, and inadequate personal protection, all of which accompany poverty.[376]

GENDER

> *Then there was the pain. A breaking and entering when even the senses are torn apart. The act of rape on an eight year old body is a matter of the needle giving because the camel can't. The child gives because the body can, and the mind of the violator cannot.*
>
> MAYA ANGELOU

One's gender and marital status may help predict one's victimization,[377] although much may depend on the setting. For example, outside the home men far surpass women in victimization,[378] yet inside the home we have only begun to discover the much greater victimization of women.[379] Accordingly, being a wife and not a husband substantially increases one's victimization in the home,[380] yet outside that setting men, and divorced or single women, suffer the most crime.[381]

Among crimes committed outside the home, women most risk getting raped,[382] followed by other traditional crimes, and by some special to certain women, such as the victimization of female hospital personnel.[383] At home women not only risk rape by their husbands, but also battering at an alarming rate.[384] Women get little protection for these crimes, thanks to social biases, entrenched by law, myth, culture, and literature[385] that allow men to rule the home and that second-guess women's victimization in the streets.[386] Ironically, while the women's liberation movement has encouraged (as well it should) battered women to "come out," and thereby perhaps helped reduce this victimization of women, it has also encouraged women to leave the home (for work and other pursuits) for a setting where they may be subjecting themselves to greater victimization by other crimes.[387]

AGE.   Along with some women, children and the elderly seem to best exemplify people who, because of their physical condition, find themselves vulnerable to crime. Age strongly predicts victimization and injury.[388] The elderly, for example, often isolate themselves in their homes, except for occasional departures, because they so fear crime.[389] While they mostly risk street victimization, we have learned increasingly about "granny bashing," or elderly victimization at home by their own families.[390] The elderly frequently have those characteristics most associated with victimization outside the home as well, including low incomes, low mobility, high crime neighborhoods, public transit, and defenselessness.[391] Consequently, they suffer repeat victimizations, yet have relatively little resilience for each new attack.

Children, from young infants to older juveniles, bear considerable victimization as well.[392] Like women and the elderly, they risk victimization both inside and outside the home. As children age, their risks shift from the home to the street. While we continue learning about juvenile victimization in public settings,[393] the most recent research has emphasized children's victimization in the home.

In 1981, 851,000 cases of child abuse were reported, up 50% in just five years, with as many as 5000 children dying each year as a result. While this undoubtedly reflects an increasing willingness to report, it may also indicate an actual crime increase. Yet those reported may comprise as little as 10% of all cases.[394] One report estimates that 1 of every 100 children get abused, that it has occurred historically, and that it affects children of all classes.[395] Some of that crime occurs as sexual victimization,[396] others as abduction (sometimes by one's own parents),[397] but most comes as child battering. Some children, such as the hyperactive, precocious, premature, adopted, lower-class, younger, nonwhite, stepdaughters, and children of abused parents, seem most susceptible.[398] Others have found male children somewhat more susceptible, but female children more likely to be injured.[399] As with women, the victimization rate might climb considerably in national statistics as we increasingly pry open the doors of the home and family.

OFFENDERS AS VICTIMS. Some people suffer an increased risk of criminal victimization by being criminals themselves. Criminals in general, especially those in prison or those committing vice or "victimless" crimes, experience a high crime rate. Offenders generally suffer various kinds of victimization from their arrest through their imprisonment, and from the accompanying procedures and conditions they experience. Some of this victimization, such as police beatings, seriously questions government behavior.

Offenders, both inside and outside prison, bear extensive crime committed by officials and private individuals, often fellow inmates,[400] often racially motivated,[401] and at rates at least as high as crime outside prison.[402] They may suffer thefts, robberies, rapes, assaults, homicides, extortion, and other crimes. Rape is epidemic in some prisons.[403] One study shows prison assaults eleven times higher than prison records show.[404] Official crimes in prison include unwarranted beatings, solitary confinement, and the deprivation of food, water, and other rights and needs.[405] Others might be victimized by having been wrongfully accused, tried, and punished for crimes they did not commit, such as revealed in recent studies showing 25 wrongful executions since 1900 and at least 6000 wrongful felony convictions annually.[406] We can explain much of this victimization not only by the criminal atmosphere in which offenders find themselves, but their lack of protection, rights, and legitimacy.

VICTIMLESS OFFENDERS AS VICTIMS. Likewise, while offenders generally increase their chances of victimization by being forced to live with other criminals, offenders without victims[407] (that is, largely vice criminals) bear a special crime burden. On the street, the secrecy, stigma, and illegality of their actions prevent them from receiving protection, and legitimize their victimization by other offenders.[408] Biased enforcement and social conditions also help make people like prostitutes,[409] homosexuals,[410] and drug users[411] highly susceptible to criminal victimization. Because of their criminal label, they often find themselves embroiled in serious crimes with real victims, often themselves. Drug users, for example, constitute 31% of all homicide victims in Philadelphia.[412]

OTHER VICTIMS. Many others suffer criminal victimization to varying degrees as well. Some recent research has emphasized some increasingly frequent and important victims, such as tourists and other inexperienced people,[413] students,[414] auto drivers and pedestrians,[415] and bystanders.[416] In sum, who gets victimized? To varying degrees, we all do. Yet some people bear a much greater burden than others, particularly given our unequal opportunities for avoiding victimization or for coping with it should it come. Those victims warrant our greater attention.

Where Victimization Occurs

Just as our stereotypes about criminals and victims predict who victimizes and who gets victimized, they also suggest where victimization predominates. If, for a moment, we remain bounded by our current criminal definitions, then the places we assume bear the burden of crime might meet our preconceptions. Even so, our stereotypes of street crime may be somewhat misleading.

First, most "street" crime does not occur in the streets at all. Most pickpocketing and purse snatching, for example, happen in nonresidential buildings and public transit.[417] Much property and violent crime occurs in the home. In 1980, twenty-four million households were victimized, almost one of every three in the nation.[418] Although in the home violence among strangers appears less, family violence more than compensates.[419] Much common crime occurs in other institutions as well, such as public buildings, private offices and businesses, and in prisons. The annual cost of crime in schools, for example, exceeds $200 million.[420] Consisting of mostly larceny and minor assaults, it accounts for 8% of all victimization, yet as much as 90% may go unreported. Poorer schools bear more victimization than wealthier ones.[421]

We commonly assume that if the wealthier (our stereotypical victim) get victimized by the poor (our stereotypical offender), then it occurs where the wealthier live or work or play. Yet the poor will more likely commit (both personal and property) crimes in their own poor neighborhoods than elsewhere. And, since criminality pervades the population, wealthier neighborhoods will likely be most (but not exclusively) victimized by wealthier criminals. Businesses will also be more likely (but not exclusively) victimized by their own employees or management than by outsiders.

Certainly, business sites and wealthier neighborhoods and "playgrounds" can suffer significant victimization, although predominantly as property losses. Some of this victimization results from "spillovers" of crime from other areas, or even some calculated targeting of more lucrative locations.[422] Yet the most serious and most extensive crime occurs in poor neighborhoods and businesses. While crime rates appear to be increasing in rural,[423] small-town,[424] and suburban areas, cities bear the greatest burden.[425] The thirty-two largest cities, for example, with 16% of the population, suffer three-quarters of all robberies.[426] Most urban victimization, however measured, occurs in poor, nonwhite ghettos,[427] committed not only by residents, but also extensively by outsiders.[428]

Economic wealth and class provide useful, but imperfect, indicators of where victimization will occur. Significant crime occurs in the "suites" as well as in the "streets" (to use the popular, but misleading cliché), but is committed mostly by those we expect to see in those settings. While the poor might be naturally inclined toward victimizing those with greater resources, they usually do not do so.

Economic factors seem to motivate crime at different class levels, for different reasons. More broadly, regions with high unemployment (such as the Northeast) or poverty (such as the rural South) frequently have high crime rates, yet economically healthier regions (such as the Southwest) have considerable victimization as well. Economic competition can produce crime just as does economic stagnation, particularly with wealth poorly distributed. Interestingly, while poor, Third World neighborhoods have the same relatively higher crime rates as poor American neighborhoods, the overall American crime rate far exceeds that of developing nations, despite our great wealth. Yet affluence and urbanization need not produce crime, as many other developed nations demonstrate. Both indicators begin to recede when wealth becomes more evenly distributed.[429]

Finally, recent research designed to help Americans assess their security when travelling shows that their risks decline dramatically not when they stay home, but when they leave. With more killings than in the rest of the world combined, most crime in the world occurs in the United States.[430]

CONCLUSION

Criminal victimization in the United States occurs at overwhelming levels, including much property crime and extensive violence. Yet we often misunderstand American crime, particularly in how we define crime and criminals in the law and in how they are portrayed and conveyed in the media.

Our social reality of victimization contains many misconceptions about crime's form, setting, perpetrators, and victims. Our selective criminal definitions unnecessarily exclude much harm and wrongdoing which, taken together, far surpass the damage from those acts we do define as criminal. Yet, even within official definitions, broad segments of the population, across classes, commit crime, and not merely some specialized group. Victimization is also felt throughout the population, although poor, young, nonwhite males bear the greatest burden and, as we continue to discover more family violence, women and children increasingly share the load. We get victimized significantly by those we know, and not merely by strangers. Many victims have previously been offenders, and vice versa. Most crime is committed not in the streets, or in wealthier neighborhoods (by poor offenders), but rather in homes and buildings in poor neighborhoods (by poor offenders), and in wealthier settings (by wealthier offenders).

In the previous chapter, we examined victims' historic role and contemporary reemergence. In this chapter, we have begun to more specifically analyze the victimization experience as a prelude to the victim's involvement in the criminal process. We thus have examined the victimization level; and who, what, and where it strikes. But we have done so only within the confines of a limited "social reality" of victimization.

We must penetrate this social reality to discover the actual scope of victimization if we ever hope to understand the problem and take steps to eliminate it. We will later suggest that we might do so by applying human rights standards that significantly broaden victimology's scope and power, overcome the limits of official crime definitions in identifying victimization, and help us stress the underlying causes of suffering. Unfortunately, in getting to victimization's

sources—the most fruitful direction for handling the crime problem—our misleading perceptions of crime and victimization impede
our progress. We move now to consider the various theories of victimization, and the unnecessary dead end to which most of them
have thus far lead us.

4

Casting Blame: The Sources of Victimization

I am the masculine American man
I kill therefore I am

PHIL OCHS

Why does man kill? He kills for food. And not only food:
frequently there must be a beverage.   WOODY ALLEN

Criminals do not attack merely for food, although that might be one reason. In fact, almost endless reasons for crime have been suggested. These many causes, most of which we regard as separate and distinct, have made victimization appear almost inevitable. We often act, almost complacently, as if we can do very little about crime,[1] except perhaps to keep it within manageable levels. Such conclusions profoundly affect victims.

A Prevailing Fatalism

We hear, for example, that we cannot discover crime's ultimate causes and, even if we could, they themselves have no causes and, thus cannot be changed.[2] Others argue that the intractable causes of human behavior constitute the causes of crime. The pain and distress associated with crime should be viewed not as symptoms of disease, but as growing pains. Even if we knew the causes we may not be able to control them.[3] Others tell us that we cannot make a conclusive case for any mode of crime control.[4] Finally, we hear that criminological theory concerns itself almost entirely with the roots of crime, and yet the problems of crime, as currently understood, are susceptible to only approximate solutions of very limited potency.[5]

This pessimism may be unnecessary. A couple of those who tell us that crime constitutes an irreducible fact of life, for example, nevertheless show us, in their study of the Law Enforcement Assistance Administration, that the program failed to affect crime because it ignored the problem.[6] This may characterize our fatalism about eliminating crime: we assume we cannot change it, yet aside from treating its symptoms, we may not have really tried.[7]

In fact, criminology has spent relatively little effort discovering the roots of crime. Most studies claiming to analyze the "etiology" of crime do not look at causes or sources of *crime* at all. At most, many study the causes of *criminals*, taking a narrow, individualized analysis of lawbreakers, finding various reasons, and concluding that either everything causes crime or that we cannot say, for sure, that anything causes crime.[8] Or they suggest that crime results because the police do not do their job or because judges sentence too leniently or because civil liberties block enforcement efforts or because victims take inadequate precautions. But these theories ask us to believe that crime occurs merely because we have not done enough to physically prevent it.[9] They tell us little about the forces generating criminal behavior.

In assessing whether we know crime's origins, we seem to hold ourselves to unreasonably high standards, inapplicable in other scientific fields. If we do not know *all* the causes of crime, we assume we know none. If we cannot precisely trace how some factor specifically *causes* crime, we reject it. We cannot assume that poverty causes crime, apparently, because we do not know precisely *how* poverty leads to crime and, besides, not all poor people commit crime.

Some argue that we should ignore the sources of crime because even if we found them, we could do nothing about them. Existing programs have failed. We have limited resources. If government cannot conceivably devise a feasible solution, then we should not even theorize about crime's causes. Since social scientists have not "proven" the causes of crime, they act ideologically and not scientifically when they provide opinions to policymakers.[10]

Such views may vastly exaggerate our ignorance and inability to prevent crime at its sources. Since most criminologists do *not* examine sources, they cannot have attributed crime to poverty. Those few who do, often do so out of context and prescribe welfare programs without addressing the root sources of poverty or crime at all. As we shall see, we do know much about crime's sources, and probably can take steps to eliminate them. We need not rely on government programs, but in any case, our crime theories and theorizing must never depend, as some suggest they should, on whether the solutions our theories imply seem politically feasible. Also, we do not abandon science for ideology when we, as experts thoroughly immersed in a specialized field, make recommendations based on evidence strongly associating crime with certain factors and conditions, even if we have been unable to offer definitive scientific "proof." Is a science useful only when it has completed definitive studies on every question it has ever asked?

Suppose physicians or medical researchers told us that they (and we) could not examine the causes of disease or provide any remedies because they did not know all the sources. They could not act because although they knew the main sources they could not tell us precisely how they caused the disease, because disease will always be with us, and because we cannot change the ultimate causes of disease precisely because they are ultimate. Or suppose they told us that we could not use aspirin to cure our pains because we do not know precisely how the remedy works. Would we not protest?

In criminology, we seem to reject possible causes because we find cases where those causes do not *necessarily* lead to crime. Since we cannot predict all crime, or identify all causes, we conclude that we must ignore underlying sources and muddle through, hoping that the "growing pains" will subside on their own. Yet this may amount to what C. Wright Mills once called "crackpot realism," or a call for realism that not only unnecessarily perpetuates problems but makes them worse. As Laurence Sherman of the Police Foundation has argued, we used to put leeches on sick people to get the blood out and, if they did not get better, we put more leeches on: thus describes our level of discussion about crime.[11] As Jeffrey Reiman has suggested, to believe we can do nothing about crime, we must believe

> That the United States, with virtually limitless resources, capable of spending hundreds of billions of dollars to fight a hardly believable "threat" in Vietnam, cannot summon the resources and will to do battle with a threat that haunts almost everyone in our society and makes them fearful to walk the streets and hardly more secure at home; that the United States, with technology and information beyond the dreams of any previous generation, indeed any previous civilization, capable of placing a being on the moon and a heart in a human being, cannot figure out at least "some" of the causes of some crime and eliminate those causes; and that the United States, with over a million law enforcement and criminal justice personnel, with training and literally billions of work-hours of experience in the "fight against crime," has not developed the expertise even to dent the rising crime rate much less to reduce it. This is just too much to swallow.[12]

We do not know all the sources of crime, nor perhaps what specifically causes all crime to occur. But we do have much knowledge, and we may know the predominant sources of crime. Those "real-ists" who claim that our crime derives considerably from social and historical forces that police and courts cannot alter surely tell the truth.[13] We cannot reduce crime by tinkering with the police or the courts, but only by changing broader social conditions. Our failure stems not from our technical incapacity, but rather from our un-willingness to make the fundamental changes that significantly re-ducing crime would require.

What passes as causes or sources of victimization rarely fulfill the meaning of those words at all. We often needlessly complicate our knowledge of crime's origins, usually confusing symptoms with causes, and separating interrelated factors as if they had no com-mon sources. Consequently, the crime problem, which we will never easily solve, nevertheless appears much more intractable than need be. An almost limitless proliferation of "causes" has emerged, from reactionary, conservative, liberal, and radical perspectives. While we can never hope to examine them all, and while we will specifically ignore the more "exotic" crime sources (such as fluoridation or rock music), we can address the major theories, unearth their weak-nesses, and in particular suggest their implications for victims and victimology.

The Likely Culprits?

We can roughly divide (with some overlap) crime's supposed causes into: (1) regulatory failures, (2) criminal characteristics, (3) victim precipitation, and (4) structural forces. They amount to institution blaming, offender blaming, victim blaming, and system blaming. In-stitution blaming, or regulatory failures, refer to various inadequa-cies in the law, in enforcement practices and resources, in correc-tions, and in controlling various external correlates of crime. Offender blaming, or offender characteristics, refer to various acquired or in-herent traits, such as sickness or evil or upbringing, which cause people to commit crime. Victim blaming, or victim precipitation, de-scribes those acts of omission or commission that increase one's risks, if not invite crime. System blaming, or structural forces, represent those political, economic, social, and bureaucratic conditions, and structural characteristics that might induce crime.

Our basic understanding and treatment of the causes and per-petrators of crime often seem no more sophisticated, or logical, than Samuel Butler's description of Erewhonian trials:

> "Prisoner at the bar, you have been accused of the great crime of laboring under pulmonary consumption and . . . you have been found guilty. . . . It pains me to see one . . . brought to this distressing con-dition by a constitution which I can only regard as radically vicious; but

yours is no case for compassion: this is not your first offence: you have
led a career of crime, and have only profited by the leniency shown you
. . . to offend yet more seriously against the laws. . . . You were convicted of aggravated bronchitis last year . . . you have been imprisoned
on no less than fourteen occasions for illnesses of a . . . hateful character. . . . It is all very well for you to say that you came of unhealthy
parents . . . excuses such as these are the ordinary refuge of the criminal; but . . . there is no question of how you came to be wicked, but
only . . . are you wicked or not? . . . the law may . . . have its inevitable hardships. . . . But yours is no such case . . . . had not the
capital punishment for consumption been abolished, I would certainly
inflict it now. It is intolerable that an example of such terrible enormity
should be . . . unpunished. Your presence in the society of respectable
people would lead the able-bodied to think more lightly of all forms of
illness. . . . You may say that it is not your fault . . . that if you had
been born of healthy and well-to-do parents, and been well taken care
of when . . . a child, you would never have offended . . . nor found
yourself in your present disgraceful position. If you tell me that you had
no hand in your parentage and education, and that it is therefore unjust
to lay these things at your charge. . . . I answer that whether . . . your
fault or no, it is a fault in you . . . against [which] . . . the commonwealth shall be protected. You may say that it is your misfortune to be
criminal; I answer that it is your crime to be unfortunate. I do not hes-
itate . . . to sentence you to imprisonment, with hard labor, for the rest
of your miserable existence. During that period I . . . entreat you to
repent . . . and to entirely reform the constitution of your whole body.
I entertain but little hope that you will pay attention . . . you are already
too far abandoned" . . . though the feeling of the court was strongly
against the prisoner, there was no . . . violence against him. . . . Indeed, nothing struck me more during my whole sojourn in the country
than the general respect for law and order.[14]

We can do much better. Reviewing our various crime theories
constitutes no idle activity, particularly from the victim's perspective. We seek not to reestablish the eternal "truth" that we either
do not know crime's causes, or that the sources are endless, or that
we can do nothing about them. We do want to review the differing
implications for victims of accepting or rejecting the various crime
theories, or of concluding that we either can or cannot eliminate
victimization's major sources. We will also examine the political uses
of various crime theories, the interests they may serve, and the barriers they might pose to eliminating crime. And, we hope to reveal
some workable and feasible solutions for victimization. We may try
to do many things for victims, ranging from providing better protection, to greater court involvement, to better compensation and
services. But, while we must pursue these objectives, we help victims most by identifying and eliminating the primary sources of victimization in the first place.

INSTITUTION BLAMING:
REGULATORY FAILURES

The criminal law has, from the point of view of thwarted virtue, the merit of allowing an outlet for those impulses of aggression which cowardice, disguised as morality, restrains in their more spontaneous forms. War has the same merit. You must not kill your neighbor whom perhaps you genuinely hate, but by a little propaganda this hate can be transferred to some foreign nation against whom all your murderous impulses become patriotic heroism.   BERTRAND RUSSELL

Many argue that crime occurs because we fail, both directly and indirectly, to regulate it. Typically, they suggest that various failures of law, enforcement, punishment, resources, and external control create crime. Most of the blame falls on the criminal justice process.[15]

Nonenforcement

> *The word illegal means nothing in Duluth,*
> *where only law and order reign supreme.*
>
> GORE VIDAL, *Duluth*

> *Don't worry, I won't kill you;*
> *If anyone takes your life, it will be the law.*
>
> LONE RANGER (TO BAD GUY)

We often criticize the law and those who create and interpret it. Some argue that we enforce it inadequately, suggesting stricter laws and harsher punishments for common criminals. A few argue for criminal laws that encompass harms and wrongdoing not now defined as crime.[16] Others blame "soft" judges for promoting plea bargaining, excessive appeals, and defendant's rights, and for applying those protections at trial, concluding that civil liberties coddle criminals. Yet we have little reason to believe that these legal failures cause crime. We already have virtually the strictest laws in the world. Ironically, the strictest societies, including ours, have the most severe crimes.[17] Although encompassing other wrongdoers into the criminal law might promote equity, it would not eliminate the sources of lawbreaking. And civil liberties hardly provide protection for most offenders; they are usually honored more in the breach.[18]

Many failures of enforcement and correction have been suggested as crime sources. We have blamed crime on officials, especially the police, for their unprofessionalism, poor personnel, improper behavior, and even lawbreaking.[19] Official lawlessness breeds disrespect, as common criminals begin to see the real criminals as bribed police, slumlords, ripoff merchants, bribed corporate executives, and corrupt Presidents and Vice Presidents.[20] Some argue that inadequate or ineffective enforcement causes crime. Many suggest that we prematurely label youths as criminal, thus encouraging criminal careers.[21] Others find the source in the counterproductive incentives provided criminal justice personnel, which encourage them to place organizational needs and personal advancement ahead of preventing crime. We often accuse the courts of promoting crime by providing criminals a "revolving door" characterized by overprotection, lenience, and inadequate punishments. In general, we criticize enforcement and correctional objectives, such as deterrence, rehabilitation, isolation, reform, retribution, and prevention, either for their failure or their inappropriateness as goals in the first place.

Yet these problems, to the extent they really exist, do not cause crime either. We have done much to improve official professionalism, have tried an endless array of patrol and enforcement techniques (lavishly funded over the past decade), and have taken measures to reduce official corruption,[22] yet crime has not declined.[23] We do overlabel criminals, but this fails to explain why offenders break the law the first time, before the label has been applied. In fact, our "revolving door" is largely myth, particularly for the crimes we most fear.[24] The average prison term has doubled since 1965, during our greatest crime surge.[25] Our so-called crackdowns show no signs of working either.[26]

Officials do have discordant professional, organizational, and personal motives, many of their goals do conflict, and several seem counterproductive and inappropriate.[27] But all these problems fail to address the roots of crime. They rely, almost entirely, on questionable deterrence theories that would control crime through efficiency and punishment.[28] At best, they suggest secondary, not primary, "causes" of crime, or factors which, although they do not fundamentally generate crime, often make the crime problem worse.[29]

In other words, focusing on criminal justice failures falsely converts crime into an almost purely technical problem. Yet, as a social malady, the police cannot be expected to solve the crime problem.[30] Conceivably, we could reduce crime partially to a technical challenge, but not until we identify and largely eliminate the major sources of victimization. Then, we might more reasonably view crime prevention as physical control, strenuously reinforced by social norms and conditions that have removed the major incentives for crime.[31]

Nonregulation

RESOURCES. While many place the crime problem entirely in criminal justice hands, others attribute it to broader regulatory failures.

Some claim that criminal justice cannot solve the problem without sufficient resources and other support from the broader society. A few see the impossible task assigned to criminal justice, given the enormous incentives for crime that exist beyond enforcement lapses. Consequently, they blame crime on a general public unwillingness to support crime control efforts and our failure to regulate other social conditions that might stimulate crime in the first place.

In this vein, we have lamented our inability to control the effects of spending cuts, urbanization,[32] federalism,[33] affluence,[34] a burgeoning youth population,[35] the environment,[36] public health,[37] the media,[38] economic growth and development,[39] bystanders and the public generally,[40] and third parties who might facilitate victimization.[41] Many have identified these, and our failure to regulate them, as the major sources of crime. While we will discuss them all in greater detail (later in this chapter), now we can suggest that these "causes" either do not correlate with crime, or describe symptoms of more fundamental forces, or portray failures of self-protection, not underlying sources.[42]

By and large, regulatory failures represent either symptoms of crime or administrative lapses that largely occur after criminal forces have already begun. They might make the crime problem somewhat worse, but hardly constitute its source.[43] Some regulatory failures, such as overcriminalization, prisons, and handguns, while still secondary to crime's major, underlying causes, may help increase crime significantly, however. Although eliminating these problems would only begin to reduce crime, they deserve our attention in addition to crime's underlying social sources.

HANDGUN PROLIFERATION

> *Society creates gunmen and then gets excited when their guns go off.*
>
> BRUCE FRANKLIN

Handguns contribute significantly to crime, not to mention accidents.[44] A new handgun is sold every 13 seconds in the United States, and over one-half of all American households have at least one gun,[45] with as many as 200 million in circulation.[46] Over 30,000 deaths occur each year from handguns,[47] with at least 200,000 injuries and maimings. While 29 Americans were killed *each day* in 1979 with handguns, 8 people were killed *all year* with handguns in Great Britain, 34 all year in Switzerland, 21 in Sweden, 52 in Canada, 8 in Israel, and 42 in West Germany.[48] Almost all police officers who die on duty get killed with handguns.[49] A dramatic increase in gun use in committing crimes has occurred, including robberies (over 100,000), assaults (over 65,000), homicides (over 15,000), and suicides (over

12,000).[50] Firearms cause six times more accidental death than they wound intruders.[51]

Most handguns acquired for household and business protection either end up in the illicit gun market (having been stolen or misplaced) or end up being used against their owners, often with deadly consequences.[52] If offenders now using guns committed just as much crime, but with a knife (the next deadliest weapon), 80% fewer fatalities would result.[53] In sum, easy access to handguns not only vastly increases the death rate due to homicides and accidents, but it may provide a crucial difference in whether many crimes are committed in the first place. The proliferation and ready availability of handguns does not *cause* crime, but it does contribute substantially to facilitating crime and to helping justify armed police. Serious regulation would not end crime or its motivating forces, but it could significantly reduce those crimes that, by our failure to regulate appropriately, we practically invite.

Overregulation

OVERCRIMINALIZATION.   Ironically, crime might increase as much by overregulation as by underregulation. Many argue that overusing the law to criminalize behavior that fails to directly harm others generates unnecessary crime, simply by definition. But, as suggested earlier, it also creates a much bigger crime problem beyond this commonsense notion,[54] including secondary crime, nonenforcement, organized crime, and police crime.[55]

THE PRISON SYSTEM.   Prisons provide another example of overregulation. Simply put, many believe we imprison most people unnecessarily, for excessive terms, in intolerable conditions,[56] and for purposes that may have more to do with political or social control than crime control.[57] In combination, the system creates more crime. The United States has used prisons traditionally to punish crimes, yet although we incarcerate more than any other nation (and for longer than all but two countries),[58] this has not reduced crime,[59] and undoubtedly increased it.[60] Higher punishments have, in fact, correlated with increases in the crimes we seek to prevent, or with new crimes (such as murders committed by abductors when kidnapping receives the death penalty),[61] or sometimes with reduced prosecutions and convictions (from prosecutors and juries reluctant to impose such stiff penalties in practice).

Putting people in prison isolates offenders from their communities, imposing a stigma and a prison record that ex-convicts often find so indelible that committing more crime may be their only option.[62] By imprisoning people for long periods, in intolerable conditions that not only breed crime (upon release) but produce it (in prison) at alarming rates, we only harden prisoners to the criminal world and help teach or reinforce the skills and psychology of crime that often guide their behavior when released.[63] Most prison wardens admit that only a tiny fraction of their inmates provide any danger to the community. Prisons do not reform, or deter, or (with what little we devoted to the effort) rehabilitate. Their only function seems to be to further criminalize. Making prisons more "humane" will not solve the problem.[64] Yet we could, as other nations have, vastly reduce incarceration and help lessen some crime our system now seems to generate.

Implications

Crime does not originate in the criminal justice system's failure— although it certainly has failed—or in other administrative lapses. Of the many shortcomings of American criminal justice, some flaws contribute marginally to increasing crime. Others, like overcriminalization, the prison system, and inadequate handgun control, significantly add to the crime rate. Yet none of these regulatory failures describes a fundamental crime source.

Nevertheless, Americans widely accept regulatory failures as causing crime. What impact does this belief have? Politically, while it negatively assesses official behavior, it levels only very superficial criticism. Certainly, the American public has not denounced officials for overcriminalization, overpunishment, and inadequate handgun control. Instead, we view the problem as one of inadequate resources and administrative inefficiency, hardly a fundamental critique of the system's operation. For victims, the regulatory theory implies that their interests lie in improving the system's efficiency, in lobbying against defendant's rights, and in seeking a niche for themselves in the criminal process—conclusions that have important strategic implications, particularly if the regulatory theory, as we suggest here, is basically wrong. To see, let's explore the other theories of crime's origins, beginning with the offender as the possible source of victimization.

OFFENDER BLAMING: CRIMINAL CHARACTERISTICS

No one has the right to take another person's life. Or torture them or do anything to them to change their situation. That's antisocial and I don't give a damn what the cause is. . . . They're trying to find excuses to give people leeway to do whatever the hell they want to. And that's stupid. **No one forces anyone to do anything.**

A Crime Victim

Rich Man: *This is a free country. No one has to do anything if they don't want to.*

Poor Man: *(Stares at rich man)*

Rich Man: *This is a free country. You wouldn't have to be poor if you didn't want to.*

Poor Man: *(Pulls out a gun)*

Rich Man: *This is a free country. You wouldn't have to be a criminal if you didn't want to.*

Poor Man: *(Shoots rich man)*

Rich Man: *(On the ground) This is a free country. I wouldn't have to be dying if I didn't want to.*

Jules Feiffer

Sure I'm crazy. You think a sane person would go around killing people?

Woody Allen Character

No doubt we have spent more effort showing how offender characteristics produce crime than any other possible source. With criminology's historical preoccupation with offenders, crime theories predominate that stress traits criminals acquire inherently, or biologically, or from their immediate surroundings.[65]

Inherent Qualities

Some have argued that crime results from inherent qualities. That is, criminals represent those people born evil and therefore incapable of living in civil society.[66] Or, alternatively, some have suggested that we all either have an evil streak, or perhaps even a basically evil nature, and criminals are those who cannot overcome tendencies such as maliciousness and greed. While much of this might be predetermined, criminals might be those who choose not to control themselves. The "riffraff theory" of crime, for example, suggests that the poor and minorities who commit much of our crime consciously "choose" that behavior because they like it, just as they "choose" to live in slums. They would live in squalor, and presumably also commit crimes, even if their incomes were doubled or tripled.[67]

Other theories often ascribe to offenders some considerable free will to choose between a criminal and law-abiding life.[68] Thus, we

attribute to offenders a series of personal failings stemming from
their unwillingness to put their lives in order. We view them as
lazy, shiftless, undisciplined, thrill seeking, unfocused, and, in particular, unwilling to work.[69] When we do not attribute crime inherently to influences such as alcohol and drugs, then we ascribe weak-
ness to offenders who use such stimulants, arguing that their habits
increase their criminality.

Biological Traits

Related theories tend to be more biological.[70] One of the earliest, for
example, argued that criminality arose from one's body or facial features.[71] A few said criminality reflected endocrine malfunctions or
chromosome abnormalities.[72] Others related it to intelligence, using
IQ testing as a guide. Some traced it to genetic roots, identifying
degenerate family trees.[73] Some argue that crime results from sickness. Many have examined the psychological roots of criminality,
attributing it to influences such as stress, depression, role models,
and various psychopathologies.[74] Others connect it to a deprivation
of body touch, contact, and movement. Some even attribute criminality to one's odor, such as the famous French detective, Vidocq,
who claimed that every branch of the criminal profession has its
own smell: "Put me in a crowd of a thousand persons, and by the
sense of smell alone, I will single out every violator of the moral
law."

According to some, a person's immediate social contacts determine criminality, particularly those encountered when young. Thus,
the family, the school, the community, and the church shape our
behavior. When these institutions either break down, or become
tainted, children fail to develop the proper values and skills of self-
control. Thus, criminals might come from bad families, or from a
rising tide of permissiveness or "moral carelessness" in social
groupings,[76] or even from a "totally lost," undisciplined, indulgent,
drug-dependent generation.[77]

Problems with Offender Blaming

Yet some of these views have long been rejected as general crime
theories in criminology, sometimes derisively. While some tiny fraction of crime might come from illnesses that provoke violent out-
bursts of violence, we have little evidence that crime results from
inherent qualities, and many of the biological flaws we have discovered have no necessary relationship with crime, or at best they
describe only symptoms of deeper social causes. Less than 5% of
those charged with sex-related offenses, for example, are diagnosed
as having an underlying psychosis. Mental illness shows no cor-

relation with greater dangerousness or unsociability.[78] The degenerative influences of facial features hardly warrant mentioning. Corporate criminals, some of our most prolific lawbreakers, hardly display the traits of laziness and shiftlessness. Despite the propaganda of classic films such as *Reefer Madness*, alcohol and drugs do not cause raping, murdering, or other crimes inherently. Even mass murder may be more a social than a psychological phenomenon.[79]

Theories emphasizing personal choices and failures hold little more validity. Traits such as laziness and indecision do not correlate with crime; in fact, they might produce the opposite. We have little evidence that deteriorating institutions cause crime and, even if they did, we would want to know what caused those institutions to decline. To the extent that we have been more permissive, we could just as easily conclude that this has provided an alternative to crime, not a cause. Social rules and values will be obeyed not merely because we thoroughly ingrain them, but because we provide social circumstances that do not pervasively contradict them. Understanding the victim's role in crime also helps us dispel the false distinction offender blamers make between "good guys" and "bad guys." In the real world, the offender's peculiarities are vastly exaggerated.[80]

A New Upsurge

While we may have thought that theories of inherent or personal evil had long faded, they nevertheless still seem to capture the public imagination,[81] part of the continuing, but misleading, social reality of victimization. Recently, a new upsurge of these claims has arisen with considerable force. *Time* magazine talks about the "savages" and the "animals" stalking the streets, waiting to attack us. President Reagan conveys visions not only of evil empires abroad but evil criminals at home. With rehabilitation now officially and perhaps professionally regarded a failure, simple theories of personal failings have reemerged. And, just when we thought that biological theories had finally died, we also find them being resurrected once again.[82]

The prominence of criminal theories emphasizing offender characteristics may have more to do with politics than evidence. Political rhetoric can exploit people's tendency to attribute crime to personal failings rather than underlying social causes.[83] Some people may have personal problems that induce them to commit crime or that put them in situations where crime might be a spontaneous choice. But those lapses have nothing to do with inherent traits, and little to do with biological or psychological lapses. If we find alcohol and drugs,[84] or family conditions,[85] or social disintegration, or personal alienation[86] associated with crime, then we must identify the sources of those maladies. We will rarely find them in individuals.[87]

Life situations and social conditions do not completely predetermine human lives. We do have free will and some ability to resist circumstances and act independently, but much less so than we normally attribute. Even in a political democracy, our choices can be severely restricted and our temptations toward lawbreaking overwhelming.[88] We must hold individuals responsible for their behavior on some level, but presumably only in a society that provides reasonable and accessible alternatives to criminality, and not incentives to do precisely the opposite.[89] Responsibility cannot be absolute, but instead must rest on circumstances.[90] Eliminating the "bad apples" from the barrel will not reduce crime. To focus on the real sources of crime, we might well examine the apples less and the barrel more.

Implications

Nevertheless, many victims and Americans believe that irredeemable offenders or immutable offender characteristics cause much crime. What impact does this belief have? Politically, it justifies significant increases in state power and punishment for social control and protection, yet promises minimal success in eliminating crime, which we can only assume will continue to emerge from the irrepressible evil forces of human nature. For victims, it means becoming more suspicious of other people (any one of whom could strike at any moment), altering one's personal behavior, upgrading one's personal security, and lobbying for stricter penalties. With this theory's inherent pessimism, victims can do little but accept the problem and live with it.

VICTIM BLAMING: VICTIM PRECIPITATION

My friends, because my horse is stolen, you have hastened one and all to tell me my faults and my shortcomings. But strange, not one word of reproach have you uttered about the man who stole my horse.   KAHLIL GIBRAN, *The Forerunner*

Mark Slackmeyer: *It's now 3:00 a.m., and we're still chatting up a storm with NRA point man Pete Springfield. Pete, I wonder if you would share with our listeners some of your truly amazing thoughts about vigilantism.*

Pete Springfield: *I'd be glad to. Crime prevention is much like nuclear deterrence, Mark. Mutual assured destruction is the key. If all of us fought back, preferably with handguns, your average scum would be forced to think twice before rolling someone for video game* *money. My feeling is that the crime victim who won't risk his life over a few bucks deserves what he gets. He invites crime by failing to resist it.*

Mark Slackmeyer: *Okay, to sum up. The real reason for street crime?*

Pete Springfield: *Permissive victims.*

GARY TRUDEAU, *Doonesbury*

Ironically, perhaps the most developed component of victimology examines the victims' role in their own victimization. Using various degrees and definitions of victim precipitation, we have explored the contribution to crime made by victim characteristics and behavior.[91] While such an analysis might have its uses, and while some insist that it merely searches for insights into offender-victim interactions, its effect has often helped blame victims for victimization.[92] In fact, in reading this literature, we would be inclined to conclude that victims constitute a major source of crime.[93]

Whether intentional or not, *crime* victims have been implicated in victimization in countless theories, and for numerous crimes, although we generally do not scrutinize, much less blame, other victims such as those affected by hurricanes or tornadoes.[94] Since victimology's early days, we have heard about victim-offender mutuality,[95] victimogenesis,[96] the vague distinction between victim and criminal,[97] victim-offender interaction,[98] the victim's personality[99] or functional responsibility[100] or active role,[101] and the processes of victim precipitation[102] and of becoming a victim.[103] Victims have been found precipitating murders,[104] child abuse,[105] rapes,[106] thefts,[107] burglaries,[108] auto theft,[109] and property crime generally.[110] Most victim typologies at least imply the victim's participation in crime. National statistics show precipitation levels of 4 to 6% for rape, 14 to 21% for assaults, 5 to 11% for robberies, and 22 to 38% for homicides.[111] Other studies show even higher rates, including 19% for rapes,[112] and as high as 67% for homicides.[113]

Earlier, we suggested that people's risk of victimization might depend on their desirability, vulnerability, availability, susceptibility, resilience, and provocativeness. Now we must consider how responsible victims are for having failed to reduce those risks. What aspects of victim behavior and characteristics might help "precipitate" crime?

Behavior

Behaviorally, victims might provoke, invite, initiate, or instigate crime, or cooperate or participate in committing crime.[114] They might precipitate crime, and be blamed because of their lifestyle,[115] relationships,[116] movement patterns,[117] or inadequate precautions.[118] For example, aspects of one's lifestyle such as time spent outside the family in public places might increase one's chances of victimization.[119] We might even blame victims for simply being conspicuous.[120] A few years ago, a Wisconsin judge refused to sentence a rapist, indicating that sexual permissiveness and the woman's provocative clothes induced the attack.[121]

During a crime, we wonder whether victims sufficiently resist their attackers,[122] although ironically, nonresistance may best avoid injury. Many suggest, for example, that resistance provokes offenders,[123] and that submissiveness in rape reduces violence,[124] yet many women's organizations recommend resistance as a response.[125] Some attribute greater blame to victims who do not resist.[126] A few even argue that most victim typologies automatically, but unjustifiably, indict victims if they offer no resistance, when the reverse should be the case: we should consider only those who do not resist as victims![127]

Characteristics

As for traits precipitating crime, we have suggested that a victim's relative attractiveness[128] or respectability[129] might be important. Certain household characteristics have been associated with crime.[130] Some fall into a "victimological cycle" of interaction with offenders.[131] People might be victim prone, or have a psychological propensity,[132] or even possess "basic inner drives"[133] leading toward victimization.

Victims may present traits or behavior that allow offenders to justify their attacks, not merely after the offense,[134] but before and during the crime.[135] As a society, we may contribute to that "self-legitimization." Particularly in our culture and our politico-economic system, we attribute extensive individual responsibility for our fate. Various "just world" theories of everyday life assume that most people get what they deserve. Our very strong stereotypes of success and worthiness help not only offenders but also the public justify victimization on some level. When we get "ripped off" or cheated we often feel ashamed, as if we were raped.[136] Often, we get treated like most rape victims when victimized by offenses such as white-collar crime: we stand accused. Or we may deny victimization: "it never happened, and besides, they deserved it."[137]

Moreover, we seem to culturally legitimize some groups of victims, such as women, the poor, minorities, and homosexuals whose victimization we often treat much less seriously than others.[138] Some believe we assume that these people precipitate crime to politically justify their victimization.[139] We blame victims most easily when they appear remote and separate from our lives,[140] or when they threaten our interests. Specific provocation may be unnecessary; some victims might precipitate and "deserve" victimization by definition.

Advantages of Victim Orientation

Understanding victim precipitation has many valuable uses.[141] It helps us better understand the origin of particular criminal events. It allows us to examine the kinds of victim-offender interactions that lead to victimization. It suggests, from a sociological perspective, that victims have a "functional responsibility" for victimization that develops not because victims have necessarily provoked the crime, but rather from their being necessary for the criminal transaction to have occurred.[142] Clarifying the victim's role in crime can also help us devise strategies for reducing risks and predicting victimization. And, to the extent that victims really precipitate crimes, we can consider such behavior when deciding how to handle the offender. With these uses, we should not be reluctant to shift our focus to the victim in understanding crime.

Dangers of Victim Orientation

The concept of victim precipitation may carry many dangers, however, some of which we have already suggested. While we cannot impede scientific study simply because our findings might be misapplied or misunderstood, we nevertheless must recognize their likely effects. For example, what will be the impact of this statement taken from a leading rape study: "in a way, the victim is always the cause of crime."[143] Victim precipitation theories may, unwittingly, rationalize our blaming victims for their victimization and for shifting the burden and responsibility of crime control onto the victim and the general public.[144] Or, worse, they might provide yet a further distraction from examining crime's sources.

Victim Blaming

Blaming crime victims may symptomize a more widespread blaming of other victims in society.[145] By taking a very individualized focus, blaming the victim identifies—or even manufactures—traits that differentiate victims from the rest of us. While our fault finding has perhaps mellowed some since the days of social Darwinism when we argued that the poor were poor because they were unfit, we attribute blame subtly nevertheless. We now claim that victims suffer because of their differences; if we can change victims and accommodate them to society, their victimization will recede. But, of course, we have only limited resources and knowledge to achieve this, and victims hold stubbornly to their behavior, so seeing results will take some time.

In fact, victims do not differ much from the rest of us and, when they do, it is less from their failures or shortcomings and more from socially inspired, if not required, behavior.[146] To reduce victimization, we should not be changing individuals, but rather social structures, for which we have plentiful knowledge and resources.

We have discovered already that victims share many characteristics with both offenders and the broader public. Thus, victims differ from nonvictims primarily because they have been less able to avoid victimization. They have suffered that fate not because they have failed personally to properly accommodate to society, but because they have had few opportunities or resources to better protect themselves, and because social conditions (not victims) promote crime regardless of their actions. Unfortunately, we have used victim precipitation politically to pressure the public to make personal accommodations to avoid crime, yet, when crime still occurs, we blame the victim for failing to take sufficient precautions.

Victim blaming holds victims responsible for some of their inherent characteristics, such as their age or sex. It criticizes those who insufficiently transform their lives to avoid crime, thus blaming them for being unwilling to curb their individual freedom and ignoring the difficulties they have in avoiding the circumstances associated with victimization. It ignores the frequent overlap of victims and offenders and simplifies the matter of responsibility. And it might significantly exaggerate how much victims really precipitate crime in the first place.[147]

For example, by having traditionally viewed rape as a sexual act, we have attributed victim blame vastly more than we would if we regarded it, properly, as a violent act. Moreover, auto thefts have been blamed on motorists by what has been called an "organized victim-blaming lobby," composed of auto makers, insurance companies, law enforcement, and civic and business groups who ignore what they contribute to such crimes.[148] Yet when victims represent established interests, such as the businesses looted during the New York City blackout, suddenly the media and law enforcement become ardent victim defenders (not blamers), ignoring how these "victims" and the police may have cheated customers, drained resources, artificially inflated prices, used deceptive advertising, distributed inferior goods, lured customers into long-term debts, used brutality and harassment, and stimulated economic exploitation and hardships generally found in ghetto life.[149] As we shall see, the victim precipitation level may vary with the particular victim, yet those that do really precipitate crimes may be precisely those we have most defended.[150]

Most important, victim blaming may divert us from crime's underlying sources. It implies that victims' failure to take proper precautions, if not their overtly provocative behavior, causes crime. Yet, at best, this only describes a process of crime, not its causes. Even if we had evidence that various protective devices or behavior really deterred crime, using them would only divert it to locations having fewer resources. Even if we could all "protect" ourselves uniformly, we still would not have addressed crime's causes, and thus, even with a police state and massive personal security, we probably could not significantly reduce it either.

Victim Defending

For similar reasons, we also should shun the other extreme: victim defending. Victim defenders argue that victimology exaggerates victim culpability and ignores the vast majority of innocent victims. They say that victim typologies concentrate so much on the victim role that they define away any possible innocence, thus vindicating offenders and downplaying their criminal role.[151] Defenders complain about excessive rights for defendants, lenient sentencing, inadequate law enforcement, and insufficient victim involvement and services. Mostly, victim defenders promote traditional, get tough, "law and order" strategies for coping with crime.[152]

Surely, victim defenders have helped us focus on victims' undeserved fate, and they can be excused perhaps in absolving victims entirely from blame. Yet some people question the defenders' devotion to victims. Or, if genuine, to which victims in particular? The political rise of the victim movement may have produced a remarkable new breed: "bleeding heart conservatives," who passionately defend victims to the death. Yet their ostensible efforts for the victim, unwittingly or not, may have helped victims much less than preserving and extending entrenched political interests and conventional, if not repressive, law enforcement practices. Ironically, these efforts may make the situation for victims worse, not better, by bolstering policies that have been counterproductive to reducing victimization.

System Defending

Politically, we must carefully distinguish between victim blamers and defenders. Some blamers probably do so unintentionally, seeking only to show that victims sometimes contribute to crime, and that crime involves complex behavior and not merely "good guys" and "bad guys." Other blamers intentionally indict victims, allegedly only to help them avoid future victimization. A few blamers attack victims to protect their clients (defendants) or to forestall an erosion of defendant's rights. Practically no victim blamers indict well-off, established people, organizations, and institutions that might be victimized. And many victim blamers seem more interested in diverting crime's responsibility onto victims and away from entrenched institutions and social conditions. A similar pattern emerges for victim defenders, with some variations. A few defenders promote victims solely because they believe victims have been too long excluded from the criminal process and from help after victimization. Some defend victims because they believe offenders have accumulated excessive rights in criminal justice. Other victim defenders do so only to better blame offenders. Defenders support victims most vigorously when they include well-off, established people, organizations, and institutions. But, most defenders seem to promote victims much less for victims and much more for bolstering and strengthening existing institutions and social arrangements. In other words, *both* victim blaming and victim defending may have more to do with "system defending."[152]

An Alternative

A third approach puts victim precipitation into a much different light. It recognizes the exaggerated distinctions we have traditionally made between victims and offenders and acknowledges that victims may contribute to victimization either directly or indirectly, even though crime victims do suffer victimization that we should not ignore or slight under any circumstances.

Although they might properly bear the primary blame for committing crimes, and although some might bear more blame than others (because they committed more serious crime or because they had less justification for committing a crime?), we might well consider how offenders might be victims, too.[153] This requires us to reject crime theories that blame victimization on regulatory failures, on offender behavior and characteristics, and on victim precipitation. That is, this view *defends* both victims and offenders, given the context of their behavior, and *blames* the system and those who, although they plead "victim" themselves, might do much more to produce or precipitate victimization than experience it.

This suggests that perhaps the most meaningful precipitation may be the victimization provoked by social structures and arrangements. For example, some believe that organizations such as businesses and government officials precipitate victimization during civil disturbances.[154] Others wonder whether excessive social control precipitates victimization, unnecessarily pitting "offenders" against what some view as "precipitating" police officers.[155] Some argue that our culture legitimizes violence and acquisitiveness, thus precipitating victimization.[156] Social structures and conditions might precipitate victimization. In other words, we must explore one final crime theory, which finds fundamental crime sources in various aspects of our political and economic system.

Implications

With the recent emphasis on victim precipitation, Americans have increasingly blamed victims, if not also themselves, for causing crime. Although precipitation has been exaggerated, and although it hardly constitutes a real crime source (as much as something that may help spark particular criminal incidents), we have incorporated it into our belief system. Thus politically, blaming victims has focused our attention away from law-enforcement failures and has made victims responsible not only for their victimization, but for preventing future attacks. Taking a very individualized view, it has attributed crime to personal failings, directing us away from institutional or structural flaws. For victims and the general public, it has inspired guilt and suspiciousness, severely limiting and changing one's activities (if not characteristics) and significantly escalating one's personal security precautions.

Altogether, from the three crime theories we have examined so far, victims and the public receive somewhat conflicting, somewhat complementary, and, undoubtedly, overall very confusing signals. Theories that stress regulatory failures, offender characteristics, and victim precipitation guide the public's attention in three different directions. Unfortunately, none of them seems to point to victimization's real sources.

SYSTEM BLAMING: POLITICO-ECONOMIC STRUCTURES

It is an outrage for reformers to spend so much time asking what can be done to ease the lot of the poor or to make the poor bear their conditions with greater dignity, when the only remedy is to abolish the condition of poverty itself. OSCAR WILDE

You will not eliminate crime by eliminating poverty, ignorance, poor health, and ugly environments. But it is clear that such conditions are demonstrably responsible for most crime.

RAMSEY CLARK, *former U.S. Attorney General*

The law is meant to provide us all with the measure of safety we need to function. And no matter what its imperfections, it is **the** **best we have.**

MORTON BARD AND DAWN SANGREY, *The Crime Victim's Book*

Our criminal law and our social policy may be "the best we have," but they seem to be far from the best we could do. Typically, when we seek victimization's sources, our very piecemeal approach considers possible causes almost completely in isolation. We examine what causes *criminals,* for example, instead of what causes *crime.* Criminology seems to study "doers, and the prevention, control and treatment of their behavior,"[157] instead of crime's social causes.[158] We identify poor family upbringing, drug abuse, bad education, broken communities or individual corruption as sources, yet ignore their interconnectedness or their common and deeper origins. We discover long lists of possible causes, and despair at ever being able to correct so many problems, as if each comprised a separate issue, distinct from all others. We assume that the social control that might prevent crimes can only emerge from legal or administrative constraints, formally imposed, instead of from the social regulation that might more naturally flow from a just, balanced, and equitable social system. In sum, whether liberals or conservatives, we never raise fundamental questions about the viability or desirability of American mainstream life when considering what to do about crime.[159]

Our final crime theory takes a much more comprehensive approach. It claims that any social problem can be understood only within the framework of the society's social, political, and economic structures.[160] It argues that fundamental characteristics of the American system cause crime. While conventional theories sporadically identify various economic or political trends or decisions that might contribute to crime, the structural theory claims that basic, underlying structures or politico-economic forces provide crime's major sources. It suggests that crime emerges largely *because* of prevailing structural arrangements that underlie the crime symptoms or characteristics we normally, but incorrectly, identify as sources. In other words, it aims at the primary, and not merely the secondary, causes of crime.[161] Since we rarely examine theories challenging basic American structures, we will describe this perspective in somewhat greater detail.

Simply put, the structural theory argues that our political economy provides the major sources of victimization. This theory, much maligned, regularly misinterpreted or misrepresented, and rarely advocated,[162] suggests that our system produces dead-end poverty, structural inequality, ruthless competition, unequal political power, cultural violence, social alienation, repression, and social protest that underlie crime and other kinds of victimization. In fact, some argue that corporations and capitalism not only generate crime, but are themselves criminal by definition.[163] While a few of this theory's proponents treat American capitalism as a monolithic crime source, most only argue that it generates the greatest, but *not* the only, victimization. In other words, they argue that transforming our politico-economic system will not eliminate crime—it will only end most crime and most other victimization as well.

This theory argues that many factors we identify as crime's causes emerge from alterable, structural forces. It views formal regulatory controls as fighting a losing battle against social incentives far stronger than the threat of detection and punishment, even if social control could be vastly strengthened. Attributing to people a basically positive human nature, it rejects inherent or inevitable crime, or other evils. And, it argues that victims and the public contribute only marginally to precipitating their own victimization.

The structural theory of crime suggests that it results most fundamentally from certain political and economic characteristics of the society. By politics, it does not mean Democrats or Republicans (or what passes for the difference between liberals and conservatives), who differ little in their crime policies. And, by economics, it does not mean economic choice theory or merely economic development. In other words, it has nothing to do with the cost/benefit analysis some theorists say that offenders complete before deciding whether or not to commit a crime.[164] Nor does it refer to the various manifestations of economic development, such as overpopulation, urbanization, industrialization, growth, and affluence. At most, it views these as only mildly associated with crime.

Instead, the structural theory does emphasize poverty, competition, inequality, bureaucracy, political inequality, private power, and social alienation. Not all of these structural outcomes affect everyone; thus different features or effects may induce crime in different kinds of people. In a way, this theory more fundamentally confirms so-called "learning theories" of crime.[165] People in different social strata may "learn" crime through the criminal motives generated by our political economy.[166]

Economic Development

Let's begin by more specifically examining the economic development theory of crime. Simply put, overpopulation, urbanization, industrialization, growth, and affluence often do not even correspond to crime. For example, in the United States studies have shown that crime does not correlate with population density.[167] China and Japan have a comparatively low crime rate despite their great population and urbanization.[168] Sweden, despite its high industrialization, also has a comparatively low rate.

Moreover, even when these factors do correlate with crime we cannot show that they themselves create crime. We have earlier argued that we cannot reject a possible crime source, such as poverty, simply because we do not know precisely *how* it causes crime or because it does not *necessarily* produce crime. Thus, the real issue is: if we eliminated the other major crime sources, would the various measures of economic development still be associated with whatever crime remained? Partly because those measures do not strongly and consistently correlate with crime, and partly because the structural theory identifies prior and more fundamental crime sources (such as poverty and other structural by-products that would continue generating extensive crime even if we eliminated all other sources), we need not assume that crime inevitably accompanies overpopulation, urbanization, industrialization, growth, and affluence. Economic development might tell us something about crime's distribution within and between nations, and underdevelopment might explain some crime in poorer nations, but we cannot say that the "pains" of development cause crime. In other words, crime need not be the price of modernization, as we often hear, but only the price of development (unnecessarily) characterized by poverty, competition, and political and economic inequality.

Poverty and Inequality

> With all this, he had neither fear, nor regret, nor shame, nor self-pity. He had faced his position, and made a philosophy for himself. Being a beggar, he said, was not his fault, and he refused either to have any compunction about it or to let it trouble him. He was the enemy of society, and quite ready to take to crime if he saw a good opportunity.
>
> GEORGE ORWELL, *Down and Out in Paris and London*

> Not that all murders are activated by hunger. That is not the case. But, when the harvest is good, and provisions are at an obtainable price, men, lighter hearted and less miserable than usual, do not give way to gloomy passions; do not from trivial motives plunge a knife into the bosom of a fellow creature.   PETER KROPOTKIN

> In your day, fully nineteen twentieths of the crime, using the word broadly . . . resulted from the inequality of the possessions of individuals. Want tempted the poor, lust of greater gains or the desire to preserve former gains tempted the well-to-do. Directly or indirectly, the desire for money, which then meant every good thing, was the motive of all this crime, the taproot of a vast poison growth, which the machinery of law, courts, and police could barely prevent from choking your civilization outright.
>
> EDWARD BELLAMY, *Looking Backward*

More specifically, what do these structural shortcomings represent and how do they fundamentally generate crime? First, many view poverty and inequality as important crime sources.[169] For example, we know that 80% of those who pass through the criminal process come from the poorest 15% of the population.[170] These poorer people are far from alone in committing crime, and law enforcement discriminatorily apprehends and processes them. Yet we must still acknowledge that poorer people commit most common crimes. Are we to believe the correlation between poverty and crime to be only a coincidence, and that the criminal behavior of the poor really springs from other sources such as our failure to strictly regulate them, or their inherent characteristics? Perhaps the very traits that make and keep people poor constitute the very factors that cause them to commit crime? Or perhaps since all poor people do not commit crime, only the "evil" poor victimize, not the "good" poor—thus rendering their poverty irrelevant? Obviously, the structural theory rejects these suggestions.

How and why do poverty and inequality cause crime? As B. F. Skinner suggests: "It is the environment which is "responsible" for the objectionable behavior, and it is the environment, not some attribute of the individual, which must be changed."[171] Poverty produces not merely little or no income, assets and property, but also poor health, housing, education, nutrition, unemployment, and other social maladies. It may produce characteristics we often mistakenly attribute to some individuals or families inherently, such as listlessness, frustration, rage, drug abuse, sickness, psychological problems, broken homes, poor upbringing, and abusive families. It might also produce decaying communities, substandard schools, economic depression, "subcultures of violence," and declining churches and other community institutions and organizations.[172] It may prevent people and communities from being able to help protect themselves against crime or exert enough power to secure better law enforcement. Inequality may intensify poverty's frustrations by revealing to the poor, and even to the middle class, those people who do much better in our success-oriented society.[173]

The manifestations and results of poverty and inequality may produce crime by creating needs and frustrations that crime might appear to satisfy, however illusionary. It may generate crime by limiting legitimate opportunities for improvement.[174] Unemployment and underemployment, for example, provide good predictors of crime, in mid-twentieth century corporate capitalism, both in the streets and at home.[175] The unemployed also suffer victimization themselves 2 to 3 times more than the employed.[176] Millions lack jobs chronically, or lack job quality or stability, which denies them economic opportunity and psychological satisfaction.[177] As Congressman John Conyers has suggested, stealing provides a private substitute for the government's failure to provide opportunities or redistribute wealth.[178] In other words, poverty may help create crimes of accommodation, survival, and resistance.[179] Crime may be one of the social costs of poverty and inequality. The "culture of poverty" from which crime emerges does not cause crime,[180] but the structural sources of that poverty may.[181]

Economic Competition

> *Got a gun from Uncle Freddy*
> *Got a station all picked out*
> *Got a plan and now we're ready*
> *Gonna take that station out*
> *Cause we've almost made it*
> *We've almost made it to the top*
>
> RANDY NEWMAN

> *Combined with other, alienating social forces, this may produce the modern equivalent of social bandits. As individuals they are not so much political or social rebels, let alone revolutionaries, as peasants who refuse to submit and in doing so stand out from their fellows, or even more simply, men who find themselves excluded from the usual career of their kind, and therefore forced into outlawry and "crime." En masse, they are little more than symptoms of crisis and tension in their society.*   ERIC HOBSBAWM, *Bandits*

Economic competition provides another structural source of crime. It operates on many levels: competition for jobs, for careers, for promotions, for profits, for property and products, for status and recognition, for personal and business survival.[182] Except for business survival in the nation's large, monopolized industries, our economic system relies on a particularly ruthless competition which has many adverse consequences, perhaps including criminal victimization.

On the lowest levels, poor people compete for very scarce resources and opportunities.[183] Most doors for advancement for the poor have been closed. With an artificially created and, in ghetto areas, astronomically high, unemployment rate, thousands of people often compete for only a few jobs.[184]

Financial institutions and large companies often either refuse to invest in poor communities or may drain what little resources they have, leaving poor people to compete for what's left.[185] Poor people not only work hard, they usually do the society's most strenuous and distasteful work, yet few can pull themselves out of the ghetto,[186] thus producing a permanent class of poor.[187] Lacking opportunities and consistently failing or being impeded in economic competition,[188] some people resort to crime either as a rational alternative to legitimate, but blocked, opportunities[189] or as an irrational expression of rage and frustration,[190] particularly when they view officials and upper classes as "crooked" but prosperous.[191] Others commit crime for social status to "prove oneself," or to "be a somebody"[192] in circumstances where being somebody legitimately is rarely possible. Tom Waits writes:

> They all wish they could be just like Romeo
> If they only had the guts
> But Romeo is bleeding but nobody can tell
> And he sings along with the radio
> With a bullet in his chest
> And he combs back his fenders
> And they all agree it's clear
> That everything is cool now that Romeo is here.[193]

Racism and Sexism

> *He had killed twice, but in a true sense, it was not the first time he had ever killed. He had killed many times before, but only during the last two days had his impulse assumed the form of actual killing. Blind anger had come often and he had either gone behind his curtain or wall, or had quarreled and fought.*
>
> RICHARD WRIGHT, Native Son

> *I see you black boy*
> *bent toward destruction watching*
> *for death with tight eyes*
>
> SONIA SANCHEZ, Homegirls and Handgrenades

We generally acknowledge that racism and sexism produce crime, but usually ignore the major sources of that discrimination. We often believe that racism and sexism emerge from misunderstandings, poor education, cultural differences, and other factors. But, most fundamentally, they may arise (or at least attain their greatest virulence) from economic conditions and competition.[194] For example, racism has often emerged around school busing. We often view this as the inevitable miscommunication between races or as their inability to coexist because of indelible differences. Yet what may really underlie racism in busing is economic competition for scarce educational resources and for the scarce economic opportunties that education might provide.[195] Not surprisingly, busing conflicts not only have generated or intensified racism, they have also produced crime and violence.

Blacks, in particular, have suffered the ravages of racism, which may explain their committing crime at levels even higher than we would expect simply from their poverty. Many argue that facing a legacy of slavery and the badge of color, blacks have learned violence in America, despite their historic pacifism, and ultimately are no longer willing to withstand the violence directed at them-selves.[196] Having experienced perpetual humiliation, discrimination, degradation, poverty,[197] and blocked opportunities (as others, arriving later, passed them by), some believe they have finally exploded in this last generation,[198] willing to "shoot their way out of this life."[199]

Sexism provides a similar theme. Critics claim that women's victimization and exploitation emerge not merely from habit, insensitivity, false stereotypes, poor education, or misunderstandings, but rather from sexism's economic and political functions.[200] In the home, for example, women suffer economic dependence and vulnerability, which often subjects them to an unbreakable cycle of battering by their husbands, whose own violence may often reflect their economic and political frustrations and insecurities in the outside world.[201] Outside the home, women's economic inferiority and vulnerability may rob them of political power that might otherwise demand relief for their victimization. The profits of pornography, sexual advertising, and prostitution legitimize the female victimization portrayed in those activities, thus acquiescing to women's criminal victimization by offenses such as rape and assault.[202] We now also see an increasing female crime rate, perhaps also reflecting the frustrations and limited opportunities sexism imposes.

Middle Classes

People do not commit crime simply because of poverty or discrimination, however. Widespread crime, lawbreaking, and other wrongdoing exist across social and economic classes. Poverty does not stimulate crime in middle- and upper-class criminals, but economic competition may. People who have never experienced insecurities and frustrations may, nevertheless, suffer those feelings for other reasons. Middle classes worry about job security and advancement, about making ends meet, about "keeping up with the Joneses," about planning for the future, and about achieving financial security.[203] Seeing, and probably working for, other people who enjoy a much more luxurious life might cause middle classes to envy that wealth, even if it far exceeds what they need. What happens when obstacles emerge, as they regularly do, that impede our climb up the ladder of success? What if our jobs or careers appear tenuous or jeopardized? What if our financial future shows questionable promise? What if we cannot maintain the competitive pace? What if our small business constantly verges on the brink of failure?[204]

If these things occur, so say many observers, we might resort to crime, not because poverty has created basic, unfulfilled needs or confined rage, but because we suffer another kind of insecurity, and because we so strongly measure our status and worth by our economic achievements.[205] In a ruthlessly competitive society, we may begin to view others as either obstacles or commodities. If we cannot overcome those obstacles or exploit those commodities legitimately, we may do so illegitimately, particularly when we view our targets either as impersonal competitors (in our dog-eat-dog world) or oppressive institutions (for which many of us might work). By responding to these irresistible incentives, we have become, according to some, a "society of frauds."[206]

Upper Classes

> *Inasmuch as great wealth is an instrument which is uniformly used to extort from others their property, it ought to be taken away from its possessors on the same principle that a sword or pistol may be wrested from a robber, who shall undertake to accomplish the same effect in a different manner.*   THOMAS SKIDMORE

Upper classes may have some similar incentives. While freed from the worries of economic insecurity, they may find themselves in an equally debilitating status insecurity. If they fail, they will not starve, but they will lose power and position and perhaps a few jobs or businesses along the way. Studies of corporate crime tell us that both managers and owners often find themselves so pushed (by either personal goals or competitive inertia) toward successfully reaching individual and business objectives by any means that they can barely recognize the line between legitimate and illegitimate business activity, much less help crossing it. For example, Ronald Secrist, who was deeply involved in the Equity Finance Corporation's massive insurance fraud a few years ago, concluded that his years in the insurance industry "gained me nothing but the option of being crooked to survive."[207] As Thorstein Veblen suggested many years ago, we often have difficulty distinguishing between praiseworthy salesmanship and a penitentiary offense, although obviously we have primarily perceived the former.

Some corporate executives claim that lawbreaking solves certain business problems that some view as their *own* victimization, and that certain government, consumer, or competitor actions "precipitate" such crimes.[208] And, in the famous electrical industry conspiracy case in the 1960s, executives claimed they had practiced price fixing so long they had lost sight of its illegality.[209] In fact, although our law gives enormous leeway to business practices, when we finally draw the line, it still often marks a limit that contradicts the competitive or other practices we so much expect from successful firms.

In other words, every natural business incentive gives us every reason to pursue activities that contravene even our very liberally drawn law of corporate and business crime. Rich criminals do not commit crime because of economic destitution or even insecurity, but perhaps because of the relentless engines and standards of business success. Much of that crime will emerge in the business world, and the rest may spill over into private lives. In the words of Pat Parker:

> *My anger rises*
> *I know who the killers are*
> *and know the killer will go untried*
> *see no court or judges*
> *no jury of peers*
> *the killers wear suits of*
> *businessmen*
> *buy ghetto apartments*
> *and overcharge the rent*
> *the killers lock Black men*
> *in prison or drive*
> *them from their homes*
> *the killers give the Black woman*
> *a job*
> *and pay her one-half of what she*
> *needs to live*
> *the killers scream about*
> *juvenile crime*
> *and refuse to build childcare centers.*
> *It won't matter what*
> *demented fool is caught*
> *for society has provided*
> *the lure.*

PAT PARKER, *Jonestown and Other Madness*

But poverty, inequality, and economic competition are not the only crime sources our political economy might produce. We must consider not only other ingredients, but what constitutes the driving force of that political economy in the first place. That is, how does corporate capitalism provide the source of poverty, inequality, economic competition, and the other foundations for crime.

Corporate Capitalism

Institutions, and especially economic systems, have a profound influence in moulding the characters of men and women. They may encourage adventure and hope, or timidity and the pursuit of safety. They may open people's minds to great possibilities or close them against everything but the risk of obscure misfortune. They may make a man's happiness depend upon what he adds to the general possessions of the world, or upon what he can secure for himself of the private goods in which others cannot share. Modern capitalism forces the wrong decision of these alternatives upon all who are not heroic or exceptionally lucky. BERTRAND RUSSELL, *Political Ideals*

Some observers might agree that poverty, inequality, and economic competition provide several of our major sources of crime.[210] But they might disagree about their origins. Liberals argue, for example, that these outcomes inadvertently emerge from economic development, and that we must either wait for those side-effects to disappear or apply government programs to ameliorate their effects. For example, we might cope with poverty and inequality through welfare programs, and with economic competition by passing stricter laws against certain white-collar wrongdoing.[211] Liberals would undoubtedly reject the view that corporate capitalism produces the problem.

Yet most structural theorists find crime's sources in our political economy's basic traits and incentives, and not in our failure to create programs to ameliorate some of its harsh characteristics. They argue that government programs will provide minimal relief— and inevitably fail—because they avoid the problem's real sources.[212] They claim that typical welfare budgets inherently deprive by standardizing and institutionalizing bare subsistence, and by their consistently punitive administration, so much so that they almost clamor to be violated.[213] Structural theorists further believe that corporate capitalism not only correlates with poverty, inequality, and economic competition, it inevitably generates and requires them. They constitute permanent, and not merely temporary, features of corporate capitalism's structural requirements.[214] As such, we cannot alter its adverse effects by ameliorating its symptoms, but only by eliminating its structural sources. In other words, we may in some way have to transform corporate capitalism and establish an alternative political economy that not only does not require poverty, inequality, and economic competition to function, but which strives purposely to avoid them.[215]

Our economic system might require wrongdoing, illegality, and crime.[216] Many argue that our modest tangible, and not merely token or symbolic, corporate regulation has resulted largely from the government's general and unchallenged acquiescence to blatant corporate abuses.[217] Our widescale nonenforcement of what modest formal regulation we have not only suggests the government's predominantly supportive role,[218] but also how regulation, even at meager levels, contradicts standard business practices. Consequently, we may be wrong to expect that mere reforms, such as improving business ethics, corporate reorganization, federal chartering, deconcentration, consumer pressure, and greater enforcement and penalties,[219] will seriously change corporate practices. Without provid-

ing viable economic alternatives and checks, punishing corporations
will often *hurt their victims* even more.

Corporations might now be even more inclined to commit crimes
in the face of falling profits, increased taxes, greater productive and
unproductive labor (i.e., managers, lawyers, advertisers) and raw
material costs, and emerging third world cartels.[220] Only strongly
supportive and pro-business government policies, such as recent
Reagan administration initiatives, may be able to curb the pressures
toward greater corporate wrongdoing and crime, but, ironically, may
enhance crime by others. Some have suggested that if we do not
check corporate crime, we risk losing the capitalist system itself.[221]
Others suggest, to the contrary, that capitalism would more likely
decline if we *did* check corporate crime; since capitalism seems to
generate that crime, only transforming capitalism can provide that
check.

Bureaucracy and Alienation

> *In practice nobody cares whether work is useful or useless, produc-*
> *tive or parasitic; the sole thing demanded is that it be profitable.*
>
> GEORGE ORWELL

> *Each person, withdrawn into himself, behaves as though he is a*
> *stranger to the destiny of all others. His children and his good*
> *friends constitute for him the whole of the human species. As for his*
> *transactions with his fellow citizens, he may mix among them, but*
> *he sees them not; he touches them, but he does not feel them; he ex-*
> *ists only in himself and for himself alone. And if on these terms*
> *there remains in his mind a sense of family, there no longer remains*
> *a sense of society.*   ALEXIS DE TOCQUEVILLE

Our political economy may produce much more than merely poverty, inequality, and economic competition. It may generate bureaucracy, social alienation, internal and external violence, repression, and militant protest, which further stimulate crime. Our political
economy creates both private and public bureaucracies, characterized by large, impersonal organizations with hierarchical controls.
In the public sphere, some believe government bureaucracies emerged
both to ostensibly regulate and to concretely accommodate corporate growth. Large regulatory agencies may have arisen to control
the excesses of business enterprise, while others, such as welfare
departments, emerged when those controls failed, or when our political economy otherwise generated social or economic casualties.
Others believe that, more likely, large public bureaucracies have
arisen more to promote, expand, and rescue our economic system

than to seriously regulate it.[222] Either way, our contact, if not employment, with distant and unwieldy bureaucracies has vastly increased.

Our economic system's development and concentration have multiplied private business bureaucracies as well, further enhancing our dealings with large, faceless organizations as employees, employers, customers, subcontractors, and so forth. Taken together, we have dramatically increased our immersion in large public and private bureaucracies, which may generate an additional and important crime source.[223] As faceless, oppressive organizations bearing considerable resources, they may inspire crimes that reflect economic needs or desires or personal frustrations and alienation.[224]

We may find it easier to "rip off" a large, impersonal victim that will not really miss what we have extracted anyway.[225] Crimes may be our way of despising such organizations, taking revenge, or cutting through "red tape" or obstacles to advancement. Besides directly attacking such organizations, we might otherwise vent our rage and despair at an inhuman society, or at some human being. The oppression, conditions, powerlessness, and alienation of the workplace, for example, may translate into criminal behavior in the "streets," and into male oppression in the home, with women and children usually bearing the rage, if not the physical attacks.[226]

Corporate capitalism may create other forms of social alienation as well. It may help create a culture devoted to greed, individualism, materialism, competition, acquisitiveness, isolation, narcissism, aggressiveness, violence, and social dislocation.[227] It may help develop values, attitudes, and behavior that imperil relationships and divide communities and social groupings.[228] Capitalist forces undoubtedly do not produce all these reactions alone, but they may account for a substantial portion. In turn, alienation may generate crime, including the offenses we often view as so senseless, but which may be much more rational than we think, given their sources and context.[229]

Violence

> *Whoever has the gun, you see,*
> *gets to tell everybody else what to do.*
> *It's the American way.*
>
> KURT VONNEGUT

> *Violence has been made comfortable*　　　　ALBERT CAMUS

> *Men murdered themselves into this democracy.*　　　D. H. LAWRENCE

Violence does not work except for the man who pays your salary.

ALICE WALKER

American capitalism may also generate substantial internal and external violence that indirectly creates models for such methods or behavior and directly produces crimes of its own.[230] We often hear that American violence has emerged from our frontier culture,[231] yet our violent culture may have deeper roots. The violence we used to conquer our internal frontiers may not have been limited to merely environmental obstacles and the dangers of the wild. Many argue that our greatest violence depleted one population (native Americans),[232] and exploited others (such as blacks, hispanics, Asians and women).[233] Critics suggest that we committed violence rarely to protect ourselves from unprovoked attacks, but rather to overcome human obstacles to accumulating property and economic resources.[234] We may have a violent culture, but its contours may have been shaped largely by the forces of economic accumulation. Violence may represent our sanctification of the deeply cherished value of property.[235] Yet, as Philip Slater suggests: "All great fortunes were initially taken from the people directly or indirectly. One important function of the police, subsidiary to their primary role of maintaining order and predictability, is to prevent any of the people from stealing it back."[236]

Others argue that we have also used violence domestically to forcibly block any and all opposition to our economic system and its supporting structures. Privately and publicly dispensed violence has been used to prevent labor organizing and opposition,[237] to repel anti-capitalist ideologies and movements, and to control those who have either been unwilling or unable to keep within the bounds of capitalist law and order.[238] As Herbert Marcuse suggests:

> "Law and Order": These words have always had an ominous sound; the entire necessity and the entire horror of legitimate force are condensed and sanctioned in this phrase [:] . . . the legitimate, organized violence required to protect the established society against the poor, the oppressed, the insane: the victims of its well-being.[239]

Most of that violence, including our history of police riots,[240] violates the law, thus producing another crime source, although not one we readily acknowledge.

Many argue that our violence has surpassed our borders as well, extending both to sporadic but routine force used to protect our foreign "interests" and wars to make the world "safe for democracy." In the guise of promoting third world development, and to not only extract valuable resources, but also (in this century) help rescue corporate capitalism's often flagging development, we seem to have used force and violence systematically to impose our system and extract other societies' wealth. We may have set an example further justifying domestic violence by our repeated involvement in wars, police actions, and other military invasions and maneuvers, almost invariably for questionable motives.[241] We should little wonder when such violence repeats itself as American criminal behavior.

Political Power

Freedom, in short, is what Kitty Genovese enjoyed: the freedom to be leisurely stabbed to death in a New York street for an hour without some small-town busybody poking his nose in her private affairs.

PHILIP SLATER, *Earthwalk*

Finally, the structural theory of crime argues that crime might also depend on political systems and the distribution of political power.[242] In the United States, we have an elaborate legal and constitutional structure that creates the foundations, if not some substance, of a formal political democracy. We have rights and powers that both protect us from government control and allow us to participate in the political system, presumably to accumulate and wield political power.

Unfortunately, formal legal protections may not necessarily guarantee real political power. Laws that assume literal equality may serve those who in reality have more resources or power. Despite our elaborate, formal protections, our ability to wield political power may depend less on our rights or our efforts, but rather on our economic wealth.[243] In other words, what political democracy provides, our economic system (with its unequal distribution of wealth and resources) may largely take away. Our constitutional protections of democracy may not merely fail to overcome the imbalances in political power caused by unequal wealth, but by providing only political democracy and not economic democracy, they fail to prevent those economic inequities from emerging in the first place. Our government may act largely to promote and perpetuate the economic system that generates those inequalities. By advancing corporate objectives, it may facilitate, and fund (with taxpayer money), social dislocation, unemployment, "modernization," community decline, capital and technology shifts, overconsumption, and inequality—thus generating a "pro-crime policy," producing an inevitably "crime-prone society."[244]

Undemocratic processes, much less totalitarian political systems, may well generate crime as well.[245] Many believe that political crime that resists oppression will likely result not merely from economic, but also political, exploitation. Blocked participation and control, unresponsive bureaucracies, ineffective voting, barriers to expression and other rights will likely generate alienation, frustration, and opposition that may produce crime. That crime might reflect rage, or revolutionary resistance, or more likely the needs or incentives generated by the political economy overall. In other words, when poor people, for example, commit crimes, they may be responding to blocked opportunities that result from both their poverty *and* their political powerlessness to overcome their economic condition. People may violate the law because, with good reason, they often do not respect the outcomes it produces or the interests it represents. Middle classes may respond, in part, to these political frustrations as well. In sum, they may react to the "unfulfilled promises" of the American system.[246]

Implications

As for existing models of alternative political economies, no others literally approximate the system the structural theory implies. Yet we may find that some aspects of an alternative system already exist and, in any case, should not rule out creating an alternative from entirely new cloth, particularly with the resources and capabilities of the richest nation in the world.[247]

Properly combining political and economic systems may significantly reduce crime. A political democracy that strongly controls the poverty and inequality produced by capitalism may reduce some common crime, but that crime will probably still continue, and white-collar and corporate crime will probably flourish, until it trades corporate capitalism for a decentralized, nonhierarchical economic democracy. Furthermore, a society that provides the rudiments of economic democracy may reduce crime, but it will persist at some level nevertheless until it trades totalitarian and bureaucratic government and institutions for a decentralized, nonhierarchical political democracy. In other words, providing the kind of political economy that will reduce victimization generally will likely also reduce criminal victimization. Even the leading neoconservative crime spokesman, James Q. Wilson, has conceded that "in a sense the radical critics of America are correct. If you wish to make a big difference in crime rates, you must make a fundamental change in society."[248]

The structural theory of crime carries implications very different from the other theories we have examined. Politically, it does not blame crime on failed regulators or failing regulations, or on offenders' inherently criminal characteristics and behavior, or on victim traits and actions, but rather on our political economy. It implies not only that the political economy primarily determines the crime level, and thus explains the major, although not all, sources of crime, but also that any serious crime policy must transform that structure.[249] Obviously, this suggests not only different, but also much grander, policies; some would argue unreasonable and unfeasible change. Nevertheless, it may be the change we need and, despite the obstacles, we could devise and implement strategies to move toward a different system.

For victims, this theory implies significantly different strategies than the ones they and their advocates have been pursuing. It suggests that victims will not find crime's cure in tougher or more efficient regulation, or in isolating evil people, or in substantially altering their own behavior. If victims and the public embraced the theory, it would push them to pursue some short-run protective strategies (probably including decriminalization, decarceration, gun control, and community crime control), to lobby for increased victim support and services, to reevaluate what role they seek in contemporary criminal justice, and to closely reconcile and integrate them into a simultaneous and long-term strategy for transforming our political economy in ways that begin to eliminate the major sources of crime.

CONCLUSION

Evaluating the sources of crime should be a vital aspect of victimology. These sources obviously also reflect the sources of victimization. Identifying them and prescribing policies to eliminate them will do more for victims than any other pursuit. Clearly, we must also act in the short run to promote victims' immediate interests, but we may be forever frustrated in ever providing them with anything more than remedial and inadequate assistance until we address the roots of their victimization.

We have examined several major views of victimization, including theories that blame institutions, offenders, victims, and our political economy. Each theory has different implications for politics, public policy, and victims. Theories emphasizing regulatory failures and offender and victim behavior and characteristics largely bolster conventional, if not "law and order," crime policies. In contrast, the structural theory not only challenges traditional law enforcement, but also questions the broader political economy in which it operates. Thus, the crime theory to which we subscribe not only directs us toward different culprits, it also may suggest significantly different forms of political change.

Our crime theory also significantly affects victims. Conventionally, we may be subscribing to a victimization theory that reflects only the social reality, instead of the objective circumstances, of victimization. What we believe causes victimization, and what we believe can or should be done about it, may reflect an ideology into which we have been socialized. That ideology might pose substantial psychological, if not physical, barriers to all but a limited array of "legitimate" or "feasible" solutions for crime. To the extent that our social reality of victimization misleads us about the actual reality of crime and its sources, we may support policies that not only ignore the causes of victimization, but which may enhance crime and make the victim's situation worse.

In any case, knowing victimization's sources is critical to posing solutions for the victim's dilemma. We will later suggest that applying human rights standards which examine and identify sources of political, economic, and social victimization will best help victimology identify the underlying causes of criminal victimization. If we accept crime theories that blame institutional inefficiency, or offenders, or victims, then victimology may forever be a science of limited possibilities, restricted to providing victims aid and comfort, and perhaps minor alterations in crime. If we accept theories that blame the American system, then we confront the formidable task of transforming our political economy. By choosing the latter path, victimology encompasses the study and promotion of human rights.

Now that we have examined at least one "reality" of victimization and suggested its possible sources, we can move, in the next chapter, to examine its impact and the response it elicits.

5

Handling Pain: The Impact of Victimization

I was severely beaten in a mugging. I got a brain concussion, a deeply lacerated scalp, a broken left elbow, a broken bone in my back, a damaged right eye, blood clots behind my right eardrum, bel palsy on the right side of my face, and a damaged right eyelid. I can't see well, can't hear, and can't walk properly.

A BROOKLYN CRIME VICTIM

Dead man lying by the side of the road
With the daylight in his eyes
Don't let it bring you down
It's only castles burning

NEIL YOUNG

Having discussed the objective and the social realities of victimization and its sources, we must now examine its impact on victims as well as nonvictims, keeping in mind that the official measures we use will significantly underestimate victimization's overall effects. Victimization influences people very diversely, ranging from minor harms, to significant repercussions, to the ultimate impact: death. We must analyze victimization's results, not merely to assess its tangible impact, but also to better understand the responses it engenders. Thus, we will consider the effects of victimization on people's quality of life and its implications for public policy. And although they experience victimization unequally, we must also examine its impact on specific groups, for whom its effects may be the harshest.

<hr>

COSTS OF VICTIMIZATION

Individual Costs

DIRECT FINANCIAL LOSSES.   Victimization generates financial and physical costs for victims in the short run, and over time, either directly or indirectly. Direct losses result when crime takes or damages property. Indirect losses may involve the medical costs of injuries, temporary or permanent work loss, lowered property values, and the costs of criminal-justice involvement. The cost of lost assets and physical injuries may subside quickly or last a lifetime. But, almost invariably, victimization has some costs.

It has been suggested that for some crimes, nobody seems to lose, since burglars get the goods, consumers get bargains on stolen property, and victims get insurance.[1] Yet, aside from this view's obvious self-contradiction, such crimes also cause insurance company losses and higher premiums, most victims will not recover insurance, and they may feel compelled to spend money on self-protection in the future. While this may be merely an atypically insensitive view, we might generally underestimate victimization's costs.

Common crime produces considerable direct losses. Residential larceny costs $2 billion, burglary $3 billion, and arson $1 billion each year.[2] We lose almost $9 billion a year in unrecovered property, property damage, and unreimbursed medical expenses.[3] Indirect losses for property and people often exceed direct losses. Even when property has not been taken, it may lose value because of damage or its connection to a crime-prone location.[4] Besides its overall financial costs, arson costs an average of $6,000 per fire, and produces 1,000 deaths and 10,000 injuries annually. Approximately 75,000 fires are set intentionally each year.

INJURIES.   Many crimes produce both financial and physical losses. Overall, about one-third of all crimes produce some bodily injury resulting in financial loss, if not physical impairment, temporarily or permanently. Injuries might be minor—or as serious as sterility or paralysis.[5] Little variation in injury occurs across demographic traits.[6] Elderly victims, for example, do not suffer greater bodily harm than other groups.[7]

Nevertheless, when taken as aggregates, instead of as merely individuals, some groups and communities bear most injuries and losses from conventional crimes.[8] Thus, victims risk injury more if victimized by non-theft crimes,[9] by acquaintances,[10] and especially by offenders whose victims counterattack or threaten to protect themselves or their property.[11] A debate rages, for example, about whether women threatened with rape should resist. It may be that women who fight back stand a greater chance of avoiding rape, but they may incur greater injury in the process. For elderly victims, reasoning with their attackers seems to produce much less injury compared to self-defense through force.[12]

Injury may depend less on victim or offender traits, and more on the circumstances of the attack,[13] except that non-stranger crime significantly increases injuries no matter what.[14] The weapon used will best determine injury. For example, less injury occurs with guns (perhaps since they best neutralize resistance), although when actually used, they produce the most severe injuries and the most likely fatalities.[15] Ironically, victims suffer injury and death significantly more when they wield guns during an attack for their own "protection." Greater injuries also seem to be produced by offenders who have been previously victimized themselves, regardless of the victim.[16]

INDIRECT FINANCIAL LOSSES.   Although not all victims suffer bodily injury, those who do bear considerable financial costs. Many require hospitalization: as many as 49% in one study.[17] Yet many and perhaps most people cannot afford those costs, and thus the number of those really requiring hospitalization might actually be much higher than those who actually arrive.[18] Many and perhaps most people lack insurance coverage, usually because they cannot afford it. Those who do go to the hospital must pay steadily escalating rates. Even those who forego hospitalization bear enormous costs for outside medical services, often required by two-thirds of those injured.[19]

Bodily and even psychological injuries usually impose additional costs of lost work time (for 21% in one study), or even completely losing one's job (for 10% in one study).[20] Sometimes victims can be easily replaced or they may incur disabilities that prevent them from working either for short or long periods, and perhaps forever, without job protections or guarantees. These victims often lack ready alternatives for jobs and resources. Bodily injury might also result in death. While death prevents some other costs, and while it might bring some survivors the financial rewards of life insurance (when covered), it might also significantly reduce the family's earning capacity, produce high funeral costs, and of course, take an even higher psychological toll.

We often find that while physical, social, and psychological costs tend to persist over time, financial costs usually decline.[21] Yet we cannot underestimate their effects. In particular, those costs are borne unequally throughout the population. Not only will certain groups be much more likely to get attacked, and perhaps injured, but they will often be those who can least cope with its costs, due either to their own material conditions or their lack of effective assistance. Blacks, for example, have much less chance of recouping their losses than whites.[22] The greatest suffering from victimization affects the poor, minorities, the less educated, and ghetto dwellers, who incur psychological, financial, and practical problems with greater intensity, for longer periods, and with the least available help.[23]

State Expenses

Victimization's costs exceed those paid by individual victims. Government, and thus taxpayers, must bear the considerable expense of systems designed to prevent, prosecute, punish, and recompense crimes. One estimate indicates that taxpayers pay $25 billion yearly for these services,[24] yet an inequitable tax structure means that middle and lower classes bear the brunt of those costs.

Our prevention and law enforcement system incurs the considerable costs of police training, salaries, equipment, maintenance, and operations. The increased spending between 1950 and 1980 nearly doubled the growth in other government social spending.[25] When victimization occurs, the state must pay for apprehending and prosecuting offenders (including prisons, probation and correctional personnel), which requires financing for courts, prosecutors, judges, defenders, other judicial personnel, and their maintenance. The state must also pay for incarcerating offenders, particularly in America where we imprison so extensively. One estimate shows that we spend $4 billion yearly to maintain prisons, and that the new ones recently proposed by the Reagan administration would cost an additional $8 to 10 billion.[26] While we routinely exaggerate the price per prisoner (by ignoring the "sunk" costs of prisons that compose most of their pricetag), the average of $12,500 yearly still suggests formidable costs.[27] Overall, criminal justice now constitutes the fifth largest employment category in the nation, with most of the costs attached to the state.

Other estimates of total costs for police, courts, prisons, and parole indicate an outlay of $26 billion in 1979, up from an estimated $4 billion in 1967.[28] We spent billions on criminal justice, mostly through the Law Enforcement Assistance Administration, during the 1970s, with no effect on reducing crime. Some wonder whether we should stop spending. Others disagree: "We've spent many, many more billions of dollars and still have welfare," argues the former Executive Director of the International Associations of Chiefs of Police.[29] Yet perhaps we have failed to stop *both* crime and poverty, despite our vast expenditures, because we have not attacked the problems at their sources, and instead have been merely content to keep both problems somewhat manageable.

In any case, we have increasing signs that people have reached the limit of their willingness to finance such programs. Some federal cutbacks and various state propositions have begun to reduce both welfare and criminal justice funding. A "fiscal crisis of the state"[30] has emerged that makes it increasingly more difficult for the government to pay the "social expenses" of coping with poverty and with crime.

Private Costs of Protection

PROTECTION.   Beyond the individual costs of victimization that result from coping with injuries and property losses, both victims and nonvictims bear the costs of attempting to protect themselves from crime, or of at least cushioning the losses when they do occur. While we must lament the great burden these costs impose on those who pay them, we might be even more concerned about the many people who cannot afford "protection" at any price or who cannot purchase the kind of security they desire.[31] The elderly, for example, often cannot afford protection, and thus most must bear the costs of isolation, including their separation from outside human contact, and from services they often require, but will not risk leaving their homes to use.[32] People have vastly different opportunities to protect themselves.[33] Ironically, many of those least capable of self-protection suffer some of the greatest fear and take the greatest precautions.[34] Many people cannot afford self-protection; those same people often suffer further from inadequate law enforcement.

Later, we will detail the various protective devices used, but for now we will emphasize only their cost. High victimization, or at least fear, has motivated people to invest in endless security devices ranging from handguns, body guards, surveillance systems, and guard dogs to simply adding more lights, locks, alarms, and other warning devices. Even the least expensive mechanisms can impose considerable costs. An average, basic security system purchased from Sears, for example, costs almost $1,000, with more sophisticated systems costing much, much more.[35]

INSURANCE.   Some people also invest in various forms of insurance policies to cover losses ranging from stolen or damaged property, to arson, to health care, to disability, to death. Unfortunately, not only does victimization or its threat impose this otherwise unnecessary expense, but not all people have equal access to its benefits. As suggested earlier, many people cannot afford insurance or cannot get others (e.g., employers) to help them bear such expenses.

Others who can buy some insurance often cannot buy adequate protection. Still others cannot get insured even when they can buy it since insurance companies will often refuse to sell coverage to certain kinds of people or to residents of what they consider to be high-crime areas.[36] Most victims also cannot find alternatives to insurance to cover their losses. While government insurance for people such as the poor or the elderly might cover some expenses, it excludes many others. Most people do not qualify for government insurance, nor can they typically qualify for restitution or compensation when they exist.[37] Another alternative for securing compensation from either the government or the offender requires a civil suit, which not only routinely fails, but costs too much to pursue. Relying on charity or on committing crimes oneself provide even less attractive alternatives.

IMPACT.   Americans spend billions of dollars yearly on crime protection, an estimated one dollar for every four dollars stolen.[38] Many others would like to increase that outlay even more, to protect themselves, but cannot afford to do so. The cost of protection suggests several things: We have enormous fears about crime that affect our expenditures, and undoubtedly considerable real crime to fortify those fears. We spend all of this money even though we would normally assume that the taxes we pay for police services would cover the cost of protection. Finally, many people's careers and livelihoods now depend on criminal justice, including both state personnel, private police, and those running security businesses of one kind or another.

Business Costs

Private firms must bear many of the same costs as individuals and governments. They incur the expense of protection, insurance, compensation, and the loss of goods, employees, and property. Although businesses frequently transfer the costs of crime prevention to consumers or labor or taxpayers, we must still recognize the great losses they incur.

Businesses lose approximately $40 billion yearly to crime.[39] They lose more money to employee theft than to external victimization, such as from shoplifting.[40] Taken together, "inventory shrinkage" cost $5.3 billion in 1974, while wholesalers' losses were $2.1 billion and manufacturers' losses were $2.8 billion from crime that same year.[41] As of the 1980s, the estimated cost of credit card fraud ranged between one-half and three billion dollars each year.[42] Between 1 and 6% of all contractor's equipment gets stolen each year by employees.[43] Even ripoffs we consider almost "natural" can cost tremendous amounts, such as a leading hotel chain which claims $3 million losses in stolen towels alone each year.[44] Businesses often install sophisticated protection systems, including not only equipment, but considerable armies of private police units.[45] They also bear the costs of business insurance and lawsuits that pursue company losses. They must pay for lost inventories, for injured employees' medical bills, and for property repairs. When losses become severe, some businesses might suffer reduced patronage and employment, higher prices, and even relocation. The costs of locating a business in a ghetto, for example, will include extra insurance, high personnel turnover, unemployment compensation, and plant and personnel security, before any crime even occurs.

Beyond the high costs of crimes committed against businesses, we have increasingly recognized that crime, its prevention, and its expenses have become almost endemic to business operations. Businesses suffer a threat not only from outside, but often even more profoundly from their own employees, whose criminality produces at least 30% of all business failures each year. This victimization not only threatens business enterprise, but since it has become so pervasive and almost institutionalized, it may also seriously question business activities and incentives.

Victimization as Big Business

While victimization produces considerable costs to individuals, governments, and businesses, it also significantly benefits others. We refer not to the gains secured by offenders, since for common criminals they will be meager and sporadic, if any at all. Instead, we refer to the gains secured by individuals and firms constituting what some have called the "criminal-justice industrial complex."[46]

While victimization provides a career for only a relatively few offenders, it creates vastly more careers for many others in the American economy. Crime prevention and indemnification constitute a multibillion dollar industry, growing about 15% per year. As we have already suggested, it provides employment for a significant portion of the population, including not only criminal-justice personnel, but also private police, insurance adjustors, social service workers, academics, security firm employees, and many others. Private and public security now constitute the nation's fifth largest employer, and corrections jobs now rank among the twenty fastest growing occupations.[47]

Victimization or its threat provides extensive business for those firms. Such businesses manufacture, or otherwise supply, equipment, automobiles, surveillance gear, computer technology, uniforms, administrative support services, insurance, medical services, and extensive private protection devices, from locks to alarms to firearms.

While we would not suggest that these businesses and personnel purposely conspire to generate a high crime rate for the tremendous profits it provides, we can at least say that they would lose much if victimization significantly declined. Has this prevented us from being more successful in reducing crime? The commerical exploitation many of these firms promote makes it difficult to assess their activities generously. We have considerable evidence of their false and fear-mongering advertisements, of inflated crime hysteria, and of exaggerated protection claims about their products.[48] We can now even buy fashionable bulletproof clothing "for today's active lifestyles."[49]

Some wonder whether we have not been experiencing a massive arms race in security hardware, with existing protection never being enough to guard against the steadily escalating criminal threat.[50] As with the nuclear arms race, one must wonder whether the net effect of this buildup is more safety or a profoundly greater danger.

Costs of Unofficial "Crimes"

The costs of victimization described above reflect only wrongdoing officially defined as criminal. Yet such definitions encompass only selective harms and exclude many of our most serious threats. If we redefined crime to reflect the objective reality of serious wrongdoing and harm, then we would pay considerably more attention to white-collar, corporate, and state crime, and the costs of official victimization would vastly escalate.

To begin with, officially designated white-collar crimes, although rarely so defined and usually escaping enforcement, now cost $100 to 200 billion yearly,[51] according to some estimates. And this may be a gross underestimation. An American Bar Association study of 283 corporations and government agencies, for example, found 49% of them victimized by computer crime alone, producing an annual loss of between $145 and $730 million. It suggested that other losses would be impossible to estimate.[52] In 1967, the President's Crime Commission found that corporate property crime exceeded common property crime by at least five times, yet even this surely and significantly underestimates the real gap.[53]

The costs borne by victims of state actions, including government violence, also compete with the expense of conventional crime, yet rarely receive punishment or even a criminal label. We could include, for example, the costs of state violations of rights, of illicit imprisonment and other punishments, and of violence from police brutality or "police riots." If we adopted international human rights standards, we might also hold the state responsible for the economic costs of racism, sexism, and poverty, which many believe the state facilitates—or at least refuses to seriously ameliorate. Discrimination, for example, has been estimated to cost nonwhites $37.6 billion and women $81.2 billion yearly.

Finally, if we were to add only a few categories of corporate wrongdoing to our criminal definitions, or more seriously consider those already illegal, victimization's costs would rise most dramatically of all, since they produce far more destruction and cost than conventional crimes. As of the late 1970s, for example, an average of 390,000 job-related illnesses (costing $30 to 50 billion yearly to treat) and 100,000 job-related (and mostly preventable) deaths occurred each year, yet this probably underestimates at least the number of illnesses by ten times. In fact, one study has shown one in four Americans with a workplace disease. Also, industrial accidents (60% of which come from unsafe working conditions) in 1970 caused 14,200 deaths, 2.2 million disabling work injuries, 245 million workdays lost, $1.8 billion in wage losses, $900 million in medical costs, and a total $23 billion total loss to the economy.

Twenty thousand people die unnecessarily each year from improper emergency care. About 3.2 million cases of unnecessary surgery occur yearly as well, costing over $5 billion, and killing as many as 16,000 people. The government will lose $2 billion alone on kickbacks to doctors, unnecessary operations, and overcharges for cataract surgery through the Medicaid program. Twenty-two percent of all prescriptions are unnecessary, causing between 2,000 and 10,000 deaths yearly. Eighty percent of those dumping hazardous waste do so illegally. Sixty to ninety percent of the 365,000 people who die each year from cancer succumb to preventable environmental forms. Water pollution costs $60 billion a year, and a 60% reduction in air pollution could save $74 billion yearly. The death rate caused by all chemicals (53,000 of which have not been tested for hazards) runs at least twelve times higher than the homicide rate.

Price fixing raises prices at least 25%, and costs as much as $265 billion yearly. In 1978, U.S. petroleum companies received $10 billion in overcharges and other pricing violations. Commerical bribery and kickbacks cost as much as $10 billion yearly. Deaths and injuries caused by defective products cost another $10 billion annually, and auto defects add another $9 billion in losses. Insider trading cases have become epidemic according to *Business Week*, producing half the market reaction to corporate takeovers before any public announcement, and millions of dollars lost to uninformed investors. Poverty alone contributes significantly to unnecessary deaths, producing malnutrition, poor health care, and infant, maternal, and adult mortality.[54] The wealthiest 10% of the population underreports at least $28 billion in taxes annually,[55] and perfectly "legal" (but perhaps effetively "criminal") loopholes cost American taxpayers $78 billion in taxes annually.[56]

We can only partially understand the financial and physical costs of "criminal" wrongdoing in the United States, partly because we often find it hard to measure, but mostly because we have excluded much "crime" from our social reality of victimization. As we move now to examine the psychological and other costs of victimization, we might consider how much we actually underestimate those burdens as well.

THE PSYCHOLOGICAL EFFECTS OF VICTIMIZATION

Personal Guilt, Blame, and Pain

Victimization's cost may far transcend merely financial or physical losses, as severe as they might already be.[57] Victimization can produce psychological repercussions that enhance our fear and sense of vulnerability, alter our attitudes about our environment, and transform our behavior. It may disrupt social relations at home, at work, in friendships and other relationships.[58] Perhaps most profoundly, victimization may alter our attitudes about ourselves.

Being victimized can produce a strong sense of invasion or intrusion even from property crimes committed in the victim's absence, much less from violent personal assaults. Having one's house or apartment burglarized, for example, can significantly violate the sanctity or safety or privacy of one's home, creating a radical sense of vulnerability.[59] While such victims escape personal violation, they must bear at least the faint stigma of victimization when their neighbors watch police officers investigate the crime on their premises.

VIOLENCE.   But a much more serious stigma can result from being a victim of violence. Victims often react to violent victimization with a combination of anger and shame,[60] and even collapse.[61] Our egos and our sense of self correspond to our ability to maintain some level of personal control, particularly in certain spaces or environments. Violent victimization assaults our egos as well as our bodies, producing a sense of defilement and lost confidence. Sometimes it may make us hate everyone.[62] Strong psychological distress may result from shattering people's assumptions about their goodness, their invulnerability, and about living in a just world.[63] Men, for example, often sustain a strong blow to their masculinity for having been unable to prevent their victimization, particularly when publicized.[64]

Undoubtedly, however, women who have been sexually assaulted bear victimization's most pervasive personal effects. Rape victims report feelings of invasion, shame, defilement, dirtiness, and stain. They often view their violation as invading not only themselves, but also their families. The woman's, or her mate's, response may destroy their sexual relations.[65] Rape victims often find their lives shattered irretrievably, even when they have suffered no personal injury or financial loss. One study suggests that sexual assaults break up 50 to 80% of all relationships.[66] Women will often radically change their perceptions of danger, particularly if the assault occurred in a place they previously considered safe.[67]

Beyond the fear their victimization often generates, these women feel the special stigma attached to illicit sexual intercourse. Many women feel guilty about their sexual violation, despite their innocence.[68] These feelings, reinforced by what many view as sexist laws and a sexist culture that promote helplessness and double standards, place a special burden on women to absorb their victimization, which some never overcome.[69] Women's acquired passivity, and their internalization of sexist, patriarchical social values may help create the circumstances for victimization. In fact, some argue that their psychological assault not only *results* from the rape, it may be the perpetrator's conscious or unconscious *purpose* in committing the offense in the first place.[70] Thus, culturally, we seem to encourage male offenders to dominate women, and women to accept their fates passively, perhaps learning a "lesson" in the process.

Family violence invariably produces adverse psychological effects as well.[71] Child rape and incest victims, for example, regularly suffer psychological trauma.[72] Incest victims often conceal their abuse for long periods, later searching hopelessly for new meaning in their later lives.[73] Victimization occurring both within and outside families can be devastating, and even produce a collapse. Perhaps the most disturbing psychological effect occurs when victims begin blaming not merely others (such as their attackers), but, more important, themselves. Victims must overcome the stigma and guilt of victimization, beyond its other significant costs.

REACTION. Victims may adapt well or badly to their victimization and newfound sense of vulnerability.[74] Those who have felt somewhat susceptible and about equally vulnerable to victimization seem to adapt better than those who either have felt unsusceptible or highly vulnerable.[75] Some victims develop a "learned helplessness," concluding that any response to victimization will be futile. This often makes them numb and passive.[76] Victims sometimes blame themselves for either causing, failing to mitigate, or tolerating victimization, often downplaying their own personal characteristics.[77] They may experience intrusive thoughts and images, nightmares, irritability, and repressed, negative self-images that interfere not only with their normal functioning, but with their psychological and physical health.[78] To minimize victimization psychologically, some victims selectively evaluate themselves and their situation. They may compare themselves to unfortunate others, focus only on their own positive attributes, create hypothetically worse worlds, construe benefits from the event, or apply coping standards that make their survival seem remarkable.[79]

Many victims become highly outraged toward their assailants. Ironically, and perhaps tellingly, victims show more rage and vengeance toward offenders who attack their property and not themselves personally. Male victims show greater hostility toward their offenders than female victims.[80] Yet feelings of revenge will only be counterproductive for victims psychologically. According to psychologists, policies that promote retribution and punishment do not further victim interests or contribute to their recovery.[81]

Some analysts have tried to explain the typical response patterns displayed by victims. One model, for example, suggests an initial stage of stress, followed by denial and numbing, then latency, with periodic intrusions of the victimization until they gradually fade forever.[82] Another has found an initial shock, disbelief and denial, followed by frozen fright and detachment, then self-degradation, and finally integration.[83] Yet another has identified an initial disorganization, then recoil, and finally gradual reorganization.[84] Unfortunately, many victims do not make it completely through these cycles, causing psychological problems to linger indefinitely.

Public Fears and Concerns

Victims often react to their victimization with fear and cautiousness. People who have been victimized, however, do not necessarily show more fear, or take more precautions, than those who have not been victimized.[85] Thus, we find that both victims and nonvictims can be significantly affected by crime.[86] We must examine how it might influence their behavior, but first we should analyze the attitudes it might promote.

Victimization, even when it affects others and not you directly, can generate "fears" that you will be next. We also know that public perceptions of escalating crime rates have caused public "concern." Are fear and concern the same thing? Perhaps not. Lower classes seem to fear crime the most, perhaps because they risk victimization more (particularly by violence), yet middle classes show more concern about crime and about appropriate public policy.[87] If we can distinguish the two, then fear seems to imply a much more immediate danger—and a much more intense psychological response—than concern. We might fear crime when we daily witness its effects on our local community, but we might be concerned about crime as a problem, even if we consider our neighborhoods relatively safe.

Ironically, those concerned about crime often have comparatively little to be concerned about, yet they usually take vastly more precautions than those who fear crime.[88] Those who fear crime the most, like the elderly and the poor, often have the least resources or opportunities with which to respond. In any case, we might keep the possible difference between fear and concern in mind when considering public attitudes even if distinguishing the two may sometimes be very difficult.

WHO FEARS. The fear of crime, particularly in urban areas, pervades the population,[89] yet people's apprehension exceeds the actual victimization level,[90] and their actual victimization experiences.[91] The public not only routinely exaggerates the crime level, it believes the level has been constantly rising, and that little or no crime existed before.[92] As already suggested, people also tend to fear the wrong crimes, or generally have fears that contradict their objective danger. Middle and upper classes often fear violent crime, from which they stand relatively immune. They also fear strangers when they will more likely be attacked by an acquaintance or someone even closer.[93] Young males, who should fear crime the most, given their high propensity for victimization, often fear it the least.[94] Women and the elderly have some of the greatest fears[95] yet their victimization level falls considerably below many other groups. In a way, many people have become victimized more by their fear of crime than by crime itself,[96] particularly tragic since many of those fears are misplaced.

Some suggest that these contradictions may not be so illogical. For example, some people may be fearful less because they risk victimization, and more because they feel totally incapable of repelling or withstanding an attack if it comes.[97] Also, those least victimized may have escaped crime precisely because their great fears have led them to relatively successful precautionary measures.[98] Finally, some people who have a low victimization risk still may find themselves in situations that widely expose them to crime, thus creating fears that no statistics will likely dispel.[99]

Much research on fear has revealed the various characteristics or predictors of those who seem most afraid. Although it provides us with a general consensus on the question, some inconsistencies emerge. Some researchers have found fear related to sex, age, the size of town, and one's knowledge of crime and one's neighborhood.[100] Others suggest that fear emerges from violent crimes, from crimes occurring in a familiar area, and from recurring crime.[101] We might have the greatest fears of strangers,[102] and wrongly attribute to outsiders crimes actually being committed by insiders. Fear might depend as much on the seriousness of the crimes with which we feel threatened as on our perceived risk of being attacked.[103] We tend to be more fearful when poor, less educated, black, female, children, or elderly, and we tend to fear strangers, the disorderly, the culturally alien, the morally corrupt, the disruptive, and those from other races, ethnic groups, and classes.[104] Demographic factors might better predict fear than psychosocial and crime-related variables.[105] We seem to be less fearful about our own neighborhoods, although not necessarily in poor communities, or when we do not feel particularly attached to our neighborhoods.[106] Moreover, "less fearful" may be only a relative good since as many as 40% indicate that they fear walking alone even in their own, what they describe as safer, neighborhoods.[107]

CULTURAL SOURCES.   Our fear of crime may be only one part of our broader feelings of danger, often culturally defined. In other words, we may fear certain kinds of people and places as criminally dangerous, yet those fears may have less to do with objective dangers or bad experiences and more to do with culturally inculcated stereotypes.[108] And crime may not be the threat we have been socialized to fear the most. Some suggest that our crime conceptions emerge less from experience and more from official definitions and cultural indicators. As such, those conceptions may serve ideological purposes, including providing misleading cues about who and what endangers us the most.[109] Consequently, we have learned not only who to fear for crime, but who may threathen our status and security generally. In other words, some suggest that middle and upper classes have been socialized to fear the so-called "dangerous classes," composed of lower-class people who threaten their social status, their opportunities, and their economic well-being.[110] Perceptions that these "classes" also threaten us the most with crime only intensify the fears we have been inclined to have in the first place.

Much has been written about the fear of crime among women, the elderly, and children. These groups seem the most likely to acquire the "victim role" even before they have actually been victimized.[111] Women, for example, often feel particularly terrorized. Surveys indicate that over one-half of all women have strong personal fears of crime.[112] Female fear may emerge not merely from crime rates, but from the threatening context many women feel,[113] a perception that may be established or intensified by cultural norms. On the other hand, women may also react directly to perceptions about specific crimes.[114] Rape, for example, may be a "bellwether" crime by which women, and perhaps also some men, judge the criminal environment and determine their fears.[115]

The elderly also fear crime profoundly, which may produce the

most adverse consequences, since they will likely significantly restrict their behavior and affect their health.[116] Some elderly fear crime
more than others, however. Their fears seem most related to their
sex, race, community, and economic circumstances.[117] Poor, nonwhite women living in depressed areas suffer the greatest fears. Sex
and age, in particular, often merge as predictors. Some have found,
for example, that storytelling about crime enhances fear, but particularly for women and the elderly, who often figure so prominently in those stories.[118] Other studies show older women to be
most fearful, particularly when living in unsheltered environments.[119]

Besides women and the elderly, children also show high fear levels, and increasingly so.[120] Much of this fear may be emerging from
school environments. Although most victimization in schools affects
property and not persons, many school children fear crime.[121] In
one study, for example, one-fifth of all school children expressed
fears of victimization.[122]

The fear of crime, as we will examine, can change behavior significantly. But how people behave can also affect their level of fear.
How people orient themselves to the crime problem, and the measures they take, can increase or decrease their fears accordingly. Those
who seek crime prevention by working for a community crime organization, or who acquire personal defense training, show significantly less fear and more control than those with similar conditions
and characteristics, but who emphasize various avoidance strategies.[123] Moreover, the fear of crime may produce more crime. If people restrict their activities, for example, because they fear victimization, crime might be less observed (or perceived as such), and thus
more committed.[124]

PERCEPTION OF CRIME.   Apart from specific fears for their own safety,
the public also has great concerns about crime, which in turn produce feelings about offenders, punishment, and public policy. A rise,
or high rate, for some crimes actually may produce no concerns
whatsoever if the public views the offenses as unimportant, or perhaps (like gambling) not even criminal in the first place.[125] Yet the
public does care about most other crimes and, as we have suggested, they believe that the crime rate has been steadily escalating.
Crime seems to routinely compete with economic issues as the public's greatest concern.[126] Actually, the two factors may be related.
Concern about crime may have more to do with economic insecurity
than criminal insecurity.[127] Crime concerns may, in fact, have less
to do with victimization's impact and more to do with its symbolic
importance.[128]

People usually view the crime problem as being bad, but worse
in places other than where they live. According to the National Crime

Survey, past victims (and blacks particularly) voice concerns about escalating crime, including property crime in their neighborhoods, and especially about violent crime all over.[129] Most people believe they have become increasingly vulnerable to victimization, particularly among the more educated and wealthy, although not noticeably greater among past victims.[130] Middle-aged people also show increasing concerns about vulnerability, but based largely on perceiving national, not local, victimization levels.[131]

If these concerns do not produce fear, they will often at least produce feelings of alienation, isolation, distrust, and suspiciousness.[132] These feelings may not be universal, but instead vary by sex, race, and the kinds of crimes causing concern.[133] Crime might alienate us from other groups, our communities, our workplace, and even our friends, neighbors, and nation.[134] Some people claim they would leave their communities if they could because of the crime problem,[135] although other reasons might actually be more important. Nevertheless, one study of those who had recently moved shows 69% saying that the crime problem was an important motive.[136] While willingness to move might be exceptional, most people at least believe that they and their neighbors have definitely changed their behavior in some way because of crime.[137]

MEDIA EFFECT.   Earlier, we suggested the media's general impact on public perceptions of crime. More specifically, some believe that the media compete with other sources in developing public awareness. Social networks may transmit separate and sometimes conflicting perceptions. It may well be that social networks, for example, provide people with cues about local crime while the media suggests the crime problem's overall scope. Some research indicates that the public views the media as either accurately reflecting crime or underestimating its seriousness.[138] If so, whatever apprehensions about crime the media generate, the public may think it is even worse.[139] This could mean that concerns about crime develop independently of the media, but more likely the media helps set a base level of fear which, through constant bombardment, escalates and assumes, in the minds of many people, a life of its own.

Public concerns and fears may influence attitudes about both offenders and their punishment. Many people express their greatest concern about those who fulfill conventional criminal stereotypes, even when many others pose equal threats. Lower classes, in fact, may most accurately perceive likely offenders. Middle and upper classes, however, often fear poor, nonwhite males, yet will more often be victimized by people much closer to their own backgrounds and characteristics. Whether politically motivated and directed, or simply happenstance, we have historically designated certain people and certain groups as scapegoats for our problems. Our common offender stereotypes, however, may be little more sophisticated than the witchcraft we attributed to some New England women earlier in our history.[140]

PUNISHING OFFENDERS. We generally find the public believing we have not been dealing severely enough with criminals, particularly with those fitting our stereotypes. At least since the 1960s backlash against Warren Court decisions on defendant's rights, the public (with some considerable political and bureaucratic encouragement) has demanded increasing penalties, and through the early 1980s it has been significantly obliged with a new upsurge in punitiveness, perhaps not unrelated to increasing demands on behalf of victims.[141] Those demands have included an increasing support for the death penalty.[142] The public also seems extraordinarily willing to allow the police to use violence. One study, for example, shows public approval of "shoot to kill" and "shoot to wound" orders for hoodlums at 32% and 64%, for ghetto rioters at 30% and 61%, and for student demonstrators at 19% and 48%, respectively.[143]

Nevertheless, some victims have been surprisingly ambivalent about punishing their attackers.[144] The desire to punish may decline as one's case develops and as new priorities emerge.[145] This may be true for the general public as well. People seem less severe in the penalties they demand when they believe victims have been well treated.[146]

PUBLIC POLICY. Finally, we must examine the relationship between public concerns and policy, if only briefly. We might assume that official initiatives have simply followed public beliefs and preferences, but more likely the reverse has been true. Although crime has long been a political issue, the politicization of crime may have achieved new levels over the last twenty years.[147] Officials and other powerholders may well resist change and increase their freedom of action by not only doing little to reduce fear, but by actually enhancing it by manipulating public opinion about crime.[148] Yet too much fear may be counterproductive, and thus lately public policy initiatives may aim at minor reductions in the fear of crime while leaving the victimization level intact.[149]

In any case, victimization and concerns about crime can substantially damage our quality of life and our perceptions of the good society. Public fears can induce people to sacrifice freedom and mobility for greater social control and order, but they can also challenge the society's viability and legitimacy. Political leaders bent on increasing their powers might find that the very conditions promoting their strength directly challenge the system they seek to rule. For this and many other reasons, the public policies we pursue about crime, and about our fears and concerns about crime, strike at the heart of political power in any society.

Personal Behavior

We must examine official and community responses more closely, but first we should consider how perceptions about crime affect personal behavior. We can, in fact, predict much behavior from one's attitudes, but not completely. Some people, for example, who have been previously victimized or who substantially risk victimization or who even fear, if not worry, about crime, nevertheless fail to change their behavior, or do so minimally.[150] This may be irrational behavior, yet they may simply be unwilling to change their lifestyle, or unable to do so because they have few alternatives or resources. Thus, some people do not react to crime, or even their own concerns, at all.[151]

PRECAUTIONS.   Nevertheless, many people do change their behavior in some way, such as by taking precautions or by making accommodations that attempt to either avoid or manage risk.[152] This might involve approaching regular activities differently or eliminating some activities altogether.[153] People might substantially reduce their own freedom and mobility,[154] such as by going out less often,[155] or by staying off the streets at night.[156] One study shows 37% of those questioned to be practicing "loss evasion" of one form or another.[157] Other research shows that between 35% and 56% change their activities, with two-thirds doing something specifically to prevent crime.[158] Many people isolate themselves, even though it might intensify their fear.[159] For others, crime does more to change *how* they do things then *what* they do.[160] They adapt instead of ceasing their activities completely.[161]

WOMEN, CHILDREN, AND THE ELDERLY.   As with attitudes, victimization seems to particularly affect the behavior of women, children, and the elderly. Women, for example, take special precautions to avoid crime, far greater than most men.[162] If previously victimized, especially by sexual assault, then their coping behavior invariably includes some stringent alterations in their behavior.[163] For example, some rape victims, particularly when dragged through the stigma of criminal trial, feel they must leave their homes, communities, or states to restore their sense of security and dignity. The victim of the recent and notorious "Big Dan's" gang rape case in southern Massachusetts, for example, withstood the onslaught of threats, accusations, humiliation, and media sensationalism until she could bear living in her hometown no more. Unfortunately, these moves may often be counterproductive to the woman's recovery.[164]

In the home, where women may risk victimization even more than outside, women will often try to accommodate attacks. At worst, they might fall into a "cycle of battering" that may induce them to rationalize the violence they suffer.[165] They might, for example, rely on some future salvation; deny their injuries, their victimization, their victimizer, and other options; or appeal to their higher loyalties to their spouse, despite the violence.[166] Because women typically lack economic security and self-defense, and fear retaliation, they may simply suffer,[167] sometimes even creating situations that induce quick bursts of violence which they can manage, instead of surprise attacks. Victims often correctly perceive resistance as enhancing the violence.[168] Part of women's victimization in the home results from their socially learned behavior around men. In other words, they learn to be victims.[169]

Children often follow a similar pattern. The so-called "child sex abuse accommodation syndrome," for example, involves secrecy, helplessness, accommodation, and delayed disclosure.[170] Juveniles have increasingly changed their behavior at school as well, including various self-defense mechanisms.[171] Finally, the elderly also often drastically alter their behavior, anticipating victimization.[172] My grandmother, for example, lived in a relatively safe neighborhood yet was so frightened by what she read and heard in the media that she rarely left her house, even when she needed groceries. And she so secured her house, including completely blocking her rear door, that she turned it into an obvious firetrap. Some senior citizens have apparently even starved to death in their homes, too afraid to leave even for food.

AVOIDANCE AND PROTECTION. Some people react to victimization simply by trying to reduce losses and, for physical attacks, might prepare to flee not fight. Yet many people do not retreat from the threat of victimization; they take steps to try to protect themselves and their households. Some pursue various "target hardening strategies" such as getting guards, mace, tear gas, or watchdogs, installing bars, locks, alarms, lights, and warning stickers. Others ask friends or the police to watch their homes. Some learn self-defense. Other engrave their property and try to buy insurance, although only half of us actually get it.[173] Some people even change their job or move.[174] A 1981 Gallup poll showed 5% with burglar alarms, 5% in neighborhood watches, 13% with special locks, 16% with guns, and 20% with guard dogs.[175] Some studies suggest that people most often resort to better lighting,[176] while others show that they most often buy guns.[177] Guns have increasingly proliferated in schools, for example, ostensibly for self-protection in many cases.[178] While those with handguns do seem to feel more secure (however illusionary), researchers doubt generally that fear inclines people toward buying guns.[179]

Although these responses may provide some people with some greater peace of mind, they represent almost exclusively individualistic reactions, with dubious effectiveness. Buying the latest gadgets for home protection may divert people from more collective strategies and from the source of the threat. But, more important, we have little evidence that these precautions actually work.[180] Furthermore, such individualized measures may degenerate into a pathology of defensiveness that not only wreaks psychological and social damage, but that will often find people harmed by their own defenses (such as through accidental shootings).[181]

STANDARD REACTIONS.   Some have devised models to describe our reactions to victimization. The "utilitarian" model, for example, has people calculating acceptable risk to determine their behavior. The "psychological" model shows people making fairly rational responses, taking into consideration the problem's seriousness and their risk and efficacy.[182] The "opportunity" model recognizes that people's ability to respond may vary significantly, based on their resources. Thus, an apparently irrational response may be dictated by limited choices.[183] Other research suggests that people create cognitive maps of where to go and when. They learn to mind their own business and manage their relationships, not necesarily withdrawing into fortresses. Social groupings will help identify strangers. Finally, people will often define social boundaries by the most obvious racial, ethnic, or class divisions.[184]

CRIMINAL RESPONSE.   Actual victimization or perceived threats may make some victims so angry, frenzied, desperate, or distraught that they respond with their own crimes.[185] People might practice, for example, illegal modes of defense.[186] Some may respond in revenge or to save their honor. The infamous Bernhard Goetz, for example, who shot four black youths (two in the back) who he claimed were about to rob him, highlights the increasing vigilantism amidst a climate of public fear and frustration. As a kind of "avenging angel" where police forces have failed, such behavior receives significant public, and even political, support.

Some victims lash out with their own crimes because of the frustrations or pains of their own victimization, such as when battered women in turn batter their children, or kill their victimizers.[187] Ntozake Shange suggests the feelings and reactions such violence may generate:

> "there is some concern
> that alleged battered women
> might start to murder their
> husbands and lovers with no
> immediate cause"
> i spit   i vomit   i am screaming

we all have immediate cause
every 3 minutes
every 5 minutes
every 10 minutes
every day
women's bodies are found. . .[188]

People frustrated with what they perceive as judicial lenience toward their offenders may commit crimes to ensure their own "justice." Finally, some might strike back at their oppressors, such as the recent case of Joanne Little killing the prison guard who raped her.[189] The rage and desperation of such incidents are conveyed strongly in the words of Jayne Cortez:

And what was Joanne supposed to do for
the man who declared war on her life . . .
This being wartime for Joanne
she did what a defense department will do in times of
war
and when the piss drinking shit sniffing guard said
I'm gotta make you wish you were dead black bitch
come here . . .
Joanne did the dance of the ice picks and once again
from coast to coast
house to house
we celebrated the day of the dead rapist punk . . .[190]

FUTILITY. As for accommodating those victimizations not defined as criminal, victims have little recourse. Responding to institutional violence and victimization may be an even more formidable task than taking precautions against individual offenders. Employees who need their jobs find it very difficult to quit so as to avoid workplace hazards or diseases. Ghetto minorities have little recourse against police brutality. City dwellers can do little to avoid the polluted air and water they must breathe and drink. Reacting individually, these and many other victims can do little about victimization. Collectively, as we shall see, they may do much better.

We might further understand the psychological impact of criminal victimization by examining the effects of victimization produced by terrorism, war, military service, and concentration camps.[191] Such effects include anxiety, physical disorders, and depression, and a susceptibility to other kinds of victimization, sometimes self-induced, such as homicides, suicides, and auto accidents. Over 40% of all Korean War and World War II veterans, for example, died of those causes,[192] and more Vietnam veterans have died from suicide (with another 450,000 attempted) than actually died in the war.[193]

While we want to better understand how victims react after victimization, we should not ignore how they react during victimization. In particular, considerable controversy surrounds the resistance victims should offer to their attackers. Although some people resist robberies, for example, most do not. Most people also cooperate with skyjackers.[194] Some suggest that resistance provides a poor strategy in property crimes, but unclear results in personal victimizations.[195] We know little about the comparative effectiveness of collective, as opposed to individual, resistance. Some argue for nonviolent resistance in all cases, but recommend against violent resistance.[196]

Resistance provides perhaps the biggest issue in sexual assaults. Here the question transcends merely the effectiveness of resistance since traditionally we have also taken nonresistance in rape as signalling either the victim's guilt or acquiescence. The advice we give to women about how to respond also differs sharply.[197] Some recommend against resistance, suggesting that it only provokes the attacker[198] or that fewer injuries result for submissive rape victims.[199] Most police officers advise against resistance as well.[200] Yet others strongly urge resistance, both for effectiveness and for maintaining one's self-esteem.[201] Some implore women to prevent their attackers from treating them impersonally.[202]

Having considered individual behavior during, after, and in response to victimization, we can now examine the role of third parties. That is, how do bystanders respond during crimes and how has the crime problem influenced our willingness to help our neighbors generally?

Bystander Behavior

At least since the infamous case of Kitty Genovese, who in 1964 died following an hour-long attack within earshot of at least thirty-eight witnesses, we have been concerned about bystander behavior during crimes.[203] The research shows an apparent decline in "good samaritans" who aid their fellow citizens.[204] The recent "Big Dan's" case in Massachusetts (where bar customers refused to help, and in fact apparently cheered a woman's rape by several men) provides only one example.

The public has shown great reluctance to help victims of violence, as well as police officers who respond to victimizations,[205] except perhaps when victims are family, close friends, or members of the same minority race.[206] Fear of one's own victimization or its consequences has helped diminish a potentially important barrier to crime,[207] and one whose further deterioration may significantly increase the public's danger.[208] This unresponsiveness may also reflect the alienation and depersonalization of modern life or of American society, although some believe it merely shows confusion and a conflict of interests.[209]

One's responsiveness may depend on the crime's social context.[210] Bystanders may not be entirely unwilling to act, but find that emergencies such as crime catch them too much by surprise.[211] Some research shows that bystander attitudes toward criminals or authorities predict their intervention much less than the behavior of other bystanders whose presence may induce participation.[212] Yet others suggest that bystander motives stem more from attitudes toward crime, criminals, and the police than a concern for the victims.[213] Some experiments have shown that direct appeals by victims to bystanders elicit the most assistance, compared to indirect or no requests.[214] Some would like to impose a legal duty on bystanders to respond.[215]

Community and Official Responses

OFFICIAL REACTION.   As suggested earlier, victimization and its threat may promote conflicting incentives among officials. Reducing crime and the fear of crime produces both advantages and disadvantages for powerholders and bureaucrats. Victimization might provide the pretext for repression,[216] or what some have called the "iron fist."[217] It might also result in "softer" or "pacification" policies designed to improve police-community relations.[218] Our increasing victimization, and our new concern for victims, have helped stimulate new programs ostensibly for preventing victimization and for assisting victims. Those programs may be largely symbolic, however, and reflect a kind of "image building" about official actions.[219] In any case, for now we will simply acknowledge these services and programs as responding to victimization and later described them in some detail.

COLLECTIVE VS. INDIVIDUAL REACTIONS.   Victimization also affects communities, and sometimes elicits a community response. Compared to our intensely individualized reactions to victimization or its threat,[220] we respond collectively relatively infrequently. Emile Durkheim arged that crime would elicit a collective response, drawing the community together, while Margaret Mead predicted a kind of "negative" unity.[221] Yet others have found it more likely to paralyze group reactions, and perhaps even help tear communities apart.[222] This disintegration may not be inevitable, although our largely individualistic politics and psychology provide a significant obstacle to community efforts.[223] A recent trend toward "victimization prevention" instead of "crime prevention" may have intensified the individualized approach.[224]

Some communities may just ignore certain kinds of "victimization," such as vice crimes, not because they cannot organize a collective response, but because they tacitly support the behavior.[225] Yet most communities do regard victimization as a problem. Aside from weakening community solidarity,[226] fear and victimization may cause people to leave their neighborhoods[227] or may justify and reinforce hostilities stemming from class, racial, and ethnic conflicts.[228] Neighborhoods will also be more fearful when in transition or when unorganized,[229] a telling observation. Crime may only affect social stability adversely when already weak, but perhaps not when strong.[230] Some people transcend their individuality and judge their quality of life based on their community's condition, in which case threatened communities mean threatened individuals.[231]

KINDS OF RESPONSES.   While we will later examine community programs in some detail, for now we can suggest the kinds of responses that have emerged. Unfortunately, they have not been entirely constructive. Spontaneous or organized vigilantism, for example, might result,[232] often with racial overtones, and official acquiescence.[233] Other reactions with a more positive face may, as we shall see, produce adverse consequences, such as programs that drastically heighten suspiciousness, blame victimization on dubious sources, and unnecessarily sacrifice liberties.[234]

Some communities rely on various strategies of informal sanctions.[235] Sometimes, specific groups will organize to challenge the problem, such as women's organizaitons that have vowed to "take back the night" from attackers, or more broadly gain political power from men.[236] Others might try to lobby for better law enforcement in their communities.[237] Some have tried to transform their communities physically, through environmental or architectural design.[238] Still others might try various forms of community policing.[239]

These community measures will likely fail, however, if they avoid the root causes of crime and neighborhood deterioration. Defensible space through environmental redesign, for example, will not automatically reduce victimization amid conditions of social fragmentation and underdeveloped strategies for social action.[241] Since community fears often transcend the crime rate, successful programs must go to the sources of perceived dangers, which cannot be achieved by building greater fortresses, using better gadgets, or enhancing state control.[241]

Finally, communities, like individuals, may be victimized by "crimes" that have not been officially defined as such.[242] Residents living near "Love Canal" in New York, for example, suffer the effects of hazardous wastes. People living in or near Harrisburg were victimized by the radiation emitted from Three Mile Island. Youngstown, Ohio, essentially a company town, has had to cope with the precipitious departure of the steel industry. Some have responded to these kinds of victimization, usually when organized, but most communities have had little recourse for such suffering.

CONCLUSION

Victimization can dramatically affect attitudes and behavior. It will often impose considerable financial and physical costs on individuals. It will stimulate state expenditures, usually borne unequally by taxpayers. Many will resort to various degrees of personal protection, which bring costs and behavioral changes. Businesses can be very adversely affected by crime, although many other enterprises benefit considerably from high levels of victimization and fear. The greatest costs of all will usually result from harms and wrongdoing that we routinely exclude from our criminal definitions.

Crime or the fear of crime will also impose notable psychological effects, which will often alter behavior. It will routinely produce guilt, self-blame, or psychological pain of one sort or another and will heighten our concerns about ourselves and our communities. And it will stimulate personal accommodations, and sometimes community reactions as well. We can also inevitably expect official responses, although they may be more symbolic than real.

We cannot overestimate the enormous impact of victimization on people's lives. Yet, as significant as the effects we have described may be, they still understate the overall victimization suffered. We will suggest that we cannot appreciate the true burden of victimization until we employ broader indicators of victimization that transcend our narrow criminal definitions. In other words, we should consider applying more universal standards of human rights.

For now, we must turn to examining the victim's encounter with public officials. That is, we will examine victims' role and experience in the criminal process, assessing their effect on law enforcement and its effect on them. As we shall see, victimization may not end with the crime.

6

Adding Insult to Injury: Victims and Law Enforcement

There is a cop who is both prowler and father
he comes from your block, grew up with your brothers,
had certain ideals.
You hardly know him in his boots and silver badge,
on horseback, one hand touching his gun.
You hardly know him but you have to get to know him:
he has access to machinery that could kill you.
He and his stallion clop like warlords among the trash,
his ideals stand in the air, a frozen cloud
from between his unsmiling lips.
And so, when the time comes, you have to turn to him,
the maniac's sperm still greasing your thighs,
your mind whirling like crazy. You have to confess
to him, you are guilty of the crime
of having been forced . . .

ADRIENNE RICH, "Rape"

The quality of a nation's civilization can be largely
measured by the methods it uses in the enforcement of
the criminal law.   WALTER SCHAFER

The system's failure is only in the eye of the victim; for
those in control, it is a roaring success!

JEFFREY REIMAN

Victimization's impact often does not end with the crime, its effects, and the victim's response. Instead, many victims become involved in the criminal process and must bear its burdens as well. We might expect that law enforcement would naturally cater to victims, yet this rarely happens.

Some argue, incorrectly, that law enforcement primarily serves suspects and defendants at victims' expense.[1] Even short of this, some say we shortchange victims by conceptualizing victimization as a blow to society or the state, instead of to individual, or even groups of, victims. While this comes closer to the truth, it still misleads. We have too much evidence to contradict the "consensus model" of criminal justice, whereby the system serves the general public interest. Instead, the criminal process seems to much better serve certain political, economic, and bureaucratic interests, although we need not assume some sort of purposeful conspiracy. Thus, powerholders may see victimization less as a threat to public interests and more to their special interests.

Whichever view we support, law enforcement definitely does not serve one group: victims. For whatever reasons, we have shown little social responsibility toward victims.[2] It has become something of a cliché to suggest that the victim suffers a "second victimization" in law enforcement, but it bears some considerable truth.

As Chapter 2 suggested, victims historically have played a much different role in law enforcement than they do today. Before the modern era, victims either completely controlled enforcement or played a major and central role. Until very recently, victims had almost completely lost their niche in the criminal process. In the last few years, however, we have worked hard to reintegrate the victim's role into law enforcement. While that trend might seem wise by definition, it actually deserves careful consideration. A greater victim role might restore the historic position of victims, but could place unwanted and inappropriate burdens on victims. In other words, we must consider whether victims really want a significantly greater role and also whether such a role best serves the victim's and the public's interests.

For example, beyond the questions of victim burdens and defendant's rights, some wonder whether we should not apply a "cost theory" to victim involvement. We might want to consider the negative costs of not satisfying victims.[3] Although dissatisfaction may not necessarily guarantee nonparticipation in the future, its effects will do little to promote law enforcement. On the other hand, a "cost theory" may unnecessarily take crime for granted, and may underestimate the impact of significantly increasing victim involvement. In an already fragile system, the increasing workloads that greater participation might generate could bring the criminal process to a grinding halt.

We must consider how politics shapes the victim's role in law enforcement. Victim involvement is hardly self-evident simply because a crime has been committed. How do restricted criminal definitions limit those who can play the victim role in the first place? What shapes victim needs and motivations in law enforcement? What costs emerge from not satisfying them? How do victim needs interact with internal, official goals, and external structural objectives?

VICTIM MOTIVES

Why do victims get involved in the criminal process or, alternatively, why do many victims fail to participate? Answering these questions might help us understand victim attitudes toward law enforcement and the barriers and incentives to participation. Aside from victim needs, officials also may want this information to create appropriate procedural reforms, and, more important, to gauge the perceived legitimacy of criminal justice, if not the political system generally.

We will examine how victims might participate in law enforcement, emphasizing their role in reporting crime, promoting an arrest, pressing charges, and giving testimony, information, or advice. While some victims participate in law enforcement for reasons beyond their control (such as when bystanders report crimes for them), many participate for very concrete reasons.

Reporting Victimization

Victims may act as the most significant "gatekeepers" of the criminal process since they predominantly control the decision whether or not to report victimizations. Although victim reports will certainly not automatically become official police reports, probably around 95% of all victimizations known to the police result from citizen reports, usually from the victims themselves,[4] although one study has shown as many as one-half coming from nonvictims.[5]

Victimization surveys have shown that the victimizations reported, or at least recorded, fall considerably short (perhaps by as much as 10 times and by at least 3 times) of the actual crime rate. Nonreporting would be an insignificant problem if it meant sparing the system trivial cases, yet the evidence suggests otherwise.[6] The so-called "dark figure" of unreported victimizations may vastly exceed those that victims and others actually report. Thus, although victims serve as important gatekeepers of many cases entering the criminal process, they participate most significantly by not becoming involved in the process at all.

Researchers have learned much about what motivates victims either to report or not report victimization, although we know much less about what motivates nonvictims who must decide whether to report crimes on victims' behalf. While reporting seems correlated with certain characteristics of victims, offenders, and crimes, victims have also offered many explanations for their decision.

NON REPORTING. Broadly considered, victims tend *not* to report victimizations to avoid further problems, because they believe that law enforcement cannot provide a solution, because of certain characteristics of the victimization or its perpetrator, or because the costs seem to outweigh the gains. More specifically, victims avoid reporting because they want to forget or reduce their losses or have pursued a private solution, such as a settlement or revenge against their attacker. Victims may also not report because they think little of law enforcement, as when they mistrust the process, do not know how to use it, believe it will provide no solution, view their evidence as insufficient or the police as incapable, too busy, or too insensitive, wonder whether the real offenders will be caught, or fear additional victimization in the criminal process. Finally, lower-class victims may experience a kind of "social learning" about how law enforcement works, which generates substantial hostility and nonreporting.[7]

Characteristics about the offender or the offense may convince victims not to report, such as when victims fear retaliation, have a relationship with the offender, do not really want the offender punished, or do not perceive the incident to be significant or perhaps any victimization at all. Reporting patterns also differ between urban and rural areas.[8] Finally, the costs of reporting may outweigh the benefits, such as when it will produce inconveniences, no payoffs, possibly cancel their insurance, or when victims just feel too confused or helpless to resort to formal mechanisms.[9]

REPORTING. When victims *do* report crime, they seem to do so either to provide some benefit for themselves, their family, or society or to give some response to the offender. For example, victims might pursue social goals when they report crimes because they believe a moral duty, believe criminal justice involvement to be a natural response, or want to help the community or aid others. Victims might pursue personal goals when they report, such as to seek insurance, social services, victim compensation, revenge, protection from future victimization, or lost property. They may want to remedy a lingering situation or may respond to the urging of others. Finally, victims might report to express anger or disapproval toward criminals or to seek retribution, punishment, or treatment for their attackers.[10]

FACTORS.   Aside from what reasons victims volunteer for either reporting or not reporting crimes, their decision may reflect characteristics of the community, the victim, the offender, the case, and the offense. For example, a crime report may depend on community traits such as its location or crime level[11] or the attitudes of its residents toward law enforcement.[12] Reporting may also hinge on victim characteristics such as age,[13] sex,[14] ego or sense of social responsibility,[15] socioeconomic status,[16] criminal involvement,[17] or past offenses.[18]

Crime reports may be determined by offender traits, such as their sex.[19] It may depend on case characteristics such as whether a suspect exists,[20] or whether the costs outweight the benefits.[21] Finally, reporting may reflect characteristics of the crime, such as the kind of offense,[22] and its severity.[23]

TIMING.   When victims do report their victimization, we have also been interested in *when* they make their report, and what determines their timing. Some studies show that most crime reports occur very soon after the event, usually within fifteen minutes.[24] Other studies have shown average delays as long as one hour.[25] This delay, if typical, may have important implications not only for law enforcement, but also for the public misgivings it might imply.

The crime's characteristics, and some situational factors, such as the time of day, will best predict when victims report.[26] Delays may occur while victims ask advice from friends and family about what to do.[27] Delay could also indicate the victim's doubts about the efficacy or appropriateness of the criminal process.

INTERESTS.   Crime reporting studies mostly suggest that many victims decide that getting involved in law enforcement will not be worth it. Their noncooperation stems predominantly from conscious choices.[28] Those who do cooperate usually report for specific reasons and to pursue particular goals. Although some participate from a sense of duty, this seems isolated and may be steadily decreasing.

We might believe that victims jeopardize their own interests by not reporting their victimization since, after all, without notification how can law enforcers pursue the perpetrators and bring them to justice? Yet nonreporting may be more rational than we might suspect.[29] The view that victim participation will be futile seems well supported in practice since reporting crimes does not produce a significantly different outcome in most cases.[30] And, if participation brings burdens beyond victimization, with no material or psychological gains in return, nonparticipation might be even more justified.

Arresting Suspects

While a "citizen's arrest" provides an option available to victims, few people actually attempt one either because of its impracticality or because it risks a suit for false arrest.[31] Instead, victims rely on law enforcers to make most arrests. But to what extent do law enforcers rely (or at least employ) victims in making or seeking those arrests? Police usually react to victim reports of victimization. While law enforcers sometimes observe crimes in progress, and bystanders sometimes report crimes against others, the police will usually only begin thinking about making an arrest if victims notify them that a victimization has occurred.

Thereafter, police officers tell us they rely significantly on victim cooperation and information to pursue suspects and eventually make arrests.[32] Yet in practice this may be true only for some offenders or victims or offenses. Factors other than victim cooperation seem to have much more to do with arrests. For example, various organizational incentives for particular police enforcement patterns might much better predict the level and kinds of arrests. If so, then the blame victims often receive for losing cases by refusing to cooperate seems unwarranted. The fact that police officers might rely, in part, on victim cooperation, and might want to encourage it, hardly suggests that victim noncooperation provides the major obstacle to arrests. To the contrary, we may find that some kinds of victims of some kinds of crimes conflict with police priorities.

Pressing Charges

A victim's ability to press charges depends, of course, on whether an offender has been apprehended and put into a position to be charged. This may, in part, reflect the victim's earlier participation. Yet even ignoring official decisions and actions that also help determine whether an offender will appear, victims hardly dominate the decision to charge, as we shall soon see. Nevertheless, we still want to know what determines whether victims will press charges when they have the chance to do so. Their rationales strongly resemble the reasons they give about crime reporting, although their incentives apparently do change to some extent over time. A victim might report a crime for one reason, yet press charges for another.

Research shows that victims fail to press charges because they have resolved the incident or received promises of restitution from the offender.[33] Some withdraw because they do not really want their attacker to be punished,[34] such as in some relationship cases.[35] Others resist because of delays, lost income, poor accommodations, or intimidation.[36] For example, one study shows that 53% had their cases delayed at least once, and 32% at least twice, causing them to withdraw charges.[37] Other studies show that intimidation causes as many as 28% to refuse to press charges.[38]

When victims do decide to press charges, the reasons can again often be classified as either pursuing social interests or personal goals or offender retribution. Sometimes victims may be pressing charges as cross-complainants[39] simply to get their accusors to drop charges.[40] Victims may clarify their motives by the time they must decide whether to press charges. While a victim's self-interest seems to dominate when reporting crime, victims may give more weight to social interests—and less attention to their offenders—by the time they press charges, although personal goals still count most of all.[41]

Other Needs and Incentives

We often assume that victims primarily participate in law enforcement either as a social responsibility, to protect themselves, or to seek punishment and revenge against the offender. When we examine the specific reasons victims often give for reporting or pressing charges, however, we often find other needs and incentives. In particular, victims seem very strongly motivated by personal, material interests.

ECONOMIC. Even when victims do not suffer crimes involving direct financial losses, their economic motivations for pursuing cases can often be very strong. For example, victims might seek insurance, restitution, compensation, government welfare payments, social services, or witness fees. One study suggests that victims pursue cases not merely to recover economic losses, but sometimes for a net financial gain, particularly when they are poor.[42] The prospect of getting witness fees, or other economic benefits, induces victims to participate, a finding public officials might want to consider.[43]

Economic incentives influence even more strongly when direct financial or property losses have been incurred. Some officials oppose the return of stolen cash or property to victims before cases have been concluded since they believe victims will drop charges after recovering their losses. Nevertheless, some victims find the criminal process to be ineffective for recovering their losses, especially in consumer fraud cases.[44] These cases, which often cause substantial economic losses, either receive no legal protection or enforcement outright or fall low among prosecutorial priorities.[45]

In those few cases where prosecutors do pursue consumer matters in criminal courts, they treat the state or society as the victim, which means that victims will have to press separate civil cases anyway, even if offenders receive criminal convictions.[46] And those convictions will not automatically guarantee civil judgments; in fact, criminal case outcomes often will be barred from civil trials.[47]

PSYCHOLOGICAL. Finally, still other needs and incentives cause victims to pursue cases. Some victims get involved seeking advice about handling a situation.[48] Similarly, victims might merely want to threaten offenders or to stop a lingering situation, without necessarily seeking formal sanctions. Beyond their civic duty, some victims really want to participate in this government process, and expect that they will be consulted and informed about their role and the proceedings.[49]

VICTIM IMPACT ON ENFORCEMENT

Aside from knowing what motivates victims to participate, we must also consider what effect they have on the criminal process. This will depend, in part, on whether and how victims participate, or otherwise exert influence, which in turn may depend on how well victims correspond to official needs. After suggesting both victim influences and official incentives, we will follow victims through the various stages of the criminal process, ranging from criminal investigations to post-trial proceedings, assessing their impact at each stage.[50]

Influence vs. Participation

To assess victims' effect on law enforcement, we must consider not only what kind of impact they might have, but also the appropriateness of their involvement in the first place. Ever since the victim's recent revival, we have almost invariably assumed that the greater the involvement the better. Yet we might well reconsider that presumption. Do victims really gain by taking a greater role? Do victims really want to increase their participation? Does involvement contradict some of the requirements and assumptions of the criminal process?

On what grounds, for example, can we extend victims new powers, influence, and participation? According to our adversarial system, offenders will not be considered offenders at all until actually convicted. Since defendants must be presumed innocent, victims can thus only be "presumed" victims legally.[51] Should victims be able to shape cases against defendants who formally cannot be presumed to be their attackers? We might recognize victims as victims to provide them assistance, but we might transgress by regarding them as legal victims whose influence we should significantly heed in processing offenders, assuming, of course, that we find the adversarial process legitimate in the first place. Ironically, in practice defendants will routinely be presumed guilty, despite our legal standards. Should we also regard presumed victims as legal victims,[52] and thus twice violate those standards?

Furthermore, do victims really want to bear the burdens of increased participation? Already, even with victims' modest involvement, they often abandon their cases because of their hardships. To be successful, victims will often have to prepare themselves for a contest, not merely with the offender, but with judicial institutions and personnel. Moreover, some victim participation may actually impede the effective processing of offenders, possibly jeopardizing crime prevention.[53]

Beyond whether victims should be more involved in law enforcement, we can assess just what effect they *actually* have. Many have argued that victims should participate more in the criminal process, to restore the victim's historic role. By that standard, we will find that victims have had little effect. Already we have seen the victim's reluctance, with apparent good reasons, to participate even in reporting victimizations or pressing charges. Those who do get involved will typically participate only in very limited ways.

Nevertheless, victims might still affect law enforcement by other means besides their actual participation. We will observe victim *influence* much more than actual victim *participation*. Victims may influence, for example, by their mere physical presence, their demeanor, or their visible characteristics. This may not nearly suit many victim advocates, it may not promote a victimological jurisprudence,[54] and it may be far less than victims' influence abroad,[55] yet some opponents would argue that criminal trials should not be "tainted" by any victim influences at all.

Official Motives

As we shall see, law enforcement officials have incentives that not only seem to contradict criminal justice ideals, but often clash with victim interests. This occurs even when we would expect victim and official goals to be identical.[56] Officials rarely receive any reward for catering to victims. As frequently embodying society's least powerful interests, victims can rarely influence judicial personnel.[57] Officially, victims will usually come second to state interests, when considered at all.[58] Victims may be viewed as interfering with official routines, efficiency, and effectiveness.[59] And excessive attention to victims might generate new programs that threaten official budgets.[60]

Officials will often view victims functionally, as possible ingredients to help pursue cases, or promote public relations, but not as people whose interests constitute ends in themselves.[61] Victims might view themselves as crucial to crime control, and certainly many officials concur, yet crime control may not really be law enforcement's primary purpose after all.[62] Some believe that arrests, trials, and punishment may be only very tenuously related to law enforcement and deterrence, and have only a remote relationship to justice.[63]

Gaps in lifestyle and background between most victims and most officials (even police officers) may prevent officials from identifying with victims.[64] Officials often hold "just world" views that may lessen their sympathy for victims who they might regard as at least partially deserving their fate.[65] Victims also symbolize official failure, a trait not likely to attract support even for blameless victims.[66] Officials also often view themselves as victims,[67] making them less inclined, and in their minds less able, to help other victims.[68]

Finally, officials often have incentives to ignore entire victim categories. Through limited criminal definitions, many victims fall outside official responsibilities in the first place, despite the great losses suffered. And among those formally recognized, officials further select those to emphasize, routinely excluding victims of white-collar and corporate crime, and often deemphasizing other, less influential victims such as women, minorities, and the poor.[69] In sum, while we might expect officials and victims to pursue similar goals, often they clash instead, sacrificing victim interests for official objectives.

Criminal Investigations

Most victims first encounter law enforcement not in some official setting, but instead in the "streets." There, most victims call for police assistance or report victimizations. Most justice will be dispensed in the streets as well,[70] as police officers use their discretion to decide which incidents and suspects to pursue and which victims to take seriously. They may promote an informal decriminalization of the laws (by ignoring cases) that deprives victims of their due recognition.[71] Since the victim's role in criminal investigations will depend considerably on interacting with law enforcers, we must consider police incentives as they react to victim interests.

POLICE MOTIVES. Ironically, the first stages of police professionalism may have contributed considerably to the victim's original marginalization from the criminal process. Making law enforcement a full-time specialization of public police officers helped supplant victims as those who would apprehend offenders and introduce them to the criminal process.[72] Specialized police work has also helped create law enforcers who often feel, if not act, isolated from others. This generates rigidity, defensiveness, and suspiciousness which may counteract victim interests.[73]

Police officers, like most other judicial personnel, usually view their work as helping to protect society from crime, even if their real function may be different.[74] While they undoubtedly interact with victims more than other officials, we have little reason to believe that they primarily conceptualize their role as protecting individual victims, much less as caring for them after victimization.[75] Coping with victims comprises only one part of their work, and not necessarily the most important one. The police often view themselves as victims,[76] and tend to regard all others as threats whether really victims, victimizers, or others.[77] In fact, some police officers *are* actual crime victims, or at least witnesses, and they compete favorably for attention in court against victims, as we might expect.[78]

What incentives motivate police officers? They respond to a combination of personal and professional goals. Since police officers rarely view themselves as social workers, they consider victim assistance as the work of others. They might grant whatever aid and comfort they can, but even that may be difficult given job pressures and redundancy,[79] and may even provoke psychological conflicts. As bureaucrats, they see each case beginning to look like every other one, making it difficult to react sensitively to each victim they confront.[80] At worst, law enforcers may invoke a kind of psychological "police brutality" against victims, as a personal defense mechanism, by treating them roughly, insensitively, or culpably.[81] But, beyond any possible personal concern, do police officers have professional goals or requirements that might make them attentive to victims?

Rarely do formal rules require certain behavior by law enforcers toward victims, although in New York the compensation board has tried to require New York City police officers to read victims their rights.[82] Informally, police officers have the greatest incentives to improve their arrest and clearance rates, and to otherwise seek promotions within the organization. Do police officers rely on victims to achieve these goals? What determines the victim role in police work and the kind of treatment they receive?

POLICE RESPONSE TIME.   If the police want to build public and victim support, then research tells us they will do so best by responding promptly to calls. This may build considerable satisfaction even short of producing tangible results.[83] The actual response time varies considerably, however. One study shows responses ranging between ten minutes and four hours.[84] This variance may have less to do with police capabilities and more with conscious decisions to respond differently.

Some cases will be ignored completely; police failed to respond at all to 23% of the calls in one study.[85] Others have great difficulty in getting through.[86] The police may respond to some cases, but fail to take them seriously; consequently they may have to "cool out" adamant complainants.[87] Police officers will apparently respond differently depending on the kind of incident and caller; even serious crimes may receive no or slow responses when reported by certain kinds of people or from certain segments of the city.[88] Many police officers consider nonwhite, lower-class callers to be second-class complainants who have a much greater tolerance for crime.[89] This may be one of the first instances of what has been called "two-class justice."[90]

CLASSIFYING INCIDENTS.   When police do respond to calls, they must decide how to treat the incident. They can be crucial for helping victims define whether a victimization has really occurred and how to react.[91] Police officers must assess the situation and the complainants to determine their own reaction, including whether they will record and seriously pursue the complaint. As with the decision to respond, they do not necessarily apply neutral and objective standards.[92] The police begin a selection process that effectively limits those victims taken seriously, in the same way they begin the "weeding out" process for offenders.[93]

Police officers will often treat black victims, for example, less seriously,[94] even in serious crimes.[95] They usually will not process family disputes, even when protection orders have been issued.[96] Some places will routinely not process black assaults or consensual statutory rapes.[97] Police will usually acquiesce to their many "informers" committing crimes because of the information they bring.[98] Police will take more seriously "outside" crimes, which they often define as their major responsibility, as compared to "inside" crimes committed completely beyond their purview.[99] They will react differently based on victims' personal attitudes and characteristics,[100] and on whatever prior dealings they have had with certain victims and suspects.[101] They will routinely respond more to crimes reported by local business elites,[102] and, generally, a higher status will produce greater attentiveness.[103] Law enforcers will also take cues about which incidents to treat seriously, from prosecutors[104] or politicians.[105]

Fully responding to all the complaints they receive would cripple the enforcement system,[106] and thus the discrimination they practice stems partly from organizational demands. One study, for example, shows that police did not record 25% of the cases they were called to investigate.[107] Even among those incidents they actually record, many have been filed cursorily and will be pursued leisurely, if at all.[108]

Many cases will be "unfounded" or "defounded" as the investigation proceeds. Unfounded cases will be struck from the books, which police officers value since it will appear to both lower the crime rate and increase the solution rate.[109] One study has shown that 20% of all rapes, 32% of all robberies, and 8% of all burglaries may be unfounded.[110] Another study in Chicago discovered 21% of all major offenses to be unfounded, 40% of which were real victimizations.[111] Defounding, on the other hand, does not eliminate a case, but does reevaluate and classify it differently, usually as a lesser offense.[112]

ARREST PATTERNS.   Victim characteristics will also help determine the arrest pattern. Because of personal or organizational objectives, law enforcers will often simply fail to enforce in certain areas, thus reducing the chances of making arrests for many victimizations. Also, if police officers have already refused to record incidents, or later label them unfounded, they will have no suspects to pursue for those victimizations in the first place.

When police do pursue suspects, obviously many factors will determine their success. One of them—victim traits—will help officers set priorities for the cases they most strenuously pursue. Those traits might include age, race, status, the victim's culpability, relationship with the offender, the victimization's damage to victims, and the suspect's status compared to the victim's.[113] Victim behavior during and after the crime may provide cues as well, such as whether the victim resisted the attack or insisted on police action.[114] Victim motives such as merely threatening offenders rather than seeking a serious arrest will affect law enforcers as well.[115]

Studies suggest that police will ignore cases unless the incident requires, in officers' minds, some decisive action, in which case they will assess the victim's legitimacy.[116] Police respond to more than simply victim traits and behavior; in fact, most arrests occur because of the direct or indirect assistance victims provide. Research indicates that about 60% of all arrests result from victim initiatives.[117] Most arrests seem to occur shortly after the crime, and much less thereafter. Victims can be very important in identifying suspects and providing police officers with the timely information they need for arrests.

Law enforcers respond selectively to victims and victimizations because of personal biases and general organizational demands. Their reactions also reflect how they believe they can best achieve their professional goals. Contrary to conventional wisdom, getting as much help from all victims may not help law enforcement, but rather confuse it. Police officers determine their goals and priorities; victims and the incidents, information, or assistance they provide will only selectively advance those objectives. Overzealous victims of minor crimes, for example, might take valuable police time away from more serious, or (from a police perspective) more rewarding, pursuits. Moreover, even in cases police would like to pursue seriously, victim involvement may exceed its usefulness relatively quickly.

FORMAL COMPLAINTS.   Once police take incidents seriously, and after victims assist law enforcers in completing reports and acquiring information, victims may first encounter an official setting by being asked to make a formal report either in a stationhouse or at a courthouse complaint office. If a victim is injured, police officers might appear in the victim's place, but otherwise most victims will appear in person. While the settings may vary, they have many common characteristics. Even with modernized facilities, the atmosphere can be overwhelming, alienating, and even frightening. Confusion reigns, as victims cannot easily fathom where to go and what to do. Rarely do special offices or instructions exist for victims, and officials rarely have the time, or apparently the inclination, to explain what must be done. Police officers often help victims through the process, but most victims have little control or understanding, much less get special attention. Usually, victims must wait long periods, not knowing why they must wait nor for how long. The atmosphere seems congested, fast-paced, threatening, and generally depressing and unappealing.[118]

Most victims will find this setting very unfamiliar, although some have been there before, either as past victims or even as past offenders. Even veterans, however, can barely negotiate the process. Victims may be asked to do several things, like viewing mug shots, helping develop a composite drawing, providing statements, and visiting the crime scene. Victims sometimes may be asked to hearings for search or arrest warrants.[119] If a suspect has already been arrested, the victim may be asked to come to a "line up" to make an identification.

Usually, through several steps, victims eventually make a formal crime report, either to police officers, police prosecutors, or to assistant district attorneys. Sometimes victims talk about their cases directly with prosecutors; other times they go through police officers. At this stage, prosecutors will begin to categorize the cases they receive, continuing the screening process begun earlier by the police.[120]

SCREENING.   Prosecutors will sometimes reject cases that police officers have encouraged victims to report. In fact, victims may be more successful with their cases when they report them directly to prosecutors instead of to the police.[121] Cases will usually be classified by criteria that determine the case's seriousness, its likely success, and its "worth" for prosecutors. Much may depend on victim complainants. Their characteristics and behavior will help determine the case's strength, including their credibility, culpability, and cooperativeness.[122]

Like police officers, prosecutors seem strongly influenced by victims' personal traits.[123] Older, white male victims, for example, will be more likely to have their cases pursued.[124] The victim's incredibility will often doom a case even if otherwise strong, at least when prosecutors rule out a plea bargain. If the victim must appear before a judge or jury in court, prosecutors seek good "standup victims."[125] Yet the victim's usefulness may reflect stereotypes more than real trustworthiness. Many cases will be dropped because of victim-offender relationships,[126] or signs of victim precipitation.[127]

When prosecutors want to discontinue cases, they will usually appeal to victims' better judgment. As police often do earlier, prosecutors will try to "cool out" victims by convincing them that their cases cannot be won, or that they may not be that serious, or that their pursuit will be a substantial burden. Despite their best efforts, prosecutors may be unable to placate many victims, even when accurately assessing their cases.[128]

VICTIM RESPONSE.   As with the police, victims may be frustrated and angered by discontinued cases, and may even respond with their own crimes. Or they may seek an alternative to conventional procedures by hiring a private prosecutor, just as some attempt citizen arrests when police will not act. Private prosecution, and the victim's prominent prosecutorial role, have suffered at least as long as restitution's decline.[129] Nevertheless, victims may legally employ private prosecutors in at least 33 jurisdictions, although they rarely do.[130] Although more widely practiced abroad,[131] private prosecution will usually be too expensive for most victims and private prosecutors are regarded quite negatively by most public prosecutors. Still, some victims may resort to "reconnoitering," or hiring private attorneys to at least collect information to provide the public prosecutor, or employ outside lawyers to monitor the prosecutor's work on certain crimes, such as those committed against local merchants.[132]

Generally, we cannot expect victims to feel very pleased about their involvement thus far, even when officials pursue their cases, since they must survive the trauma of their treatment, their minimal involvement, and the discrimination with which law enforcers often respond to their victimization.[133] Moreover, even when district attorney's take cases and pursue them, the victim's experience becomes the "prosecutor's property," thus beginning the process not only of negating the victim-offender conflict, but also the victim's involvement.[134]

Although victims often provide important information, they participate little beyond that. Nevertheless, victims do exert some considerable influence through their traits and behavior. Unfortunately, victims seem little able to increase their influence, and what influence they do exert seems to discontinue cases more than anything else. Since they have no active role, they often can only hope they have no traits that will automatically jeopardize their case. Victims may well feel alienated from law enforcement, and conclude that no justice exists, and that they have just wasted their time. Unfortunately, the victim's role will rarely improve in subsequent stages.[135]

Pre-Trial Proceedings

EARLY STAGES. Many victims will participate no further in the criminal process because their offenders or other suspects have not been arrested. If an arrest occurs, however, technically they will be elevated to the higher status of "witness,"[136] and may be called to several proceedings early in the case.

While these stages may vary from one jurisdiction to another, victims may be present at the initial appearance, where the state first accuses the suspect. Victims may also come to the next stage, the preliminary hearing, which will determine whether reasonable cause exists to believe that the suspect committed the crime. Here victims may give testimony about the case, but isolated from other witnesses.[137] If the suspect has not already been identified in a line up, the victim may be asked to do so at this time and can be cross-examined by the defense.

Then, although many jurisdictions use an "information" procedure dominated by the prosecutor, others send the case to the grand jury to decide whether to issue a formal indictment, or drop initial charges, or change them. Victims may also be called to testify at this stage.[138] Finally, the victim may appear at various evidentiary hearings if called by the defense.[139] While these possibilities for participating exist, most victims attend none of them, and thus these proceedings make decisions largely without victim influence or presence.

ARRAIGNMENT. Victims can next participate at arraignment, where formal charges will be placed, the offender's plea will be taken, and bail will either be revised or established for the first time. Although many victims never learn about arraignment, more victims appear at this proceeding than the others. Nevertheless, they mostly play little or no role.[140] Ironically, their greatest participation may be acquiescing to dropping charges.[141] Many cases end here, for one reason or another—sometimes because the judge or prosecutor has shown the victim the "advantages" of discontinuing the case. When cases do continue, it may be only to eventually arrange a settlement. Arraignment provides the first opportunity for plea bargaining yet, as we will see, victims rarely contribute to this process, and often fail to recognize it even when it occurs before their eyes.

Most victims cannot influence charges or bail setting. Those few who do, either influence by their traits or their behavior; again the victim has no formal role.[142] In setting charges, prosecutors may respond to many of the same cues that determined whether police officers took the cases seriously. Research shows that a victim can influence charges by not being a homosexual or alcoholic or addict. Charges will be more likely pressed if victims are middle aged or elderly, white, employed, and upper class, particularly when the defendant is nonwhite. Female victims will be successful when they have no promiscuous history or when they have been attacked by a stranger. Victims will be viewed more favorably when they have no arrests, have not provoked the offense, and have not violated community norms themselves.[143]

As with the earlier decision whether or not to charge, prosecutors must balance, among other things, victim needs and social needs, which frequently sacrifices the former.[144] Prosecutors will often, although not always,[145] deemphasize relationship cases, for example. Ironically, these kinds of cases often lead to the easiest arrests, many of which will be fruitless.[146] The victim's demeanor may also help determine the charges set. Reluctant victims, for example, may exert less influence, particularly in severe, nondomestic cases. Adamant victims may be strongly heeded, especially in serious crimes. In general, prosecutors tend to "bedsheet" or "overcharge"[147] suspects, which should at least temporarily please most victims who seek strict penalties. A credible and adamant victim will make overcharging even easier.

Victims likewise have little control or influence over bail. Whether defendants must post bail, and at what amount, may determine whether they will be free pending trial. We often exaggerate the danger this poses to victims and to others in the community. For the most part, we have been far more restrictive on defendants' freedom than we need be, and those released on their own recognizance rarely engage in new crimes.[148] And, contrary to conventional wisdom, when a new crime does occur, the courts generally act quickly to revoke bail and apprehend the offender, usually withholding subsequent bail.

Nevertheless, some defendants may threaten or harass victims, thereby giving victims some legitimate interests in bail hearings. A desire to protect victims competes with bail's major goal: to assure that defendants will appear at trial. It would be inappropriate and impossible to predict whether defendants will commit crimes while out on bail. Withholding bail would deny rights for defendants whose guilt has not yet been established. If we allowed victims to determine bail, few defendants would be allowed free before trial. Instead of presuming that defendants will threaten victims, and withholding their freedom, we must protect victims when they need it.

In any case, whether warranted or not, victims apparently have little role in setting bail anyway. Unfortunately, most victims claim they also have been given no special protection against defendants.[149]

CONTINUANCES. Some considerable time may elapse between arraignment and an actual trial, if one ever occurs. This may result from delays produced by various motions and continuances, as well as by the typically heavy workloads that burden most urban courts. Delays may be sought for unexpected reasons. We normally assume that defenders will seek delays to challenge police procedures or to wear down victims and other prosecution witnesses. Yet, while a few defenders may harass victims or discredit them at trial, most defense attorneys work for poor clients and never exert such efforts, or worry much about their client's rights. In fact, the greatest delays come from prosecutors who cannot manage their workloads or who want to wear down overzealous victims themselves.[150] Despite the court's otherwise great concern for efficiency, unnecessary adjournments proliferate, with as many as 80% of all dates being "continued" and 94% of all appearances being unnecessary.[151]

Victims may be completely ignored as each new court date comes and goes, or may be consistently called to court for each date only to find the trip futile.[152] Many times victims get so confused or so little information that they may wait in court all day only to learn that their case had been adjourned, in their presence, early that morning.[153] When the court routinely fails to notify victims, we must wonder whether prosecutors really rely on them for pursuing cases as much as they say. When victims do learn about court dates yet suffer endless postponements, they may become increasingly disenchanted about their role. Here, the frustration may emerge not only because victims cannot participate, but because they incur increasing expenses and lack information about their case and even any apparent symbolic importance to the process.

Ironically, while victims might justifiably become less and less interested in participating, their absence will often be blamed for losing cases. Their nonparticipation may also risk their being cited for contempt of court,[154] which may result in their own arrest and possible imprisonment.[155] A member of my family, for example, recently decided not to pursue charges against an indigent pickpocket in Boston and only fortuitously escaped an attempted arrest by uniformed police officers.

While victims await trial, they may be asked to provide pre-trial information to the prosecution. The district attorney will often want as much information as possible, and victims may be an important source. As "judicial consultants," victims may help prosecutors prepare cases as well as their own testimony.[156] Unfortunately, in many court systems the prosecutor changes at each stage,[157] and victims often find themselves repeatedly retelling their stories. Victims may feel used, if not abused, as a resource, yet lack any concrete sense of participation.[158]

Plea Bargaining

Despite some possible trial preparation, practically no cases actually go to a full trial. An average of over 90% of all cases end in a guilty plea, usually after plea bargaining. This results not only from the administrative burden of high caseloads, but also because prosecutors, judges, and defense attorneys prefer it that way. Plea bargaining occurs between prosecutors and defenders, with defendants pleading guilty to apparently reduced charges in exchange for a more lenient sentence. Since lesser charges only reduce the prosecutor's typical "overcharging" down to the actual offense, since a lenient sentence may never materialize, and since the process pressures defendants into sacrificing their rights, plea bargaining hardly provides them the "free ride" we assume. In any case, the most typical process available for victims to influence in court constitutes no trial at all.

Yet we have little evidence that victims even influence plea bargaining. Most bargaining occurs in hallways, in private offices, and even on the telephone. Not only will victims rarely be present, they will also rarely be consulted.[159] While it might seem logical to seek victims' opinion or approval, plea bargaining may give officials even less reason than trials to consult them. Officials have such strong motives for plea bargaining that victims will almost invariably provide only a threat, not an aid, to its smooth functioning.[160]

PROSECUTORIAL MOTIVES.　Prosecutors, judges, and even defense attorneys willingly pursue plea bargaining. Their personal, professional, and administrative objectives may ignore not only victims and their needs, but will negate the adversarial process as well. Prosecutors, for example, want to win big cases, compile a strong conviction rate, manage their considerable caseloads, and achieve personal advancement. In big cases, they will likely insist on formal trials and victims might find themselves involved, sometimes very significantly. But, to compile a favorable conviction rate, prosecutors rely substantially on plea bargaining. It not only boosts their percentages, it also most easily processes their caseloads and helps them win weaker cases.[161]

JUDICIAL MOTIVES.　Judges must ensure the appearance, if not the reality, of justice, yet their administrative incentives predominate. Their professional status depends primarily on how well they manage their court and its caseload. Although in some jurisdictions judges take pains to appear ignorant of negotiations, all judges accept bargaining as the most efficient processing method.[162] Just a 10% decrease in bargaining would require twice the court's current resources, thus showing its great administrative importance.[163]

DEFENSE MOTIVES. Defense attorneys also strongly pursue plea bargaining, even though it may appear to undercut their client's best interests.[164] Most defenders work for the court either as private, appointed attorneys or as public defenders, and have mostly indigent clients.[165] This substantially influences how they represent defendants. Defenders usually assume that cases will be negotiated, and offer plea bargaining to their clients as a benefit *they* have provided, not as the automatic conviction it really represents. Plea bargaining also allows defenders to control their clients.[166]

Private defense attorneys, often part of the so-called "cop out" bar, often receive a flat fee for each case, and often derive most if not all their income from the courts.[167] This gives them little incentive to pursue long, or even any, trials. Public defenders, while not depending directly on a rapid turnover of cases for their income, must nevertheless respond to their overburdened caseloads and to the judges for whom they work. Thus, they have little time or inclination for full trials either.

COURTROOM WORKGROUPS. Of course, for the few nonindigent defendants who enter the criminal process, who usually retain private, outside attorneys, the incentive structure differs, and thus plea bargaining occurs less frequently. These cases and those others that have, for some reason, not been negotiated, constitute the only full trials to which victims might contribute.

Even in less congested courts, the criminal process tends to be much less an adversarial contest than an administrative proceeding,[168] the members of which seem to have much more in common and much more to gain from cooperation. They respond to interrole reciprocity demands emerging not only from their caseloads, but also from their personal and professional objectives.[169] As such, and particularly with certain court structures and scheduling, courtroom "workgroups" emerge as the most efficient means of processing cases.[170] While we might well understand how the incentives of workgroup members might merge, where do victims fit into this process?

Victims, like defendants, will be effectively excluded from courtroom workgroups. Just as we might well wonder how well the workgroup and plea bargaining serve defendants, they apparently ignore victim needs and interests, and certainly participation, as well. Victims rarely participate in plea bargaining because the negotiations typically do not rely on their involvement.[171] In fact, as a consensual process where workgroup members have well-established standards of each case's worth and each actor's objectives,[172] victims threaten workgroup cohesiveness.[173] As unpredictable "outsiders,"[174] they provide potential uncertainties and inefficiencies that contradict bargaining's purpose in the first place. Victims will be regarded more as interferences (to harried prosecutors, for example) than aids. In fact, some judges believe that plea bargaining, even without victim participation or consultation, benefits victims anyway by sparing them the burden of testifying and attending trials.[175]

COOLING OUT VICTIMS. If victims interact with officials before or during plea bargaining negotiations, it may be more to "hide" or "cool out" victims than to promote any meaningful participation.[176] When hidden, victims will have little chance to disrupt, much less reject, the bargain struck between the prosecutor and the defense. Prosecutors may tell victims, for example, to arrive at the courthouse in the afternoon, having fully planned to plea bargain the case to conclusion in the morning.

When present, prosecutors will try to "cool out" victims by convincing them of the bargain's wisdom, or even its fairness, perhaps by deemphasizing the "deal" and asking victims to be reasonable and thankful that the case has finally ended with at least something having been done. Victims might be consoled if negotiations induced defendants to provide information about other offenders or accomplices. Prosecutors may try to wear down persistent victims by purposely requesting continuances on cases they want to bargain, if not dismiss.[177]

Even prosecutors, who might be reluctant to admit the victim's minor role, tell us that they rarely consult victims for plea bargaining. In one study, for example, 59% of the prosecutors claimed they rarely sought victim input, and only 15% said they sometimes talked to victims in very serious cases they sought to negotiate. For those relatively few who do consult victims, only 31% gave their views much weight, and 15% gave them no weight at all.[178]

As with previous stages of the criminal process, victims participate little in plea bargaining, and exert little influence. In fact, officials often purposely prevent them from interfering or influencing, perhaps not so much because they maliciously disregard victim interests, but rather because they will often threaten official objectives. Some officials may sincerely believe that plea bargaining provides victims with the greatest benefits. In any case, since negotiations settle most cases, we now need only consider the victim's possible role at the relatively few trial proceedings and in post-trial or post-settlement processes.

Trial Proceedings

By and large, the criminal process resembles an assembly line,[179] attempting to process as many cases as efficiently as possible. Its relationship to "justice" may be dubious for both victims and offenders. For victims who have pursued their cases this far, the rewards must be few. Officials end most cases before the trial, although some victims also formally drop cases on their own.[180] Nevertheless, if victims have had little role and received little benefits for their involvement thus far, perhaps they can find new meaning and rewards at full trials.

On the average, less than 10% of all completed cases actually go to a full trial. Since only about 10% of those trials have a jury, most trials occur before a single judge. Either way, full trials do at least resemble our ideal adversary process. In many cases, victims will play some role since the prosecution will rely, at least partially, on the information and perhaps even the courtroom testimony they provide. Working closely with victims, especially when they have witnessed or directly experienced the crime, would seem essential to winning cases. Yet victims still cannot be guaranteed that at least in the few trials that do occur, they will achieve some substantive participation and control.

Many trials, for example, encounter numerous delays, which eventually may leave victims wondering whether they really want to participate after all. Also, many trials eventually decay into some sort of negotiations, which again typically exclude victims. Even when trials go their full course, and even when victims ignore the frustration of repeated delays, their role may be unsatisfactory.

WITNESS MANAGEMENT. In recent years, prosecutors have devised elaborate "witness management schemes," a few based on computer programs or simulations,[181] to better control their use of victims at trial. Many prosecutors claim that absent witnesses cause their greatest case loss. For example, one study shows that victim nonparticipation accounted for 50% of all lost cases,[182] while prosecutors in New York City have claimed it costs 63% of their cases.[183]

Witness management schemes presume that victim noncooperation results from inefficient operations and confused victims,[184] yet to the extent that victims do not participate, it may be for many other reasons.[185] A major cause may be how the process alienates and burdens victims. But, more likely, prosecutors lose most of their cases on their own, while blaming victims for the problem.

While some undoubtedly do decay from victim noncooperation, the number may be exaggerated since many willing victims persistently complain that they would like to participate, but have been denied the chance.[186] Undoubtedly, some victim attrition results from inefficient notification systems, but often prosecutors merely show little interest in getting victims to court in the first place, sometimes purposely. Even at full trials, some prosecutors find it unnecessary or even counterproductive to use victims.[187] They want to avoid the almost inevitable ambiguities of guilt that victims might reveal to the judge. The victim's appearance may weaken the case by posing contradictions or hints of victim culpability.[188]

Moreover, some prosecutors may want to use victims, but wrongly anticipate their noncooperation based on past experience and so settle cases short of trial.[189] Many victims who view themselves as cooperative and willing have been perceived by prosecutors as disagreeable.[190] Particularly in certain kinds of cases such as rape, prosecutors try to avoid trials more than victims, perhaps to spare victims an ordeal.[191] Some victims labeled as uncooperative have some relationship with defendants and have been assumed, often incorrectly, to be uninterested in pursuing a trial.[192]

ATTRITION.   Aside from prosecutors' apparent and frequent disinterest, victims fail to appear at trial for other reasons. They may be tired of delays, unable to bear its inconvenience and costs, unaware of the date, or no longer interested in pursuing the case. Witness management schemes may reduce some of the administrative frustrations victims often encounter, but may not significantly increase victim participation. Actually, witness management, which often begins long before trial, often seems to have much more to do with "using" victims to satisfy official goals than anything else.[193]

We incorrectly assume that using victims to gain convictions will satisfy both official and victim needs. Victims seem as concerned about the process as the outcome.[194] They do not think of themselves as "resources"[195] and undoubtedly do not want to be treated as such. They seem to want information, participation, and control at least as much as a conviction and a tough penalty.[196] Information seems particularly important.[197] Victims would like to know about their roles, how the process works, why certain decisions have been made, and how their cases have been progressing. They would like more than simply a one-way flow of information where they must act as passive recipients.[198] Witness management programs that simply use victims as cogs in the justice machinery will not likely satisfy these needs. Without giving victims some meaningful control, status, and role, they do not promote the victim's equal role in the criminal process.

TESTIFYING.   When asked to trials, victims sometimes perform a meaningful, and presumably satisfying, role. Yet more often they participate minimally in a process designed to degrade them. Many victims get called to court for political or organizational purposes. Visible victims symbolize the court's concern, and may help prosecutors convince the judge or jury of their cases.[199]

When victims get called to court to actually testify, they may wish they had not. Even when coached by prosecutors, witnesses often encounter a threatening, confusing, alienating, and degrading process, made all the worse by unexpected and often hostile questions and treatment from judges, defense attorneys, and sometimes even prosecutors.[200] Some victims not only have their wisdom, veracity, and memory questioned, but also their character, reputation, and past behavior. Contrary to popular perception, constitutional rights provide little protection in practice for most defendants,[201] and thus defenders must work hard to build a good defense, sometimes resorting to maltreating victims.[202] Being in the witness box may be an unexpected and distasteful ordeal for most victims,[203] although not invariably.[204]

TREATMENT. As we will later examine in greater detail, victims usually find themselves poorly accommodated at the courthouse. They receive little useful information and rarely any services to make their appearance less burdensome. This treatment reflects official dispassion, conflicting objectives, and victim powerlessness. Officials routinely ignore victims' special problems and needs not only because they have no time, but because their job has hardened them to adversity and shielded them from overinvolvement.[205] They may regard the state, not the individual, as the real victim, and the trial as a process for determining criminal guilt, not for providing victim comfort. Moreover, since modern penology has stressed, until recently, deterrence and rehabilitation over revenge and restitution, prosecutors often must distance themselves from victim needs in favor of social needs.[206]

Primarily because of their routinely lower status backgrounds, victims have little power to improve their accommodations. Some advocates have argued for better treatment at court:

> Why could not his time be consumed in a more businesslike fashion? . . . Should he not be given a part of a room with a desk and a telephone where he can work on his interrupted business affairs when a necessary and unexpected delay in putting him on the witness stand occurs?[207]

This inquiry totally misconstrues typical victims, their needs, and their potential influence to acquire such accommodations. Most victims would settle for a comfortable room with a coffee pot, yet cannot even get that.

CONVICTION.   Nevertheless, victims may have some concrete influence on the major outcome of criminal trials: conviction. Although some argue that victim traits do not affect guilt or innocence,[208] other research suggests the contrary.[209] Conviction seems significantly more likely when victims come from a higher status background,[210] when their testimony corroborates other evidence of the crime,[211] and when victims have no relationship with the offender.[212] The victim's attractiveness[213] and respectability[214] also may increase convictions. Offenders will also be more likely convicted when victims are employed, young and "helpless," reputable, and white, and also when victims have not provoked the offense nor had a criminal record of their own.[215]

Finally, at trial, victims perhaps have the greatest opportunity to interact with judges. Although judges preside over most of the preceding stages, the trial may give them their first real chance to consider "live" victims, in presumably the most serious cases. Unfortunately, while this increases the victim's chances of interacting with the judge, and even though prosecutors often fear its results, one need not be concerned. In fact, victims consistently claim they have not been helped or consulted or even addressed by judges during the trial.[216] While judges will occasionally ask victims their opinion about the case, victims seem to influence more by their traits and demeanor than by their advice. At worst, some judges not only ignore victims but may even berate them, particularly women or minorities.[217]

Post-Trial Proceedings

When their cases end in acquittal, most victims will likely feel frustrated and betrayed, although often as much because of the process as the outcome. When the defendant has been convicted, the victim may feel gratified, although still concerned about what sentence will be imposed. Victims may want to influence not only the punishment delivered, but also the offender's subsequent disposition at the probation and parole boards and in prison. They might seek any punishment, or some particular punishment, perhaps a very harsh penalty. Or they may want the judge to order restitution from the offender. They may want offenders imprisoned, and made ineligible for parole or at least be informed when criminals have been released.

PUNISHMENT.   Although our incarceration rate exceeds that of all other nations,[218] we often feel that we have not punished offenders enough. Victims, in particular, may feel this way. Many victims would like to advise judges about the appropriate penalties, although this happens relatively infrequently. Like prosecutors and police officers before them, judges seem trapped by conflicting penal goals, none of which seems to argue for a very strong victim role.[219] For deterrence, judges want certainty and uniformity; for rehabilitation, the sentence must be tailored to offender needs; and for retribution, it must be oriented to the crime. If judges consider victims, then they must sacrifice either uniformity or offender needs or social goals. Moreover, appellate courts often rebuke any victim influence, arguing that crimes occur against the state not against individual victims.[220]

Despite these barriers, judges do sometimes consult victims for their opinions, although more often for information than recommendations.[221] When victims do express preferences, they usually ask for more severe sentences in property, not personal, crimes.[222] At best, victims and judges may engage in "reverse plea bargaining" whereby they undo the promises made to defendants for pleading guilty.[223] Thus, pursuing victim interests may increase the injustices against defendants. Some argue that victims should have a veto power over sentences, suggesting that victims have no less qualifications for this kind of decision than officials.[224] But we must consider the propriety of allowing victims, who often seek the severest punishment against their attackers, to determine penalties, even if that has been the victim's role periodically in the distant past.[225] The recent emergence of "victim impact statements" may steer a middle course between no role and a predominant role for victims in sentencing.[226]

As with earlier stages, however, victims influence punishment the most, not by their participation nor a formal sentencing role, but rather by their characteristics and behavior,[227] although perhaps more so abroad than in the United States.[228] While some doubt that victims influence judges and juries,[229] or see it as only one of many factors,[230] some research has shown their apparent effect on some punishments.[231]

Ironically, the influence of victims may *reduce* penalties as well as increase them. For example, even victims might mellow when asked their sentencing recommendation in the offender's presence.[232] As for judges, they may assume that victims suffer greater injuries than they do, and thus the victim's presence may reduce sentences when those injuries appear less serious.[233] Victim precipitation will often soften judicial judgments in murder cases.[234] Others may go so far as the Wisconsin judge who recently imposed no penalty on a convicted rapist, claiming that the victim's enticing dress and the general aura of permissiveness provoked the offender.[235] In fact, victim behavior during the crime can frequently affect sentencing. Victims will often reduce the sentence by having afforded the offender an opportunity, acted provocatively, used excessive self-defense, given retrospective consent, and been negligent.[236]

Yet victims may help increase sentences as well. Judges may consider individual victims if they view *them* (and not merely the state) as victims, if they favor retributive goals, and if the victim has not helped precipitate the offense.[237] Victim testimony can reveal negative things about offenders that might otherwise be ignored and thereby influence judges to impose higher penalties.[238] Juries seem to respond to victims even more than judges.[239] Attractive female victims can sometimes induce stronger punishments.[240] Punishments will be more likely when victims have a high status job, do not know the offender, and suffer an injury.[241] White victims attacked by blacks can often stimulate the most severe penalties.[242] For example, blacks will be eighteen times more likely to get the death penalty when the victim is white.[243]

PROBATION AND PAROLE.   Victims may influence subsequent stages of the criminal process, although again they play no formal role, and researchers disagree about what effect they might have. Probation officers will sometimes consult victims, but may be more interested in information than advice.[244] Victims virtually never participate in parole hearings,[245] yet may influence their outcomes when parole officers learn about their strong opposition to some convict's release. This may be particularly true with recent lawsuits against parole boards that have released prisoners who have committed subsequent crimes.

Generally, victims may not be very impressed with their power over punishments. Their greatest influence seems to arise from characteristics, and even some behavior, over which they have little control. Despite our national inclination to impose severe punishments, many victims may believe their attackers were treated leniently, even when they draw prison time. Yet prison may not be the only punishment imposed by the criminal process.

THE PROCESS AS PUNISHMENT.   One study, for example, suggests that the "process" inflicts other serious punishments beyond merely sentences.[246] The process causes offenders delays, pressures them to forego rights and plead guilty (when they might be innocent), often deprives their rights without redress, causes them lost jobs and income, regularly brings long periods of pretrial detention before conviction, inflicts costs such as lawyer's fees and bail bonds, promotes discrimination, imposes a criminal stigma, and provides them with a criminal record (which may prevent them from getting a job), even when they have not been formally sent to prison.[247] We might also underestimate the penalty and restrictions imposed by probation.

Much research suggests that the great protections and bountiful rights for offenders which some victims and victim advocates parade as evidence of a bias against victims largely function as "hollow symbols" of fairness, or at best as luxuries or reserves that can be invoked only in big, intense, and particularly difficult cases. Appeals practically never occur, trials are almost nonexistent, and formal pre-trial motions occur very rarely.[248] Exercising these rights means paying costs that exceed the reach of almost all defendants. If criminals "get away with it," it happens much more in the streets than in the criminal process,[249] and rarely at the victim's expense.

In fact, victims may know better than anyone the punishment the criminal process may impose since they suffer many of its same effects, along with defendants. For victims, the process may be the punishment too.

Summary

Law enforcement strongly emphasizes the society as victim, and much less so those individuals who have been specifically harmed by crimes. That bias emerges particularly when we consider the individual victim's role in the criminal process. At most, victims have an informal role. They actually participate very little, particularly because they fulfill no formal, institutionalized function. They participate early in a case by what they contribute to helping police officers apprehend suspects, and they make a formal complaint. They participate little thereafter, in most cases, except for giving testimony at trial; yet trials rarely occur.

Victims do seem to affect law enforcement with their behavior and their characteristics, although it may often be difficult to distinguish the victim's impact from other influences. Victims' influence seems greater earlier in their cases, and then steadily declines.[250] In some cases, particularly with serious crimes, adamant victims may have a greater impact. Ironically, one of the victim's greatest roles may be to help dismiss cases. Most of all, victims influence by their characteristics over which they have little control.

Aside from philosophical barriers that might repress the victim's role, many practical, personal, professional, and political obstacles exist as well. The criminal process, despite our adversarial ideals, has much less to do with dispensing "justice" (for either victims or offenders) and much more to do with managing caseloads. Even with more moderate workloads, judicial personnel view themselves primarily as administrators, concerned with processing cases efficiently and effectively.

Law enforcement also reflects the personal and professional goals of its personnel. Officials have incentives for personal advancement and professional interaction that fight outside interferences, including the influence of victims. Not only do victim interests often clash with judicial priorities, they represent a challenge to well-established work patterns.

Finally, victims may be impeded in law enforcement, or selectively employed, for political reasons. As primarily society's most disadvantaged people, victims (like most offenders) have little political leverage in the criminal process, which reflects the same configuration of interests and power as in the broader society. They not only play a role commensurate with their limited political power, but their relative influence as a group further splits along racial, gender, and class lines. We should not expect victims to significantly influence until they can increase their own power base or win the sympathy of more powerful segments of society. What role victims do play in the criminal process may also be political. Victim involvement performs the symbolic function not only of showing our concern for the disadvantaged, but also encouraging their support and participation in our institutions. Victims help legitimize the criminal process.

Victims play a minor role in law enforcement, mainly affecting decisions and behavior only marginally, although sometimes importantly. Yet law enforcement may affect victims considerably. We must examine the burdens, problems, and outcomes criminal justice produces for victims. Then we can consider law enforcement's impact on victim attitudes, particularly for those who actually experience the criminal process.

We should not forget, however, that *not* participating in law enforcement may also significantly affect victims. While avoidance might spare them the burdens of criminal justice involvement, we should not discount the alienation and helplessness that decision might breed.[251] Feeling unable to get satisfaction from institutions may only intensify the "little injustices" that seem to increasingly characterize our lives.[252]

ENFORCEMENT'S IMPACT ON VICTIMS

Victim Problems

In the last chapter, we examined victimization's impact on victims, including its economic, physical, and psychological costs. Unfortunately, participating in the criminal process can often increase those costs, although they will vary depending on the case's progress and the victim's status.[253] As if victimization does not create enough problems, getting involved in law enforcement causes many more.

ECONOMIC FACTORS.   To begin with, court involvement produces many economic costs.[254] Repeated appearances will often cause victims to lose income and sometimes their job. They may have to pay for child or elderly care for the day. They will have to pay transportation costs and expenses for their court dates. They will incur other intangible expenses of having their life disrupted as well.[255]

Many also complain about being unable to get their stolen, but retrieved, property returned.[256] While officials may exaggerate its effects, they often retain property because they fear that victims will drop charges if they receive it back.[257] Thus, some victims suffer problems not merely because law enforcement cannot or will not accommodate them, but because some officials believe that depriving victims may, in some ways, be functional for the criminal process.

INCONVENIENCES.   Victims often suffer many inconveniences in the criminal process. To appear in court, they will have to change their schedules, negotiate various transportation systems, and locate the building and appropriate room. Repeated appearances may restrict their plans for many months. In court, they will face delays, unnecessary trips, hostile personnel, uncomfortable accommodations, inadequate or misinformation, and repeated recountings of their story. In particular, they will seldom know what has happened or what to expect, and seldom get information about available services or about outcomes at various stages in the process.[258]

PSYCHOLOGICAL FACTORS.   Psychological problems might plague participating victims as well. They suffer from workplace and family disruptions. They must bear the frequent stigma of court involvement among their family, friends, and coworkers, even when they have done nothing wrong.[259] Sometimes they receive even broader publicity throughout their community.[260] And, quite likely, their maltreatment in court and their inability to substantively participate in their cases will further damage their already bruised sense of self-worth.

Finally, victims may be intimidated by their attackers at the courthouse. Although many overzealous victim defenders exaggerate the problem, some victims may, nevertheless, have to wait in the same room with offenders or their families and friends, withstanding their taunts or threats and occasionally having to fight off their physical attacks.[261]

RECOMPENSE.   Victims might find some consolation for these problems if they could gain some satisfaction from either participating in their case or from its outcome, or from receiving some compensation for their troubles, but these rarely occur. As we will see, victims usually seem less than pleased by their court involvement, and they rarely receive any financial consolation for their participation. Although other, external compensation sources for victims exist, only a limited few come from the criminal process, and most victims rarely receive their benefits. First, many victims look to law enforcement officials for advice about various external services that might help them cope with their victimization, yet officials usually have no information or offer fragmentary leads that provide victims with little help. And some of the help they do receive, such as emergency hospital treatment, tends to be woefully inadequate and insensitive.[262] Second, victims might receive the witness fees most jurisdictions have been authorized to pay. Yet most victims get no witness fees at all, and those who do receive amounts totally inadequate to cover their costs,[263] especially for certain groups such as women, children, the elderly, minorities, and the poor.

Victims might also help offset their costs for appearing in court and for their victimization generally through offender restitution or state compensation. Yet neither source awards payments for court expenses[264] and most victims will find neither alternative available to them. For reasons we will soon examine, courts rarely order offender restitution and even in those states where compensation programs exist, only very few victims ever receive awards.[265]

Case Outcomes

Although we have emphasized the importance of less tangible aspects of victim participation in the criminal process, such as information and recognition, some victims no doubt seek particular ends as well. For a few, these may be their only goals. Several possible objectives may interest victims, depending on their circumstances, their reasons for pursuing their case, their needs, and, of course, their personal preferences.

Victims who purposely pursue their cases only to a certain point, perhaps merely to threaten their abusers, may be very satisfied merely to see offenders arrested and charged. Other victims may demand at least a conviction, perhaps settling for a plea bargain. Some victims want their offenders convicted and punished in some way. Others may want specific punishments or sufficiently severe penalties. Many victims seek some economic objectives, such as having their property returned or receiving compensation or services.

As we have known for some time, law enforcement provides a "funnelling process' whereby among the vast multitude of crimes and criminals only a portion actually enter the system. Those cases also significantly decline as we move through each stage in the criminal process, from arrest to sentencing,[266] although much less than has been recently portrayed.[267] Consequently, those victims who demand particular punishments will often be disappointed. A few convictions may also be overturned on appeal. We have already seen that victims will rarely satisfy their economic needs through their court involvement, since they will rarely receive either restitution, compensation, witness fees, or their stolen property. As for other objectives, most offenders, particularly in property crimes, never get caught, much less arrested, charged, prosecuted, convicted, sentenced, and imprisoned. We have a somewhat better record for violent crimes (particularly for homicides), yet overall can offer victims few tangible outcomes to justify their involvement.

Victim Attitudes

OFFENDER. Few studies have examined victim attitudes toward their offenders. Some evidence, however, shows that although other concerns, besides punishing offenders, emerge during their case, many victims still remain very angry with their assailants throughout.[268] Most victims feel no guilt about having pursued their case, although a significant minority do.[269] We do not know whether their regret comes from having forgiven their attacker or from the case's frustrations. Some other evidence suggests that victim anger toward offenders declines over time.[270]

CRIME AND PUNISHMENT. Victims have strong feelings about crime and punishment, particularly for their own cases. Many believe that we should promote much tougher law enforcement to curb crime, although not significantly more so than nonvictims.[271] A surprising number believe that poverty and racism cause the most crime and must be eradicated.[272] Victims also often feel that they will be revictimized.[273]

As for their case, many victims show dissatisfaction when their offender has been acquitted or when they find the punishment too lenient, while satisfaction increases with convictions and "proper" punishments.[274] Another study shows 68% finding the punishment too lenient, 29% about right, and 3% too severe.[275] Other research indicates that over one-half the victims were dissatisfied with their case's outcome, with about one-quarter somewhat satisfied, and only 14% very satisfied. Almost one in ten did not care.[276] Those at least somewhat satisfied were mostly pleased that something had been done, or because they felt more protected now. One in five people were satisfied because of the punishment and one in ten felt some justice had been done.[277] Almost one-half of those dissatisfied protested the lenient punishment, 15% had wanted restitution, 11% felt they had wasted their time, 9% thought they had not received protection, 7% were not kept abreast of their case, 5% felt the dispute had not been resolved, and 4% were actually unhappy because the punishment was too severe.[278]

LAW ENFORCEMENT. Much research has examined victim attitudes toward law enforcement personnel, particularly for their treatment of offenders or victims or their work generally. Victims sometimes find judges too lenient compared to prosecutors and the police, although they accuse the latter of ignoring many crimes as well.[279] Other victims show a similar pattern, although many accuse all officials of being too lenient.[280]

POLICE. Overall, most studies show the police receiving the greatest support from victims for their work, with less approval for prosecutors and even less for judges.[281] This corresponds to general public attitudes about these officials as well,[282] although satisfaction seems somewhat lower for each official among actual victims.[283] Although police officers receive the greatest support comparatively, most victims still question their work to varying degrees.[284]

Feelings toward the police improve mainly when they treat victims well, have a good attitude, and respond promptly to calls.[285] The elderly seem favorably disposed toward the police,[286] but women and particularly blacks and lower classes strongly disapprove police behavior.[287] Female victims seem more pleased when dealing with female police officers in family disputes.[288] Many believe the police are corrupt but a strong majority still support them.[289] Victims seem to become increasingly dissatisfied with the police as their case progresses.[290]

PROSECUTORS AND JUDGES. Victims have mixed views of prosecutors and judges as well. Some believe that prosecutors do the best they can, but act ruthlessly, and feel that judges show considerable intelligence, and some concern for victims but behave too leniently and probably take bribes.[291] Some support officials even when they experience inadequate participation and unsatisfactory outcomes.[292]

Most others show considerable disenchantment.[293] While some victims seem more favorably disposed toward judges and prosecutors as their case progresses,[294] most feel just the opposite.[295] Attitudes seem to improve when victims develop a more personal relationship with officials, but this rarely happens.[296] Many hold the judge most responsible for their dissatisfaction.[297] As with the police, women and blacks seem most dissatisfied with these officials.[298] Those among the most dissatisfied seem to be victims who do not report their victimization, perhaps due to an earlier experience or a negative preconception.[299]

INVOLVEMENT. Victim attitudes toward law enforcement depend not only on officials, their offenders, and their case outcomes but also on their court involvement. Most victims complain about not participating enough in the criminal process, but we must clarify what that means. One study, for example, shows most victims feeling overinvolved,[300] yet they were also very dissatisfied with their role in court. Less than half claimed it was worth coming to court. Thus, it appears that victims rebel against meaningless involvement in the criminal process, which they regard as a waste of time, but would most likely welcome some more substantive participation.

FUTURE PARTICIPATION. Despite their frequent dissatisfaction with the criminal process, many victims still claim they will get involved again.[301] These attitudes do not necessarily predict future participation since supporters may not act after all, particularly given the costs of cooperating.[302] The disgruntled may still participate in a new situation, perhaps from a sense of public duty. Nevertheless, these attitudes do provide some guide to how victims evaluate law enforcement. In fact, the process has not been building victim support. Victims express less willingness to participate than the general public, and recidivist victims show a steadily declining interest in cooperating.[303]

Summary

By participating in the criminal process, victims regularly suffer new problems beyond those their victimization already provides. Those new burdens include economic costs, psychological problems, physical inconveniences, and offender intimidation. Victims might willingly bear those burdens if they found their participation worthwhile and their case outcomes satisfactory, yet this rarely happens. They seldom get the treatment they think they and their offenders deserve, their involvement lacks substance and purpose, and the economic needs they hope to satisfy usually go unattended.

Not surprisingly, victim attitudes toward their offenders, their case outcomes, their involvement, criminal justice officials, and law enforcement generally, tend to be rather negative. Police officers fare better than prosecutors and judges, and victims seem somewhat willing to participate again despite their dissatisfaction, but much more grudgingly than they would had they not actually experienced the criminal process. Law enforcement affects victims significantly, but also mostly negatively.

FEMALE VICTIMS AND LAW ENFORCEMENT

It's the same
The whole world over
Happens all the time
The woman who's the victim
Gets convicted of the crime.

SI KAHN

A victim's experience in the criminal process depends on many factors, but certain traits may portend more difficulties than usual. We have already suggested that some kinds of victims, such as women, the elderly, children, minorities and lower classes, have greater problems than others.[304] While we cannot dwell on each of their experiences, we should examine the special plight of at least one of those groups: women.

Sexist Laws

Many argue that we not only have a sexist society, but that our laws have institutionalized sexism.[305] Our rape laws provide a good example.[306] Women suffer the typical array of property and violent crimes, but also bear the special burden of battering and sexual assault.[307] These offenses can produce harm enough simply from the social, physical and psychological injuries they provide. Exposing their attack and pursuing their attackers impose a hardship on almost all victims, but even more dramatically affect female victims of battering and sexual assault. To emphasize their special problems, we will examine the role in law enforcement of women who have been sexually assaulted.[308]

To begin with, we have a startlingly ambivalent attitude toward sexual assault and toward women as victims.[309] The way we address the problem suggests that women have been designated as "culturally legitimate" victims.[310] Examining how we respond to sexual assault victims, the laws we pass, and our approach to enforcement and prevention will show why.

Traditionally, we have viewed women as men's property. Many argue that rape laws have served much more to protect (or require retaliation for) men's property (females) than to protect women from sexual assaults.[311] Our laws seem to routinely define rape very narrowly, and require standards of proof that far transcend our usual norms. We have long considered rape to be a sexual, and not a violent, offense, which has left false doubts about whether victimization has really occurred. We scrutinize women's past sexual history and their past sexual relations with their offenders. Showing that a woman has been willing to have sex, and may act or dress enticingly, loses many rape cases. To prove their case, women have had to corroborate the assault with at least one other witness and show they resisted the offense.[312] All of these requirements emerged from our traditional rape laws.[313]

Rape Reform Legislation

Recently, thanks primarily to the women's movement, some significant legal changes have occurred. New legislation has removed many of the old restrictions, sometimes holding husbands responsible for raping their wives.[314] And rape shield laws have prevented a woman's prior sexual conduct from being used at trial.[315] But, while some changes have occurred, dramatic shifts have not. Although the corroboration requirement has sometimes been deleted, most cases without corroboration will be discouraged or, if pursued, lost.[316] Even significant legislative changes have only minimally affected women's role in criminal justice. Gains made thus far may have been severely (but unjustifiably) compromised by the recent, nationally publicized, case of Gary Dotson, a convicted rapist imprisoned in Illinois for six years, whose victim, Cathleen Webb, dramatically reversed her story, claiming she lied about having been raped.[317]

Response

Sexual assault will often shatter a woman's life. Aside from whatever physical and financial losses she might incur, she will also be very personally and intimately violated. Deciding how to respond often becomes a very difficult decision. Even inexperienced victims can well imagine the additional trauma, pain, and stigma they will likely bear by pressing their case. Some refrain from fear, or because they want to forget, and sometimes even because they feel sorry for their attacker.[318] These and other reasons have made rape one of the least reported victimizations,[319] with no more than one in ten reported and perhaps as little as one in one hundred. When rape victims do report their case, they usually feel either strongly committed to protecting their community against other rapes or a strong sense of revenge against the offender.

When a woman has been sexually assaulted, she will usually be taken directly to a hospital if she calls the authorities, although sometimes police will insist on pretreatment interrogations that may be quite lengthy.[320] Some women will not report the victimization, or will delay their report until they become sure what to do, in which case they may find their way to a hospital on their own. In any case, women typically encounter their first round of insensitivity, difficulties, and degradation when seeking medical assistance from personnel who frequently embarrass them, second-guess their actions, and callously disregard their needs.[321]

Women may receive similar treatment from police officers who, besides their frequent insensitivity, will often criticize and blame victims, or discredit their stories through sharp and brusque interrogations.[322] The police expect immediate reports of victimization while most victims will need time to decide what to do. Many women will be discouraged in pursuing their case either because police officers doubt their story or inform them that even their true story will fail in court. Cases might also be impeded by how police officers record offenses, the first of several opportunities for court personnel to downgrade if not dismiss cases that victims would otherwise like to pursue.

Screening

The screening process begins with police decisions and continues until trial.[323] Officials will more likely discontinue cases or reduce charges if the victim and offender have a past or present relationship, if no force or weapon or roughness was used, if the assault lasted less than fifteen minutes, and if the victim has a low income, no job, a weight problem, a psychiatric history, or receives welfare, uses alcohol, has been a runaway or in trouble with the police. Cases of anal intercourse and multiple offenders will also less likely be pursued.[324] Police officers will typically devote very little enforcement effort to rape cases, especially for black victims.[325] When they do apprehend offenders, they are usually either black or gang rape offenders. Police officers have organizational incentives to clear rape cases, but not necessarily to complete good investigations that ensure the rapist's successful prosecution.[326] Although many recent, innovative programs have attempted to improve police and medical responsiveness to sexual assault victims, most of the traditional problems still linger.[327]

Screening continues with prosecutors, who will often either eliminate cases or strongly urge victims to spare themselves the ordeal of trial.[328] They will encourage a plea bargain by reducing charges and try to convince victims to play along. Prosecutors often seem barely less abrasive and insensitive than police and hospital personnel. Before the victim even enters the trial, if it occurs at all, she will usually feel victimized merely by the degrading treatment she has already received.

Some women drop their case by failing to appear at one of several pre-trial hearings. Cases evaporate particularly at the preliminary hearing where about 15% of all victims fail to appear. Others end because of repeated delays.[329] Besides the informal attacks on their credibility and sex life, victims will also often suffer through repeated examinations, lie detector tests, interrogations, and countless recapitulations of their story.[330]

Trial

The bravest and most steadfast victims may survive this treatment and insist on pursuing their cases to a full trial, before either a judge or jury.[331] Ironically, their greatest pain may be yet to come. The defense will use various arguments that focus less on proving the defendant's innocence and more on discrediting and defaming the victim.[332]

These arguments exploit various myths about female behavior. Defense attorneys may claim the victim has identified the wrong assailant and try to show that she was too distraught to make a proper identification. Exhibiting too much emotion will therefore call into question the victim's credibility, yet showing too little will produce suspicions about whether the rape ever occurred.[333] Alternatively, the defense may argue that the victim gave specific or implied consent to intercourse (by showing the victim's sexual history), or provided enticements. Finally, the defense may argue that a rape never occurred by disparaging the victim's attractiveness or suggesting her spitefulness.[334] At trial, most victims will be dragged through a very degrading process, to the point where victims often end up on trial much more than defendants. Except for the strongest of witnesses, the experience will likely intensify whatever psychological trauma they may have suffered from the victimization itself, and will enhance, in particular, their feelings of worthlessness and self-blame.

Judges, and especially juries, seem reluctant to find defendants guilty.[335] Among those convicted, only a little more than one-half go to prison. Juries, in particular, seem uninfluenced even by beatings that accompany many rapes or routinely discover some kind of victim precipitation; they seem to apply a standard much stricter than merely "beyond reasonable doubt."[336]

Impact

Frequently lacking a conviction or punishment and having played a traumatic role in pursuing the case, those victims who survive through the trial rarely view the process with any satisfaction.[337] Although sometimes even a grueling trial may help a few victims achieve some psychological release,[338] most victims gain little from being involved and routinely suffer further harms, usually from official maltreatment. The sexual assault victim must bear the usual costs and problems that face all victims in the criminal process, plus an extra dose of publicity, insensitivity, and degradation, not to mention having to relive the victimization. It should not surprise us, therefore, that rape victims show some of the greatest dissatisfaction with criminal justice and its personnel and the greatest reluctance to participate in law enforcement again.[339] The trial's impact may be so severe, particularly from its notoriety and publicity, that victims often feel they must leave their jobs and even their communities, such as in the infamous "Big Dan's" case in Massachusetts where the case was won, yet the rape victim was virtually driven out of town.

While we could never fully describe law enforcement's impact on female victims of sexual assault, we have at least begun to suggest some of their special problems and some of the great degradation they often must bear. As with other kinds of victims and victimizations, rape victims must withstand a process that provides them with no formal role except for possibly being put on trial themselves. Not only will the process bypass or contradict their interests, but officials will often have incentives that either ignore victim needs or further intensify them. Female victims bear special burdens because they typically wield little political clout and often lack legitimacy for even being labelled as a victim in the first place.

Conclusion

We can now see why participating in law enforcement further victimizes most victims. Although the likely costs of participation may not be the primary reason why most people do not get involved, nonparticipation, for this reason alone, may be rational. Most victims who do get involved seek more than merely doing their civic duty. They often seek specific outcomes for themselves, their property, and their assailants, and a specific role in the process.

Victims do have some impact on law enforcement, but rarely what they would like. Since they have no formal, institutionalized role in the criminal process, they seldom participate substantively and actively in their case. They affect law enforcement not primarily by their participation, but by the influence their behavior and characteristics have on official decisions. Victims are not burdened by competing with offenders (who usually share most of the same circumstances and characteristics) for rights and attention,[340] but rather by the personal, professional, organizational, and political needs, motives, and preferences of officials. Women, blacks, lower classes and others with low status bear the effects the most, yet almost all suffer as essentially the "victims of enforcement."

Although victims exert relatively little influence on law enforcement, the process often profoundly affects them, usually intensifying their victimization. The criminal process not only largely fails to deliver victims the outcomes and participation they desire, it also generates many new problems and costs, which in turn produce negative victim attitudes toward law enforcement and a reluctance to participate again.

Examining the victim's treatment in law enforcement only begins to reveal its apparent inefficiencies, ineffectiveness, and oppressiveness. The process excludes, through selective criminal definitions or enforcement, many of the most serious crimes and criminals, and thus provides no effective mechanism to check that victimization. It seems also to pursue counterproductive policies for reducing crime, thereby failing to prevent victimization, if not needlessly generating new victims. It provides a process where no more than one-half of all victims feel confident or willing to take their cases, thus leaving them with no recourse. For those victims who do use the process, it often maltreats and degrades them, prevents their effective participation, blocks their objectives, and ultimately uses them for official purposes.

It regularly brings maltreatment and injustice for offenders as well, the fervent cries of some victim defenders notwithstanding. Defendants routinely find themselves pressured into waiving rights, or otherwise denied protections, while having little or no effect on victims' treatment. And, although the process often provides officials with significant personal and professional gains, some believe that it often victimizes them as well by encouraging them to pursue illicit, insensitive, and even illegal and repressive behavior to satisfy internal organizational goals and external political objectives.

We might well explore alternatives to conventional law enforcement or at least question whether victims should really participate more in the existing criminal process. Pursuing these alternatives could begin by placing criminal law enforcement within the broader context of promoting human rights. This would suggest mechanisms for preventing victimization that do not simultaneously cause further, or their own separate, victimization. Such a system would promote and protect victims' rights as well as defendants' rights, not merely against official maltreatment in the criminal process, but against a criminal process that may, by definition, victimize politically and organizationally.

Having examined the characteristics of criminal victimization, its possible sources, its likely effects, and the impact of the process we have ostensibly designed to prevent victimization and provide redress, we can now consider the various victim services that have been proposed, and in some cases already implemented, to help victims through their ordeal of victimization, but also, ironically, through the trauma of participating in law enforcement.

7

Victim Advocacy: The Functions of Doing Good

Hopefully, we are at the threshold of an era when . . . pressures will result in progressive programmes rather than political placebos to provide for the victim of crime.
                                        DUNCAN CHAPPELL

As we have seen, crime victims typically suffer many pains from their victimization and its aftermath. The damage comes not only from the crime, but also from their treatment thereafter, especially in the criminal process. For about twenty years now, victim advocates have been proposing, if not implementing, various programs designed both to recognize victim interests and to satisfy their needs. Beyond their ostensible goals, however, these programs may fulfill other, often unrecognized and political functions, quite apart from victims themselves.

We must examine victim advocacy, and evaluate its effectiveness. To do so, we will summarize the various problems victimization and the criminal process generate for victims. Then we will examine the various programs, the needs they address, and their impact.[1] Finally, we will consider the broader functions of victim programs and who besides victims they may serve.

VICTIM PROBLEMS

Victimization and the victim's involvement in the criminal process usually create many problems for which victims traditionally have no recourse. The crime itself may produce psychological, financial, practical, and medical problems such as fear, trauma, lost wages, medical expenses, family and work disruptions, and injuries, to mention only few. In the criminal process, victims develop further problems and some understandable expectations. They often find themselves inconvenienced, poorly treated, threatened, exploited, or ignored. They may incur significant expenses for transportation, lost wages, repeated appearances, or child care. They often expect information about their case and their role, some meaningful participation, and a satisfactory case outcome, all within a reasonable time period. Perhaps above all, victims seek protection from further victimization in the future.

What kind of programs and approaches have we created to address these problems? How well have they worked? What other functions do they perform?

APPROACHES TO VICTIM ASSISTANCE

We can best understand the various kinds of victim assistance by examining the help each seeks to provide and by analyzing each program's origins, form, and sustenance. By knowing whether the assistance has been created and funded by private or government sources, whether it exists within or outside government and the criminal process, and whether it helps many constituencies or only crime victims, we may better evaluate the programs and their future. As we shall see, these programs differ widely in their form, strategies, and ideologies. We have no united victim movement, but instead a series of victim movements, often pulling in different directions.

Victim Services

Victim services attempt to assist victims with inconvenices and with psychological and medical problems that result from their victimization. They may serve victims generally, but many emphasize special victims, such as women, children, and the elderly.

Crisis Intervention programs provide emergency victim services, particularly for victims of violence. They specialize in satisfying immediate physical and psychological needs. Programs such as Transition House for Battered Women in Cambridge, Massachusetts, the Safespace Shelter in Dade County, Florida, and the Sexual Assault Program in Washington, D.C., may provide volunteer assistants, shelters, and drop-in or call-in programs. They may have public or private origins and funding (often from special interests such as women's groups), work closely with medical facilities but outside criminal justice, and serve specialized victim interests.[2]

Medical Facilities such as the Women's Medical Center in Washington, D.C., provide victims with medical assistance after their victimization. Most medical facilities, such as hospitals and out-patient clinics, serve multiple populations, yet some health services have been provided for victims in particular.[3] Some hospitals, for example, offer special services (such as the Victim Counseling Program of the Boston City Hospital), usually in emergency rooms, to crime victims as well as to accident and health victims. Others have specific rape treatment units or procedures.

Besides hospitals, some clinics give special treatment to certain kinds of victims, and a few handle special cases, such as sexual assault victims, exclusively. The larger institutions get funding either through government revenues or private fees, and either their staffs or outside interests initiate whatever special programs they offer victims. The smaller clinics may accept private fees, but also depend on private donations, government funding, or donated labor, and their specialized efforts for victims usually result from interest groups, most typically women's organizations. Obviously, medical facilities operate independently from criminal justice.[4]

Mental Health Facilities, such as the numerous community mental health clinics, closely resemble medical facilities, except that they emphasize the short-term and long-term psychological problems that may afflict victims. They also range from large to small, with comparable structural and financial characteristics. The psychological help victims need, however, may last much longer than their medical problems and require much more particularized attention. Consequently, more psychiatrists and psychologists specialize in victim problems such as the mental effects of sexual assault, battering, incest, and other violence. Aside from the informal counseling that may occur in courthouse victim/witness programs, mental health facilities operate independently from criminal justice.[5]

IMPACT.   Although victim services reach many more people now than a few years ago, they have numerous difficulties.[6] Many victims never get help because they have not been referred to any, or appropriate, programs. Many others seek assistance but find that either they have no access or that their needs surpass program capacities.[7] Some victims discover appropriate programs, which could provide some valuable help, but their welfare stigma or their likely bureaucratic frustrations keep many victims away.[8] Assistance such as mental health programs may need greater outreach, advocacy, and financial support.[9] Crisis and emergency intervention programs seem relatively successful, but only in serving a rather narrow range of victims. And, even then, they might suffer from ideological divisions such as in women's centers, where members have often split between pursuing social change and merely providing services.[10] These services, designed to reduce inconveniences and fill medical and psychological needs, provide a good beginning, but usually fall far short of satisfying most victims' needs.[11] Finally, interagency competition sometimes arises between the mental health and criminal justice systems, as they battle to determine the proper disposition of victims.

Victim Reimbursement

Victim reimbursement programs attempt to repay victims for their losses from their victimization and its aftermath. The resources come from several places.

Compensation programs provide victims with government payments to restore their losses. They also try to improve victim attitudes toward criminal justice and government and increase their willingness to cooperate. These programs, which exist in most American states and also abroad, have emerged through official initiatives and from external public and special pressures. As with the leading American plan, in New York, for example, they almost invariably serve victims exclusively. Except for a few plans (such as the Massachusetts program, which dispenses compensation through the courts), most schemes exist separately from criminal justice but seek a very close relationship. Their funding comes from government revenues and criminal fines.[12]

Restitution programs require offenders to use their resources to repay victims for their losses. Existing in states such as Minnesota, Iowa, Georgia, California, and Maryland, the payments may come as money or labor given directly to victims, or given indirectly, or even given to the community. Theoretically, restitution can be ordered from courts in virtually any jurisdiction. Some more specialized programs exist that help arrange jobs for offenders to either pay or work off their obligation. Restitution arose as a correctional alternative advocated by those concerned about victims, prison reform, and correctional efficiency. It provides a service to victims (and sometimes the community), operates (when used) within the criminal process, and receives funding from individual offenders, except for the administrative costs of special programs, which come from government revenues.[13]

Civil Actions allow crime victims to bring lawsuits against their offenders, apart from and usually after any criminal case, to gain financial damages. Crime victims may also sue third parties, holding them liable in the victimization for failing to take proper precautions. The civil courts, of course, serve many other purposes and many other kinds of "victims." Aside from administrative costs, which government largely pays, civil courts get resources partially from those who file suit (as filing fees), but mostly from litigants who lose their case. The United States and many other nations take pains to separate their civil and criminal processes, although other nations allow some interaction and even a joint procedure.[14]

Insurance comes in several forms, including private insurance, government crime insurance such as the Fair Access to Insurance plans, and government welfare programs such as medicaid and unemployment compensation. Many nations provide very broad social insurance (sometimes coordinated with victim compensation plans, as in New Zealand) or tightly regulated private insurance, but the United States emphasizes independent private insurance. With the latter, potential victims must secure individual policies, while government insurance relies on individual applications, based on need or right, depending on the nation. Insurance arose to indemnify many kinds of potential losses or needs, and only sometimes targets crime victims for particular attention. It can emerge from either government or private sources and will be financed either by government revenues or private premiums. Insurance plans have no direct relationship with criminal justice.[15]

IMPACT.   All the various forms of repayment have difficulties. Although perhaps more people have crime insurance today than ever before, it imposes a considerable cost and, in fact, most people still have no coverage.[16] Many people cannot afford a policy or find insurance companies withholding coverage because of their location. Although a U.S. federal government program ostensibly guarantees some crime insurance,[17] few have received its benefits. Even those who can afford insurance often find themselves underinsured. Thus, with few exceptions, insurance will reimburse few victims after victimization.

Civil actions also have problems. Rarely can victims afford the time and cost of civil suits. Criminal convictions can rarely be used as proof in criminal trials.[18] These and other factors make it very difficult to win against offenders. When victims do win, their offenders rarely have funds to reimburse them and, even if they do, victims often have difficulties collecting.[19] While third-party suits aim at people who will more likely be able to pay (such as Connie Francis' successful rape suit against Howard Johnson's), victims still rarely recover,[20] and the trend may breed unnecessary paranoia.

We know even more about the impact of restitution and compensation. Some restitution plans have worked quite successfully, within their natural limitations. The Minnesota program, for example, helped less serious offenders integrate into the community, partly by earning wages on work release to restitute their victims.[21] Studies show many victims seem satisfied when repaid.[22] Yet restitution has some considerable philosophical and practical problems.[23] Briefly, courts have been very unwilling to use the restitution option, although victims seem very supportive. When judges try restitution sentences, offenders rarely have resources or jobs and thus victims cannot recover. The programs would be boosted significantly by government subsidies.[24]

Finally, compensation programs have provided valuable aid to some victims,[25] yet they have helped very few victims overall, thanks to their inaccessibility and restrictive requirements. While excluding property crime victims entirely, less than one percent of all violent crime victims apply and no more than a third of them recover—and then insufficiently to cover their losses.[26] Besides reimbursement, these programs try to lower crime rates and improve victim attitudes and cooperation in criminal justice, yet have largely failed.[27] They have not reduced the crime rate or improved clearance and conviction rates.[28] They have also not increased crime reporting or willingness to prosecute or favorable attitudes.[29] In fact, one study shows that applicants to compensation programs have significantly worse attitudes than nonapplicants.[30] In sum, while these various reimbursement methods have provided valuable assistance for some victims, they have been inaccessible to most.[31] Efforts to improve coverage through federal funding have been consistently blocked by fears of escalating costs.

Criminal Justice Reform

Criminal justice reform, pursued by various victim advocacy programs, seeks various changes in the criminal process that would help promote victim interests, such as rights, information, better treatment, just outcomes, and greater involvement.

Special Training programs, such as those pioneered by the Dallas Police Department, help criminal justice and other personnel (especially police officers) interact better with victims. Since police officers traditionally receive no special training to help and interact with victims, these programs sensitize them to victim needs and problems. Aside from this general training, special projects—such as the New York City Police Department's Sex Crimes Analysis Unit—may be available, which specialize in sexual assaults, family violence, or elderly victimization. These programs result either from outside pressures or from internal policies designed to promote better police-community relations. They cater specifically to victims, often to particular victims, and receive regular department expenditures. Obviously, they work integrally within criminal justice.[32]

Victim/Witness Assistance Programs provide varied services to victims and witnesses, mostly to help them participate in the criminal process. Programs such as the National Victim/Witness Resource Center in Alexandria, Virginia, the Victim Service Agency (of the Vera Institute of Justice) in New York City, the Victim Service Council of St. Louis, the Victim Witness Advocate Program of Pima County, Arizona, and the Victims Assistance Project of Multnomah County, Oregon, supply victims with information about their role, their case, and the process; with help in getting to court and finding the correct rooms; with an alert system to remind them of court appearances and to prevent unnecessary trips; and with conveniences such as refreshments and a place to wait. They help victims through their cases and promote their continued participation. Some groups, like Senior Victim Services, the Center for Creative Living, Parents United and Child, Inc., provide services to specific populations, such as the elderly and children.

A few jurisdictions operate more sophisticated witness-management schemes that may use computer technology to help program victim involvement in criminal cases and avoid victim attrition. Other jurisdictions have victim advocates who much more aggressively pursue victim interests in court by developing a closer personal relationship with victims, by pursuing greater victim control and input, and by promoting victim rights at each stage of the process.[33] Most victim/witness programs develop at police headquarters or prosecutor's offices, and get funding primarily from the federal government. They work closely with criminal justice agencies.[34]

Victim Rights initiatives try to assist victims and to provide them specific rights in the criminal process. These protections include the right to dignity and compassion, safeguards against intimidation, information (about procedures, assistance, their case, and their offender), legal counsel, reliable police response, access to the prosecutor, reparations, job and property protection, due process (including speed, input, and impact statements), and conveniences. These rights have been pushed by organizations such as the National District Attorneys Association, the National Organization of Victim Assistance, and the President's Task Force on Victims of Crime, and have been enacted into federal and state legislation domestically and into laws abroad as well. These rights may come at the expense of defendant's rights or official powers. Victim rights obviously affect criminal-justice processes, and many of them require some expenditures that must be borne considerably, if not completely, by the government.[35]

Adversarial Reform proposals have many variations, but they all try to alter the criminal process to eliminate obstacles to victim interests. One reform brings back the private prosecutor, who formally pursues cases when the public prosecutor refuses to act. A second reform promotes an expedited process that reduces procedural complications and the adversarial contest.[36] A third reform makes the process more accessible to victims by shifting cases systematically to night or weekend court, such as the Night Prosecutor of Columbus, Ohio, and of the Southeast Chicago Commission. A fourth reform reduces defendant's rights, such as by eliminating or weakening the exclusionary rule, to try to increase convictions. A fifth reform adopts an "adhesion" or "parte civil" procedure that unites the civil and criminal process into one procedure, and allows victims to sue simultaneously for civil damages. These reforms come from various victim advocates, they alter the criminal process, and they often incur additional government costs.[37]

IMPACT. Some special law enforcement projects for victims, such as sexual assault units, have produced significant improvements,[38] yet officials still have few incentives to consider victim needs. Evaluations of victim/witness programs have shown some positive results (less inconveniences and court appearances) but officials may have gained much more than victims from programs that help manage witness involvement and reduce institutional costs.[39] In other words, they may be cost effective, but for whom?[40] Also, although victim/witness programs had grown to 410 by 1980, federal funding cutbacks reduced them to 200 by 1982.[41] Piecemeal rights have been protected in some jurisdictions, but few have created a formal role for victims.[42] In the value conflict between participation and management, the latter continues to dominate.[43]

If anything, services have overshadowed any increase in victim participation.[44] Few adversarial reforms to promote victim interests have been implemented or evaluated either. While we cannot negate their potential, they have provided victims with little assistance so far. We cannot expect that victim advocates, as outsiders, have achieved very much.[45] Even providing better information, which many victims find so important, still seems relatively scarce.[46] In sum, while some important changes in criminal justice have been initiated, particularly with victim/witness programs, reforms have not institutionalized victims into the criminal process, have helped protect few rights, only sporadically generate better official treatment, do not reduce crime, and rarely produce for victims any more satisfactory outcomes. The greatest gains so far have been to reduce victim inconveniences in the criminal process.

Legislative Reform

Legislative reform tries to establish victim programs (such as victim compensation) and to change the criminal law to promote victim rights and interests and reduce victimization.

Decriminalization would eliminate some categories of the criminal law and also reduce those offenses punishable by prison. Decriminalization, such as promoted by the National Organization for the Reform of Marijuana Laws (NORML), responds to evidence that overlegislating produces unnecessary victims by stimulating crimes that would otherwise not occur. Decriminalizing drug use, for example, would eliminate those crimes committed to support one's drug consumption, thus reducing the number of crime victims. Decriminalization and decarceration have also been proposed, entirely apart from victim interests, for other (largely offender-oriented) purposes. Together they reduce the criminal justice role and expenses, but sometimes require alternative treatment programs.[47]

Criminalization initiatives, such as those from the President's Task Force on Victims of Crime and from Mothers Against Drunk Drivers, would impose stricter penalties to deter criminal behavior. Traditionally, we have criminalized common criminal behavior, but this has also been recommended recently for white-collar and corporate "crimes" which have largely escaped criminal penalties. Criminalization has been long advocated by multiple interests, including some victim advocates. It enhances the law enforcement role, and requires more personnel, prisons, and government resources.[48]

Special Legislation proposals target the problems of general and specific victim populations, particularly their role in criminal law and the criminal process. Legislation has been passed, for example, to protect children in court, and for missing children, such as the Federal Missing Children's Act of 1982. The most significant new laws promote the interests of female victims. Rape legislation has helped redefine women in the law and changed the rules for proving sexual assault, eliminating corroboration requirements, "shielding" past sexual histories, and "staircasing" penalties. The 1982 Federal Victim and Witness Protection Act helped develop the U.S. Attorney General's Guidelines for Victim and Witness Assistance. And the Victim Assistance Act of 1984 allows the U.S. Treasury to "collect" up to $100 million for victims, mostly from federal criminal defendants. Special legislation emerges from pressure exerted by special interest groups (such as parent's or women's organizations), it may impose additional government expense, and it changes the criminal law or process to promote special victim interests.[49]

Procedural Rights initiatives would alter the allocation of rights and powers in the criminal process. They might promote victim rights alone, or do so together with eliminating defendant's rights. An increase in victim rights might come at the defendant's expense or may reduce official powers, or both. Increased victim powers might also increase official powers, ostensibly on victims' behalf. Altering procedural rights presumes that the balance of procedural protections will determine victim interests. Procedural reform has been promoted by law enforcement officials, law and order supporters, and many victim advocates, such as the National Organization of Victim Assistance. It usually strengthens the criminal process and the formal victim role within traditional criminal justice.[50]

Victim Lobbying builds organizations that advocate victim interests in government agencies to produce desirable public policy. These groups have included both specialized organizations concentrating solely on victims or broader organizations that have taken a partial interest in victims. Such groups include the National Organization of Victim Assistance, the National Victims Organization, Victims for Victims, Mothers Against Drunk Drivers, the American Bar Association, the National District Attorneys Association, and the National Organization of Women. These organizations solicit lobbying funds from their members and outside sources and work for victim interests within traditional legislative and criminal-justice process.[51]

IMPACT. Little decriminalization has occurred in the United States, except for a somewhat more lenient attitude toward marijuana use. Abroad, however, "hard" drug use has been decriminalized (in Britain, for example), producing decreasing drug use and decreasing crime.[52] Americans have been more inclined to criminalize or to increase current penalties, primarily for common offenses, and rarely for white-collar crime. Periodic toughening of the criminal law has occurred routinely in this century, yet has never reduced victimization; in fact, the evidence suggests the opposite. Moreover, psychologists warn that punitiveness will be counterproductive for victims.[53]

Legislation for particular victims—and for victim rights generally—has emerged increasingly in the last few years, particularly in Wisconsin, Nebraska, Washington, Oklahoma, Massachusetts, and California, with victim bills of rights pending in several other states as well. Yet a large gap remains between the law and its implementation.[54] Even some revolutionary changes in sexual assault law have shown few results, according to some evaluations, except perhaps to help inform public opinion.[54] On the other hand, recent laws and judicial decisions have largely eroded defendant's rights, yet neither has tangibly promoted victim objectives in the criminal process nor reduced victimization. Simply improving victim rights may not be the solution anyway. Formal rights do not provide much real protection for defendants and thus may do little more for victims. Also, increasing rights without changing the sources of victimization and rights violations may be counterproductive.[55]

Finally, an organized victim lobby has emerged, composed of victim advocates, some public officials, some professional advocates (such as lawyer's groups), special constituency groups (such as women's and senior citizen's organizations), and specialized victim organizations, such as the National Organization of Victim Assistance and the National Victims Organization. Certainly, these groups, although sometimes ideologically opposed, have aided victims significantly, at least symbolically, by attracting public attention, stimulating a Presidential task force, and securing important legislation.

Unfortunately, while some of that legislation has created victim assistance programs, victim lobbyists must acknowledge that many fewer tangible gains for victims have occurred than they might have hoped. In sum, while legislative reform has achieved some significant symbolic victories for victim rights, victims have only modestly improved their situation and their chances of continued victimization usually remain as high as ever.

Crime Reduction

Crime reduction seeks to help victims by devising strategies to reduce crime and victimization, largely by increasing victim participation.

Victimization Avoidance seeks to prevent victimization by focusing on victims, and inducing them to take various precautions or other measures. It may require behavioral changes, as, for example, limiting where people go and when. It may require various methods of "target hardening," safety equipment, weapons, surveillance devices, guards, and booby traps. It may require training in self-defense or resistance. In general, it tries to curb the various ways that victims might precipitate or facilitate crime by having taken insufficient precautions. These measures arise from police departments and victims groups, may involve private solutions or close coordination with law enforcement, and cost millions of dollars annually, usually borne privately.[56]

Community Crime Control involves many strategies that often contradict each other. It emphasizes crime prevention through organized efforts, usually in neighborhoods. It may be used together with individualized, victim avoidance strategies, but also focuses on criminals and on organizing groups of people, often into "neighborhood watches." In the one direction, local organizations may become auxiliaries to the police department, reflecting its goals, priorities, and methods. At the furthest extreme, it may abandon officials and begin vigilante actions, such as those of the "Marshalls" of Restore Our Alienated Freedoms (ROAF) of Boston, that take the law into their own hands, distributing "justice" in the streets.

On the other hand, local organizations, such as the Guardian Angels of New York and other cities, may pursue crime control independent of authorities, and may put crime within the context of broader community problems. Other groups, such as the House of Umoja in Philadelphia, Centro de Orientacion y Servicios in Ponce, Puerto Rico, and the Community Boards Program of San Francisco, combine prevention methods with strategies to rectify victimization's underlying sources, while monitoring official behavior.[57] This might also embrace community corrections, which integrate offenders back into the community.[58]

In between, various environmental approaches to crime prevention, such as the many "Crime Prevention Through Environmental Design" (CPTED) projects, put "eyes on the street" by using different architectural or spatial techniques.[59] Some programs will aim at specific victim groups such as Women Organized Against Rape (WOAR) and the Elderly Anti-Victimization Program of Washington, D.C. Community control strategies may arise from authorities or from neighbors, may be well integrated or independent of law enforcement, may have a single, crime control purpose or multiple goals, and will require some, and often extensive, expenditures borne either privately or by government.[60]

Enforcement Crackdowns increase police forces, resources, and mobilization to try to reduce victimization through prevention. Groups such as the Victims Committee of the International Association of Chiefs of Police and Victim Advocates for Law and Order (VALOR) call for more prosecutions, convictions, and punishments. Crackdowns might require more personnel, increased surveillance, enhanced patrols, additional equipment, new control methods, or reduced rights for suspects. In recent years, crackdowns have been promoted in the name of victims and supported by law and order adherents and some victim advocates. They may focus on all crimes, or on particular, target offenses. They often require greater government spending and, of course, are integral to traditional criminal justice.[61]

IMPACT. Enforcement crackdowns have not reduced victimization either, even when advanced using the latest equipment, technology, and methods.[62] Considerable effort and expense has gone into avoiding victimization, and some of these measures have undoubtedly reduced crime and fear for some people. Nevertheless, we have little evidence that protective devices effectively prevent crime,[63] and while restricting one's personal freedom might reduce criminal victimization,[64] it incurs a severe tradeoff. Moreover, it appears that victimization avoidance strategies do much less to reduce fear than crime prevention strategies,[65] and may even increase it.

We have mixed reports about community crime control. We have few really independent community programs to evaluate, and thus can only assess other, more dependent, approaches. Certainly, vigilantism, for example, has produced no positive effects, for victims or anyone else, particularly when initiated and led by police officers.[66] Some believe, however, that community projects tied to police departments have been successful. Crime watch and auxiliary programs may have helped law enforcement and reduced fear and crime in many neighborhoods.[67]

On the other hand, others believe that such programs have pursued narrow, police objectives, have stimulated fear and suspiciousness, promoted greater official controls, and failed to reduce crime, or merely displaced it to neighborhoods that cannot organize or afford such programs. The plans seem to be punitive and short-lived, and ignore community needs and crime's sources, emphasize questionable protective gadgets, throw blame onto victims, promote a one-way communication from the police to the community, and perpetuate stereotypical views of crime and criminals.[68] While some important models have been pioneered, we have little evidence that various crime reduction strategies have lessened victimization or even the fear of crime.

Structural Alternatives

Structural alternatives have been devised to improve victim treatment and outcomes, particularly to give greater access and control and even to facilitate significant social change.

Diversion creates alternatives to traditional criminal justice that might reduce complications, increase victim involvement, provide greater access, as well as correctional options that may reduce future victimization. These methods go beyond traditional diversion to juvenile and family courts and instead create new mechanisms, including consumer complaint divisions, such as the New York City Consumer Advocacy Unit, anti-discrimination boards, such as the Massachusetts Commission Against Discrimination, and offender treatment plans, such as the Highfields Program in New Jersey. They treat criminal offenses as civil wrongs in exchange for greater public access, although may be available only for selective offenses. Typically, they originate either from officials concerned with judicial effectiveness or from external, special interest organizations such as consumer groups. They will often be official government programs, with public revenues, that maintain a relationship with criminal justice but also strong independence.[69]

Mediation also relies on diverting cases from the criminal process. As with Dorchester's "Urban Court," Brooklyn's Dispute Resolution Center, and the various Victim Offender Reconciliation Projects in the Midwest, it requires a program, usually staffed by nonprofessionals, who provide a nonofficial forum for reconciling disputes through a neutral third party.[70] Potential participants, such as victims and offenders in relationship cases, can substitute mediation for the criminal process. As such, the disputants lose their victim and defendant status and become equals.[71] Mediation programs cannot impose punishments, but will help enforce agreements mutually arranged. They resemble the neighborhood justice centers that have originated to handle civil disputes,[72] increasing victim control, resolving disputes informally, and reaching more mutually satisfactory and lasting solutions. Mediation has originated from official sources and victim advocates, usually receives government financing and operates outside, but closely related to, criminal justice.[73]

Popular Justice seeks a fundamental social restructuring. Its various forms presume that existing structures impede justice, and thus they seek some politico-economic transformation combined with alternative judicial mechanisms. Popular justice approaches, such as the National Alliance Against Racism and Political Repression and the Prisoner's Union, try to not merely supplement traditional criminal justice, but to transform and replace it, as a part of broader social change. It promotes decentralized, popularly controlled, social structures, including judicial institutions, guided not merely by criminal definitions but by human rights standards. Popular justice pursues objectives beyond crime control, considering crime within the context of broader social problems and structures.[74] It adopts informal, dispute resolution mechanisms such as mediation, but mostly aims at eliminating the sources of crime and conflict in the first place. It might, like the Self-Defense Guard in North Carolina, initially seek self-protection from the police and vigilante groups. It strongly emphasizes victim interests, but defines itself broadly to include all victims. Popular justice would operate independently from traditional government and criminal justice institutions; indeed, it would seek to replace them.[75]

IMPACT. As with the small claims movement,[76] many programs diverting cases from the criminal process have had only moderate success. Even the best funded and staffed consumer protection divisions, for example, have been very ineffective in checking abuses and in providing victims with a more accessible and helpful forum.[77] Mediation programs and their civil analogs have apparently worked much better, showing much more promise for resolving disputes, and already satisfying many victims and other parties.[78] About 150 of these centers had arisen in the United States by 1980, with the federal government adding its own legislation that same year.

We can say little about so-called popular justice since we have practically no experience with this strategy.[79] Nevertheless, several studies of popular justice in nations such as Chile (under Allende), revolutionary Portugal (1974–75), various nonindustrial societies, and post-revolutionary Cuba, China, Nicaragua, and Mozambique show some considerable advantages for participants, if only on the procedural level, by increasing popular influence, participation, control, and access.[80] In the United States, we have tested few structural alternatives thus far, and certainly no appropriate alternative politico-economic systems upon which they might be based. Our limited evidence suggests, however, that victims might benefit significantly from alternatives to current processes and victim roles that portend greater access and control along with better treatment and outcomes.

International Protections

International protections would transcend narrow and nationalist concepts of criminal wrongdoing in favor of regional or international efforts to regulate crime, promote victim rights, and provide protections.[81]

International Covenants and Programs seek international or regional standards for protecting victim rights. This approach appeals to the United Nations and regional organizations such as the Council of Europe to establish covenants on broad victim rights or on specific rights such as victim compensation. It also promotes victim interests through international nongovernmental professional organizations, such as the Scientific Committee on Victims of the World Federation of Mental Health. From such covenants and programs would flow international or regional norms and protections that might influence national behavior toward victims.[82] International covenants arise primarily from victim advocates, protect and promote conventional crime victims, require no initial, but probably future, outlays, and operate independently from government and criminal justice but impose standards upon them.

International Human Rights initiatives go beyond establishing international covenants. They try to conceptualize an international criminal law that identifies how nationalism provides the source of much victimization.[83] They define victims much more broadly than official and public conceptions, and encompass equally or more severe (but currently excluded) victimizations produced not only by individuals but also by states and other social institutions, such as large corporations and public bureaucracies.[84] This approach brings victims, more broadly defined, within the larger framework of international human rights, seeking protections from various "crimes against humanity." Besides international protections, this method calls for alternative institutions and social arrangements to reduce victimization's sources. An international human rights approach, like the local popular justice strategy, promotes victims through social transformation and seeks not merely to supplement government and criminal justice, but to transform and replace them.

IMPACT. Victim advocates have stimulated some considerable international interest in devising covenants to promote victim rights, and we may well soon see such instruments adopted by the United Nations. Recently, the UN Institute on the Prevention and Control of Crime, the Committee on International Criminal Law of the International Law Association, the 1980 Caracas Declaration of the United Nations, the International Association of Penal Law, and the 1984 Draft Resolution on Victims of Crime and Abuses of Power of the 7th United Nations Congress on Crime Prevention and the Treatment of Offenders have also emphasized victim issues.[85] We have made few strides, however, toward devising an international criminal law or incorporating criminal victimization within broader, international human rights. Even when rights have been formally recognized in covenants, their enforcement has met many persistent obstacles. Crime victims have so far received little direct assistance or rights from international protections.

Implications

This review of victim programs reveals some important barriers to satisfying victim needs, and shows some services working better than others. Obviously, financing has been a major obstacle, despite evidence that costs may not be nearly as high as we assume.[86] Victims have also found many programs very inaccessible because of low visibility, inadequate information, and eligibility requirements. Some programs have been well integrated into criminal justice, while others have clashed. Some schemes promote a close working relationship with law enforcement, but receive little cooperation. Others have specifically sought independence only to find themselves coopted by criminal justice, in various ways.

Despite the many programs, some victim groups, such as homosexuals, mental patients, prison inmates, and victims of arson and corporate crime, still seem rather systematically excluded from benefits. Some have also challenged the programs' equity, wondering whether paying for victim services for some groups robs financing for preventing crimes against others.[87] Some criticize the programs, despite their apparently worthy goals, for being inadequate "bandaids" that divert attention from victimization's sources.[88] Finally, beyond each program's external value, many internal conflicts often emerge that limit their effectiveness, such as fragmentation, competition, unclear victim and professional needs, inadequate information, and splits on appropriate ideologies.

Beyond these limitations, other characteristics may help determine success. The most successful programs have been aimed at certain target victims, and been run privately and independently (from criminal justice) by major advocate groups (either generating their own financing or accepting no-strings government funding).[89] Government control, despite its greater resources, may not provide victims the greatest assistance.

THE FUNCTIONS OF VICTIM ADVOCACY

Overall, although some important developments in victim rights and assistance have occurred in the last twenty years, the gains often seem much more symbolic than tangible. Despite our best efforts, and despite some significant changes, most victims still incur considerable, unresolved problems from their victimization and criminal justice involvement. Perhaps we risk being too impatient for rapid results, yet maybe the reason for such modest gains lies elsewhere.

We have thus far analyzed assistance exclusively from the victim's perspective and ignored other, competing motivations for such programs, completely apart from (and perhaps contradictory to) victim interests. Although victim programs may not entirely satisfy these other goals, understanding them may help explain why we have achieved comparatively little for victims. To do so, we may risk appearing unduly cynical about personal, professional, and institutional motives, particularly when many people and organizations may be making very sincere efforts to help victims. Yet to ignore the possibility of competing incentives will, in the long run, do victims the greatest disservice.

We must examine why so many victim programs have emerged without having asked victims their own preferences and needs.[90] Perhaps we have viewed their problems as obvious, believing we could safely predict the assistance victims really want. Yet we could just as easily suspect that creating victim programs (whether consciously and intentionally or not) served functions or purposes beyond merely satisfying victim needs.[92] They might include institutional, professional, entrepreneurial, or political motives.

Institutional Motives

Some competing institutional motives may be innocent enough, since we might welcome policies that can pursue different goals simultaneously. On the other hand, we might find none of those objectives satisfied, or that some goals (other than victim interests) predominate over others. For example, some victim programs, such as witness management schemes, try to ease criminal court workloads and better manage the victim's role in resolving criminal cases. Unfortunately, this will not necessarily satisfy victim needs, problems, or expectations.[93] Restitution, to take another example, might be promoted partly to help repay victim losses, yet many times it has been pursued more as a correctional alternative that might be more effective and efficient in reducing prison overcrowding and promoting rehabilitation.[94] Perhaps in this case no conflict arises, although promoting restitution as primarily a rehabilitative device for offenders may be rejected by many judges who might more readily accept it as a pro-victim policy.

Furthermore, we must examine how victim policies might either contradict or promote official goals—or perhaps both simultaneously. For example, we might find that substantially improving victim treatment contradicts police officers' tendency to resist change and outside interferences in their daily work.[95] On the other hand, promoting victims might well pave the way for tougher policing, less burdened by concerns about offender rights and police methods. From this contradiction, we should not be surprised that law enforcers often publicly proclaim their concern for victims, and perhaps encourage better police-community relations, while making few actual accommodations for victims in their daily work.

Professional Motives

Some victim programs create new organizations whose members may find their own personal or professional interests competing with victim interests. Personnel might find that their desire for funded projects pushes them toward programs that may not best serve victim needs. Psychologists may find that beyond their humanitarian desire to assist and treat victims, the programs they participate in also serve professional research interests and goals. Lawyers may find that beyond their sincere concerns for victims advocacy may bring more legal jobs or legal work. Social scientists may find their research opportunities significantly expanded by a growing victim movement. It would be too much to suggest that some social service providers intentionally avoid solving their clients' problems to preserve their jobs,[96] yet conflicting personal motives may help explain some of the obstacles victim assistance faces.[97]

Entrepreneurial Motives

Some people might have entrepreneurial motives for stressing the victim's plight. For example, focusing attention on the great dangers victims (or potential victims) face from possible victimization and offering services to address those needs might make very good business sense. We know that hospitals have sometimes jumped into new services for the profits of handling new or newly discovered populations. Insurance companies profit from increased premiums for crime insurance.

Security companies also profit when people purchase the many protective devices they offer. We might argue that businesses merely offer services, for profit, *after* we and they recognize certain victim problems. But, since their "services" often do not meet victim needs, yet appear in sensationalist and frightening advertisements as the victim's only recourse, perhaps we should not be so generous. Business propaganda will frequently help develop needs (often hysterically) more than respond to them, and may make us feel guilty (i.e., "you wouldn't want to endanger your family, would you?") for not buying their services or products.

Political Motives

The foregoing motives may have already suggested several political purposes for victim assistance beyond victim interests. We will examine a few more, but largely reserve our analysis of the politics of victim advocacy to Chapter 9. Victim services may help political interests control the labeling of victims and victimization, and build public support and social control.

As suggested earlier, the civil liberties movement of the 1960s focused, in part, on violations of defendant's rights. Not only did judicial decisions attempt to curb those violations, but we began to wonder whether offenders were not victims too. Some argue that the services, such as victim compensation, that began to emerge by the end of the 1960s and early 1970s functioned as the state's method of regaining control over defining victims. By limiting services only to certain victims, government regained definitional control and distinguished legitimate and illegitimate victims, which not only excluded offenders but also many other victims as well.[98] Victim compensation rules, for example, exclude victims who facilitate or otherwise "precipitate" victimization, who delay in reporting crimes or filing claims, who have present or past relationships with victims, who fail to satisfactorily cooperate with the court or the compensation board, who fail to show financial destitution, and many others. Beyond the labeling process that the requirements achieve, they also eliminate most victims from even being considered for compensation.[99]

Victim services have also helped build public backing for government and criminal justice.[100] Again, by the end of the 1960s, a backlash against defendant's rights made victims a perfect vehicle for promoting political support. While undoubtedly many politicians and administrators sincerely supported victim interests, their strategic mobilization of victim programs shows other motives as well, including a desire to build constituency support in general on a "no-risk" political issue and a quest to restore strong and unrestrained police forces.[100] Regardless of their modest impact, victim services have generated strong public support and provided considerable political mileage.[101]

Finally, some suggest that victims provide the best alternative to formal laws and bureaucracies for promoting social control; that is, for preventing anti-social behavior.[103] Officials might resist the decentralization and decriminalization this would require, yet nevertheless may view it as a promising direction politically. More likely, however, victims and victim programs have already been used to promote quite a different kind of social control. As we will discuss more fully, they seem to have been used primarily to help promote politically sensitive criminal-justice policies and appease and control potentially disruptive social elements.[104]

Summary

We need not suspect a conspiracy to recognize that victim services might serve many other functions or purposes besides merely assisting victims. Perhaps we can serve victims and other interests simultaneously, but so far victim advocacy may have served competing interests at least as well as—and perhaps better than—victims. Those competing interests have not only done better, but may have also limited victim gains in the process. In fact, ulterior interests, and not victim interests, may have been all that many political elites, professionals, entrepreneurs, and administrators had in mind: the symbolic politics of victim programs, without delivering tangible results. They may amount largely to the "political placebos" some have feared. If so, then the future of victim advocacy must be seen and confronted in this light.

CONCLUSION

Victims develop a variety of problems and expectations from their victimization and criminal-justice involvement, including financial, practical, psychological, and medical needs, and many inconveniences. They also develop some new concerns about being protected from victimization in the future. To respond to these needs, various approaches and programs have been pursued.

Victim advocacy has included services such as crisis intervention, and medical and mental health services. It has pursued victim reimbursement schemes such as compensation, restitution, civil actions, and insurance. It has sought criminal-justice reforms such as special training, victim/witness assistance programs, victim rights, and adversarial reform. It has initiated legislative reforms such as decriminalization, criminalization, special legislation, procedural rights, and victim lobbying. It has promoted crime reduction strategies such as victimization avoidance, community crime control, and enforcement crackdowns. It has suggested structural alternatives such as diversion, mediation, and popular justice models. And it has proposed protections through international covenants and human rights.

Victim programs have met victim needs and expectations very unevenly. While some either have achieved significant results or shown some promise, most have poorly addressed victim problems. The programs showing the greatest success often aim at particular victims, are privately run by advocate groups, operate separately from criminal justice, and seek financial independence.[105]

Victim services may fill other functions beyond providing assistance to victims. They may be promoted for institutional motives such as easing workloads, or better managing victim involvement, or pursuing alternative correctional policies. Victim assistance may also reflect professional motives for research, employment, and funding. It may be pursued for entrepreneurial motives such as making profits from selling medical care, protective devices, and insurance. And it may have political motives such as controlling the social definition of victimization and building public support and social control for government and criminal justice.

Unfortunately, these competing motives or purposes have often outpaced the satisfaction of victim needs and expectations, perhaps so much so that they actually impede victim interests. This may merely reflect the unfortunate and unintended inertia of political, professional, entrepreneurial, and administrative interests, or it could signal a conscious neglect of victim needs, the formal programs notwithstanding. It could represent, in other words, the outward, symbolic politics of victim advocacy, with little substance underneath.

We have now examined the evolution of victims and victimology, the reality and social reality of victimization, its sources, the impact of victimization and law enforcement, and victim advocacy. Throughout, we have suggested that we might well advance victims and victimology to their next developmental stage by exploring their relationship to universal human rights standards. Now, we turn to more specifically examine the kinds of victims and victimization this might include. In particular, we will consider human rights victims: the victims of oppression.

8

Oppression: Victims and Human Rights

Crime threatens the social order in the same way as totalitarianism.

CHARLES SILBERMAN, *Criminal Violence, Criminal Justice*

We are in a world in which we must choose between being a victim or an executioner—and nothing else. Such a choice is not easy. It always seemed to me that in fact there were no executioners—only victims. In the last analysis, of course. But this is a truth that is not widely known. ALBERT CAMUS

It is probably quite true literally that in the history of human thinking the most fruitful developments frequently take place at those points where two different lines of thought meet . . . if they are at least so related to each other that a real interaction can take place, then one may hope that new and interesting developments may follow. WERNER HEISENBERG

In examining victims and victimology thus far, we have frequently suggested their relationship to human rights. We can now make that link much more explicit. By embracing a broader, human rights conception of victimization, we can provide victims new rights and protections and move victimology toward a fuller development as a scientific discipline and vehicle to promote victim interests. For the moment, we can explore how this development might look by briefly sketching the relationship between victims, victimology, and human rights. Although in this context we can only examine oppression[1] suggestively, we will use the same approach for considering human rights victims that we have already used for crime victims. This time, we will review the evolution of human rights victims and protections; the social reality, sources, and impact of oppression; and human rights enforcement and advocacy. We will consider these issues largely within the American domestic and foreign policy context, although obviously they could be similarly addressed internationally, or for other nations.[2]

This analysis will begin clarifying the similarities between crime victims and human rights victims, their plight, its impact, and our response. We will see the intersection between victimology and human rights inquiry, and between crime and oppression. We will observe a rather consistent, but unfortunate, pattern in how we understand and treat both kinds of victimization.

This will provide mutual advantages. Unlike victimology, the human rights field has little scientific claim and a considerably smaller literature examining issues of victimization. As a much more developed science, victimology can offer human rights a methodology and a set of victimological theories and questions, not to mention considerable comparative data on other victims: namely, crime victims. With its emphasis on crime, victimology can help human rights inquiries more clearly theorize the "crimes against humanity" it now only partially operationalizes. For victimology, a human rights framework provides a broader conception of victimization and victim rights. It can help us examine our current criminal and victimological definitions to compare those victimizations we define as criminal to those (despite their greater harm) we do not. It will also help promote victimology's increasingly international trends.

A human rights focus can help us examine victimization's sources and the relationship between the causes of crime and the causes of oppression. We might find, for example, that oppression produces the main conditions for personal and property crimes. As suggested earlier when considering crime's structural sources, victimization may result primarily from adverse social, political, and economic conditions. If so, then a human rights analysis will detect those conditions; the following review will begin doing precisely that. It may well be that if we do not understand and assess our human rights conditions and record, we will never identify the major sources of victimization (both from crime and oppression), and thus be perpetually unable to offer victims much more than merely remedial aid and comfort. If we take the following human rights evaluation seriously, we might also question why victimology routinely accepts the state's legitimacy and official criminal definitions.

In sum, this analysis will allow us to consider a "new" victimology that transcends the "old" victimology's criminological constraints, and which, ironically, may only bring victimology back to its original purposes. As the pioneer Beniamin Mendelsohn suggested over forty years ago, victimology is the science of studying victims—not just *crime* victims, but *all* victims.[3] Human rights will help us see the victims we have thus far ignored, and the sources of those victims with whom we have thus far been preoccupied.

THE EVOLUTION OF HUMAN RIGHTS

Origins

Philosophers have long pondered social justice questions, yet the concept of human rights has emerged largely in the modern era. We may derive our current ideas of rights from predecessors such as divine rights and natural rights. While some argue that rights did not really emerge until the growth of individualism, this may only reflect a Western bias and definition. Even as we expand our human rights definitions, we tend to ignore Eastern thought or other sources, defined not merely individually, but collectively.

In any case, we largely associate the Western development of rights with leading philosophers. Rights were considered by Locke in relation to political or civil society, by Montesquieu in relation to the spirit of laws, by Rousseau in relation to the social contract, by Voltaire in relation to tolerance, by Kant in relation to civil constitutions, and by Mill in relation to liberty and representative government.[4] Interestingly, we also partly owe our human right conceptions to two philosophers who also pioneered the field of criminology: Bentham and Beccaria.[5] Rights also appeared in landmark documents such as the Magna Carta, the English Bill of Rights, the U.S. Declaration of Independence and Bill of Rights, and the French Declaration of the Rights of Man and Citizen.

These philosophers and charters largely emphasized natural rights, and, indeed, the American and French revolutions emerged from this perspective. Yet, by the nineteenth century, natural rights had been challenged by people like Marx for being merely formal, individualistic, and procedural, and for ignoring the material conditions on which substantive rights depend, both for exercising political rights and for enjoying economic rights.[6] Combined with the more communal rights conceptions emerging from non-Western cultures, the Marxian view of social and economic rights arose to compete with Western, individualized political and civil rights.

Modern Era

By the end of the nineteenth century, some global agreement on rights began to emerge, first as international protections about slavery and medical personnel in wartime.[7] In the early twentieth century, a more social and economic definition of rights stimulated both the Russian and Mexican revolutions. The League of Nations arose partly to curb the injustices of war, to protect racial and national minorities, and to promote national self-determination. It was followed by the International Labor Organization, which began protecting workers' rights. Then, in the mid-1940s, we vastly expanded international human rights by adopting the United Nations Charter and the Universal Declaration of Human Rights, and established new institutions such as the World Health Organization (WHO) and the United Nations Educational, Scientific, and Cultural Organization (UNESCO), concerned with specialized rights and protections.[8] At about the same time, victimology arose from some of these same international, human rights goals.[9]

Thereafter, various specialized protections against offenses such as genocide, torture, and racial and sexual disrimination were adopted. Borrowing from earlier concepts of self-determination, sovereign rights gained prominence, especially in the 1950s and 1960s, as dozens of developing nations won independence in the name of national liberty from the yoke of foreign dominance. By the mid-1960s, many of these same nations began joining the socialist countries in promoting collective rights coequal with Western individual rights. What emerged were two separate and more detailed charters, the International Covenant on Civil and Political Rights and the International Covenant on Economic, Social, and Cultural Rights.[10]

Finally, in the mid-1970s, Jimmy Carter injected human rights into American foreign policy, which helped push them into the international limelight as they never had been before.[11] Despite the Reagan administration's complete retreat,[12] and despite our refusal to ratify almost all these covenants,[13] international human rights still remain as important criteria for evaluating American and world politics. The Algiers Universal Declaration of the Rights of Peoples in 1976, the first rights covenant produced by public representatives and not governments, added a much needed popular dimension to human rights as well.[14]

American Conception

In the American context, human rights have been individualistic even beyond most other Western nations. Beginning with the Declaration of Independence and then the Bill of Rights, we have a long political and civil rights tradition, bolstered by a sometimes activist Supreme Court. Unfortunately, many believe that our formal protections have been very narrowly conceived and frequently ineffective. Despite our Bill of Rights' long history, many of its clauses received little formal court recognition until the mid-twentieth century. The Warren Court's "civil liberties revolution" of the 1950s and 1960s significantly expanded our commitment to political and civil rights, yet formal court decisions hardly ensured actual enforcement. Ironically, by the time Jimmy Carter called for promoting international human rights, many Americans wondered why he had ignored such glaring rights violations at home.

The Carter human rights policy ostensibly emphasized violations in the American sphere of influence around the world. In the Western hemisphere, it built upon the American Declaration of the Rights and Duties of Man of 1948 and the American Convention on Human Rights of 1969, and invoked national legislation that would withhold foreign aid to gross human rights violators. Many argue that the policy imposed few restrictions, however, even on those few nations ostensibly sanctioned, considering the various exemptions, and alternative sources the legislation allowed.[15] Instead, the policy may have been more devoted to rescuing the battered American reputation after Vietnam and to denouncing Soviet bloc violations while largely turning its head to offenses in the American sphere. It may have been much more of a political or symbolic policy, and less devoted to substantial human rights protections.

At home, no presidential administration during the 1970s showed concerns for domestic human rights, although again the Carter record seems somewhat better by comparison. In fact, during this period, the Burger Court pursued a sweeping (although not complete) counterrevolution to the earlier Warren Court decisions, persistently whittling away political and civil rights protections.[16] Furthermore, it made no progress in expanding our concept of rights to include economic and social protections, as had other Western nations.

Human Rights Movement

By the early 1980s, international human rights violations approached crisis proportions and domestic American rights denials steadily increased, both significantly fomented by Reagan administration policies. Nevertheless, the international human rights movement presses steadily on, despite recent setbacks. Domestically, the women's rights movement persists, and the quiet, decentralized, but very mobile citizen's movement makes steady progress pursuing political and civil rights and new conceptions of community and economic and social democracy. Increasingly, the United States finds itself pressed to reduce violations at home and in its foreign sphere and to adopt a broader, more universal concept of human rights.

Some apparently believe that one group of human rights victims—crime victims—can best progress by riding a conservative law-and-order wave both internationally and at home. For them, infringing others' rights, particularly those of suspects, defendants, and offenders, will best promote victim rights. From this perspective, international human rights has nothing to offer either crime victims or victimology. Others, however, have increasingly recognized the relationship between victim rights and human rights, and have seen the false distinctions and choices the law-and-order movement holds for victims. Instead, they understand how promoting victim rights depends on promoting human rights generally. From this perspective, international human rights offers a promising new direction for victims and victimology.

Cultural Perspectives

Culturally, most Americans have embraced the narrow American human rights conception, often measuring oppression simply by whether or not a nation holds national elections, for example. We often seem willing to join forces with officials who blame victims of oppression for their fate, concluding that they must be either unworthy or unloyal. Nevertheless, victims of oppression have apparently received a much more sympathetic ear from the literary world than crime victims. Although rarely available to the American public as local drugstore paperbacks, a growing American and Latin American literature of oppression has emerged, nevertheless. Works such as Alice Walker's *The Color Purple*,[17] E. L. Doctorow's *The Book of Daniel*,[18] Manlio Argueta's *One Day of Life*,[19] James Baldwin's *Nobody Knows My Name*,[20] Marge Piercy's *Woman on the Edge of Time*,[21] Edward Galeano's *Nights of Love and War*,[22] Gabriel Garcia Marquez's *One Hundred Years of Solitude*,[23] Ariel Dorfman's *Widows*,[24] Jay Cantor's *The Death of Che Guevara*,[25] and Carlos Fuentes' *The Death of Artemio Cruz*[26] have immeasurably expanded our understanding of human rights victims. And they may ultimately help sensitize and mobilize us against oppression. For example, consider this from Carolyn Forche:

What you have heard is true. I was in his house. His wife carried a tray of coffee and sugar. His daughter filed her nails, his son went out for the night. There were daily papers, pet dogs, a pistol on the cushion beside him. The moon swung bare on its black cord over the house. On the television was a cop show. It was in English. Broken bottles were embedded in the walls around the house to scoop the kneecaps from a man's legs or cut his hands to lace. On the windows there were gratings like those in liquor stores. We had dinner, a rack of lamb, good wine, a gold bell was on the table for calling the maid. The maid brought green mangoes, salt, a type of bread. I was asked how I enjoyed the country. There was a brief commercial in Spanish. His wife took everything away. There was some talk then of how difficult it had become to govern. The parrot said hello on the terrace. The colonel told it to shut up, and pushed himself from the table. My friend said to me with his eyes: say nothing. The colonel returned with a sack used to bring groceries home. He spilled many human ears on the table. They were like dried peach halves. There is no other way to say this. He took one of them in his hands, shook it in our faces, dropped it into a water glass. It came alive there. I am tired of fooling around he said. As for the rights of anyone tell your people they can go fuck themselves. He swept the ears to the floor with his arm and held the last of his wine in the air. Something for your poetry, no? he said. Some of the ears on the floor caught this scrap of his voice. Some of the ears on the floor were pressed to the ground.[27]

Scientific Pursuits

Finally, victimology also offers much for studying human rights scientifically. International human rights encompasses a large and far greater scope of issues (and rights) than victimology. But victimology has much greater depth. Victimology offers human rights a series of theories and methodologies by which to organize and pursue our understanding of oppression, its shapes, sources, impact, and remedies. As we will see, for example, we have progressed only very modestly in assessing the financial, physical, psychological, and human costs of oppression. We know little about effective rights enforcement mechanisms and their impact on human rights victims. We have little information about the problems and needs of victims of oppression and how to provide effective relief.

We might apply various victimological concepts to human rights as well. Do victims of oppression bear a "functional responsibility" for their victimization? To what extent do human rights violations emerge from domestic social control mechanisms? Have we designated, either implicitly or explicitly, some people or peoples, or groups as "culturally legitimate" victims, thereby warranting no effective protections?

Obviously, victimology does not have all the answers, but can offer much to systematically analyze and understand victims and, ironically, could provide even more answers by adopting a broader, human rights perspective. That perspective, for example, would help reveal oppression's impact on criminal victimization and help us understand victimization's sources. For these and other reasons, the interchange between victimology and human rights would be mutually beneficial.

THE SOCIAL REALITY OF OPPRESSION

Conceptualizing Oppression

DEFINING OPPRESSION. Within the American context, human rights has shared victimology's propensity for narrowly defining victims and victimization. American human rights largely recognizes only political and civil rights, including free expression and religion, due process, equality of opportunity, and especially property. It largely disregards, both theoretically and practically, protections of economic and social rights such as guarantees of decent housing, food, shelter, work, and living standards.[28] Instead of embracing more universal human rights conceptions, which encompass various cultural, religious, and ideological differences, American human rights has recognized only those consistent with liberal capitalism, although some academics and activists accept a broader definition.

Moreover, American human rights not only limits the breadth of its protection (by excluding many other internationally recognized rights) but also its depth. Its individualized rights ignore what many see as the more important rights of peoples and groups.[29] Some believe it defines and protects people artificially outside their social memberships and context, and ignores the disparate material conditions that block the effective enjoyment of formal political and civil rights. For example, if individuals have widely varying wealth and capabilities, then the "equality of opportunity" formally granted may be only a hollow pretension. If with those same distinctions, we all equally receive the right to free expression but our access, and our power to persuade, depend largely on material advantages, then some people will inevitably be more equal than others, regardless of legal protections. Individual rights may not merely fail to guarantee rights or equality, they may actually institutionalize inequalities.[30] In any case, just as we define crime victims and criminal victimization selectively, so too do we selectively define oppression and its victims.

MEASURING OPPRESSION. American human rights also often measures oppression selectively. To begin with, since it already defines human rights only partially, it would naturally ignore some kinds of violations completely. It excludes by definition economic, social, and cultural rights which, according to many reports, are violated extensively both domestically and in the American foreign sphere. Even within its preferred rights conception, it takes a relatively narrow view.

We often measure human rights very formalistically. If we formally establish a constitutional or statutory right, then we often assume its protection or implementation. When we find some court cases challenging the violation of those rights, we often view them as aberrations instead of reflecting systematic behavior, and when courts catch the violations, we assume the rights will thereafter be automatically protected. This ignores, however, the "politics of rights," which requires not only that rights be formally written, but also recognized and activated, and, finally, actually implemented in order to really be protected.[31] This will not happen automatically, but largely depends on the political and economic power of those seeking the rights.

Measuring oppression will also reflect our information sources.[32] In foreign policy, for example, we have relied on State Department reports about violations in nations in our sphere. They have rather consistently claimed improvements in the human rights records of our client states, thus allowing us to extend foreign aid without interruption and to console ourselves about the steadily improving situation. Often, these reports receive support from surveys produced by human rights organizations such as Freedom House.[33] Yet we might well be wary of both sources.[34] State Department reports officially assess nations to which we seek continuing and close ties and they rely on data largely provided by local, state-controlled newspapers, American embassies, and the very governments we seek to evaluate. Groups such as Freedom House only selectively evaluate human rights and profess a clear pro-Western, capitalist bias.

Moreover, we find that alternative, more neutral sources of human rights information virtually always contradict official American evaluations, often overwhelmingly.[35] Reports completed by United Nations missions, and by human rights organizations such as Amnesty International and the International Commission of Jurists, have found a steady escalation of human rights violations, much of it concentrated in the American sphere. In any case, just as we measure criminal victimization in ways that may distort its true proportions, so too do we measure oppression in ways that significantly underestimate human rights violations.

IDEOLOGY, MEDIA, AND PUBLIC OPINION. As with crime victims, we often develop a very distorted view of human rights victims. We may become socialized by official definitions and measurements and by prevailing ideologies and media coverage. Most Americans need not be convinced about the American version of human rights since it has been the only view we have learned. While we consider ourselves to be a very humanitarian people, we largely support negative freedoms (from government interference), and otherwise believe that people should be allowed to sink or swim on their own. We seem to widely disdain those who cannot successfully compete, including ourselves. We readily blame victims for their fate.[36] After the National Guard killed four students at Kent State, for example, totally untrue rumors claimed that the students were filthy and had lice, and that the killings had spared the parents embarrassment since the slain girls were pregnant. After the My Lai massacre, the common American reaction was: "It never happened—and what's more they deserved it!"[37]

Moreover, our selective perception may become all the more reinforced by biased research, education, and media coverage.[38] Although we consider ourselves to have the freest education and press in the world, reflecting our strongly democratic values, many believe otherwise. Under the mantle of scientific objectivity and free expression, academia and the media may help ingrain official conceptions and distortions of human rights.[39] They may only selectively examine human rights, emphasizing those most congruent with prevailing ideologies and policies. They seem to relentlessly emphasize political and civil rights violations in the Eastern bloc, while largely ignoring similar violations, not to mention massive economic and social deprivations, in the American sphere.[40] We hear endlessly about our Eastern bloc hero, Lech Walesa and his "brutal" treatment, while ignoring hundreds of comparable labor leaders tortured and killed in American client states.

Critics believe we receive superficial human rights analyses that ignore international standards and tolerate the conditions that produce violations in the first place. We ignore significant domestic violations and, when we acknowledge offenses in our sphere at all, we insist that things have been getting better. We call massive human rights violators such as El Salvador democratic merely because they have held national elections.[41] And we learn that we must fear *individual* terrorists when actually *state* terrorism produces incomparably more damage.[42]

Some view this as a kind of "brainwashing under freedom," where under the guise of an open society, we nevertheless become systematically propagandized into a rigid and narrow perspective. Taken together, the biases promoted officially and by substantial sectors of academia and the media may distort our conception of oppression, for ideological purposes. To examine, accept, or adopt broader human rights conceptions and alternative definitions and measurements would likely challenge American state legitimacy by revealing our involvement in oppressive activities or our support for them. Our social reality of oppression, while contradicting objective circumstances, may perform certain ideological functions for the American system.

Level of Oppression

> *Lord, let me not be silent while we fight*
> *In Europe Germans, Asia Japanese*

> *For setting up a Fascist way of might*
> *While fifteen million Negroes on their knees*
> *Pray for salvation from the Fascist yoke of these United States*
>
>   CLAUDE MCKAY

KINDS OF OPPRESSION.   As the foregoing official reports and our prevailing ideology suggest, America prides itself on practicing democracy and protecting human rights at home and on leading the "free world" abroad. Consequently, we should have little to report about American oppression, especially at home. Yet, ironically, the research showing American oppression, although written by minority voices, and largely inaccessible to the American public, has grown so voluminous that we can only very briefly review it here.[43] To do so, we will examine both political/civil and economic/social rights in America, and then the impact of American policy on human rights in the developing nations in its orbit. For victimology, this review may suggest the social, political, and economic conditions upon which criminal victimization may rest.

POLITICAL AND CIVIL RIGHTS

> *I eat Watergate*
> *with my breakfast*
> *every morning*
> *and wonder*
> *how many*
> *will die*
> *that day*
> *by a warning shot*
> *in the back*
>
>   ROSS LAURSEN

> *I am very familiar with the problems of the C.I.A.*
> *and the problems of South Africa and the problems*
> *of Exxon Corporation and the problems of white*
> *America in general and the problems of the teachers*
> *and the preachers and the F.B.I. and the social*
> *workers and my particular Mom and Dad/I am very*
> *familiar with the problems because the problems*
> *turn out to be*
> *me*
> *I am the history of rape*
> *I am the history of the rejection of who I am*
> *I am the history of the terrorist incarceration of*
> *my self*
> *I am the history of battery assault and limitless*

armies against whatever I want to do with my mind
and my body and my soul and
whether it's about walking out at night
or whether it's about the love that I feel or
whether it's about the sanctity of my vagina or
the sanctity of my national boundaries
or the sanctity of my leaders or the sanctity
of each and every desire
that I know from my personal and idiosyncratic
and indisputably single and singular heart
I have been raped . . .

JUNE JORDAN, *A Poem About My Rights*

Since the American human rights conception emphasizes political and civil protections, our record here should be particularly good, yet much research indicates otherwise. To begin with, many suggest that far from only failing in practice, American law may actually institutionalize repression. In other words, instead of creating mechanisms for avoiding or correcting political and civil rights violations, it may incorporate various violations such as classism, sexism, racism, intrusiveness, and violence.

This research suggests, that despite our highly vaunted anti-discrimination initiatives, for example, American law may institutionalize sexism and racism, despite equal protection initiatives.[44] It also argues that American law promotes classism by sanctifying property competition and accumulation among people with vastly different means. And, as suggested earlier, this research claims that American criminal law incorporates biases and double standards that not only ignore considerable wrongdoing by some classes, but discriminates against other classes as well.[45]

Other research illustrates political and civil rights violations in practice, either through corruption (such as bribery, kickbacks, evasion, and collusion) or intentional policies.[46] Many argue, for example, that we have significantly obstructed free expression by selectively barring speech, press, and participation, by chilling critical thought through private and public ideological propaganda, and by surveillance and harassment through illegal electronic techniques, red-baiting, false arrests, intimidation, dirty tricks, intelligence agencies (such as by the FBI, CIA, NSA, IRS, and the White House), data banks, grand juries, military and corporate spying, and special police operations (such as COINTELPRO, infiltration, and break-ins), among many other things.[47]

Much research questions our highly tauted "equality of opportunity," suggesting that apart from the many predetermined inequities that would distort any competition, even formal equality in the chances offered for advancement and success falls considerably short for the bulk of the population generally, and particularly for certain people such as women and minorities.[48] Others find inequities in procedural protections, denying due process in administrative, civil, and criminal proceedings.

In criminal justice, for example, many have found that, contrary to conventional wisdom claiming that civil liberties "handcuff" authorities, officials have instead widely violated protections against searches and seizures, self-incrimination, inadequate legal representation, entrapment, double jeopardy, unfair trials, excessive bail, unnecessary incarceration, parole and sentencing discrimination, and cruel and unusual punishments.[49] Still others suggest that we have political trials and prisoners—that is, people tried and punished for their political beliefs and activities who have not necessarily violated the criminal law.[50]

Some considerable research reveals the widespread use of official violence, by groups such as police officers, the national guard, military and mental hospital personnel, and prison guards. In criminal and mental institutions, for example, studies show widespread brutality, torture, and lethal force, involuntary drug and behavioral experiments, forced sterilization, inhumane confinement and living conditions, and even murder, not to mention the death penalty's questionable and discriminatory application.[51] Other studies show that in other domestic settings widespread official violence has been used to repress groups such as labor, students, civil rights and anti-war demonstrators, homosexuals, prostitutes, alcoholics and drug addicts, criminal suspects, minorities, and the poor.[52] Some argue, in fact, that the police have historically initiated most violence between themselves and other groups, thus suggesting the term "police riots."[53] Still others cite even more pervasive official violence against groups such as blacks, Indians, Haitians, and Mexicans.[54]

Finally, although human rights conventionally emphasize state violations of individual and collective rights, philosophically and practically we need not remain so confined. Thus, we could consider criminal victimization as violating human rights as well, even though private individuals and not merely the government commit such crimes.[55] As we have discussed extensively already, criminal victimization can produce devastating losses, comparable in some instances to other human rights violations.

In any case, this brief review suggests some substantial challenges to American political and civil rights. Although the American system has promoted many rights and developed a sophisticated judicial system apparently available to vigorously challenge rights violations, many believe that in practice the tendencies toward oppression have significantly outweighed the quest for freedom.

ECONOMIC AND SOCIAL RIGHTS

> *Early on, I discovered the range of injustice*
> *Hunger was not just hunger*
> *But rather the measure of the man.*
>
> PABLO NERUDA

American law and policy provide few economic and social rights. Contrary to some nations that claim they either lack the resources or development to provide "positive" rights, the American system has the means, but not the will. Consequently, despite our apparently humanitarian welfare programs, much research shows the inadequate American protections for health, education, welfare, nutrition, sustenance, shelter, employment, environment, and working and living conditions, despite the nation's obvious capability to do so. A recent study of the quality of life in the world's leading 100 nations ranks the United States 45th, despite its incomparable means, only one notch ahead of the Soviet Union.[56]

In health and the environment, for example, many believe that Americans often suffer from unnecessary surgery, inadequate emergency care, hazardous products, untested drugs and additives, malnutrition, workplace hazards, oil spills, deforestation, strip mining, air and water pollution, nuclear radiation, and environmental diseases such as cancer.[57] As for living standards, the nation's official poverty rate approaches one in five Americans, with some suggesting that as many as half of all Americans lack a minimum decent living standard.[58] Some stress our high unemployment, inadequate education, and substandard housing for many Americans, in general,[59] yet economic destitution affects some groups much more than others, according to many studies. People such as women, Vietnam veterans, immigrants, blacks, Indians, and other minorities, deviants, or unpopular groups can expect to suffer much more significantly from these maladies.[60] Many believe these and other deprivations result primarily from corporate capitalism and our unwillingness to control it. They cite corporate violations not only of living standards for the poor and minorities, but also for most workers, consumers, taxpayers, and communities in general.[61]

This suggests some considerably adverse social conditions and incentives for most Americans, and particularly for the poor. If accurate, and if we have reason to believe that such conditions and incentives provide significant sources of criminal victimization, then these human rights findings have important implications for victimology.

EXPORTING OPPRESSION

> *Those husbands themselves are the ones responsible for the criminal*
> *and terrorist activities against the country, which have obliged the*

*armed forceses to intervene with the efficiency and virility for which
we are known and feared.* ARIEL DORFMAN, Widows

*But it so happens that when the native hears a speech about Western
culture, he pulls out his knife—or at least he makes sure it is within
reach.* FRANTZ FANON, *The Wretched of the Earth*

*I have a daughter/mozambique
I have a son/angola
our twins
salvador and johannesburg/cannot speak
the same language
but we fight the same old men/in the new world*
NTOZAKE SHANGE, *A Daughter's Geography*

Other research has emphasized rights violations outside the United States but within the American sphere of influence. Undoubtedly, some oppression in American client states emerges from within, yet many investigators argue that America has exported much of it.

Much research has connected American policy to political and physical repression, particularly in Asia and Latin America. It has revealed various techniques used by the United States and American multinationals to assist governments and other interests in controlling their populations, including arms sales, economic aid, military and police training (in areas such as surveillance, torture, and counterinsurgency), military hardware and equipment, and even more direct assistance such as election fraud, political assassinations, and American-sponsored overthrows. Beyond its direct political ramifications and human destruction (from things such as political killings and disappearances), fomenting militarism and security states in these nations also wastes valuable resources that could otherwise be used to meet economic and social needs.[62]

Research also suggests the negative effects of American policy on economic and social rights. While the American government and corporations routinely claim they promote economic and social progress in developing nations, much evidence suggests otherwise. Studies have shown the adverse effects of American public and private policy on poverty,[63] hunger and malnutrition,[64] work,[65] land, resources, and environment,[66] and trade and finance.[67]

Finally, research also shows the adverse consequences of American policy on sex, race, ethnicity, and culture in developing nations. Studies reveal direct or indirect support for discrimination, exploitation, and even the systematic destruction of women, certain races, and other minorities (such as supporting South African apartheid and the murder of indigenous Latin American populations.)[68] Other reports show the pervasive effect of American culture and propaganda on altering and destroying local cultures, through television, advertising, consumerism, and so forth.[69]

This evidence, if accurate and representative, says much about human rights violations in the American sphere, yet apparently very little directly relevant to victimology and criminal victimization at home. Yet, indirectly, it may, along with other evidence, seriously question the apparent American devotion to human rights, and bear significantly on at least how victimology regards the state, its legitimacy, and its motivations. Presumably, a disregard for rights abroad suggests a similar disregard at home, thus perhaps questioning our support for state actions in criminal justice.

Who Oppresses

Given traditional human rights conceptions, we can almost identify oppressors by definition. Human rights initiatives typically seek to protect people against government actions—thus, government oppresses. Yet we should be more precise.

In the American context, repression can result from government policies at many levels, from national to local governments. Yet we primarily associate repression with the national government, partly because it controls greater resources and wields greater power. Nevertheless, much repression may come from state governments as well, especially in our federal system, in areas such as criminal justice, for example. Also, while oppression might emerge from deliberate government policies, some might also arise indirectly from official misbehavior and rampant bureaucracy.

We also might well consider other, nongovernmental oppressors. Increasingly, we have begun to recognize the adverse impact of private policies and activities on human rights. If we include criminal victimization in our concept of human rights violations, as perhaps we should, then individual or collective offenders, and not merely governments, also oppress. And, even more significantly, we have also learned about the deprivation of human rights produced by large, private institutions, such as corporations. Thus, multinational corporations, many of which are larger and more powerful politically and economically than most nations, may oppress human rights, too.

Who Suffers Oppression

By now, the victims of oppression should have become fairly obvious. In an important way, oppression affects us all, not only tangibly, but also symbolically as common members of the human race. Some bear its burdens much more than others, however. And they bear striking similarities to the people we have already identified as the primary victims of criminal offenses, which suggests an important relationship and some mutual origins. Oppression most severely affects women, minorities, indigenous populations, deviants, workers, the poor, and the politically unpopular. In other words, it hurts the most powerless people both in America and in its client states.

Where Oppression Occurs

Predictably, oppression occurs mostly where the oppressed largely live and work. Yet these locations often reveal particular social conditions. Those most oppressed largely live in similar locations, characterized by poverty, insecurity, and deprivation. Thus, oppression occurs considerably in these locales; in fact, it significantly contributes to their poverty in the first place. In the United States, many argue that considerable oppression occurs in the streets, private offices, and the workplace, but most happens in depressed ghetto districts populated disproportionately by nonwhites. In turn, according to critics, third world nations, in their subordinate position, suffer American oppression, except for isolated elites. Within those nations, nonwhites, living in much more widespread, extensive, but often similar ghettos, suffer the greatest oppression of all.

THE SOURCES OF OPPRESSION

What is a dream to you, is a nightmare to us.   MALCOLM X

Assuming that at least some of the foregoing oppression actually occurs, what produces it? As with the sources of criminal victimization, many theories abound and each has significantly different implications for victims and their advocates. Some "explain" the violations by denying they occur in the first place, such as when third world dictators deny torture and disappearances, or when the American government and corporations deny complicity or involvement in domestic or third world oppression. Or, as in criminology, oppression is often considered inevitable, with multiple sources, few of which can be remedied.

Otherwise, people usually blame one or more of four sources: (1) institutions, (2) enemies, (3) victims, or (4) the system. Institution blaming claims that violations emerge from inadequate political and economic development. Blaming enemies relies on national security arguments that justify internal crackdowns for self-protection. Victim blaming either accuses victims of subversion or blames personal failures for their victimization. System blaming argues that human rights violations result from structural flaws in the domestic or international political economy and in domestic and international relations.

Institution Blaming

In the American context, many believe we can blame oppression primarily on institutional failures, just as they have been held responsible for criminal victimization. That is, we claim we still have flaws in our welfare system, or gaps in our civil liberties and constitutional protections, or have not yet devised more effective checks on official wrongdoing. This suggests, in other words, that we have been making steady progress, and must merely promote rights vigilantly, against institutional contradictions in the future.

For the developing nations in the American sphere, many believe violations emerge from inadequate development. They claim that oppression inevitably accompanies growth and progress, and that violations will decline over time as they develop greater means and sophistication. Some, advocating a kind of "lifeboat ethics," go further and suggest that the most unfit must be sacrificed in a world of inadequate resources. Others claim they have just been unable so far to exercise firm controls over the excesses of their police and militaries. Finally, others have discovered miraculously the distinction between the "authoritarian," but gradually reformable, nations in the American sphere, and the "totalitarian," and unredeemable, nations in the Soviet sphere.[70]

Politically, institution blaming reinforces existing structures, reassuring us that violatons result only from correctible flaws, which we can reform and eliminate eventually. It suggests that we may be more successful in controlling corporate oppression in the future as well. For victims, institution blaming asks them to wait patiently for future improvements and a less oppressive life. This perspective closely parallels the institution blaming we have already examined for criminal victimization and has similar implications.

Enemy Blaming

Another argument blames internal and external enemies for rights violations. In the American context, for example, officials have long argued that some rights must be sacrificed to protect national security. Thus, government must take actions to directly and indirectly suppress outside infiltration from foreign agents and internal subversion from communists, socialists, demonstrators, labor organizers, and other radicals. It must also maintain the public order to ensure the public peace and efficient government operations.

For the developing nations in the American sphere, many argue similar themes. We usually justify their using oppression to fight communist infiltration from abroad. Thus, they must suppress the free press, students, organizers, labor leaders, and radicals. Often, they must even repress, even indiscriminantly and violently, entire population groups, such as peasants, either because the nation suspects their subversiveness or because it must make sure, just in case. As in America, third world clients frequently claim to be protecting themselves from terrorist groups.

Politically, blaming enemies suggests that oppression will remain only temporarily, until one's enemies can be defeated. Then we can lighten government controls and reallocate resources. For victims, this often asks them not only to have more patience, but to unite to support government attempts to root out internal and external subversion. Although an imperfect comparison, enemy blaming in human rights resembles offender blaming in victimology and criminal victimization. The state often views criminals not merely as criminal lawbreakers but as national threats, and even enemies of the society, which often justifies uncontrolled, perhaps even repressive, police responses.

Victim Blaming

As with criminal victimization, some argue that human rights victims themselves represent an important source of violations. Some blame victims directly, while others suggest their contributory responsibility. In both the American and third world context, many blame victims of political, civil and violent repression for their subversive beliefs and activities, arguing that such victims bring justifiable repression upon themselves. When less inclined to directly blame victims, we then often stress the oppressor-victim relationship, and how victims trigger (if not necessarily deserve) repression. This view strongly resembles the "functional responsibility" argument in victimology.

Alternative versions of the functional responsibility argument have also been offered. One suggests that we might too readily bend to oppression, that it relies in part on public acquiescence, and that we may have ignored viable resistance strategies.[71] The other argues that human rights victims bear some responsibility for enslaving themselves to blind patriotism. This view blames nationalism as the major source of oppression and castigates victims for so willingly and energetically supporting it.[72]

The other major perspective emphasizing victims blames them not for their subversiveness but for their inadequacies. This prevails particularly to justify economic and social oppression. In the American context, we claim that minorities, women, the poor and other oppressed peoples suffer their fate because they work too little, or because they lack intelligence, or cleverness, or drive. In this modern-day version of social Darwinism, deprived people merely fail to take advantage of their opportunities.[73] Similarly, in the third world, we likewise blame lazy victims. In fact, some imply that some cultures may be inherently inadequate or violent, and thus oppression represents a natural condition at least into the near future.[74]

Politically, victim blaming will usually divert attention from institutional or systemic flaws, and from official wrongdoing, and rest responsibility with victims themselves. This view forestalls demands for reform or fundamental change, suggesting that public policy cannot remedy victim characteristics and behavior. For victims, it not only means (like institution and enemy blaming before it) that they must patiently await some relief from oppression, but that they will never significantly enjoy better conditions (i.e., less oppression) until they change themselves and their associates. Victim blaming in human rights bears consierable similarity to victim blaming in victimology.

System Blaming

Finally, some locate the basic sources of oppression in systemic structures. In particular, they find it in nationalism and the structure of international relations, in legal and bureaucratic structures, in American foreign and domestic policy goals, and in international economic dependence, business objectives, and corporate capitalism.

NATIONALISM.   Some blame oppression on the structure of international relations, arguing that ardent nationalism and national competition create the conditions for rights violations. According to this view, our patriotism causes us to justify the internal repression used to fight external threats and encourages people to ignore domestic deprivation and destruction in a "love it or leave it" mentality. People may defend with their lives the very structures that oppress them. National competition justifies the massive concentration of resources for military production, thereby increasing political and civil repression due to war and military rule, and the economic and social oppression caused by inadequate resources for basic needs.[75]

In the American context, fear and machismo help promote gun proliferation domestically, causing considerable criminal victimization as a result. Some find similar sources for the great proliferation of military weapons internationally, this time causing considerable oppression as a result. We cannot easily separate domestic victimization from international oppression, or victimology from human rights.

INSTITUTIONALIZATION.   Others locate oppression in legal and bureaucratic structures. Some believe not only that our legal and administrative structures may periodically malfunction, causing rights violations, but that oppression has been institutionalized fundamentally into those structures. For example, large bureaucracies, by their nature, may inevitably ignore human needs and invoke self-serving rules that routinely alienate and discriminate. The law may institutionalize classism, racism, and sexism, and provide fundamental support for corporate capitalism, a system to which many attribute considerable political and economic oppression.[76]

AMERICAN POLICY. Some believe that oppression emerges from American foreign and domestic goals. Critics, for example, argue that rather than serving the benevolent purposes of making the world safe for democracy abroad, and ensuring pluralistic democracy at home, the American system primarily promotes the domestic and foreign goals of our economic system. At home, although American government may perform other tasks, it may function most fundamentally to remove impediments and provide support for capitalist expansion. This requires government policies such as welfare programs that quell social rebellion against economic oppression, and policies such as legal, ideological, and violent controls to fight political and violent challenges to capitalist survival. Abroad, while American foreign policy may have several objectives, most fundamentally, it may function to promote particular business interests in client states and protect and promote capitalism internationally.[77]

POLITICAL ECONOMY. As already implied, some find the sources of oppression in international capitalism itself. As with "system blamers" in victimology, many believe capitalism inherently erodes democratic procedures and outcomes. Our political economy may not only produce, but actually require, the maldistribution of resources, wealth, and income in society, causing inequalilty and poverty and thus automatically guaranteeing the deprivation of economic and social rights such as health, education, employment, and shelter for much of the population.

Given this economic maldistribution and the impact of economic wealth on political power, corporate capitalism may inevitably prevent effective political democracy. It may promote inequitable access to expression, participation, and influence, cause procedural discrimination, and bias public policy toward special interests, among other things. It may dominate the media, education, and other socializing institutions, thus successfully ingraining the ideology of free market capitalism. And, since corporate interests have predominant, although hardly complete, influence over government actions, we should not be surprised, say the critics, when the state promotes economic policies, and political, control measures (including legal, civil, political, and violent repression) that further corporate goals. But these structural arguments say even more about oppression and American policy toward oppression. Domestically, our political economy may generate resistance that powerholders fear, often unnecessarily (given its meagre power). What opposition they cannot check through welfare lures, or ideological and legal persuasion and restrictions, they may repress physically, if not violently. Thus, critics believe that oppression occurs to restrict opposition to unbearable or objectionable conditions, structurally imposed.

Domestic oppression may have important links to criminal victimization as well. While common or white-collar criminals rarely commit crimes to promote subversive or revolutionary political aims, their acts may nevertheless reflect some level of rebellion, or at least reaction, against social conditions. Criminal victimization may derive primarily from structural sources, and particularly from our prevailing political economy. From this perspective, the conditions it produces (such as poverty, inequality, alienation, discrimination, and competition) may not only reflect social oppression, but also the basis for substantial criminal victimization (in response), either from a sense of accommodation, frustration, or survival. If we expand our human rights conceptions to include violations produced by individuals and institutions (and not merely states), then when criminal victimization results, it too causes oppression. A dialectical relationship emerges. If for no other reason than this, we might well further study the interaction between crime and oppression, through some fusion of victimology and human rights.

THE AMERICAN SPHERE.   Abroad, critics argue that the same politico-economic system causes oppression, both politically and economically, in the American sphere. But, beyond what violations our economic system might cause alone, American foreign and corporate policy may intensify the oppression. Both may operate primarily to promote capitalism (sometimes against imaginary communist threats) and particular business interests. Both seem to seek pliable, responsive, tightly controlled client states, willing to further oppress their populations to fight communism and promote a "favorable business climate" for American corporate enterprise.[78]

International economic dependence may force client states to rely on their American benefactors. In exchange for their loyalty, so say the critics, American government provides third world leaders with the tools of military and police oppression such as training, equipment, personnel, and resources, with which pliant military dictators or receptive civilian leaders trade their public's interest for American foreign and corporate policy objectives: namely, to be fervently anti-communist, to strongly promote capitalism, and to ensure attractive business conditions for American capital and production.[79]

IMPLICATIONS. Politically, system blaming means that reducing oppression will come not by blaming victims, or by first fighting external threats, or by piecemeal institutional reform, but only through fundamental political and economic change. If part of the transition to reducing criminal victimization requires domestic gun control, then part of the transition to reducing oppression will require international arms control. For victims of oppression, it suggests that they must choose between living in perpetual (or only very slowly receding) oppression and participating in a fundamental structural transformation based both on short-run protective strategies and on long-run, alternative goals, precisely the choice structural theorists pose for crime victims.

THE IMPACT OF OPPRESSION

There is no suffering, no torture anywhere in the world which does not affect our everyday lives.　　　　　ALBERT CAMUS

Each indignity visited upon a human being, each torture, is irreducibly singular and inexpiable, yet everytime a human being is flogged, stoned, deprived of self-respect, a specific black hole opens in the fabric of life.　　　　　GEORGE STEINER

Sometimes I feel so bad I ask myself who in the world have I murdered?　　　　　ALICE WALKER

As with criminal victimization, oppression imposes many costs, and oftentimes much more severely and pervasively. Thus, we must examine the financial, physical, property, and human costs of oppression. In particular, oppression can produce the same feelings of guilt, fear, and blame generated by criminal victimization and we must consider those repercussions as well. As with crime victims, victims of oppression may respond to their victimization in many ways, both individually and collectively; we must analyze that behavior as well. We have considerably less information about the effects of oppression to examine compared to the volume of victimological materials. Here, as in many other areas of future research on oppression, the victimology literature may serve as an important guide.

The Costs of Oppression

Sporadically, we have begun to quantify oppression. For example, we know that at least 20,000 people disappeared during the Argentine military regime in the 1970s, and probably another 6,000 under similar circumstances in Chile. In the United States, for example, we hear estimates of the total homeless ranging between one-half

and two and one-half million people, with as many as 4,000 per-
ishing each year.[80] Nevertheless, to quantify oppression's overall costs
would be an overwhelming task. For now, we can largely make only
qualitative observations.

The denial of human rights imposes both tangible and intangible
costs for individuals, groups, and sometimes entire peoples. Unlike
with criminal victimization, where states and corporations may be
victimized (along with individuals), here states and corporations do
the victimizing. As with criminal victimization, however, governments, and especially corporations, can gain much from oppression.
They achieve political and economic control, promote personal and
ideological goals, and reap significant profits, while bearing few losses
or sacrifices.

In any case, as with criminal victimization, individuals must bear
oppression's financial and property costs. Yet, from oppression, victims may have to carry those costs permanently, for life. People unnecessarily denied a decent standard of living, for example, will be
perpetually derived of finances and property, which in turn will help
deprive them of much else. A people denied their right to a clean,
natural environment may not only find themselves deprived but future generations deprived as well. Victims of oppression must bear
injuries, and frequently death, from torture, murders, disappearances, poverty, diseases, homelessness, ignorance, hopelessness,
powerlessness, joblessness or unsafe work, unsafe products, and
medical practices or no medical care at all.

The Psychological Effects of Oppression

While we have researched oppression's symptoms considerably, we
know little about its general psychological effects. Perhaps we have
best begun to understand those effects, not from traditional scien-
tific research, but rather from first-person accounts, such as Elie
Wiesel's *Night*,[81] Jacobo Timerman's *Prisoner Without A Name, Cell
Without A Number*,[82] Richard Wright's *Black Boy*,[83] Carolina Maria de
Jesus' *Child of the Dark*,[84] Claude Brown's *Manchild in the Promised
Land*,[85] Dick Gregory's *Nigger*,[86] Maya Angelou's *I Know Why the Caged
Bird Sings*,[87] Paule Marshall's *The Chosen Place, The Timeless People*,[88]
and Toni Morrison's *The Bluest Eye*.[89]

Research suggests the psychological impact of many individual
symptoms of oppression. We have examined the effects of ignorance, illness, workplace alienation, poverty, inequality, powerlessness, homelessness, and many other marks of oppression.[90] Yet perhaps our most extensive research emphasizes the survivors of Nazi
Germany and other captives.[91] These and other studies, some done
by victimologists, have revealed the wide array of emotional reactions, including guilt, fear, rage, horror, dread, revenge, mourning,

lost or intensified identity, empathy, and ambivalence. As with crime victims, victims of oppression often blame themselves for their suffering, even when they clearly bear no responsibility.

Individual and Collective Behavior

Oppression, like criminal victimization, produces various behavioral responses, from rebellion on the one extreme, to resistance, submission, accommodation, and support, on the other. Some have examined the criteria determining whether or not victims submit or rebel. Others have analyzed its effects on individual family life. A few have examined the "temptations" of oppression in exchange for a certain kind of predictability or security.[92]

As with criminal victimization, some victims of oppression may respond by doing nothing, usually because they have no other recourse. Others will respond individually either to repel or accommodate oppression. Still others will organize on some level for their mutual defense, if not for some fundamental change. Their response, as with reactions to criminal victimization, may as easily be counterproductive as useful to escaping oppression. Nevertheless, these responses go to the heart of any victimological or human rights advocacy we pursue since external concern and assistance will likely fail without capturing the "hearts and minds" of the oppressed. As we shall examine subsequently, designing measures for victim advocacy and protection must do more than create programs and remedial or legal structures—they must beckon victims to help liberate themselves.

VICTIMS AND HUMAN RIGHTS ENFORCEMENT

While crime victims often focus as much on their own influence and participation in law enforcement as on its outcomes and effectiveness, victims of oppression want protection more than anything else. Relatively speaking, both the domestic American and international mechanisms for protecting human rights and preventing oppression have been notably underdeveloped compared to domestic American criminal law enforcement. Since few victims of oppression have any access to protective mechanisms, questions of victims' role, participation, and influence rarely emerge. If and when human rights victims gradually gain greater access to enforcement mechanisms, we will begin being able to assess their impact, much as we have already examined the effects of crime victims on criminal law enforcement.

For now, we have been emphasizing better, usually legal, structures to grant relief from oppression. As with criminal victimization, institutional reforms and legal mechanisms have predominated over policies that aim directly at the oppression's sources, which have been relatively ignored. In other words, mostly we have sought piecemeal and temporary remedies for victims following their victimization, instead of pursuing policies, structures, and systems that might prevent oppression in the first place.

Enforcement Mechanisms

Aside from limited laws and covenants that identify human rights and exhort governments and their organizations to respect them, various institutional mechanisms try to actually promote enforcement. They range from international to regional to national in structure.

Internationally, we find that the United Nations, including its General Assembly, Security Council, Economic and Social Council, Human Rights Commission, and the International Court, offers some limited protections.[93] These mechanisms mainly respond to violations of the Universal Declaration of Human Rights, specialized covenants, and separate covenants on political/civil and economic/social rights. Regionally, the mechanisms include the Nuremberg Trials in Europe,[94] and the human rights commissions and courts of Europe[95] and those emerging in Africa and Asia. Most relevant to the American context, the Interamerican Commission and Court on Human Rights respond to violations of the American Declaration of the Rights and Duties of Man and the American Convention on Human Rights.[96]

Other attempts at promoting human rights occur through unilateral foreign policymaking. In the American context, the United States has signed the Helsinki Accords with Europe and the Soviet Union and has passed legislation to restrict aid to human rights violators in the Americas and elsewhere. Domestically, we find possible relief for American rights violations in the American court system. At the very least, American courts have the power to enforce rights recognized by the U.S. Constitution and those adopted through foreign and international treaties. Our judiciary could also enforce rights through invoking international customary law. Compared to crime victims, victims of oppression seem (at least formally) to have many more mechanisms from which to choose to seek protection, although we could well begin to use regional and international mechanisms against criminal as well as other victimization.

The Impact of Enforcement

Except in the domestic American context where victims of political and civil rights violations may bring civil suits to domestic courts, actual victims rarely appear physically before the other mechanisms we have discussed. Thus, instead of examining enforcement's impact on victim needs, problems, roles or attitudes, we will only consider its effect on outcomes—that is, on providing effective relief. Research has shown very disappointing results. Access has been minimal, many cases have been impeded, few have been won, and practically none have actually been implemented. Thus, even in providing remedies after violations (much less prevention), the available mechanisms have had little success. Moreover, they have largely ignored nongovernmental violators such as multinational corporations, whose activities have escaped largely unscathed.[97]

In the American context, some research suggests that neither American foreign policy nor domestic courts have offered effective relief. In fact, both mechanisms may do more to intensify human rights violations than to remedy or prevent them. On the negative side, many suggest that American foreign policy creates the conditions for oppression and then specifically adds its power to promote violations. As for domestic courts, many find them bound by laws that institutionalize rights violations such as racial, sexual, and class discrimination.

On the positive side, even if we attribute good intentions to American foreign policy and domestic courts, some still find little effective relief. Cutoffs of American aid and adverse publicity against human rights violators, much less "quiet diplomacy," have only superficially reduced oppression. While some grant the importance of many landmark civil rights court decisions, many nevertheless find effective protection often considerably lacking.

Critics cite inadequate access and ineffective compliance after court decisions as major problems. American courts offer to protect only a relatively narrow array of rights in the first place. The American human rights conception, as reflected in our Bill of Rights, emphasizes political and civil rights while largely excluding economic, social, and cultural rights. Since the United States has not ratified most of the international human rights covenants, including their much fuller array of protections, they do not automatically apply in American courts. The demands about prisoner's rights raised by the Attica inmates several years ago, for example, came directly from international covenants and standards,[98] yet not only did we ignore them legally, some believe we violently murdered many of those who invoked them. While American courts could apply international covenants domestically, even without our formal ratification, as a part of international customary law, they have practically never done so.[99]

In sum, human rights enforcement has much yet to accomplish, particularly if it relies only on formal, legal mechanisms that "force" nations and institutions not to violate rights, instead of also correcting oppression's root sources. Human rights enforcement has undoubtedly been even less effective for victims of oppression than criminal law enforcement has been for crime victims. Nevertheless, crime victims might well benefit from human rights enforcement, particularly if regionally or internationally administered. Enforcement mechanisms that do not rely on nation states can only help victims of both crime and oppression since national governments may contribute most to producing or facilitating both kinds of victimization in the first place.[100] Right or wrong, these possible new connections between victimology and human rights deserve our attention.

HUMAN RIGHTS ADVOCACY

We victims and victimizers, we're part of the same humanity, colleagues in the same endeavor to prove the existence of ideologies, feelings, heroic deeds, religions, obsessions. And the rest of humanity . . . What are they engaged in?　　　　　　JACOBO TIMERMAN

All I ask is that, in the midst of a murderous world, we agree to reflect on murder and to make a choice.　　　　　　ALBERT CAMUS

Problems and Needs

Since victims of oppression do not routinely (and often never) encounter an enforcement process, we can speak little about their problems due to formal procedures, as we have with crime victims. For victims of oppression, the major problem is simply being oppressed, and their major need is some remedy and relief. A few approaches to human rights advocacy help victims cope with victimization after the fact. Other approaches seek some procedural reform to promote better protections and remedies. Still others propose structural alternatives that often aim at oppression's sources.

Approaches to Advocacy

SERVICES AND COMPENSATION.　Compared to what has recently become available for crime victims, victims of oppression have little access to services and compensation. Nevertheless, some help does exist. To begin with, some nongovernmental human rights groups, such as Amnesty International and the International Committee of the Red Cross, and intergovernmental organizations such as the United Nations High Commissioner for Refugees, provide some semblance of crisis intervention for individual violations. The organization will immediately intervene, offering support to friends and family of repressed individuals and often directly to victims as well. Church groups will often work in oppressed communities to improve conditions. Other organizations, such as holocaust support groups, still exist to help victims after their ordeal. The International Rehabilitation and Research Center for Torture Victims has recently opened in Copenhagen, Denmark, providing medical and psychological services and research.

Even these few services largely reach only the isolated, individual victim. None have aimed at the much larger human rights problem: large groups of people systematically repressed. Finally, victims rarely get compensated for their losses. Some reparations have been paid through the Nuremburg trials to survivors of Nazi Germany, and Americans can attempt to sue officials for denying their rights, but few recover.

PROCEDURAL REFORMS. Both governments and nongovernmental organizations have promoted administrative and legislative reforms to provide better enforcement and greater rights. For enforcement, reforms give better access to individual and public petitions and suits (by liberalizing the sovereign immunity protections of offending governments), make nongovernmental institutions such as multinational corporations subject to enforcement, and enhance investigatory and enforcement powers.

To promote greater rights, nongovernmental groups, community organizations, and even some governments have lobbied for new legislation. Domestically, pressure from groups such as the American Civil Liberties Union (ACLU) and the National Association for the Advancement of Colored People (NAACP) for civil rights legislation and judicial decisions has extended rights protections at least formally, and reforms such as the Freedom of Information Act have perhaps helped check arbitrary government surveillance of individuals and groups. Internationally, advocates have promoted new, comprehensive human rights covenants, or specialized covenants for particular rights or victims, such as crime vicitims. These initiatives help promote greater rights and protections and greater implementation powers.

NONGOVERNMENTAL ADVOCACY. Aside from sporadically providing services and lobbying for new rights and better enforcement, nongovernmental organizations, both domestic and international, use many other tactics to help the oppressed. Particularly in recent years, many human rights groups, large and small, generalized and specialized, have arisen, producing what can only be called a "human rights movement."

These groups, emerging from professional organizations in fields such as law, medicine, theology, and publishing, and from numerous other specialized organizations, have acted individually and jointly to promote victim interests. Beyond merely relying on official enforcement mechanisms, most human rights groups use many other tactics, particularly investigations and reports, publicity and external political pressure.[101] Institutes, conferences, and clearinghouses have also proliferated which, along with other publicity, attempt to bring human rights more centrally into the public's consciousness.

STRUCTURAL ALTERNATIVES. Some victims and advocates have found existing mechanisms very inadequate for providing relief or protection. Consequently, they have promoted alternatives, most of which aim directly at oppression's sources, and much less at providing remedial relief after the fact. They respond to victimization not with submission, or even merely avoidance, but rather with resistance, if not rebellion.

Domestically, many have sought alternatives to official procedures for fighting oppresson. Most have centered on the recent proliferation of American community organizations.[102] Ranging from welfare to tenants to feminist to hunger organizations, they have pursued a kind of "popular justice" locally, using unconventional, direct action tactics to build movements, resist oppression, and promote rights.[103] Some have taken another step—arming themselves. Several years ago, for example, the Black Panthers armed for what they claimed was self-defense against police repression. Others, more modestly, have promoted alternative structures such as neighborhood courts, to bring power and access to local communities against governments and large corporations.

Internationally, advocates have pursued many alternatives as well. Some nongovernmental organizations, for example, promote much more than merely individual cases and rights, by examining oppression's sources and proposing fundamental alternatives. Organizations such as the Movement for a New Society,[104] Oxfam America,[105] and the World Policy Institute[106] in the United States, the Center for the Study of Developing Societies in India,[107] the Sarvodaya movement in Sri Lanka,[108] and the Bariloche Institute[109] in Argentina have promoted international, grass roots movements for human rights, based on alternative structures and values. A large gathering of nongovernmental leaders, groups, and national liberation organizations created the first popular human rights covenant in Algiers: the Universal Declaration of the Rights of Peoples. Both the Bertrand Russell Peace Foundation in England and the Lelio Basso International Foundation for the Rights and Liberation of Peoples in Italy have held numerous Popular Tribunals around the world to hold governments accountable for oppression.

Some have worked to help communities make international connections and gain new consciousness, empowerment, and control against oppression.[110] Others have promoted schemes for value transformation,[111] for local self-reliance,[112] global equity,[113] or "horizontal communities."[114] Some church workers have promoted so-called "liberation theology," emphasizing popular, community empowerment against oppressive structures.[115] Some national liberation movements have followed similar paths.[116] More broadly, many in the developing world seek a new international economic and information order that helps redistribute political and economic power and resources between the developed and the developing nations.[117] Still others have gone further, convinced they must resort to violence to fight their unrelenting oppression. A few create armed revolutions and topple entire governments, such as in Nicaragua.[118]

These responses obviously do not guarantee the absence of oppression in the future, but they have been united by many common goals, designed to strike at its sources. This kind of advocacy, both domestically and internationally, directly opposes authoritarianism, centralization, bureaucracy, nationalism, and corporate capitalism, seeking political and economic democracy instead.

INTERNATIONAL PROTECTIONS. Obviously, human rights initiatives emphasize international protections, unlike for criminal victimization which has only recently taken such steps. Whether or not international protections have yet effectively helped victims, victimology might well consider the major reasons for the global approach. Human rights advocates have severely questioned the will of domestic governments, as the major perpetrators, to effectively prevent oppression. Advocates also doubt whether governments will provide effective relief even for violations they did not directly cause. Also, nations and nationalism may represent two of the major sources of oppression, directly and indirectly, by definition. We may need an international criminal court to help avoid the adverse effects of national competition on rights.[119]

In victimology, similar observations have been made. While governments seem less directly responsible (than individuals) for criminal victimization (except for what they commit themselves), they may be indirectly responsible for creating conditions conducive to victimization. We may well doubt whether governments will effectively provide for crime victims, in any case, given the lowly position and power most victims hold. In response, some victimologists have condemned nations and nationalism as counterproductive to crime victim interests, and called for international protections.[120]

The Impact of Advocacy

Much has been done, particularly in the last decade, to promote the interests of human rights victims and much has been achieved. New rights and protections, new enforcement and investigatory mechanisms, and a new global consciousness have all arisen from human rights advocacy. Many people have been relieved from one form of oppression or another, if not protected from future violations. Many human rights victims credit advocates with their release or protection, and some national human rights records have improved.

Despite these good efforts, human rights advocacy has been unable to cope with the steady rise, generally, in violations. Victims can avail themselves of few services and reparations. Procedural reforms and new rights protections rarely produce the effective enforcement they seek. Structural alternatives have made some progress, but have not yet captured most people's imaginations nor significantly affected current violations. Even nongovernmental organizations, which United Nations officials find indispensable to their work, and which have much more success comparatively than government efforts, still face overwhelming obstacles.

To begin with, nongovernmental groups have incredibly meager resources, which make their limited success all that much more remarkable.[121] Not only must human rights groups operate with insufficient funding, they must also compete with organizations having vastly greater resources, such as governments, corporations, and interest groups that oppose human rights initiatives. In the U.S. Congress, for example, relatively small human rights groups struggle to compete against corporations, business associations, offending foreign governments (in the American sphere), and their public relations organizations for stronger legislation connecting American foreign policy to human rights.[122]

Finally, some believe that most human rights groups, for all their worthy work on one level, largely miss the real world of oppression. They take a piecemeal, individualized approach based on the most publicized cases, which ignores much more pervasive, collective repression and misconstrues the human rights problem in the first place. It may pursue human rights violations more as separate and isolated incidents unconnected to an overall pattern of oppression, thus ignoring their social and structural roots.[123]

In sum, as with advocacy for crime victims, human rights advocacy has done much, but achieved much less than proponents have hoped. Like crime victims, most victims of oppression remain victimized or subject to future victimization, much as if victim advocacy had not even existed. Official initiatives have produced few results, and thus many have turned to nongovernmental, and even structural alternatives that show much more potential yet still linger very far from their goals.

The Functions of Human Rights Advocacy

Given the enormous efforts at human rights advocacy, we might wonder why initiatives have not had more success. As suggested, the problems may lie with intractable nationalism, ineffective enforcement, inadequate resources, a formidable competition, and even perhaps a failure to aim at oppression's structural sources. Yet, as with advocacy for crime victims, some of the problem might lie in the competing functions victim advocacy serves. Competing professional and entrepreneurial motives may be less significant in human rights work, although some find that a lucrative American arms trade (that helps repress developing peoples) provides tempting profits. Institutional motives, such as the inherent organizational inertia toward growth, development, and new tasks, may help explain the expansion of many institutions into human rights work, but hardly appear inconsistent with victim goals. Political motives, however, do offer a significant, competing purpose for advocacy in human rights.

We cannot assume that all those advocating human rights either really seek those rights or have no complementary purpose that puts real rights progress secondary. Some organizations will overtly oppose human rights initiatives, although with their elevation in the public's consciousness in recent years, blatant opposition has become very rare. Other institutions may oppose or use human rights covertly.

Many nations, for example, vigorously work in international organizations such as the United Nations to promote human rights, ultimately by signing international rights covenants. Yet those same nations simultaneously flagrantly violate human rights at home even as they champion human rights abroad, and show no signs of changing their future policies simply because they have approved the covenants. Some multinational corporations have condemned repression, yet their pro-victim stance seems designed mostly to help avoid further attacks on their own human rights records.

In the American sphere, nations such as El Salvador and the Philippines, for example, have rather strong records on ratifying international documents, yet horrendous records in practice. Not all nations that sign covenants fail to take human rights seriously and we ought to encourage many more ratifications, but some nations advocate rights more for favorable publicity than to provide actual protections. Finally, many believe that the American government, as in most other nations, violates human rights domestically while purporting to promote human rights abroad. Recent initiatives such as the Carter policy may have had much more to do with rescuing America's bruised reputation after Vietnam and Watergate and with seeking leverage in ideological disputes with the Soviet Union than with substantively promoting human rights.[124]

These cases suggest that human rights advocacy, similar to crime victim advocacy, may have important, but less obvious, political purposes beyond promoting victim interests. While we attribute few ulterior motives to most human rights organizations, we cannot say as much for the few corporate initiatives and many government actions taken ostensibly to promote human rights. As with advocacy for crime victims, human rights advocacy may have more to do with the symbolic advantages of championing rights than with seriously pursuing any substantive protections or fundamentally eradicating oppression in the first place.

CONCLUSION

The foregoing analysis suggests why we should further explore the relationship between victimology and human rights inquiry. To begin with, our review of crime victims and victimology, and human rights victims and human rights shows considerable similarities, and a few differences, from which we might learn. Indeed, the comparative data alone may warrant connecting the two fields.

In the last fifteen years, for example, both a (crime) victims movement and a human rights movement have arisen, the former promoted more through conservative politics, and the latter more through liberal politics. Both victimology and human rights inquiries, at least in the American context, have used narrow, and perhaps distorted, definitions of criminal victimization and oppression, respectively, thus excluding many victims. Officials may have also used selective definitions, buttressed by media and other reinforcements, to pursue ideological objectives such as legitimizing state actions. In other words, the state's reaction to crime and oppression may reveal an overall pattern of response that may place victims secondary to other objectives.[125]

Crime and oppression share some strikingly similar trends and characteristics in their victimization level, who gets victimized, where, and even by whom. When identifying victimization's sources, victimology and human rights inquiries have both blamed administrative institutions and victims, much less so than systemic structures. Similar financial, physical, and psychological costs beset both crime victims and victims of oppression, although they may linger much longer, if not indefinitely, for the latter.

Psychologically, both kinds of victimization promote self-blame on the one hand and outrage on the other, and a range of behavioral responses from passive to active, and from individualized to collective. In enforcement, victims of oppression have an even smaller role than crime victims, but either way, neither receive very much relief or protection. Victim advocates have also vigorously championed the rights and interests of victims of both crime and oppression, using some similar strategies and producing some significant gains. Yet advocacy has reduced victimization only marginally, perhaps due in part to its competing motives.

Beyond these comparisons, which may suggest to victimologists the new directions that could result from relating criminal victimization to human rights, we have much else to gain.[126] We can examine existing overlaps between victimology and human rights inquiries, such as the *rights* of crime victims in victimology and the *crimes* against humanity in human rights. We can expand these concepts to provide crime victims with more rights, and victims of oppression with greater protections. The two fields can gain individually and mutually through their interactions.[127]

Human rights inquiry, for example, can adopt victimology's scientific methodology, along with a more developed set of theories and research questions. It might learn about more effective protective mechanisms and how to involve victims more in enforcement. Victimology, on the other hand, can benefit from developing more international standards and protections for victims. Its emphasis on crime diverts victimology's attention toward individual offenders and away from government. Taking a more human rights approach will bring the government back into victimology's purview and allow us to consider the "political victims" the state may generate.[128]

Together, both victimology and human rights inquiry gain from developing new definitions. If we experience even only a portion of the alleged human rights violations in the American sphere, it still considerably challenges state legitimacy. It may well force victimologists to reconsider the official definitions they have thus far largely accepted. A human rights framework can help victimology decide which other victims, for example, to include. Likewise, human rights inquiries can expand our concept of crimes against humanity and consider how crime victims might also be human rights victims. These redefinitions and revelations, for both victimology and human rights, will broaden our rights and our crimes, yet they will be even more valuable for helping us understand and pursue victimization's sources.

We have some reason to believe that crime "causes" oppression. Directly, crime creates oppression by fostering fear and insecurity, causing psychological wounds, and restricting freedoms. Indirectly, a criminal society may create an atmosphere that justifies unrestrained police behavior, which oppresses victims and the public as well as offenders. In turn, oppression may create criminal victimization since it helps produce desperate circumstances, political and economic inequalities, and a climate of violence. Taken together, they let us see that even if victims may sometimes contribute to their own victimization, crime and oppression arise more significantly either from common institutions, which fail to prevent it or, more likely, from structural sources, which cause it in the first place. Within victimology and human rights, we can pursue what John Rawls has called "the primary subject of justice . . . the ways in which the major social institutions distribute fundamental rights and duties."

Finally, connecting victimology and human rights inquiry reveals their political relationship. We have discovered several common patterns of official response to both crime victims and victims of oppression. We might well suspect that the most effective means for significantly reducing both kinds of victimization will emerge from common political initiatives, directed toward many common targets. As we continue exploring these relationships, we may find that victimology and human rights increasingly converge. Under its original definition as a science that studies all victims, victimology could well encompass human rights. As a "new" victimology, it would represent not only a much stronger science, but also provide a much more powerful tool of social justice analysis by which to examine all victims and victimization.

9

The Politics of Victimization

*My point is not to grieve for the victims and
denounce the executioners. Those tears, that anger,
cast into the past, deplete our moral energy for the
present. And the lines are not that clear. In the long
run, the oppressor is also a victim. In the short run
. . . the victims, themselves desperate and tainted
with the culture that oppresses them, turn on other
victims.*

HOWARD ZINN, *A People's History of the U.S.*

*All people who live subject to other people's laws are
victims. People who break laws out of greed,
frustration, or vengeance are victims. People who
overturn laws in order to replace them with their own
laws are victims. . . . We outlaws, however, live
beyond the law. We don't merely live beyond the
letter of the law—many businessmen, most
politicians and all cops do that—we live beyond the
spirit of the law. In a sense, then, we live beyond
society. We have a common goal, that goal is to turn
the tables on the nature of society. When we succeed,
we raise the exhilaration content of the universe. We
even raise it a little bit when we fail.*

TOM ROBBINS, *Still Life with Woodpecker*

*The struggle of man against power is the struggle of
memory against forgetting.*

MILAN KUNDERA, *The Book of Laughter and Forgetting*

Victims have progressed significantly in the last quarter century, but
they have not yet shaken their second-class status. When victimized, they lack confidence in receiving the aid they need, and for
good reason—they often must tolerate inadequate services, cultural
insensitivity, political insignificance, and official maltreatment. The
many worthy initiatives for victim rights and services have provided
valuable help, yet have been impeded by numerous obstacles. Most
important, we have been very unsuccessful in preventing victimization in the first place.

To understand the barriers to victim advancement, we must examine the victim's political role. We have frequently suggested the
relationship between victims and politics. Now we can summarize
them generally. We will examine the impact of politics on the rise
of victims and victimology, on creating our social reality of victimization, on the sources and impact of victimization, on law enforcement, on victim advocacy, and on human rights. Victims cannot be
understood apart from their political power or their position and
function generally in our political economy.

To prevent victimization, and to further victim rights, we might
well consider new vehicles for increasing victims' political influence.
As an applied science, victimology might also consider political influences on its work. Our quest both to better understand victims
and to promote their interests may depend substantially on victimology's embracing some new directions, preferably a "new" victimology, encompassing both criminal victimization and human rights
violations.

POLITICS, SCIENCE, AND POWER

*In any society, the dominant groups are the ones with the most to
hide about how a society works. Very often, therefore, truthful
analyses are bound to have a critical ring, to seem like postures
rather than objective statements. . . . For all students of human
society, sympathy with the victims of historical processes and
skepticism about the victor's claims provide essential safeguards
against being taken in by the dominant mythology. A scholar who
tries to be objective needs these feelings as part of his (sic) working
equipment.*   BARRINGTON MOORE

The rise of victims and victimology has reflected numerous political clashes. Victims first began losing their equal status and prominent criminal justice role in conflicts with the emerging power of the state. As governments took greater interest and received increasing benefits from controlling law enforcement and the definition of deviance, the victim's role receded. Victims remained largely powerless for centuries, until the mid-twentieth century when they gained new influence. Their rise corresponded to post-World War II humanitarian initiatives, to the vigorous organization and lobbying of victim advocates, and mostly to the conservative politics of law and order that have dominated America since the late 1960s.

In our conservative, success-oriented society, victims have often suffered not only as crime victims, but also as cultural victims. This has made their resurgence more difficult, yet ultimately their rise may depend mostly on their political functions. Insufficiently supported and promoted, victims will probably achieve little political power and substantive relief. Yet, even when relatively influential, their real power may depend just as much on their political uses as on their political victories. In other words, victims may perform certain functions that governments now find valuable to promote.

Research suggests that victims may function to bolster state legitimacy, to gain political mileage, and to enhance social control. By championing the victim's cause, government may deflect criticism about ineffective law enforcement, and portray itself as the friend of victims, instead of as possibly their greatest threat. Victims may provide considerable political advantage for officials seeking re-election and political support, such as by sponsoring popular victim compensation programs. And victims may help promote greater social control, not benevolently as an age-old formula for reducing victimization,[1] but rather as a rationale for enhancing state power.

Victims have risen partly through some progressive initiatives taken by the women's and human rights movements, and related efforts, but mostly from the hardline, conservative law-and-order backlash against defendants' rights and rampant crime. Most pro-victim policies have been promoted in the name of reducing defendants' rights and enhancing criminal punishments. In fact, national, conservative support would likely have been even greater had it not been impeded by other, conservative themes of fiscal austerity and state's rights.[2] Since 1980, the hardline efforts for victims have redoubled.

Victimology seems less directly affected by these political developments, yet their influence shows nevertheless. Begun as a broad, humanitarian concern for human rights and all victims, victimology has evolved very narrowly. It quickly abandoned all victims for an almost exclusive emphasis on crime victims. It has almost invariably accepted state definitions of victimization. And it has often championed victim policies invoked to strengthen government power and weaken defendants' rights.

Nevertheless, some important countertrends have emerged as well. Our emphasis on victim precipitation has made it more difficult to readily blame offenders for the entire crime problem, although it has not helped victims much. Victimology has also helped reveal the failure of get-tough, crime control policies. We have been warned about the dangers of a conservative mentality in victimology.[3] Some have promoted victim rights before the United Nations, fitting them into the international human rights tradition.[4] Finally, a few others have urged us to transcend state-defined boundaries of victims and victimization, both in our advocacy and our victimology.[5] Emilio Viano suggests, for example, that

> The problems researched, the way in which the research is conducted, and the strategies devised to reach a solution tend either to support and reinforce society's status quo or undermine it. In this sense, social research is inescapably political, although usually (and ironically) only the research aimed at changing the system is so labelled.[6]

The victim's evolution thus far reflects more than merely happenstance and good intentions; it shows the interplay of science and politics. The victim's future will likewise depend on political choices and political power.

POLITICS AND SOCIAL REALITY

Our understanding of victims and victimization may be shaped by forces beyond merely objective circumstances. Some argue that we often conceptualize a social reality of victimization that not only misleads us, but which may serve various political purposes. We may have absorbed misconceptions not unrelated to special interests and state objectives. We have developed stereotypes about who victimizes, who gets victimized, and what victimizations provide the greatest harms. Based on these conceptions, we often fear those people who objectively may represent much less of a threat than others who we relatively ignore.

Some believe our limited social reality of victimization reflects a worldview almost perfectly suited to maintaining existing political, social, and economic arrangements. As such, it may serve as an ideology, reflecting certain beliefs, and having certain goals and functions. That ideology's development and inculcation may begin with how we define victimization in the first place. The legislative process, reflecting special interests more than general public interests, may selectively define the criminal law, ignoring many harmful actions and actors while encompassing others, and even criminalizing many acts that have no apparent victims at all. Official definitions may help ingrain stereotypes and perceptions publicly, and help control certain populations much more than others. Our definitions, often reflecting an imbalance of political power, seem to emphasize lower-class wrongdoing while largely ignoring much more harmful upper-class wrongdoing. Overcriminalization, wrought by double standards, extends law and enforcement into the lives of (again, mostly lower-class) people who produce no victims, and yet who get defined as criminal and become subject to greater social controls.

Likewise, measuring crime and conveying victimization publicly may also reflect prevailing political configurations. We may rely on official indicators that only selectively portray the crime problem and that respond to crime waves that have less to do with crime levels and more with organizational and political needs. Besides our misleading measures, our concept of victimization gets further distorted by its media portrayal. The media's concept of victimization seems to faithfully reproduce official definitions and measures; provide superficial, misleading, and sensationalist accounts; convey false stereotypes and scapegoats; and ingrain and intensify an astounding level of social violence. The media may inculcate, in other words, a social reality of victimization almost perfectly suited to promote not only its own private and public goals, but also state objectives. Among other things, this may help intensify a considerable public fear of crime and help justify enhanced state control and power and reduced rights and freedoms. By breeding insecurity, it may promote the public's "escape from freedom."[7]

In this ideological process, the victim may play a considerable role. Especially in recent years, the political use of victims has helped promote government power and justify our hardline response. Victims could as easily represent the state's failure, but by coopting victims and the victim movement, the state may use them to portray its apparent concern and promote its legitimacy instead. As such, victims may help perform an ideological and political function, justifying state actions and deflecting attention from the interests it promotes and the much more extensive harms it commits. Our social reality profoundly affects our responses to public problems.

THE POLITICAL ECONOMY
OF HELPLESSNESS

Victims face many problems, such as how to take precautionary measures, how to cope with victimization's financial and psychological effects, and how to avoid further victimization in law enforcement. Victimologists and victim advocates have worked hard to eliminate these problems, yet we have done comparatively little to solve the victim's greatest dilemma: how to escape victimization in the first place. We refer not merely to protective devices or behavior, but rather to the sources of victimization, whose elimination or reduction will be the only really effective protection against crime. We have paid relatively little attention to victimization's sources because, like most criminologists, we often assume that we either can never know the causes, or that we cannot remedy them in any case.

Yet this may be more a political decision, unwittingly or not, than a scientific conclusion. Our futility may reflect a "political economy of helplessness" more than objective barriers to reducing victimization. Some believe that we may fail to examine sources, and take action against them less because we cannot do so, and more because to do so would challenge American mainstream life,[8] particularly our political economy. We must examine the political uses of various crime causation theories and their impact on victims.

Our prevailing crime theories blame regulations, criminals, or victims. We stress either institution blaming or offender blaming or victim blaming. Intentionally or not, each one may amount much more to "system defending." Institution blaming finds crime's sources in regulatory failures, particularly in law enforcement and criminal justice. Politically, it pleads for greater resources, efficiency, and power for law enforcement, and asks victims to be more cooperative and supportive, but not to expect much against the intractable crime problem. Offender blaming finds crime's sources in the inherent traits either of all people or in a select group of evil people. Politically, it suggests that we can only be more vigilant in identifying, punishing, and isolating the dangerous criminal element. Victims must constantly be on their guard and help authorities root out the threat. Victim blaming finds crime's sources in victim traits and behavior, and warns victims to reform their precipitatory habits. Politically, it diverts the blame for crime onto its victims, and implores them to change their behavior to avoid crime. The opposite view, victim defending, usually only shifts the blame back to offenders and institutions.

But these theories may only reveal some of the more important symptoms of crime. While they sometimes indicate important factors upon which we could immediately act, like overcriminalization, the prison system, handgun proliferation, and certain victim behaviors, they usually ignore the primary sources of victimization. They deflect attention away from the American system—that is, away from basic American political, economic, and social structures. They emphasize secondary symptoms of crime, against which we can hope to achieve little. Instead, critics believe the best evidence for victimization's sources lies in structural characteristics of the American system which, in their view, produce the factors on which most crime rests: poverty, inequality, racism, sexism, classism, competition, bureaucracy, alienation, violence, and political inequities.

In other words, to challenge criminal victimization fundamentally, we must stop defending a system that produces victimization generally.

Obviously, this view has substantially different implications for both politics and victims than conventional crime theories. Politically, it suggests that reducing victimization will rely on fundamental structural reform. For victims, it suggests not that they should cooperate and support conventional political and administrative forces, but rather challenge them. The structural theory of crime proposes a new "social reality" of victimization upon which victims and the public could act.

Whichever view we support, we must acknowledge that politics and political ideology may influence our theory of victimization and even our willingness to seriously discover and eliminate its sources. We act politically not merely by questioning the American system, but also by defending it or refusing to examine its effects. We do not act unscientifically by acknowledging our political philosophies, but only when we allow them to predetermine our science or its scope.[9] As Albert Hirschman has suggested:

> It is then possible to visualize a kind of social science that would be very different from the one most of us have been practicing: a moral social science where moral considerations are not repressed or kept apart, but are systematically commingled with analytic argument, without guilt feelings over any integration; where the transition from preaching to proving and back again is performed frequently and with ease; and where moral considerations need no longer be smuggled in surreptitiously, nor expressed unconsciously, but are displayed openly and disarmingly.[10]

THE POLITICS OF MISERY

Victims suffer considerably from actual victimization, and many of the rest of us suffer anticipating the crimes that might strike us. Yet this misery may have political influences as well. To begin with, the suffering and other repercussions we acknowledge in fact only encompass part of the victimization we could easily recognize. We often ignore the impact of the victimization we do not officially define as criminal. These definitions reflect political decisions, however, that do not necessarily represent the limits of objective, "criminal" behavior or social harms. These may not be neutral political decisions reflecting public interests or even the popular will, but rather decisions that direct our attention toward certain harms and away from many others whose emphasis would substantially challenge the conventional American system. Thus, we do not even consider much of our most serious misery and suffering.

We often ignore the politics of how we react to crime and victimization as well. Politics not only shapes our social reality of victimization, but also our fears and concerns. We live in perhaps the most heavily armed and guarded society in history, yet our insecurities seem almost unsurpassed as well. While some of our fears bear some considerable substance, many do not reflect objective dangers as much perhaps as official views generated for government purposes, or arbitrary perceptions for private (such as media) objectives. Some believe we suffer a psychological victimization from developing unnecessary insecurities and from the political manipulation of our fears. We not only feel terrorized, we often respond by supporting policies that may only intensify our insecurities and even increase our chances of victimization. Worst of all, beyond breeding a hatred and suspiciousness of others, we may also begin to loathe and blame ourselves.

Our financial costs of victimization have political implications as well. We steadily escalate state expenses, paid unequally through taxpayer revenues, for controlling crime and violence, despite its persistent ineffectiveness. We rely on law enforcement expenditures to pay the "social costs" of crime; the costs some would say emerge inevitably from an unjust social system. Instead of paying the "costs" of eliminating victimization's sources, we seem to muddle on, spending ever-increasing amounts for the continuing failure of conventional responses. People continue supporting policies that may not promote their bests interests.

We also ignore this burden's unequal costs. Relatively speaking, those people most victimized have the least resources to cope with their attacks. They often have no material means or opportunities to afford better self-protection and often receive the least public protection as well. Meanwhile, certain interests profit considerably from our insecurities, pandering to our fears and benefiting from the billion dollar industry in protective devices. We can hardly ignore the effects of unequal economic and political power on our ability to cope with victimization, or even profit from it.

THE POLITICS OF DISENCHANTMENT

When victimized, we expect authorities to defend us, helping us to effectively reduce our suffering and redress the wrongs committed against us. Instead, we often find ourselves further victimized in the law enforcement process. While we have long recognized this "second" victimization (in fact, it has substantially propelled the victim movement), we rarely consider its political sources.

Victims of enforcement arise from both state and organizational politics. To begin with, law enforcement may not fundamentally seek to reduce victimization. Criminal justice may have more to do with political or social control than with crime control. Thus, law enforcement may primarily perform political functions beyond its ostensible activities. Moreover, it reflects official and selective criminal definitions, frequently pressed discriminantly against some offenders and offenses while ignoring many others, and often corresponding to the society's overall distribution of political and economic power. It begins a process that some view as "weeding out the wealthier" from consideration, thus also ignoring the extensive victimization they produce. Thus, many victims have no claim for relief or remedies since their victimization has not been officially recognized.

When recognized, their experience may reflect their political and economic power and status. While officials encourage victim participation ostensibly to help enforcement, some believe it has much more to do with bolstering the government's legitimacy and support. When they try to participate, most victims find it impossible, often relegated to influencing by their demeanor and characteristics, when they have any effect at all. When they sometimes participate more extensively, they often find themselves mechanically employed through some kind of witness management scheme. In the rare instance when they participate in a full trial, they often find themselves on trial as much as the offender. These may be the typical victim experiences because typical victims have little political status or power, coming largely from middle- and especially lower-class backgrounds.

Besides this general powerlessness, victims regularly clash with criminal justice's internal organizational politics. They symbolize official failures, and represent outsiders whose participation will more than likely interfere in official routines. Contrary to our adversarial ideals, criminal justice personnel usually form cooperative "work-groups," which seek rapid case dispositions, usually through plea bargaining, free from outside participants and surprises. Personal objectives bolster these organizational goals, making it especially difficult for victims to become institutionalized into a process that already routinely considers crime as a victimization of society, not individual victims. In a way, crime victims suffer from what officials consider as their own victimization and exploitation by the criminal justice system. Victims suffer not by competing with defendants, whose rights are regularly honored in the breach, but rather by competing with official objectives. For victims, and undoubtedly others, the process is the punishment. And for particular victims, like women, the punishment can be especially brutal.

Victimization by law enforcement hardly occurs inadvertently, but reflects instead a clash of political interests, some bolstered by considerable power, and others having relatively little. Reforming the criminal process to promote victim interests may depend not merely on invoking victim rights or sensitizing officials to victim needs, but rather on addressing entrenched official incentives and even American criminal justice's purposes in the first place. Until that time, we might question any increase in victim participation in a process that will almost invariably alienate, and not satisfy, victims.[11]

THE SYMBOLIC POLITICS OF ADVOCACY

Victimization and the criminal process create many problems for victims. In response, we have developed various programs to promote victim needs and rights. Yet much of this victim advocacy, while it has made some important progress, has nevertheless been much less successful than we had hoped. The limits of advocacy, if not some of its motives, may reflect some important political obstacles.

For all their calls for greater victim participation, officials usually do quite well with little victim (save symbolic) involvement at all. Within criminal justice, officials often consider victims as a threat or interference in their activities. And victim programs may be even more threatening, unless tailored to official objectives. Witness management schemes, for example, may promote official goals, but expensive victim assistance programs may drain scarce resources and thus be resisted. Community crime control closely connected to law enforcement and reflecting official views and approaches may be embraced as improving police-community relations, but popular justice initiatives promoting independent, alternative organizations and techniques that question social structures and police functions will be opposed. This suggests that only victim advocacy carefully tailored to parallel official goals will likely be successful, even if such schemes do not serve victim interests very well or perhaps at all.

More broadly, some believe that victim programs may promote particular political ideologies and certain state interests. Ideologically, victim advocacy may hide quite another political agenda: the desire to curb defendant's rights and bolster the state's enforcement power. It may promote other state interests as well. Victim programs such as victim compensation emerged ostensibly to satisfy victim needs before we even determined their scope or victim preferences. The programs arose while (if only briefly) we were increasingly questioning victimization's sources and wondering whether offenders were not also victims. Some believe that this "opening" in our conventional social reality of victimization may have challenged the state's legitimacy and its ability to control the definition of victims. Victim compensation programs may have emerged to recoup the state's control over labeling victims. The schemes, providing little substantive assistance, did nevertheless redefine the victims society would recognize—namely, the narrow array of victims encompassed by their restrictive eligibility requirements.[12]

Programs such as victim compensation may have had other political goals as well. They may have enhanced the state's legitimacy by conveying the government's apparent concern for victims. They may have emerged for symbolic, political purposes designed to promote victim and public support and enhance social control. Most plans, for example, cover only very selective victimizations, despite public perceptions to the contrary. If very few even qualify, then even fewer actually apply (about 1% of all violent crime victims), and only about one-third of them receive any payments, in amounts often less than what they believe they deserve. While programs often receive considerable general publicity, actual application information is usually very difficult to obtain and rarely a regular part of the victim's initiation to the criminal process.[13]

Aside from inaccessibility, ineligibility, and low visibility, the programs are usually chronically underfunded. Officials have often seen the political advantages of advocating victim interests, but have balked at its potential costs. In fact, in some states, politicians have promoted the programs, announced their support to their constituents, but then voted against appropriations, or for funding totally inadequate to the task. The plans often seem to represent symbolic policies with little tangible or substantive assistance, unbeknownst, of course, to all but those few who apply. The public lauds its politicians for their concern, hoping it will never need the assistance, yet, if it ever should, it will effectively find little or no help forthcoming. Compensation programs may amount to the "political placebos" some advocates have feared.[14] But the political uses of victim advocacy may go even further.

Compensation plans emerged not only when we began suspecting the offender's own victimization, but also amid government efforts to quell social protest and domestic disorder. Some believe that welfare programs have been used in this century to regulate social disruptions and the lower classes, expanding and contracting to correspond to periodic disenchantment.[15] As essentially welfare programs themselves, compensation plans may have served similar or complementary purposes, arising as they did during a period of considerable lower-class disorder. Aside from how they complement conventional criminal justice policies, compensation plans may have had more to do with social control than with victim interests.[16]

We need not, and should not, deprecate the many sincere and important efforts at victim advocacy by acknowledging the politics of victim programs. Instead, it only suggests that some victim advocacy, most notably many official initiatives, may have purposes that place victim interests secondary, if it promotes them at all. For good reason, most sincere and experienced advocates have prescribed programs independent from government, if not basically challenging government structures and objectives. To really promote victim interests successfully, we may need strategies that transform victims into a potent and independent political force, and which second-guess apparent government benevolence.

THE POLITICAL ECONOMY
OF OPPRESSION

We have suggested a relationship between victims of crime and victims of oppression, between victimology and human rights inquiry, and between crime and oppression. Their interaction shows the importance of human rights to crime victims. Our examination of human rights has revealed many of the same political considerations that have characterized victimology and criminal victimization.

The human rights movement, both domestically and abroad, has reflected various political conflicts and struggles. The apparently liberal promotion of human rights in the mid-1970s helped stimulate the issue's resurgence, but imposed clear limitations on how far our human rights policy would extend. Often used symbolically to rescue America's bruised international image and to wage ideological battle with the Soviet Union, our policies sought much less than they promised and achieved even less than that. By the early 1980s, the not-so-crusading "human rights crusade" suffered an abrupt American reversal, reflecting conservative, cold-war politics. Yet despite these setbacks, international initiatives and domestic movements proceeded apace, offering new hope for a more conducive political climate in the near future. Even culturally, while we sometimes blame victims of oppression for their fate, an emerging and sympathetic literature of oppression has helped raise the public's awareness of steadily increasing violations.

Nevertheless, we still may suffer from a very limited social reality of oppression. We usually conceptualize a much lower victimization level than objectively occurs, particularly at home and in our "backyard." This stems largely from selective human rights definitions that encompass only part of those internationally recognized rights. For ideological and political purposes, the American rights conception excludes economic and social rights whose serious protection might question the foundations of the American political economy. Our measures of rights violations reflect similar biases, often ignoring significant violations even within our limited rights conception. Finally, our media and other engines of socialization may also help ingrain official rights conceptions and self-evaluations that divert public attention from alternative views and from concrete and serious violations, allowing us to console ourselves for our exemplary record.

As with criminal victimization, we often support theories that hold institutions, or our enemies, or even victims themselves, responsible for oppression, diverting attention from human rights theories that challenge our nationalism and our political economy. Explanations of oppression may have less to do with objective sources and more to do with political or ideological defenses of conventional structures and systems. We emphasize temporary or inevitable factors producing infringements, apparently ignoring what some view as the intentional rights violations we commit to promote special interests and conventional institutions. We often ignore how oppression constitutes crime itself and how it provides a major source of additional criminal victimization. Ending oppression, like ending crime, may depend more on political decisions and forces than on misleading technical crusades to control excesses, improve enforcement, eradicate enemies, and reform victims.

Our social reality of oppression may substantially underestimate the impact of oppression, excluding much suffering and misery. Our enforcement measures, sometimes well intended, have been ineffective, often reflecting the political barriers to implementation that emerge from national sovereignty and ideological clashes. Our human rights advocacy, while having achieved much, still falls far short of offering effective relief, again due largely to political obstacles. Human rights initiatives rarely challenge the structure of international relations, nor the social, political, and economic sources of oppression, acting instead largely to provide remedial, albeit valuable, relief. Again, we need not disparage rights advocacy by suggesting its political barriers and the possibility that we must pursue significantly different political strategies.

In sum, our ability to cope with oppression may depend on many of the same political factors that affect our battle against criminal victimization. In fact, the two maladies may have many connections and many common sources, and thus we might pursue their reduction jointly, not separately as we have in the past.

POLITICS AND THE NEW VICTIMOLOGY

This is the moment, in books of this kind, where one is supposed to offer concrete suggestions for some sort of action. "Enough diagnosis, time for prescription." I do not know why this is so— why books of social analysis should ape the format of a market research report or an engineer's memorandum. The recommendations that are made always seem fatuous to me—either so vague and

*general as to be implicit in the analysis itself, or so concrete and
trivial that one could have offered them without going through any
of the analysis. I want to state here that I intend to violate the
traditional form: I have no suggestions to offer. I have described a
way of being and its pathological consequences. This implies that
some sort of reversal of this way of being—this attitude of mind—
would be helpful, but how one arrives at it cannot be prescribed but
only discovered.*   PHILIP SLATER, Earthwalk

*The naming of the intolerable is itself the hope. When something is
intolerable, action must follow, subject to all the vissicitudes of life.
But the pure hope resides first and mysteriously in the capacity to
name the intolerable as such: and this capacity comes from afar—
from the past and from the future. This is why politics and courage
are inevitable. The time of the torturers is agonizingly but
exclusively the present.*   JOHN BERGER

Like Philip Slater and John Berger, we will end with no grand scheme
or solution. Ideally, the analysis stimulates some possible remedies
and answers. Yet we can hardly resist suggesting a few directions,
some of which we have already mentioned.

The study of victims of both crime and oppression cannot be separated from understanding political and economic systems. Thus,
we must consider political and economic solutions and probably not
those that merely tinker with institutions and processes, but those
that go to the heart of our political economy. Consequently, any
new directions we prescribe for victims, victimology, and human
rights must be made within that context. Ending victimization may
require significant social, political, and economic alterations, yet despite the obstacles, much has been done already to clear the path
for that change.

Some believe that progress for victims has emerged from a multi-
step process, beginning with acquiescence and tolerance, then recognition and consciousness, then "coming out," then new public
policy, and finally implementation and enforcement.[17] Another version shows an initial period of harm, suffering, and injury, followed
by a new perception of victimization, then by having victims claim
some status from authorities, and finally official recognition and responses.[18] But, while these steps may have produced some worthy
reforms, they may not be nearly enough to basically eliminate or
significantly reduce victimization because they do not strike centrally at the structures from which most violations emerge.

Instead, we might well pursue some quite different directions,
which encompass local and international political movements, victim rights and human rights, and political and economic democracy.
Victim advocates might wed their concerns and efforts for victims

of both crime and oppression, creating local community organizations and movements pursuing short-term victim interests and longerterm political and economic change. They might embrace various versions of "popular justice" that create alternative institutions, restore informal "conflicts" and dispute resolution, revitalize victims as vehicles of community and social control, and vigorously pressure existing institutions for tangible concessions. As independent, nongovernmental organizations, they might promote a new perception of victimization, and a broader analysis of its social sources, seeking simultaneously a social redefinition of crime and oppression based not merely on rights but also on popular needs.[19]

A new victim movement might pursue broader goals of political and economic democracy, recognizing the relationship between crime and oppression.[20] It might acknowledge its relationship to the international human rights movement and its quest for global change, making increasing connections among new organizations and institutions across national boundaries and cultures.[21] These directions constitute not merely idle speculations or dreamlike utopias, nor does any serious quest for their achievement represent naive idealism. Instead, they may represent the only realistic course away from a nation and world of victimization. As Paul Wachtel has suggested "Nothing is as naively utopian as continuing in our present course . . . hoping for . . . technology to bail us out at the last minute."[22] Or, as C. Wright Mills argued,

> Does not utopian mean merely: what acknowledges other values as relevant and possibly even sovereign? But in truth, are not those who in the name of realism act like crackpots, are they not the utopians? Are we not now in a situation in which the only practical, realistic down-to-earth thinking and acting is just what these crackpot realists call "utopian"?[23]

Finally, and perhaps most important, we must consider our scientific endeavors. We cannot clearly or honestly separate our science and our politics: our politics inevitably gives direction to our science, but it need not and should not preordain it. Our scientific conclusions must stand the test of empirical reality, but we should make good use of the knowledge we accumulate. Victimology has always been at least a somewhat applied science, but it can do much more. A "new" victimology might embrace a broader definition of victimization that brings all victims, or at least many more victims, within its purview. We might well pursue a "new" victimology of human rights, recognizing that victim rights stand inextricably connected to universal rights protections.[24]

To do so already acknowledges a political decision. It means pursuing, through our scientific study, a discipline guided not by conventional, law-and-order interests and policies, but rather by progressive goals of democracy and social change. Above all, if we take our victimological science and our victim advocacy seriously, then we should not avoid being consciously political, for surely we are unconsciously political in any case. Howard Becker has observed that some people urge scientists

> Not to take sides, to be neutral and do research technically correct and value free . . . one would have to assume, as some apparently do, that it is indeed possible to do research uncontaminated by personal and political sympathies. . . . I . . . argue that it is not possible and, therefore, the question is not whether we should take sides, since we inevitably will, but rather whose side are we on? . . . It is odd that when we perceive bias, we usually see it in these circumstances . . . because it is easily ascertained that a great many more studies are biased in the direction of . . . officials than the other way around. . . . We can never avoid taking sides. So we are left with the question of whether taking sides means some distortion is introduced into our work so great as to make it useless. . . . Our problem is to make sure that, whatever point of view we take, our research meets standards of good scientific work, that our unavoidable sympathies do not render our results invalid. . . . We take sides as our personal and political commitments dictate, use our theoretical and technical resources to avoid distortions we might introduce into our work, [and] limit our conclusions carefully.[25]

As scientists, we must not betray our greatest calling. Bertold Brecht once put it this way:

> The practice of science would seem to call for valor. She trades in knowledge, which is the product of doubt. And this new art of doubt has enchanted the public. The plight of the multitude is old as the rocks, and is believed to be basic as the rocks. But now they have learned to doubt. They snatched the telescopes out of our [the scientists'] hands and had them trained on their tormentors: prince, official, public moralist. . . . Word is passed down that this is of no concern to the scientist, who is told he will only release such of his findings as do not disturb the peace, that is, the peace of mind of the well-to-do. Threats and bribes fill the air. Can the scientist hold out on the numbers? . . . For what reasons do you labor? I take it that the intent of *science* is to ease human existence. If you give way to coercion, science can be crippled. . . . Should you, then, in time, discover all there is to be discovered, your progress must become a progress away from the bulk of humanity. . . . As a scientist . . . for some years I was as strong as the authorities, but then I surrendered my knowledge to the powers that be, to use it, no, not *use* it, *abuse* it, as it suits their ends. I have betrayed my profession. Any man who does what I have done must not be tolerated in the ranks of science. (*emphasis mine*)[26]

Similarly, Bertrand Russell argued that "the aim of *politics* should be to make the lives of individuals as good as possible" (*emphasis mine*).[27] Together, our obligation to help relieve human suffering seems clear enough. If our "political science" or other science does not contribute to that end, then what value has it?[28]

Notes

NOTES FOR CHAPTER 1

1. Robert P. Rhodes, "Political Theory, Policy Analysis, and the Insoluble Problems of Crime," in John A. Gardiner and Michael A. Mulkey (eds.), *Crime and Criminal Justice* (Lexington, Mass.: Lexington Books, 1975), 22.

For alternative roles political science could be performing, see Theodore Roszak (ed.), *The Dissenting Academy* (New York: Pantheon, 1969); Marvin Surkin and Alan Wolfe (eds.), *An End to Political Science* (New York: Basic Books, 1970); David Ricci, *The Tragedy of Political Science* (New Haven: Yale University Press, 1984); George Beam and Dick Simpson, *Political Action* (Chicago: Swallow Press, 1984); Philip Green and Sanford Levinson (eds.), *Power and Community: Dissenting Essays in Political Science* (New York: Vintage, 1970); Michael Parenti, "The State of the Discipline: Everyone's Favorite Controversy," *PS* (Spring, 1983), 189; Robert Goldstein, "The FBI and American Politics Textbooks," *PS* (Spring 1984), 172; Roy Preiswerk, "Could We Study International Relations As If People Mattered?" in Richard Falk, et al. (eds.), *Toward A Just World Order* (Boulder, Colo.: Westview Press, 1982), 175; Ernest Wilson, "Why Political Scientists Don't Study Black Politics, But Historians and Sociologists Do," *PS* (Summer 1985), 600.

2. Emilio Viano, "Victimology: The Development of a New Perspective," *Victimology*, 8 (1983), 26.

3. Mark Satin, *New Age Politics* (New York: Delta, 1978).

NOTES FOR CHAPTER 2

1. Geoffrey MacCormack, "Revenge and Compensation in Early Law," *American Journal of Comparative Law*, 21 (1973), 69.

2. David L. Decker, David Shichor, and Robert M. O'Brien, *Urban Structure and Victimization* (Lexington, Mass.: Lexington Books, 1982).

3. Eduard Ziegenhagen, *Victims, Crime and Social Control* (New York: Praeger, 1977).

4. *Ibid.*

5. Stephen Schafer, *Introduction to Criminology* (Reston, Va.: Reston Pub., 1976), 143.

6. Ziegenhagen, note 3 *supra.*

7. Emilio Viano, "Violence, Victimization, and Social Change: A Socio-Cultural and Public Policy Analysis," *Victimology*, 8 (1983), 54.

8. *Ibid.*

9. Stephen Schafer, *The Victim and His Criminal* (New York: Random House, 1968).

10. Ziegenhagen, note 3 *supra*, 39.

11. Schafer, note 5 *supra*, 148.

12. *Ibid.*

13. Viano, note 7 *supra.*

14. Schafer, note 9 *supra.*

15. Ziegenhagen, note 3 *supra.*

16. Viano, note 7 *supra.*

17. Decker, Shichor, and O'Brien, note 2 *supra.*

18. Schafer, note 5 *supra.*

19. Viano, note 7 *supra.*

20. Ziegenhagen, note 3 *supra.*

21. Viano, note 7 *supra;* Schafer, note 5 *supra.*

22. Ziegenhagen, note 3 *supra.*

23. Schafer, note 5 *supra.*

24. *Ibid.*, 23.

25. William McDonald, "Towards a Bicentennial Revolution in Criminal Justice: The Return of the Victim," *American Criminal Law Review*, 13(1976), 649; William McDonald, "The Role of the Victim in America," in Randy E. Barnett and John Hagel (eds.), *Assessing the Criminal: Restitution, Retribution and the Legal Process* (Cambridge: Ballinger, 1977), 295.

26. Ziegenhagen, note 3 *supra*, 69; McDonald, *ibid.*

27. Ziegenhagen, *ibid.*, 68.

28. Bruce R. Jacob, "Reparation or Restitution by the Criminal Offender to His Victim: Applicability of an Ancient Concept in the Modern Correctional Process," *Journal of Criminal Law, Criminology and Police Science*, 61(1970), 152; McDonald, note 25 *supra.*

29. Ziegenhagen, note 3 *supra*, 68.

30. McDonald, note 25 *supra*, 662.

31. Schafer, note 5 *supra*, 149.

32. Alan T. Harland, "One Hundred Years of Restitution," *Victimology*, 8(1983), 194.

33. Schafer, note 5 *supra*, 28.

34. Ziegenhagen, note 3 *supra*; Schafer, note 5 *supra*, 30.

35. Ziegenhagen, *ibid.*, 143.

36. Viano, note 7 *supra*.

37. Maurice Brown, "Literature: A Third Eye on Victims," in Jacqueline Scherer and Gary Shepard (eds.), *Victimization of the Weak* (Springfield, Ill.: Charles C Thomas, 1983), 249; Edith Flynn, "Report of the Discussion Sections of the Second International Symposium on Victimology," *Victimology*, 2(1977), 32.

38. See, for example, Bertold Brecht, *The Mother* (New York: Grove Press, 1978).

39. Eugene Ionesco, *Victims of Duty* (New York: Grove Press, 1958); William Faulkner, *The Sound and the Fury* (New York: Random House, 1946); Franz Kafka, *The Trial* (New York: Schocken Books, 1968); see also Ruth Noy and Avery Sharron, "Child Abuse in Kafka's Eyes: The Victim's Invisible Metamorphasis," *Victimology*, 9(1984), 296.

40. Albert Camus, *The Rebel* (New York: Penguin, 1971).

41. Arthur Lapan, "The Victim in Contemporary Literature," in Israel Drapkin and Emilio Viano (eds.), *Victimology: Theoretical Issues* (Lexington, Mass.: Lexington Books, 1974).

42. Gordon L. Harper, "Saul Bellow—The Art of Fiction: An Interview," *Paris Review*, 37(1965), 48.

43. Saul Bellow, *The Victim* (New York: Vanguard Press, 1947).

44. Ralph Ellison, *The Invisible Man* (New York: Vintage, 1947); F. Scott Fitzgerald, *The Great Gatsby* (New York: Scribners, 1956); Arthur Miller, *The Death of a Salesman* (New York: Penguin, 1976); Allen Ginsberg, *Howl* (San Francisco: City Lights, 1956); Richard Brautigan, *Trout Fishing in America* (New York: Dell, 1971).

45. Fyodor Dostoyevski, *Crime and Punishment* (New York: Modern Library, 1950).

46. Susan Kress, "Doubly Abused: The Plight of Crime Victims in Literature," Paper presented at Second International Symposium on Victimology, Boston, 1976; John Lewin, "The Victim in Shakespeare," in Emilio Viano (ed.), *Victims and Society* (Washington, D.C.: Visage Press, 1978), 451.

47. Truman Capote, *In Cold Blood* (New York: Signet, 1965).

48. George Garrett, "Crime and Punishment in Kansas: Truman Capote's *In Cold Blood*," *The Hollins Critic*, 3(1966), 1.

49. Anthony Burgess, *A Clockwork Orange* (New York: Ballantine Books, 1962).

50. Kress, note 46 *supra*.

51. Norman Mailer, *The Executioner's Song* (New York: Ballantine Books, 1978).

52. Franz Werfel, *The Murdered One is Guilty* (Munich: Kurt Wolff Verlag, 1920).

53. Judith Rossner, *Looking for Mr. Goodbar* (New York: Simon and Schuster, 1975).

54. Kress, note 46 *supra*.

55. Gary Kinder, *Victim: The Other Side of Murder* (New York: Dell, 1982).

56. Judith Krulewitz and Janet Nash, "Effects of Rape Victim Resistance, Assault Outcome and Sex of Observer in Attitudes About Rape," *Journal of Personality*, 47(1979), 557.

57. S. M. S. Ahmed, "Visibility of the Victim," *Journal of Social Psychology*, 107(1979), 253.

58. Diane Hamlin, "The Nature and Extent of Spouse Assault," *The Victim Advocate* (Alexandria, Va.: National District Attorneys Association, 1978), 3.

59. N. L. Kerr, "Beautiful and Blameless: Effects of Victim Attractiveness and Responsiveness on Mock Jurors' Verdicts," *Personality and Social Psychology Bulletin*, 4(1979), 479.

60. P. M. Mazelon, "Stereotypes and Perceptions of Victims of Rape," *Victimology*, 5(1980), 121; S. Kanehar and M. B. Kolsawalla, "The Nobility of Nonviolence: Person Perception as a Function of Retaliation to Aggression," *Journal of Social Psychology*, 102(1977), 159; B. Thornton, R. M. Rychman and M. A. Robbins, "The Relationship of Observer Characteristics to Beliefs in the Causal Responsibility of Victims of Sexual Assault," *Human Relations*, 25(1982), 321; L. G. Calhoun, J. W. Selby and L. J. Warring, "Social Perception of the Victim's Causal Role in Rape," *Human Relations*, 29(1976), 517.

61. Kurt Weis and Sandra S. Borges, "Rape as a Crime Without Victims and Offenders? A Methodological Critique," in Viano, note 46 *supra*, 230.

62. Michael Lerner, "Evaluation of Performance as a Function of Performer's Reward and Attractiveness," *Journal of Personality and Social Psychology*, 1(1965), 355; Martin Symonds, "Victims of Violence: Psychological Effects and Aftereffects," *American Journal of Psychoanalysis*, 35(1975), 19; B. W. Godfrey and C. A. Lowe, "Devaluation of Innocent Victims: An Attributional Analysis Within the Just World Paradigm," *Journal of Personality and Social Psychology*, 31(1975), 944; G. McDonald, "Factors Affecting Responsibility Attributed to a Rape Victim," *Journal of Social Psychology*, 113(1981), 285.

63. William Ryan, *Blaming the Victim* (New York: Vintage, 1976); Kurt Weis and Sandra Weis, "Victimology and the Justification of Rape," in Israel Drapkin and Emilio Viano (eds.), *Victimology: Exploiters and the Exploited* (Lexington, Mass.: Lexington Books, 1974), 3; L. A. Libow and D. W. Doty, "An Exploratory Approach to Self-Blame and Self-Degradation by Rape Victims," *Journal of Orthopsychiatry*, 49(1979), 670.

64. Charles Silberman, *Criminal Violence, Criminal Justice* (New York: Vintage, 1978), 120.

65. Ezzat Fattah, "The Use of the Victim as an Agent of Self-Legitimation: Toward a Dynamic Explanation of Criminal Behavior," in Viano, note 46 *supra*, 105; Hans Goppinger, "The Victim as Seen by the Offender,"

Paper presented at Second International Symposium on Victimology, Boston, 1976; Weis and Weis, note 63 *supra*.

66. David Rodney Watson, "Some Conceptual Issues in the Social Identification of Victims and Offenders," in Viano, note 46 *supra*, 60.

67. D. R. Watson, "The Presentation of Victim and Motive in Discourse: The Case of Police Interrogations and Interviews," *Victimology*, 8(1983), 31.

68. R. J. Smith, K. Tritt, and A. Zollman, "Sex Differences in the Social Perception of Rape Victims in West Germany and the United States," *Journal of Social Psychology*, 117(1982), 143.

69. V. V. Stanciu, "Victim-Producing Civilizations and Situations," in Viano, note 46 *supra*, 28.

70. The following discussion borrows considerably from Beniamin Mendelsohn, "The Origin of the Doctrine of Victimology," in Israel Drapkin and Emilio Viano (eds.), *Victimology* (Lexington, Mass.: Lexington Books, 1974), 3; Stephen Schafer, "The Beginnings of Victimology," in Drapkin and Viano, *ibid.*, 17; Hans Joachim Schneider, "The Present Situation in Victimology in the World," in Hans Joachim Schneider (ed.), *The Victim in International Perspective* (Berlin: Walter de Gruyter, 1982), 1.

71. Mendelsohn, note 70 *supra*.

72. Weis and Weis, note 63 *supra*.

73. Beniamin Mendelsohn, "Victimology and the Technical and Social Sciences: A Call for the Establishment of Victimological Clinics," in Drapkin and Viano, note 42 *supra*, 25.

74. Hans von Hentig, *The Criminal and His Victim* (New Haven: Yale University Press, 1948).

75. Henry Ellenberger, "Relations Psychologiques Entre le Criminel et sa Victime," *Revue Internationale de Criminologie et de Police Technique*, 2(1954), 1.

76. Margery Fry, "Justice for Victims," *Observer*, 10(November 1957), 8.

77. Marvin Wolfgang, *Patterns of Criminal Homicide* (Philadelphia: University of Pennsylvania Press, 1958).

78. O. Iturbe, "Victimologia, Nuevo Enfoque Criminologica de la Victima del Delito," *La Revista Penal y Penitenciaria*, 87–90 (Enero-Diciembre, 1958), 199; Shufu Yoshimasu, "Studien Iber 200 Morder von Ihren Kriminellen Lubenskurven aus Gesehen," *Folia Psychiatria et Neurologia Japonica* (1958); R. Souchet, "La Victimologie," *Etudes Internationales de Psycho-sociologie Criminelle*, 4(1958), 13; W. H. Nagel, "Victimologie," *Tijdschrift voor Strafrecht*, 68(1958), 1.

79. "Compensation for Victims of Criminal Violence: A Roundtable," *Journal of Public Law*, 8(1959), 191.

80. "Symposium on Victims of Crime," *Minnesota Law Review*, 50(1965), 213; "Symposium on Victim Compensation," *Southern California Law Review*, 44(1970), 22; "Symposium on Victimization and Victimology," *Journal of Criminal Law and Criminology*, 72(Summer 1981), 704; Ronnie Janoff-Bulman and Irene Hanson Frieze (eds.), "Reactions to Victimization," *Journal*

of Social Issues, 39(1983), 1; Martin S. Greenberg and Barry Ruback (eds.), "Criminal Victimization," *Journal of Social Issues,* 40(1984), 1.

81. Stephen Schafer, note 9 *supra.*

82. LeRoy Lamborn, "Toward a Victim Orientation in Criminal Theory," *Rutgers Law Review,* 22(1968), 733.

83. Israel Drapkin and Emilio Viano (eds.), *Victimology* (Lexington, Mass.: Lexington Books, 1974); Israel Drapkin and Emilio Viano (eds.), *Victimology: Theoretical Issues* (Lexington, Mass.: Lexington Books, 1974); Israel Drapkin and Emilio Viano (eds.), *Victimology: Society's Reaction to Victimization* (Lexington, Mass.: Lexington Books, 1974); Israel Drapkin and Emilio Viano (eds.), *Victimology: Crimes, Victims, and Justice* (Lexington, Mass.: Lexington Books, 1974); Israel Drapkin and Emilio Viano (eds.), *Victimology: Violence and Its Victims* (Lexington, Mass.: Lexington Books, 1974); Israel Drapkin and Emilio Viano (eds.), *Victimology: Exploiters and the Exploited* (Lexington, Mass.: Lexington Books, 1974).

84. Flynn, note 37 *supra.*

85. Hans Joachim Schneider, *The Victim in International Perspective* (Berlin: Walter de Gruyter, 1982).

86. Ezzat Fattah (ed.), *Reorienting the Justice System: From Crime Policy to Victim Policy* (New York: Macmillan, 1985).

87. Gilbert Geis, et al., "Toward the Alleviation of Human Suffering" Rapporteurs' Report of Fifth International Symposium on Victimology, Zagreb, 1985.

88. Emilio Viano (ed.), "Proceedings of the International Study Institute on Victimology," *Victimology,* 1(1976), 1.

89. Emilio Viano (ed.), "Proceedings of the Second International Institute on Victimology," *Victimology,* 8(1983), 1.

90. Emilio Viano (ed.), "Proceedings of the First World Congress on Victimology," *Victimology,* 5(1980), 93.

91. Emilio Viano (ed.), "Proceedings of the International Seminar on Victimology," *Victimology,* 8(1983), 283.

92. Emilio Viano (ed.), "Proceedings of the Third International Institute on Victimology," *Victimology,* 10(1985), 1.

93. Koichi Miyazawa, "Society and the Victim: Attitudes and Policies," in Israel Drapkin and Emilio Viano (eds.), *Victimology: Society's Reaction to Victimization* (Lexington, Mass.: Lexington Books, 1974), 5; Andrew Karmen, *Crime Victims* (Belmont, Calif.: Brooks/Cole, 1984), 149.

94. Ziegenhagen, note 3 *supra.*

95. Karmen, note 93 *supra.*

96. Weis and Borges, note 61 *supra.*

97. Robert Elias, *Victims of the System: Crime Victims and Compensation in American Politics and Criminal Justice* (New Brunswick, N.J.: Transaction Books, 1983).

98. Daniel Moynihan, *The Politics of a Guaranteed Income* (New York: Harper and Row, 1973), 101; Ziegenhagen, note 3 *supra,* xiii; Elias, *ibid.,* 28.

99. Institute for the Study of Labor and Economic Crisis, *The Iron Fist and the Velvet Glove: An Analysis of the U.S. Police* (San Francisco: Crime and Justice Associates, 1982).

100. J. J. M. van Dijk, "The Position of the Victim in Criminal Proceedings: Backgrounds and Perspectives," *Justitiele Verkenningen*, 6(1982), 10.

101. Frances Fox Piven and Richard A. Cloward, *Regulating the Poor: The Functions of Public Welfare* (New York: Vintage, 1971).

102. David Miers, "Victim Compensation as a Labelling Process," *Victimology*, 8(1983), 213.

103. Andrew Karmen, "Crime Victims, Conservatives and Liberals," Paper presented at First World Congress on Victimology, Washington, D.C., 1980.

104. John Stookey, "The Victim's Perspective on American Criminal Justice," in Joe Hudson and Burt Galaway (eds.), *Restitution in Criminal Justice* (Lexington, Mass.: Lexington Books, 1977), 21; Elias, note 97 *supra*; Robert Elias, "The Politics of Evaluating Victim Services," Paper presented at the Victims of Crime Conference, International Society of Criminology, Vancouver, 1983; Robert Elias, "Community Control, Criminal Justice and Victim Services," in Fattah, note 86 *supra*; Robert Elias, "Alienating the Victim," *Journal of Social Issues*, 40(1984), 103; Ezzat Fattah, "Some Recent Theoretical Developments in Victimology," *Victimology*, 4(1979), 198.

105. Harry Boyte, *The Backyard Revolution* (Philadelphia: Temple University Press, 1980).

106. Fattah, note 104 *supra*; Karmen, note 93 *supra*; Katherine Saltzman, "Women and Victimization: The Aftermath," in Jane Roberts Chapman and Margaret Gates (eds.), *The Victimization of Women* (Beverly Hills, Calif.: Sage, 1978), 269.

107. Sam Walker, "What Have Civil Liberties Ever Done for Crime Victims? Plenty!" *Academy of Criminal Justice Sciences Today* (October 1982), 4.

108. *Ibid.*

109. Stanley Johnston, "If You Want Peace, Prepare for Law: People as Victims of Their Own Political Bigotry," Paper presented at International Institute of Victimology, Bellagio, 1975; Stanley Johnston, "Instituting Criminal Justice in the Global Village," in Viano, note 46 *supra*, 325; Stanley Johnston, "Toward A Supra-National Criminology: The Right and Duty of Victims of National Government to Seek Defense Through World Law," in Drapkin and Viano, note 42 *supra*, 37.

110. Sarah Ben David, "Celebration Honoring Pioneer of Victimology," *World Society of Victimology Newsletter*, 1(1982), 34.

111. LeRoy Lamborn, "Toward A United Nations Declaration of Crime, Abuses of Power, and the Rights of Victims," Paper presented to the Ninth International Congress on Criminology, Vienna, 1983; Irvin Waller, "Declaration on the Protection and Assistance of Victims of Crime," Paper prepared for the Committee on the Code of Conduct for the Protection and Assistance of Victims, World Society of Victimology, 1983; LeRoy Lamborn, "The Proposed United Nations Declaration on Justice and Assistance for Victims," Paper presented at International Meeting on Criminality and Development, San Jose, 1984; LeRoy Lamborn, "Vers une Declaration de Nations Unies sur la criminalite, les abus de pouvoir et les droits de victimes," *Annales de Droit de Lieqe*, 2(1984), 205; "Special Issue: "Towards A United Nations Declaration on Justice and Assistance for Victims," *World Society of Victimology Newsletter*, 3(1983–84); LeRoy Lamborn, "The Proposed United Nations Declaration on Justice and Assistance for Victims of Crimes or Other Acts Involving the Abuse of Power: Defining 'Abuse of Power'" Paper presented at Fifth International Symposium on Victimology, Zagreb, 1985.

112. Patrick B. McGuigan and Randall R. Rader, *Criminal Justice Reform* (Chicago: Regnery Gateway, 1983); David S. Davis, "The Production of Crime Policies," *Crime and Social Justice* (1983), 121; U.S. Department of Justice, Attorney General's Task Force on Victims of Crime, *Final Report* (Washington, D.C.: Author, 1981); President's Task Force on Victims of Crime, *Final Report* (Washington, D.C.: U.S. Government Printing Office, 1982); W. Miller, "Ideology and Criminal Justice Policy: Some Current Issues," *Journal of Criminal Law and Criminology*, 2(1973), 141.

113. Christopher Birkbeck, "Victimology Is What Victimologists Do. But What Should They Do?" *Victimology*, 8(1983), 270; H. J. Schneider, *Victimology: Science of Crime Victimology* (Tubingen: J. C. B. Mohr, 1975).

114. M. E. Wolfgang and S. I. Singer, "Victim Categories of Crime," *Journal of Criminal Law and Criminology*, 69(1978), 379.

115. Schafer, note 5 *supra.*

116. Ziegenhagen, note 3 *supra.*

117. Nils Christie, "Conflicts as Property," *British Journal of Criminology*, 17(1978), 1.

118. Fattah, note 65 *supra.*

119. Weis and Borges, note 61 *supra.*

120. Schafer, note 70 *supra.*

121. Kurt Weis, "'Victimologie' and 'Viktorologie' in der Kriminologie," *Monatsschrift fuer Kriminologie und Strafrechtsreform*, 55(1972), 1970.

122. Fattah, note 104 *supra.*

123. Daniel Glaser, "Victim Survey Research: Theoretical Implications," in Drapkin and Viano, note 70 *supra*, 31; "Conclusions and Recommendations, International Study Institute on Victimology, Bellagio, Italy, July 1–12, 1975," *Victimology*, 1(1976), 130; J. P. S. Fiselier, "Methods of Research in Victimology," *Ned. T. Criminol.*, 17(1975), 241; Heather McKay and John Hagan, "Studying the Victim of Crime: Some Methodological Notes," *Victimology*, 3(1978), 135.

124. Edith Flynn, "Theory Development in Victimology: An Assessment of Recent Progress and of Continuing Challenges," in Schneider, note 85 *supra*, 96.

125. Gerben J. N. Bruinsma and Jan P. S. Fiselier, "The Poverty of Victimology," in Schneider, note 85 *supra*, 87; G. J. N. Bruinsma and J. P. S. Fiselier, "Victimology, or All-Out Empiricism," *Journal of Criminology*, 21(1979), 180.

126. Ken Levine, "Empiricism in Victimological Research: A Critique," *Victimology*, 3(1978), 77.

127. David Lewis Smith and Kurt Weis, "Toward An Open Systems Approach to Studies in the Field of Victimology," in Viano, note 46 *supra*. 43; Guglielmo Gulotta and Luisella de Cataldo Neuberger, "A Systemic and Attributional Approach to Victimology," *Victimology*, 8(1983), 5.

128. Shirley Feldman-Summers, "Conceptual and Empirical Issues Associated with Rape," in Viano, note 46 *supra*, 91.

129. Clyde Franklin and Alice Franklin, "Victimology Revisited: A Critique and Suggestions for Future Directions," *Criminology*, 14(1976), 177; Bruinsma and Fiselier, note 125 *supra*.

130. Weis and Weis, note 63 *supra*.

131. Weis and Borges, note 61 *supra*.

132. Lynn Curtis, "The Conservative New Criminology," *Society*, 14(1977), 3; Lynn Curtis, "Victims, Policy and the Dangers of a Conservative Mentality," Paper presented at Second International Symposium on Victimology, Boston, 1976; Robert Elias, "Transcending Our Social Reality of Victimization," *Victimology*, 9(1985), 3; David O. Friedrichs, "Crime Victimization: Positive and Problematic Dimensions of the Radical Criminological Perspective," Paper presented at First World Congress on Victimology, Washington, D.C., 1980; Lee Bridges and Liz Fekete, "Victims, the 'Urban Jungle,' and the New Racism," *Race and Class*, 27(1985), 47.

133. For example, see William H. Parsonage, "Introduction," in William H. Parsonage, *Perspectives on Victimology* (Beverly Hills, Calif.: Sage, 1979), 7; Gerhard O. W. Mueller, "Toward A Whole Victimology Within a Whole Criminology," in Schneider, note 85 *supra*, 1.

134. Mary C. Sengstock, "Eclipse of the Individual Victim in Radical Victimology," Paper presented at the Annual Meeting of the American Society of Criminology, Tucson, 1976.

135. Frank Carrington, *Victims* (New Rochelle, N.Y.: Arlington House, 1975).

136. S. S. Ostrovmov and I. V. Frank, "On Victimology and Victimization," *Soviet Law and Government*, 15(1976–77), 70.

137. Inkeri Anttila, "Victimology: A New Territory in Criminology," in Drapkin and Viano, note 42 *supra*, 5.

138. Hans Goppinger, "Criminology and Victimology," in Drapkin and Viano, note 42 *supra*, 9.

139. William H. Nagel, "The Notion of Victimology in Criminology," in Drapkin and Viano, note 70 *supra*, 13.

140. Levine, note 126 *supra*.

141. For example, Vahakn N. Dadrian, "An Attempt at Defining Victimology," in Viano, note 46 *supra*, 40; Miyazawa, note 92 *supra*; Viano, note 8 *supra*; Marlene Young-Rifai, "Victimology: A Theoretical Framework," in Schneider, note 85 *supra*, 65; Bosko Jakovljevic, "Types of Victims and A Concept of Victimology" Paper presented at Fifth International Symposium on Victimology, Zagreb, 1985.

142. Ben David, note 110 *supra.*

143. Mendelsohn, note 73 *supra.*

144. *Ibid.,* 29.

145. Richard Quinney, "Who Is the Victim?" *Criminology,* 10(1972), 314.

146. Martha R. Burt, "A Conceptual Framework for Victimological Research," *Victimology,* 8(1983), 261; Flynn, note 124 *supra.*

147. Viano, note 8 *supra,* 15.

148. Kathleen Barry, "The Social Etiology of Crimes Against Women," Paper presented at Third International Institute on Victimology, Lisbon, 1984; Kathleen Barry, Charlotte Bunch, and Shirley Castley, *International Feminism: Networking Against Female Sexual Slavery* (New York: International Women's Tribunal Centre, 1984); Kathleen Barry, *Female Sexual Slavery* (New York: New York University Press, 1984).

149. Viano, note 8 *supra,* 16.

150. Jacqueline Scherer, "Theories in Social Vulnerability: Research Avenues in Victimology," Paper presented at Third International Institute on Victimology, Lisbon, 1984; Jacqueline Scherer, "An Overview of Victimology," in Scherer and Shepard, note 37 *supra,* 8.

151. Birkbeck, note 113 *supra.*

152. Stanciu, note 69 *supra.*

153. Fattah, note 104 *supra.*

154. Jeffrey H. Reiman, "Victims, Harm and Justice," in Drapkin and Viano, note 42 *supra,* 77; Ziegenhagen, note 3 *supra.*

155. For example, Barry Krisberg, *Crime and Privilege* (Englewood Cliffs, N.J.: Prentice-Hall, 1975); Ian Taylor, Paul Walton, and Jock Young (eds.), *Critical Criminology* (London: Routledge and Kegan Paul, 1975); Ian Taylor, Paul Walton, and Jock Young (eds), *A New Criminology* (New York: Harper and Row, 1973).

156. Robert Elias, "A 'New' Victimology: The Dialectic of Criminology and Human Rights," Unpublished paper, 1984; David O. Friedrichs, "Victimology: A Consideration of the Radical Critique," *Crime and Delinquency* (April, 1983), 283; Elias, note 132 *supra.*

157. Herman Schwendinger and Julia Schwendinger, "Defenders of Order or Guardians of Human Rights?" in Taylor, Walton, and Young, note 155 *supra,* 113; Weis and Weis, note 63 *supra;* Guglielmo Gulotta, "Collective Victimization," Paper presented at Third International Institute on Victimology, Lisbon, 1984.

158. Lech Falandysz, "Victimology in the Radical Perspective," in Schneider, note 85 *supra,* 105.

159. Weis and Weis, note 63 *supra.*

160. Zvonimir P. Separovic, "Victimology: A New Approach in the Social Sciences," in Drapkin and Viano, note 42 *supra,* 15; P. Holyst, "On Victimological Theory," in Schneider, note 85 *supra,* 56.

161. Aglaia Tsitsoura, "The Role of the Victim in the Framework of Crime Policy: International Aspects," *Victimology,* 8(1983), 47; Aglaia Tsitsoura,

"Victimology and the Council of Europe," in Schneider, note 85 *supra*, 4.

162. Johnston, note 109 *supra*.

163. M. I. Bassiouni, "Draft Resolution on Victims of Crime and Abuses of Power," United Nations Document E.Ac 57 (1984).

164. LeRoy Lamborn, note 111 *supra*; Waller, note 111 *supra*.

165. Elias, note 156 *supra*; Separovic, note 160 *supra*; Schwendinger and Schwendinger, note 157 *supra*; Hugo Bedau, "Are There Really Crimes Without Victims?" in Drapkin and Viano, note 42 *supra*, 66; Luisella de Cataldo Neuberger, "An Appraisal of Victimological Perspectives in International Law," Paper presented at Third International Institute on Victimology, Lisbon, 1984; Gilbert Geis, et al., "Toward the Alleviation of Human Suffering" Rapporteurs' Report of Fifth International Symposium on Victimology, Zagreb, 1985.

NOTES FOR CHAPTER 3

1. Murray Edelman, *The Symbolic Uses of Politics* (Urbana: University of Illinois Press, 1964); Murray Edelman, *Politics as Symbolic Action* (Chicago: Markham, 1971); Murray Edelman, *Political Language* (New York: Academic Press, 1975); Derek Roebuck, "Victims of Language" Paper presented at Fifth International Symposium on Victimology, Zagreb, 1985.

2. Richard Quinney, *The Social Reality of Crime* (Boston: Little, Brown, 1970).

3. Jeffrey R. Reiman, *The Rich Get Richer and the Poor Get Prison: Ideology, Class and Criminal Justice* (New York: John Wiley, 1979); Richard Quinney, "Who Is the Victim?" *Criminology*, 10(1972), 314; Quinney, *ibid.*

4. William E. Connolly, *Appearance and Reality in Politics* (Cambridge: Cambridge University Press, 1981).

5. Stewart Hall, et al., *Policing the Crisis: Mugging, the State and Law and Order* (London: Macmillan, 1978), vii.

6. William J. Chambliss, "Toward a Radical Criminology," in David Kairys (ed.), *The Politics of Law: A Progressive Critique* (New York: Pantheon, 1982), 230; Herman Schwendinger and Julia Schwendinger, "Defenders of Order or Guardians of Human Rights?" in Ian Taylor, Paul Walton, and Jock Young (eds.), *Critical Criminology* (London: Routledge and Kegan Paul, 1976), 113; Herman Schwendinger and Julia Schwendinger, "Social Class and the Definition of Crime," *Crime and Social Justice* (Spring–Summer 1977), 4; Andrew Hopkins, "Class Bias in the Criminal Law," *Contemporary Crises*, 5(1981), 383.

7. Reiman, note 3 *supra*, 55; C. Brants, "Definition of Victimhood: A Critical Exploration of the Limits of Victimology," *Tijdschrift voor Criminologie*, 24(1982), 325.

8. Stuart A. Scheingold, *The Politics of Law and Order: Street Crime and Public Policy* (New York: Longman, 1984), 11; William J. Chambliss, "The State and Criminal Law," in William Chambliss and Milton Mankoff (eds.),

Whose Law, What Order?: A Conflict Approach to Criminology (New York: John Wiley, 1976), 66; Aryeh Neier, *Only Judgment: The Limits of Litigation in Social Change* (Middletown, Conn.: Wesleyan University Press, 1982).

9. Troy Duster, *The Legislation of Morality: Law, Drugs and Moral Judgments* (New York: Free Press, 1970); Chambliss, *ibid.*

10. Emilio Viano, "Violence, Victimization and Social Change: A Socio-Cultural and Public Policy Analysis," *Victimology*, 8(1983), 59; Joseph A. Scimecca, "The Implications of the Sociology of C. Wright Mills for Modern Criminological Theory," *International Journal of Criminology and Penology*, 3(1975), 145; Ralph Miliband, *The State in Capitalist Society* (New York: Basic Books, 1969); G. William Domhoff, *The Powers That Be* (New York: Vintage, 1978); Michael Parenti, *Democracy for the Few* (New York: St. Martins, 1980); Benjamin Page, *Who Gets What from Government?* (Berkeley: University of California Press, 1983); C. Wright Mills, *The Power Elite* (New York: Oxford University Press, 1957); Edward Greenberg, *Serving the Few: Corporate Capitalism and the Bias of Government Policy* (New York: John Wiley, 1974); Richard Quinney, *Critique of Legal Order: Crime Control in Capitalist Society* (Boston: Little, Brown, 1974); Charles McCaghy, *Deviant Behavior: Crime, Conflict and Interest Groups* (New York: Macmillan, 1976).

11. Kai T. Erikson, *Wayward Puritans* (New York: John Wiley, 1966); Emile Durkheim, *The Division of Labor in Society* (Glencoe, Ill.: Free Press, 1947); Michael Lewis, *The Culture of Inequality* (New York: New American Library, 1978), 73.

12. Reiman, note 3 *supra*, 35; Jack Douglas, "Crime and Justice in American Society," in Jack Douglas (ed.), *Crime and Justice in American Society* (Indianapolis: Bobbs Merrill, 1971), 15.

13. Chambliss and Mankoff, note 8 *supra*; William J. Chambliss and Robert B. Seidman, *Law, Order and Power* (Reading, Mass.: Addison Wesley, 1971).

14. Laura Shill Schrager and James F. Short, "How Serious a Crime? Perceptions of Organizational and Common Crimes," in Ezra Shotland and Gilbert Geis (eds.), *White Collar Crime: Theory and Research* (Beverly Hills, Calif.: Sage, 1980); Laureen Snider, "Traditional and Corporate Theft: A Comparison of Sanctions," in Peter Wickman and Timothy Daily (eds.), *White Collar and Economic Crime* (Lexington, Mass.: Lexington Books, 1982).

15. Quinney, note 10 *supra*, 105; Christopher Holliday, "The Elusive Victim: Conceptual Orientations," in Jacqueline Scherer and Gary Shepard (eds.), *Victimization of the Weak* (Springfield, Ill.: Charles C Thomas, 1983), 213; Gary Shepard, "Victims, Values and the Social Structure of Everyday Life," in Scherer and Shepard, *ibid.*, 232.

16. Cleobis H. S. Jayewardene and Hilda Jayewardene, "The Victim and the Criminal Law," in Hans Joachim Schneider (ed.), *The Victim in International Perspective* (Berlin: Walter de Gruyter, 1982), 391.

17. Dan A. Lewis (ed.), *Reactions to Crime* (Beverly Hills, Calif.: Sage, 1981), 12; Yet, the concept of victimization conveyed, in part, through the criminal law, may not be inescapably shaped by powerful interests. When public definitions begin to deviate from official versions, some policies and perspectives might emerge to symbolically re-entrench or revalue the victim label. With the 1960s due process revolution, for example, characterized by a more sympathetic view of offenders, the clear distinction between victims and criminals began to fade. As pre-established labels and definitions started to blur, some began considering offenders as possible victims. Since more prisoners denied responsibility for their crimes, blaming society and downplaying their own free choice, the conventional victim label became threatened. Some view official criticisms of offender rehabilitation in favor of retribution as attempting to reestablish the line between criminals and both victims and the society. Others argue that victim compensation plans may have emerged at this time primarily to reestablish official definitions of victims. As we shall see, those programs significantly redefined the social label of victim through their eligibility requirements, which ostensibly separated "real" victims from unworthy pretenders. See David Miers, "Victim Compensation as a Labelling Process," *Victimology*, 5(1980), 3; Ezzat Fattah, "Becoming a Victim: The Victimization Experience and Its Aftermath," *Victimology*, 6(1981), 29; Jayewardene and Jayewardene, *ibid.*

18. Chambliss, note 6 *supra*, 230.

19. David M. Gordon, "Capitalism, Class and Crime in America," *Crime and Delinquency* (April 1973), 179.

20. Snider, note 14 *supra*.

21. Marshall Clinard and Peter C. Yeager, *Corporate Crime* (New York: Free Press, 1980).

22. Hugo Bedau, "Are There Really 'Crimes Without Victims'?" in Edwin Schur and Hugo Bedau (eds.), *Victimless Crimes: Two Sides of a Controversy* (Englewood Cliffs, N.J.: Prentice-Hall, 1974), 101.

23. William J. Chambliss, "A Sociological Analysis of the Law of Vagrancy," *Social Problems*, 12(Summer 1964), 67; Caleb Foote, "Vagrancy Type Law and Its Administration," *University of Pennsylvania Law Review*, 104(1956), 1; Michael Tigar and Madeleine Levy, *Law and the Rise of Capitalism* (New York: Monthly Review, 1977).

24. Diana Gordon, "Equal Protection, Unequal Justice," in Leslie Dunbar, *Minority Report: What Has Happened to Blacks, Hispanics, American Indians and Other Minorities in the Eighties* (New York: Pantheon, 1984), 125.

25. Duster, note 9 *supra*.

26. Gary T. Marx, "Social Control and Victimization," *Victimology*, 8(1983), 80.

27. See, for example, U.S. Department of Justice, Attorney General's Task Force on Violent Crime, *Final Report* (Washington, D.C.: Author, 1981).

28. Inkeri Anttila, "Who Are the Victims of Crimes?" Paper presented at Second International Symposium on Victimology, Boston, 1976.

29. Schwendinger and Schwendinger, note 6 *supra*, 116.

30. Reiman, note 3 *supra*, 68; Robert Elias, "Crimes That Don't Count," *The Progressive* (September 1981); Mark Green and John Berry, "White Collar Crime Is Big Business," *The Nation*, June 8, 1985, 706.

31. M. R. Burt and R. E. Estep, "Who Is the Victim?" *Victimology*, 6(1981), 1.

32. Nadine Taub and Elizabeth M. Schneider, "Perspectives on Women's Subordination and the Role of Law," in Kairys, note 6 *supra*, 117; Na-

dine Taub, "Adult Domestic Violence: The Law's Response," *Victimology,* 8(1983), 152; Jennifer James, "The Prostitute as Victim," in Jane Roberts Chapman and Margaret Gates (eds.), *The Victimization of Women* (Beverly Hills, Calif.: Sage, 1978), 175; Karen DeCrow, *Sexist Justice* (New York: Vintage, 1974).

33. Kurt Weis, "On Theory and Politics of Victimology and General Aspects of the Process of Victimization," in Edith Elizabeth Flynn and John P. Conrad (eds.), *The New and the Old Criminology* (New York: Praeger, 1978), 185.

34. Barry Krisberg, *Crime and Privilege* (Englewood Cliffs, N.J.: Prentice-Hall, 1975), 52.

35. Reiman, note 3 *supra,* 49.

36. The law also orients us toward a rights-based or deserts-based justice without regard for natural differences when it might better use a needs-based definition of crime that describes it as obstructions to meeting people's needs. If enforced, needs would be met and traditional crime (committed to meet needs) would decline. See Larry L. Tifft, "The Coming Redefinition of Crime: An Anarchist Perspective," *Social Problems,* 26(1979), 392.

37. Viano, note 10 *supra,* 57.

38. Erik Olin Wright, *The Politics of Punishment* (New York: Harper and Row, 1973); Charles Silberman, *Criminal Violence, Criminal Justice* (New York: Vintage, 1978).

39. Krisberg, note 34 *supra,* 13.

40. William A. Ryan, *Blaming the Victim* (New York: Vintage, 1976).

41. Gregg Barak, *In Defense of Whom? A Critique of Criminal Justice Reform* (Cincinnati: Anderson, 1980), 127.

42. See Duster, note 9 *supra,* for example, for the law's role in labelling and socializing certain kinds of drug use as immoral.

43. Stanley Aronowitz, "Law, the Breakdown of Order and Revolution," in Robert Lefcourt (ed.), *Law Against the People: Essays to Demystify Law, Order and the Courts* (New York: Vintage, 1971), 152.

44. Barak, note 41 *supra,* 127.

45. D. R. Watson, "The Presentation of Victim and Motive in Discourse: The Case of Police Interrogations and Interviews," *Victimology,* 8(1983), 31.

46. The International Association of Chiefs of Police recommends against arrest even if applicable laws exist. See Fattah, note 17 *supra,* 29.

47. M. A. Straus, "Sexual Inequality, Cultural Norms and Wife-Beating," *Victimology,* 1(1976), 54; Fattah, note 17 *supra;* Viano, note 10 *supra,* 68.

48. Kurt Weis and Sandra Weis, "Victimology and the Justification of Rape," in Israel Drapkin and Emilio Viano (eds.), *Victimology: Exploiters and the Exploited* (Lexington, Mass.: Lexington Books, 1974), 21.

49. Kurt Weis and Sandra S. Borges, "Rape as a Crime without Victims and Offenders? A Methodological Critique," in Emilio Viano (ed.), *Victims and Society* (Washington, D.C.: Visage Press, 1976), 230.

50. Jeffrey A. Reiman, "Victims, Harm and Justice," in Israel Drapkin and Emilio Viano (eds.), *Victimology: Theoretical Issues* (Lexington, Mass.: Lexington Books, 1974), 86; Lefcourt, note 43 *supra*.

51. Weis, note 35 *supra*, 183; Schwendinger and Schwendinger, note 6 *supra*, 137.

52. Edwin M. Schur, "The Case for Abolition," in Schur and Bedau, note 22 *supra*, 3; Edwin M. Schur, *Our Criminal Society: The Social and Legal Sources of Crime in America* (Englewood Cliffs, N.J.: Prentice-Hall, 1969), 291; Sawyer F. Sylvester, "Iatrogenics, Law and Decriminalization," in Sawyer F. Sylvester and Edward Sagarin (eds.), *Politics and Crime* (New York: Praeger, 1972), 1; Joseph J. Fitzpatrick, "Cultural Differences, Not Criminal Offenses: A Redefinition of Types of Social Behavior," in Sylvester and Sagarin, *ibid.*, 119; Edwin M. Schur, "The Trend Toward Decriminalization: Some Sociological Observations," in Sylvester and Sagarin, *ibid.*, 108; David J. Pittman, "Decriminalization of the Public Drunkenness Offense: An International Overview," in Sylvester and Sagarin, *ibid.*, 127; Francine Watman, "Sex Offenses Against Children and Minors: Victimological Implications for Decriminalization," in Sylvester and Sagarin, *ibid.*, 137; Mary D. Howard and John R. Howard, "Toward A Theory of Decriminalization," in Sylvester and Sagarin, *ibid.*, 148; Robert C. Bourchowitz, "Victimless Crimes: A Proposal to Free the Courts," *Judicature*, 57(1973), 69; Edith Flynn, "Report of the Discussion Sections of the Second International Symposium on Victimology," *Victimology*, 2(1977), 32.

53. Jethro Lieberman, *The Litigious Society* (New York: Harper and Row, 1981).

54. Ira Shor, *Critical Teaching and Everyday Life* (Boston: South End Press, 1980).

55. Lois Forer, *The Death of the Law* (New York: McKay, 1975).

56. Burton M. Leiser, *Liberty, Justice and Morals* (New York: Macmillan, 1979).

57. Bedau, note 22 *supra*.

58. Robert S. Weppner and James A. Inciardi, "Decriminalizing Marijuana," *International Journal of Offender Therapy and Comparative Criminology*, 22(1978), 115; Paul Friday, "Issues in the Decriminalization of Public Intoxication," *Federal Probation*, 42(1978), 33.

59. Milo Tyndel, "Offenders without Victims?" in Drapkin and Viano, note 50 *supra*, 55.

60. S. Wachter, "High Cost of Victimless Crimes," *Record*, 28(1973), 357; Aryeh Neier, *Crime and Punishment: A Radical Solution* (New York: Stein and Day, 1976); Norval Morris and Gordon Hawkins, *The Honest Politician's Guide to Crime Control* (Chicago: University of Chicago Press, 1970).

61. Brian Grossman, "The Discretionary Enforcement of Law," in Sylvester and Sagarin, note 52 *supra*, 65.

62. James, note 32 *supra*.

63. Reiman, note 3 *supra*, 32; Samual Walker, *Sense and Nonsense About Crime* (Monterrey, Calif.: Brooks/Cole, 1985), 197.

64. *Ibid.*, 33.

65. "Dutch Drug Policy," *Parade,* June 17, 1984, 23.

66. DeCrow, note 32 *supra*, 212.

67. Jerome Skolnick, *Justice Without Trial: Law Enforcement in A Democratic Society* (New York: John Wiley, 1966).

68. James, note 32 *supra,* 198.

69. Dorothy Bracey, "The Juvenile Prostitute: Victim and Offender," *Victimology,* 8(1983), 151; Jacqueline Boles and Charlotte Tatro, "Legal and Extra-Legal Methods of Controlling Female Prostitution: A Cross-Cultural Comparison," *International Journal of Comparative and Applied Criminal Justice,* 2(1978), 71.

70. Jonathan Rubinstein, *City Police* (New York: Farrar, Straus and Giroux, 1973).

71. American Friends Service Committee, *Struggle for Justice* (New York: Hill and Wang, 1971), 118.

72. Morris and Hawkins, note 60 *supra*, 5.

73. *Ibid.,* 6; William J. Chambliss, "Vice, Corruption, Bureaucracy and Power," in Chambliss and Mankoff, note 8 *supra*, 162.

74. Jack Newfield and Paul Dubrul, *The Permanent Government* (New York: Pilgrim Press, 1982).

75. Evelyn L. Parks, "From Constabulary to Police Society: Implications for Social Control," In Chambliss and Mankoff, note 8 *supra*, 129; Isidore Silver (ed.), *The Crime Control Establishment* (Englewood Cliffs, N.J.: Prentice-Hall, 1974); Stephen Spitzer, "The Rationalization of Crime Control in Capitalist Society," *Contemporary Crises*, 3(1979), 187; George Leonard, *The End of Sex* (New York: Bantam, 1983), 180.

76. John Blackmore, "Are Crime Rates Really Soaring?" *Police Magazine,* 4(1981), 35; Chambliss, note 6 *supra*; John E. Conklin, *The Impact of Crime* (New York: Macmillan, 1975), 25; Michael Milakovich, "Politics and Measure of Success in the War on Crime," *Crime and Delinquency,* 21(1975), 1; Silberman, note 38 *supra,* 27.

77. Kurt Weis and Michael Milakovich, "Who's Afraid of Crime? Or, How to Finance a Decreasing Rate of Increase," in Sylvester and Sagarin, note 52 *supra*, 31; Krisberg, note 34 *supra*, 70.

78. Wesley G. Skogan and Michael G. Maxfield, *Coping with Crime: Individual and Neighborhood Reactions* (Beverly Hills, Calif.: Sage, 1981).

79. Michael R. Gottfredson, Michael J. Hindelang, and Nicolete Parisi (eds.), *Sourcebook of Criminal Justice Statistics, 1977* (Washington, D.C.: U.S. Department of Justice, 1978), 397.

80. Bruce Johnson, "Is Crime Really Increasing?" Paper presented at Second International Symposium on Victimology, Boston, 1976.

81. Leroy C. Gould, "Crime and Its Impact in an Affluent Society," in Douglas, note 12 *supra*, 83.

82. Frank Browning, "Nobody's Soft on Crime Anymore: Rethinking America's Impossible Problem," *Mother Jones* (August 1982), 28.

83. Ted R. Gurr, *Rogues, Rebels and Reformers* (Beverly Hills, Calif.: Sage, 1976), 62.

84. See, for example, Baldey Raj Nayar, *Violence and Crime in India: A Quantitative Study* (Dehli: Macmillan, 1975).

85. H. J. Vetter and I. J. Silverman, *The Nature of Crime* (Philadelphia: W. B. Saunders, 1978), 33.

86. Albert D. Biderman, "Victimology and Victimization Surveys," in Israel Drapkin and Emilio Viano (eds.), *Victimology: Crimes, Victims and Justice* (Lexington, Mass.: Lexington Books, 1975), 153; Daniel Glaser, "Victim Survey Research: Theoretical Implications," in Israel Drapkin and Emilio Viano (eds.), *Victimology* (Lexington, Mass.: Lexington Books, 1974), 31; Philip H. Ennis, *Criminal Victimization in the U.S.: A Report of a National Survey* (Washington, D.C.: U.S. Government Printing Office, 1967); James Garofalo and Michael J. Hindelang, *An Introduction to the National Crime Survey* (Washington, D.C.: U.S. Government Printing Office, 1977); Michael Hindelang, *Criminal Victimization in Eight Cities* (Cambridge: Ballinger, 1976); Robert Elias, *Victims of the System: Crime Victims and Compensation in American Politics and Criminal Justice* (New Brunswick, N.J.: Transaction Books, 1983), 9.

87. Wesley G. Skogan, *Comparing Measures of Crime: Police Statistics and Survey Estimates of Citizen Victimization in American Cities* (Washington, D.C.: American Statistical Association, 1974); Wesley G. Skogan, "Validity of Official Crime Statistics: An Empirical Investigation," *Social Science Quarterly* (1974), 12; Wesley G. Skogan, "Measurement Problems in Official and Survey Crime Rates," *Journal of Criminal Justice*, 3(1975), 17; Wesley G. Skogan, "Dimensions of the Dark Figure of Unreported Crime," in Wesley G. Skogan (ed.), *Sample Surveys of the Victims of Crime* (Cambridge: Ballinger, 1975), 75; Paul D. Reynolds and Dale A. Blyth, "Sources of Variation Affecting the Relationship between Police and Survey Based Estimates of Crime Rates," in Drapkin and Viano, note 86 *supra*, 201; James Inciardi, "Criminal Statistics and Victim Survey Research," in Viano, note 49 *supra*, 173; M. A. Howard, "Police Reports and Victimization Survey Results: An Empirical Study," *Criminology*, 12(1975), 433; J. E. Eck and L. J. Riccio, "Relationship between Reported Crime Rates and Victimization Survey Results: An Empirical and Analytical Study," *Journal of Criminal Justice*, 7(1979), 293.

88. David L. Decker, David Schichor and Robert M. O'Brien, *Urban Structure and Victimization* (Lexington, Mass.: Lexington Books, 1982).

89. D. Seidman and M. Couzens, "Getting the Crime Rate Down: Political Pressure and Crime Reporting," *Law and Society Review*, 8(1974), 457; M. D. Maltz, "Crime Statistics: A Historical Perspective," *Crime and Delinquency*, 23(1977), 32; M. J. Greenwood and W. J. Wadychi, "Crime Rates and Public Expenditures for Police Protection: Their Interaction," *Review of Social Economics*, 31(1973), 138; N. Walker, *Crimes, Courts and Figures: An Introduction to Criminal Statistics* (Middlesex: Penguin, 1971).

90. Weis and Milakovich, note 77 *supra*.

91. D. J. Black, "Production of Crime Rates," *American Sociological Review*, 35(1970), 733; J. Piliavin and S. Briar, "Police Encounters with Juveniles," *American Journal of Sociology*, 70(1965), 206; James Q. Wilson, *Vari-*

eties of Police Behavior (Cambridge: Harvard University Press, 1968); Rubinstein, note 70 *supra.*

92. Skogan, note 87 *supra;* Anne L. Schreider, "Methodological Problems in Victim Surveys and Their Implications for Research in Victimology," *Journal of Criminal Law and Criminology,* 72(1981), 818; Andrew Karmen, *Crime Victims* (Belmont, Calif.: Brooks/Cole, 1984), 43; R. Hood and R. Sparks, *Key Issues in Criminology* (London: Weidenfeld and Nicolson, 1970); A. D. Biderman and A. J. Reiss, "On Exploring the 'Dark Figure' of Crime," *Annals,* 374(1967), 1; James A. Nelson, "Implications for the Ecological Study of Crime: A Research Note," in William H. Parsonage (ed.), *Perspectives on Victimology* (Beverly Hills, Calif.: Sage, 1979), 21; Anne L. Schneider, "Victimization Surveys and Criminal Justice System Evaluation," in Skogan, note 87 *supra,* 135; Michael Hindelang, "Victimization Surveying: Theory and Research," in Schneider, note 16 *supra,* 151; Albert Biderman, "Time Distortions of Victimization Data and Mnemonic Effects" (Washington, D.C.: Bureau of Social Science Research, 1970); M. R. Gottfredson and M. J. Hindelang, "A Consideration of Telescoping and Memory Decay Biases in Victimization Surveys," *Journal of Criminal Justice,* 5(1977), 205; A. L. Schneider and D. Sumi, "Patterns of Forgetting and Telescoping: An Analysis of LEAA Survey Victimization Data," *Criminology,* 19(1981), 400; Robert G. Lehman and Albert J. Reiss, "Response Effects in the National Crime Survey," *Victimology,* 3(1978), 110; S. H. Decker, "Official Crime Rates and Victim Surveys: An Empirical Comparison," *Journal of Criminal Justice,* 5(1977), 47.

93. Howard, note 87 *supra.*

94. Carolyn Rebecca Block and Richard L. Block, "Crime Definition, Crime Measurement and Victim Surveys," *Journal of Social Issues,* 40(1984), 137.

95. James Levine, "The Potential for Crime Over-Reporting in Criminal Victimization Surveys," *Criminology,* 14(1976), 307; Frederic Dubow and David Reed, "The Limits of Victim Surveys," in Skogan, note 87 *supra,* 151; Wesley G. Skogan, "Methodological Issues in the Measurement of Crime," in Schneider, note 16 *supra,* 203.

96. B. K. E. Penick and M. E. E. Owens (eds.), *Surveying Crime* (Washington, D.C.: National Academy of Sciences, 1976).

97. Dubow and Reed, note 95 *supra.*

98. As we shall soon see, the government faces a dilemma between its simultaneous desire to portray the least amount of crime possible and the advantage of showing an even more alarming figure. See Milakovich, note 76 *supra.*

99. Marie G. Argana, "Development of a National Victimization Survey," in Drapkin and Viano, note 86 *supra,* 171; Ennis, note 86 *supra;* Richard W. Dodge, Harold R. Lentzner and Frederick Schenk, "Crime in the U.S.: A Report on the National Crime Survey," in Skogan, note 87 *supra,* 1; R. W. Dodge, *Criminal Victimization in the U.S.: 1973–78 Trends* (Washington, D.C.: U.S. Department of Justice, 1980); Lehnen and Reiss, note 92 *supra.*

100. Jan J. M. van Dijk and Carl H. D. Steinmetz, "Victimization Surveys: Beyond Measuring the Volume of Crime," *Victimology,* 8(1983), 291; D. Thissen and H. Wainer, "Toward the Measurement and Prediction of

Victim Proneness," *Journal of Research on Crime and Delinquency*, 20(1983), 243.

101. Block and Block, note 94 *supra*.

102. A. Schneider, *Methodological Approaches for Measuring Short-Term Victimization Trends* (Eugene, Ore.: Oregon Research Institute, 1975); James A. Inciardi and D. C. McBride, "Victim Survey Research: Implications for Criminal Justice Planning," *Journal of Criminal Justice*, 4(1976) 147; Wesley G. Skogan, *Victimization Surveys and Criminal Justice Planning* (Washington, D.C.: U.S. Department of Justice, 1978); Irvin Waller, "Victimization Studies as Guides to Action: Some Cautions and Suggestions," in Schneider, note 16 *supra*, 166.

103. M. E. Wolfgang and S. I. Singer, "Victim Categories of Crime," *Journal of Criminal Law and Criminology*, 69(1978), 379.

104. James Garofalo, *Public Opinion About Crime: The Attitudes of Victims and Nonvictims in Selected American Cities* (Washington, D.C.: U.S. Department of Justice, 1977); Deidre A. Gaquin, "Measuring Fear of Crime: The National Crime Survey's Attitude Data," *Victimology*, 3(1978), 314.

105. Nelson, note 92 *supra;* Marlene A. Young-Rifai, "Methods of Measuring the Impact of Criminal Victimization Through Victimization Surveys," in Schneider, note 16 *supra*, 189; James Garofalo, "Victimization Surveys: An Overview," in Burt Galaway and Joe Hudson (eds.), *Perspectives on Crime Victims* (St. Louis: Mosby, 1981), 98.

106. Joseph Peters, "The Philadelphia Rape Study," in Drapkin and Viano, note 86 *supra*, 181.

107. Albert Biderman, et al., *Report on a Pilot Study on Victimization and Attitudes toward Law Enforcement: Field Surveys I* (Washington, D.C.: President's Commission on Law Enforcement and Administration of Justice, 1967); National Criminal Justice Information and Statistics Service, *A National Crime Survey Report (Cincinnati)* (Washington, D.C.: U.S. Department of Justice, 1979); J. F. Shenk, *Criminal Victimization of New York State Residents, 1974–77* (Washington, D.C.: U.S. Department of Justice, 1978); National Criminal Justice Information and Statistics Service, *Criminal Victimization Surveys in San Francisco* (Washington, D.C.: U.S. Department of Justice, 1977); U.S. Justice Statistics Bureau, *Criminal Victimization of California Residents* (Washington, D.C.: U.S. Government Printing Office, 1981).

108. Marshall B. Clinard, "Summary of Comparative Crime Victimization Surveys: Some Problems and Results," Paper presented at Second International Symposium on Victimology, Boston, 1976.

109. J. Braithwaite and D. Biles, "Crime Victimization Rates in Australian Cities," *Australian and New Zealand Journal of Sociology*, 16(1980), 79; John Braithwaite and David Biles, "Overview of Findings from the First Australian National Crime Victims Survey," *Australian and New Zealand Journal of Criminology*, 13(1980), 41; John Braithwaite and David Biles, *Crime Victimization in Australia: A Comparison with the U.S.* (Canberra: Australia Institute of Criminology, 1980); William Clifford, "Victimology in Australia," *Victimology*, 8(1983), 35; Louis Waller, "Victims of Crime: Some Australian Developments," in Schneider, note 16 *supra*, 279; Stanley Johnston, "Victimology and Victim Services in Australia," *World Society of Victimology Newsletter*, 1(1981), 38; A. A. Congalton, *Who Are the Victims?* (New South Wales: Bureau of Crime, 1975); Australian Bureau of Statistics, *General Social Survey: Crime Victims* (Canberra: Author, 1979); David Biles, "The Australian Victim Survey Methodology" Paper presented at Fifth International Symposium on Victimology, Zagreb, 1985; Maartje Bozinovic, "The Victimization of Ethnic Workers in Melbourne" Paper presented at Fifth International Symposium on Victimology, Zagreb, 1985.

110. Hazel G. Genn, "Some Findings of a Pilot Survey of Criminal Victimization in England," in Viano, note 49 *supra*, 285; Hazel G. Genn, "Findings of a Pilot Survey of Victimization in England," *Victimology*, 1(1976), 253; Richard F. Sparks, "Crimes and Victims in London," in Skogan, note 87 *supra*, 43; R. I. Mawby, "The Victimization of Juveniles: A Comparative Study of Three Areas of Publicly Owned Housing in Sheffield," *Journal of Research on Crime and Delinquency*, 16(1979), 88; Richard F. Sparks, Hazel G. Genn, and David J. Dodd, *Surveying Victims: A Study of the Measurement of Criminal Victimization, Perceptions of Crime and Attitudes To Criminal Justice* (Chichester: John Wiley, 1977); M. Hough and P. Mayhew, *The British Crime Survey* (London: Home Office Research Study No. 76, 1983); S. J. Smith, "Victimization in the Inner City: A British Case Study," *Home Office Research Bulletin*, 14(1982), 24; Michael Hough, "The British Victimization Survey" Paper presented at Fifth International Symposium on Victimology, Zagreb, 1985.

111. J. P. Fiselier, "Victims of Crime in the Netherlands," in Viano, note 49 *supra*, 268; Jan J. M. van Dijk and Carl H. D. Steinmetz. *The Burden of Crime on Dutch Society, 1973–79* (The Hague: Netherlands Justice Ministry, 1978); J. Fiselier, "Notes on Some Policy Implications of Victim Surveys," *Tijdschrift voor Criminologie*, 25(1983), 129; J. P. S. Fiselier, *Victims of Crime: Research on Unrecorded Crime* (Utrecht: Ars Aequi Libri, 1978); J. J. M. van Dijk, "Victimology in the Netherlands," *World Society of Victimology Newsletter*, 1(1981), 51; G. J. A. Smale and H. L. P. Spickenheuer, "Feelings of Guilt and Need for Retaliation in Victims of Serious Crimes Against Property and Persons," *Victimology*, 4(1979), 75.

112. E. Stephan, "Results of the Stuttgart Survey of Victims Taking Comparable American Data into Account: An Interim Report," *Kriminalistik*, 29(1975), 201; Gerd Kirchoff and Claudia Thelen, "Hidden Victimization by Sex Offenders in Germany," in Viano, note 49 *supra*, 277; Hans Goppinger, "The Victim as Seen by the Offender," Paper presented at Second International Symposium on Victimology, Boston, 1976; Gerd Kirchoff, Claudia Kirchoff and Paul Friday, "A Cross-Cultural Study of the Incidence of Hidden Sexual Victimization and Related Aspects," Paper presented at Second International Symposium on Victimology, Boston, 1976; H. D. Schwind, "Interim Report on Research on Unreported Crime in Goettingen," *Kriminalistik*, 28(1974), 241; Egon Stephan, "Personality and Attitude Measurement in Two Studies of Self-Reported Delinquency and Victimization," *International Journal of Crime and Penology*, 5(1977), 275; H. D. Schwind, "Victimology in Policy and Judiciary Practice," *Kriminalistik*, 33(1979), 514; Hans-Heiner Kulne, "The Reality of Victims Rights in the German Criminal Procedure" Paper presented at Fifth International Sym-

posium on Victimology, Zagreb, 1985; Wolfram Schadler, "Experiences from the Victim and Witness Assistance Center in Hanau" Paper presented at Fifth International Symposium on Victimology, Zagreb, 1985.

113. Kiochi Miyazawa, "Society and the Victim: Attitudes and Policies," in Israel Drapkin and Emilio Viano (eds.), *Victimology: Society's Reaction to Victimization* (Lexington, Mass.: Lexington Books, 1974), 5; Kiochi Miyazawa, "Victimological Studies of Sex Crimes in Japan," in Viano, note 49 *supra*, 295; Tetsuya Fujimoto, "The Victimological Study in Japan," in Schneider, note 16 *supra*, 128; Y. Takahashi, H. Nishimura and S. Suzuki, "A Study of Violence Among Pupils in Junior High Schools," *Reports of National Research Institute of Police Science*, 23(1982), 108; Fumie Kumagai, "Filial Violence in Japan," *Victimology*, 8(1983), 173; K. Mushino, "Victims of Organized Crime and the Process of Victimization," *Reports of National Research Institute of Police Science*, 20(1979), 101.

114. Marshall B. Clinard, *Cities With Little Crime: The Case of Switzerland* (New York: Cambridge University Press, 1978); Marshall B. Clinard, "Comparative Crime Victimization Surveys: Some Problems and Results," *International Journal of Criminology and Penology*, 6(1978), 221; Paul Brenzikofer, "Efforts for Victims of Crime in Switzerland," in Schneider, note 16 *supra*, 136; Martin Killias, "Victimization Surveys in Europe: How to Adopt American Methods to European Budgets—Preliminary Lessons from the French Swiss Victimization Survey" Paper presented at Fifth International Symposium on Victimology, Zagreb, 1985.

115. S. Leppa and R. Sire, *Individual Victims of Property Crime between 1972 and 1975: A Comparison* (Helsinki: Research Institute of Legal Policy, 1976); K. Aromaa, "Victimization to Violence: A Gallup Survey," *International Journal of Criminology and Penology*, 2(1974), 333; K. Aromaa, *Three Victim Surveys: Gallup Surveys on Victimization to Violence* (Helsinki: Research Institute of Legal Policy, 1977); Kauko Aromaa and Teuvo Peltoniemi, "Family Violence Studies and Victimization Surveys in Finland," *Victimology*, 8(1983), 195.

116. Louis F. Freed, "A Victimological Assessment of the Problem of Crime in the Republic of South Africa," in Drapkin and Viano, note 113 *supra*, 55; H. G. Dijdom and W. J. Schurink, "Victims of Serious Crime in Soweto," *Humanitas*, 5(1979), 39; W. J. Schurink, "Data on Primary Victimization Related to the General Group Premise of Subcultural Theories of Deviancy and Juvenile Delinquency," *Humanitas*, 4(1978), 277.

117. Knut Sveri, "Comparative Analyses of Crime by Means of Victim Surveys: The Scandinavian Experience," in Schneider, note 16 *supra*, 209; Preben Wolf, "A Comparative Study of Victims of Crimes in Three Scandinavian Countries (1970–74)," Paper presented at Second International Symposium on Victimology, Boston, 1976; Ragnar Hauge and Preben Wolf, "Criminal Violence in Three Scandinavian Countries," in Nils Christie (ed.), *Scandinavian Studies in Criminology* (London: Tavistok, 1974), 25.

118. G. Gulotta and M. Riboni, "Victimology in Italy," *Victimology*, 7(1982), 156; Guglielmo Gulotta, "Victimization and Victimological Orientations in Italy," *Victimology*, 8(1983), 23; P. Nuvolone, "The Victim in

Criminogenesis: Criminological and Legal Problems, with a Brief Survey of Italian Law," *Etud. Int. Psycho-Soc. Crim.*, 26(1975), 49.

119. A. Normandeau, "For a Canadian and International Charter of Rights for Crime Victims," *Canadian Journal of Criminology*, 25(1983), 463; J. L. Evans and G. J. Leger, "Canadian Victimization Surveys: A Discussion Paper," *Canadian Journal of Criminology*, 21(1979), 166.

120. George Kellens, "Report on Victimology in Belgium," *World Society of Victimology Newsletter*, 1(1981), 42.

121. B. Edquist and S. Wennberg, "Recent Legislation and Research on Victims in Sweden," *Victimology*, 8(1983), 310; Annika Snare, "Sexual Violence Against Women: A Scandinavian Perspective," *Victimology*, 9(1984), 195; Klas Lithner, "The Legal Position of Victims in Swedish Law Since 1948" Paper presented at Fifth International Symposium on Victimology, Zagreb, 1985; Klas Lithner, "Swedish Legislation on Government Responsibility to Victims of State Activities or Because of Loss of Liberty" Paper presented at Fifth International Symposium on Victimology, Zagreb, 1985.

122. Menachem Amir and Sarah Ben David, "Victimology in Israel," *World Society of Victimology Newsletter*, 1(1981), 50.

123. Louise Shelley, "The Geography of Soviet Criminality," *American Sociological Review*, 45(1980), 111; V. I. Polubinskij, "Toward A Criminal Victimology?" *State and the Law Series*, 2(1977); S. S. Ostroumov and L. V. Frank, "On Victimology and Victimization," *Soviet Law and Government*, 15(1976–77), 70.

124. V. N. Rajan, "Crime Victimization Research Program and Policy Planning in Developing Countries," *Victimology*, 5(1980), 193; V. N. Rajan, *Victimology in India* (New York: Asia Books, 1981); Nayar, note 84 *supra*; D. P. Saxena, "Study of Victim in Future Criminological Research in India," *Indian Journal of Criminology*, 6(1978), 94; Yedla C. Schimhadri, "Victimology in India," *World Society of Victimology Newsletter* 1(1981), 47.

125. Nwokocha K. U. Nkpa, "Victimization of Babies in Nigerian Urban Centers," *Victimology*, 5(1980), 251; Nwokocha K. U. Nkpa, "Armed Robbery in Post-Civil War Nigeria: The Role of the Victim," in Viano, note 49 *supra*, 158; F. Odekunle, "Victims of Property Crime in Nigeria: A Preliminary Investigation in Zaria," *Victimology*, 4(1979), 236; F. Odekunle, "Victims of Crime in a Developing Country: A Nigerian Study," Paper presented at Second International Symposium on Victimology, Boston, 1976; Nwokocha K. U. Nkpa, "The Practice of Restitution to Victims of Crime in a Traditional Society," Paper presented at Second International Symposium on Victimology, Boston, 1976; Olufunmilayo Oloruntimehin, "The Victim in the Criminal Justice System: the Nigerian Case," in Schneider, note 16 *supra*, 403; Charles E. Okaeri, "Community Responsibility and the Victim in Nigerian Society," in Viano, note 49 *supra*, 440.

126. Stanley K. Fisher, "The Victim's Role in Criminal Prosecutions in Ethiopia," in Drapkin and Viano, note 86 *supra*, 73.

127. Charles Cutshall and Paul E. McCold, "Patterns of Stock Theft Victimization and Formal Response Strategies Among the Ila of Zambia," *Victimology*, 7(1982), 137.

128. Mohammed Shaalan, Ahmed Shawki El-Akabaoui, Sayed El-Kott, "Rape Victimology in Egypt," *Victimology*, 8(1983), 277.

129. Marcela Marquez de Villalobos, "Victims of Crimes in Metropolitan Panama," Paper presented at Second International Symposium on Victimology, Boston, 1976.

130. Laercio Pellegrino, "Victimology in Brazilian Penal Law and Law Reports," Paper presented at Second International Symposium on Victimology, Boston, 1976; Laercio Pellegrino, "The Adoption of Victimological Principles in Brazil's New Penal Law," *World Society of Victimology Newsletter*, 1(1981), 45.

131. Christopher H. Birkbeck, "Victimization Surveys in Latin America: Some First Experiences," *Victimology*, 8(1983), 7.

132. Louis Rodriquez Manzanera, "Victimization in a Mexican City: The Example of the City of Jalapa in the State of Veracruz," in H. J. Schneider (ed.), *Das Verbre Chensopfer in der Strafrechtspflege: Psychologische, Kriminologisch, Strafrechtliche und Strafverfahrensrechtliche Aspeckte* (Berlin: Walter de Gruyter, 1982), 25.

133. Tibamanaya Mwene Mushanga, "The Victimization of Wives in East and Central African Communities," Paper presented at Second International Symposium on Victimology, Boston, 1976; 133. Birkbeck, note 131 *supra*; John Hatchard, "Self-Protection by Victims: The Development of Instant Justice in Zambia" Paper presented at Fifth International Symposium on Victimology, Zagreb, 1985; George Liundi, "Instances of Actual or Potential Collective Victimization Through Abuse of Power in Selected African Nations" Paper presented at Fifth International Symposium on Victimology, Zagreb, 1985.

134. Tony Platt, "Street Crime," in Tony Platt and Paul Takagi (eds.), *Crime and Social Justice* (Totowa, N.J.: Barnes and Noble, 1981), 17; Thomas Cronin, et al., *U.S. Against Crime in the Streets* (Bloomington: Indiana University Press, 1981); Ira Magaziner and Robert Reich, *Mending America's Business* (New York: Harcourt Brace Jovanovich, 1982), 22.

135. Alfred Biderman, "Sources of Data for Victimology," *Journal of Criminal Law and Criminology*, 72(Summer 1981), 789.

136. William F. McDonald, "Criminal Justice and the Victim: An Introduction," in William F. Mcdonald (ed.), *Criminal Justice and the Victim* (Beverly Hills, Calif.: Sage, 1976), 28.

137. Terence Thornberry and Robert Figlio, "Victimization and Criminal Behavior in a Birth Cohort," in Terence Thornberry and Edward Sagarin (eds.), *Images of Crime: Offenders and Victims* (New York: Praeger, 1974), 28.

138. Kirchoff, Kirchoff, and Friday, note 112 *supra;* Stephan, note 112 *supra*.

139. "Conclusions and Recommendations, International Study Institute on Victimology, Bellagio, Italy, July 1–12, 1975," *Victimology*, 1(1976), 130.

140. Robert E. Ford and Lydia Keitner, "The Circular Population: The Victims and Offenders of Violent Offenses," Paper presented at Second International Symposium on Victimology, Boston, 1976.

141. Lee Bridges and Liz Fekete, "Victims, the 'Urban Jungle,' and the New Racism," *Race and Class*, 27(1985), 45, 60; Chambliss, note *supra*, 231.

142. Egon Stephan, note 112 *supra*; Ennis, note 86 *supra*.

143. Skogan and Maxfield, note 78 *supra*.

144. Howard Zinn, *The Twentieth Century: A People's History* (New York: Harper and Row, 1984), 310.

145. Scheingold, note 8 *supra*, 68.

146. Many have argued that schools, universities, commissions, institutes, and task forces typically reflect only a narrow range of perspectives, usually consistent with prevailing, mainstream ideologies. See, for example, Quinney, note 14 *supra*; Viano, note 10 *supra*, 60; Schrager and Short, note 14 *supra*, 29; David S. Davis, "The Production of Crime Policies," *Crime and Social Justice* (1983), 121; Tony Platt and Paul Takagi, "Intellectuals for Law and Order: A Critique of the New 'Realists'," in Platt and Takagi, note 134 *supra*, 30; Cyril Robinson, "Criminal Justice Research: Two Competing Futures," *Crime and Social Justice*, 23(1985), 110.

147. Margaret T. Gordon and Linda Heath, "The News Business, Crime and Fear," in Lewis, note 17 *supra*, 227; Conklin, note 76 *supra*, 18.

148. "The Curse of Violent Crime," *Time*, March 23, 1981, 16.

149. Gary Kinder, *Victim: The Other Side of Murder* (New York: Dell, 1982).

150. Conklin, note 76 *supra*, 22; M. Fishman, "Crime Waves as Ideology," *Social Problems*, 25(1978), 531; Jeffrey Schrank, *Snap, Crackle, and Popular Taste: The Illusion of Free Choice in America* (New York: Dell, 1977), 20, 29.

151. "The Curse of Violent Crime," note 148 *supra*, 16.

152. Gould, note 81 *supra*, 83.

153. Joseph Boskin, "The Media Image of Law Enforcement," unpublished paper, n.d.

154. Guy Cumberbatch and Alan Beardsworth, "Criminals, Victims and Mass Communications," in Viano, note 49 *supra*, 72; Conklin, note 76 *supra*; Ursula Schneider, "The Presentation of Victims of Crime in Television Movies and Documentaries," in Schneider, note 16 *supra*.

155. Cumberbatch and Beardsworth, *ibid.*

156. Institute for Study of Labor and Economic Crisis, *The Iron Fist and the Velvet Glove: An Analysis of the U.S. Police* (San Francisco: Crime and Justice Associates, 1982), 10.

157. *Ibid.*

158. This suggests that we might require television programs to provide their audience with a warning message, perhaps: "*WARNING*: This program may not portray reality and, where it does, much of the official behavior you see violates the criminal law and the Constitution."

159. Scheingold, note 8 *supra*, 63.

160. Katherine Saltzman, "Women and Victimization: The Aftermath," in Chapman and Gates, note 32 *supra*, 269; Laura Lederer, *Take Back the Night* (New York: Morrow, 1980).

161. James Gilsinan, *Doing Justice* (Englewood Cliffs, N.J.: Prentice-Hall, 1982), 215.

162. W. Schramm, J. Lyle and E. Parker, *Television in the Lives of Our Children* (Palo Alto: Stanford University Press, 1961), 155.

163. Karmen, note 92 *supra*, 5.

164. George Gerbner and Larry P. Gross, "Living with Television: The Violence Profile," *Journal of Communications* (April 1976), 1.

165. Linda Lichter and Robert Lichter, *Prime Time Crime* (Washington, D.C.: The Media Institute, 1983).

166. Scheingold, note 8 *supra*, 63.

167. Gerbner and Gross, note 164 *supra*.

168. Bertram Gross, *Friendly Facism: The New Face of Power in America* (New York: M. Evans, 1980), 310.

169. Robert LeJeune and Nicholas Alex, "On Being Mugged: The Event and Its Aftermath," *Urban Life and Culture*, 2(1973), 259; Skogan and Maxfield, note 78 *supra*, 143.

170. Tom R. Tyler, "Assessing the Risk of Crime Victimization: The Integration of Personal Victimization Experience and Socially Transmitted Information," *Journal of Social Issues*, 40(1984), 27; LeJeune and Alex, *ibid.*, 278.

171. Ezzat Fattah, "Perceptions of Violence, Concern About Crime, Fear of Victimization and Attitudes to the Death Penalty," *Canadian Journal of Criminology*, 21(1979), 22.

172. Schrank, note 150 *supra*, 18.

173. Conklin, note 76 *supra*, 20; Scheingold, note 8 *supra*, 63; Gordon and Heath, note 147 *supra*, 227; Skogan and Maxfield, note 78 *supra*.

174. M. McPherson, "Realities and Perceptions of Crime at the Neighborhood Level," *Victimology*, 3(1978), 319; V. H. Jaycox, "The Elderly's Fear of Crime: Rational or Irrational," *Victimology*, 3(1978), 328; Schrank, note 150 *supra*, 32.

175. Gordon and Heath, note 147 *supra*, 240; Rob I. Mawby and Judith Brown, "Newspaper Images of the Victim: A British Study," *Victimology*, 9(1984), 82; Schrank, note 150 *supra*, 32.

176. Conklin, note 76 *supra*, 28; Carl E. Pope and R. L. McNeely, "Race, Crime and Criminal Justice: An Overview," in R. L. McNeely and C. E. Pope (eds.), *Race, Class and Criminal Justice* (Beverly Hills, Calif.: Sage, 1981), 9.

177. Garofalo, note 104 *supra*.

178. J. J. M. van Dijk, "Public Attitudes Toward Crime in the Netherlands," *Victimology*, 265.

179. Cumberbatch and Beardsworth, note 154 *supra*, 73; Jane Briggs-Bunting, "Behind the Headlines: News Media Victims," in Scherer and Shepard, note 15 *supra*, 80.

180. Schur, note 52 *supra*, 73.

181. Scheingold, note 8 *supra*, 64.

182. Harold Lasswell, *World Politics and Personal Insecurity* (New York: Free Press, 1965), 30.

183. David Knouse, *Language, Labelling and Attribution* (New York: General Learning Press, 1971), 11.

184. Charles D. Elder and Roger W. Cobb, *The Political Uses of Symbols* (New York: Longman, 1983), 73; Furthermore: "The use of ambiguous, but potent, symbols shows that the identification of a situation or interests is less a matter of fact and more a matter of political definition," in Eugene Skolnick, *The Politics of Protest* (Washington, D.C.: U.S. Government Printing Office, 1969), 3.

185. Browning, note 82 *supra*, 29.

186. Quinney, note 14 *supra*.

187. John A. Schaar, "Legitimacy in the Modern State," in Philip Green and Sanford Levinson (eds.), *Power and Community: Dissenting Essays in Political Science* (New York: Random House, 1970), 276; Jurgen Habermas, *Legitimation Crisis* (Boston: Beacon Press, 1973); Alan Wolfe, *The Limits of Legitimacy* (New York: Free Press, 1977); David Friedrichs, "Violence and the Politics of Crime," *Social Research*, 48(1981), 135; David Friedrichs, "The Legitimacy Crisis in the U.S.: A Conceptual Analysis," *Social Problems*, 27(1980), 540; Claus Mueller, *The Politics of Communication: A Study in the Political Sociology of Language, Socialization and Legitimation* (New York: Oxford University Press, 1973).

188. David Rudovsky, "The Criminal Justice System and the Role of the Police," in Kairys, note 6 *supra*, 242; Weis and Milakovich, note 77 *supra*.

189. The fear of crime may have become "a social enterprise that provides entrepreneurs with political and pecuniary profit." in Scheingold, note 8 *supra*, 28.

190. The media may use language to both exaggerate and sanitize, yet may also deflect attention from government and alternative sources of victimization. See Edelman, note 1 *supra*. Crime may also provide a convenient symbol for focusing our general concerns about unwelcome changes in the social order. See Scheingold, note 8 *supra*, 226.

191. Selectively using words to create alarm may provide an important means of social control. See G. Sorel, *Reflections on Violence* (Glencoe, Ill.: Free Press, 1950); Paul Takagi, "A Garrison State in 'Democratic' Society," *Crime and Social Justice* (1974), 27.

192. *Time* magazine, for example, has portrayed cities as "jungles" and offenders as "savages," which may perpetuate false stereotypes and help entrench existing political relations. It may imbed its vision of crime deeply into the public culture. The media seem to portray selective images about individual offenders, victims and crimes, and an overall view of crime that may resemble ideology more than reality. See Pat Carlen, "Radical Criminology, Penal Politics and the Rule of Law," in Pat Carlen and Mike Collison (eds.), *Radical Issues in Criminology* (Totowa, N.J.: Barnes and Noble, 1981), 7.

193. The media may promote a false ideology that criminal justice functions primarily to control and eliminate crime instead of promoting interests, protecting property largely for the few, and controlling the population. See Robert Lefcourt, note 32 *supra*.

194. Some believe the media emphasizes crime committed by blacks against whites, despite its statistical insignificance. The recent switch to newly examining black-on-black crime may not have redressed the balance as much as it now has conveyed, by its presentation, the impression that blacks have been destroying themselves, completely apart from the actual context of their broader victimization by social and economic conditions. See Bernard D. Headley, "Black-on-Black Crime: The Myth and the Reality," *Crime and Social Justice* (1983), 50; Lewis, note 11 *supra*, 78.

195. The media and government may collude to pursue mutual interests, if only indirectly. Offenders may be "created" by appealing to our collective need for scapegoats for our problems, including crime, thus also creating new victims. See Gilbert Geis and Ivan Bunn, "Witches: The Nonesuch Victims," in Schneider, note 16 *supra*, 247; Offenders may become "sacrificial victims in society's attempt to obstruct disintegrative forces." See Jayewardene and Jayewardene, note 16 *supra*.

196. Our ideological conception of crime and criminals may blame crime (as well as poverty) on the poor, give middle classes a sense of "comparative advantage" and a scapegoat for their problems, divert attention from crime's social origins and from the harmful actions of the wealthier, and then prescribe punitive solutions. We may view poverty as a sign of failure, but not as a source of crime. See Reiman, note 3 *supra*, 140, 156; Lewis, note 11 *supra*, 75.

197. Some believe that crime in the streets has frequently been manufactured and exploited by presidential candidates and Presidents since at least Lyndon Johnson. See Cronin, note 134 *supra*, 168. Their response seems more symbolic than a way of really addressing the problem. Ronald Reagan's repeated distortions and ravings have been dutifully reported by the media. See Karmen, note 92 *supra*, 45.

198. James Michener, *Kent State: What Happened and Why* (New York: Random House, 1971).

199. Parenti, note 10 *supra*; Michael Parenti, *Inventing Reality* (New York: St. Martins Press, 1985); John Downing, *Radical Media* (Boston: South End Press, 1983); Robert Cirino, *Don't Blame the People* (New York: Vintage, 1971); Reiman, note 3 *supra*, 157.

200. Hall, note 5 *supra*.

201. *Ibid.*, 53. Such collaboration may help bolster official power and legitimate a freer hand for police control activities. See Hall, note 5 *supra*, 118.

202. Scheingold, note 8 *supra*, 76.

203. *Ibid.*, 54.

204. Cronin, note 134 *supra*, 181.

205. James Inciardi and Anne Pottieger (eds.), *Violent Crime* (Beverly Hills, Calif.: Sage, 1978); Lynn Curtis, *Criminal Violence* (Lexington, Mass.: Lexington Books, 1974); Duncan Chappell and John Monahan (eds.), *Violence and Criminal Justice* (Lexington, Mass.: D.C. Heath, 1975).

206. Hugh Davis Graham and Ted Robert Gurr, *Violence in America* (New York: New American Library, 1969).

207. Schur, note 52 *supra*, 125.

208. John E. Conklin, *Robbery and the Criminal Justice System* (Philadelphia: J. P. Lippincott, 1972); Morton Hunt, *The Mugging* (New York: Antheneum, 1972); Yona Cohn, "Crisis Intervention and the Victim of Robbery," in Drapkin and Viano, note 113 *supra*, 17; John M. MacDonald, *Armed Robbery* (Springfield, Ill.: Charles C Thomas, 1975).

209. John Allen, *Assault with a Deadly Weapon: The Autobiography of a Street Criminal* (New York: Pantheon, 1977); Chappell and Monahan, note 205 *supra*.

210. S. Palmer and J. A. Humphrey, "Offender-Victim Relationships in Criminal Homicide Followed by Offender's Suicide," *Bulletin of Life Threatening Behavior*, 10(1980), 106.

211. Michael W. Agopian, "Parental Child Stealing: Participants and the Victimization Process," *Victimology*, 5(1980), 263.

212. Schur, note 52 *supra*, 128.

213. Bruno M. Cormier, "Mass Murder, Multicide and Collective Crime: The Doers and the Victims," in Israel Drapkin and Emilio Viano (eds.), *Victimology: Violence and Its Victims* (Lexington, Mass.: Lexington Books, 1974), 71; Chanoch Jacobsen, "Condoned Mass Deviance Its Victims," in Drapkin and Viano, *ibid.*, 91.

214. Mark Kelman, "The Origins of Crime and Criminal Violence," in Kairys, note 6 *supra*, 244.

215. Michael J. Hindelang, Michael R. Gottfredson, and James Garofalo, *Victims of Crime: An Empirical Foundation for a Theory of Personal Victimization* (Cambridge: Ballinger, 1978); Pawel Horoszowski, "Homicide of Passion and Its Motives," in Drapkin and Viano, note 213 *supra*, 3; Klaus Sessar, "The Familiar Character of Criminal Homicide," in Drapkin and Viano, *ibid.*, 29; Stuart Palmer, "Characteristics of Homicide and Suicide Victims in Forty Non-Literate Societies," in Drapkin and Viano, *ibid.*, 43; Stephen Schafer, "Changing Victims of Changing Homicide," in Drapkin and Viano, *ibid.*, 25; Neville H. Avison, "Victims of Homicide," in Drapkin and Viano, *ibid.*, 55; Marvin Wolfgang, *Studies in Homicide* (New York: Harper and Row, 1967); B. M. Cormier and C. C. Angliker, "Psychodynamics of Homicide Committed in a Semi-Specific Relationship," *Canadian Journal of Crime and Correction*, 14; Yoshio Akiyama, "Murder Victimization: A Statistical Analysis," *FBI Law Enforcement Bulletin*, 50(1981), 8; Gloria Count van Manen, "Macrostructural Sources of Variation in Homicide Victimization Rates in the Capital City," in Viano, note 49 *supra*, 255; John A. Humphrey and Stuart Palmer, "Stressful Life Events and Criminal Homicide Offender-Victim Relationships," *Victimology*, 8(1983), 115; W. Wilbanks, "Homicide Victimization Rates in Dade County," *Victimology*, 4(1979), 305; Margaret Zahn, *Homicide in the Twentieth Century* (Philadelphia: Temple University Press, 1979).

216. Schur, note 52 *supra*, 127; *Democratic Fact Book: Issues for 1982* (Washington, D.C.: Democrats for the 1980s, 1982), 173.

217. Karmen, note 92 *supra*, 51.

218. Michael Agopian, et al., "Interracial Rape in a Northern City: An Analysis of 63 Cases," in Thornberry and Sagarin, note 137 *supra*, 91; Samuel Smithyman, "The Characteristics of Undetected Rapists," in Parsonage, note 92 *supra*, 99; Donna D. Schram, "Rape," in Chapman and Gates, note 32 *supra*, 53; M. Amir, *Patterns of Forcible Rape* (Chicago: University of Chicago Press, 1971); LeRoy Schultz, *Rape Victimology* (Springfield, Ill.: Charles C Thomas, 1975); W. Eromberg and E. Coyle, "Rape: A Compulsion to Destroy," *Medical Insight*, 22(1974), 21; Susan Brownmiller, *Against Our Will: Men, Women and Rape* (New York: Simon and Schuster, 1975); Susan Griffin, "Rape: The All-American Crime," *Ramparts*, (September, 1971), 25; Weis and Weis, note 48 *supra;* Steve Nelson and Menachim Amir, "The Hitchhike Victim of Rape: A Research Report," in Drapkin and Viano, note 48 *supra*, 47.

219. Barbara Starett, quoted in Theodore Roszak, *Person/Planet: The Creative Disintegration of Industrial Society* (Garden City, N.Y.: Doubleday, 1979), 43.

220. "Private Violence," *Time*, September 5, 1983, 19.

221. Schram, note 218 *supra;* Eugene J. Kanin, "Date Rape: Unofficial Criminals and Victims," *Victimology*, 9(1984), 95.

222. Viano, note 10 *supra*, 55.

223. Patsy Klaus (ed.), "Victims of Crime," *Bureau of Justice Statistics Bulletin* (November 1981).

224. Edward Sagarin and Donal E. J. MacNamara, "The Homosexual as a Crime Victim," in Drapkin and Viano, note 48 *supra*, 73.

225. Stephanie Riger, "On Women," in Lewis, note 17 *supra*, 53.

226. Smithyman, note 218 *supra*.

227. Nancy Gager and Cathleen Schurr, *Sexual Assault: Confronting Rape in America* (New York: Grosset and Dunlap, 1976).

228. Marjorie Brown Roy, *Rape Defendants in the Commonwealth of Massachusetts, 1974–78* (Boston: Massachusetts Probation Office, 1979).

229. Raymond Eve, "Empirical and Theoretical Findings Governing Child and Adolescent and Sexual Abuse," Paper presented at Third International Institute on Victimology, Lisbon, 1984; Sharon Howell, "Twisted Love: Pedophilia," in Scherer and Shepard, note 15 *supra*, 98; Imogene L. Moyer, "Differential Power and the Dynamics of Father-Daughter Incest" Paper presented at Fifth International Symposium on Victimology, Zagreb, 1985.

230. Agopian, note 218 *supra*.

231. Murray Straus, note 47 *supra*, 1; S. Kappel and E. Leuteritz, "Wife Battering in the Federal Republic of Germany," *Victimology*, 5(1980), 225; Ellen S. Cohn and David B. Sugarman, "Marital Abuse: Abusing the One You Love," *Victimology*, 3(1978), 11; Barbara Star, "Comparing Battered and Non-Battered Women," *Victimology*, 3(1978), 32; Del Martin, "Battered Women: Society's Problem," in Chapman and Gates, note 32 *supra*, 111; Richard Harris and Rosyln Bologh, "The Dark Side of Love: Blue and White Collar Wife Abuse," Paper presented at Third International Institute on

Victimology, Lisbon, 1984; Mildred Pagelow, "Preliminary Report on Battered Women," Paper presented at Second International Symposium on Victimology, Boston, 1976; Maria Roy (ed.), *Battered Women: A Psychosociological Study of Domestic Violence* (New York: Van Nostrand Reinhold, 1977); Suzanne K. Steinmetz. *The Cycle of Violence: Aggressive and Abusive Family Interaction* (New York: Praeger, 1977); U.S. Civil Rights Commission, *Battered Women: Issues of Public Policy* (Washington, D.C.: Author, 1978); Gerald Erchak, "The Escalation and Maintenance of Spouse Abuse: A Cybernetic Model," *Victimology*, 9(1984), 247; Richard Gelles and Claire Pedrick Cornell, *Intimate Violence in Families* (Beverly Hills, Calif.: Sage, 1985); Susan Schecter, *Women and Male Violence* (Boston: South End Press, 1984); Masamachi Itoh, et al., "The Battered Child Syndrome" Paper presented at Fifth International Symposium on Victimology, Zagreb, 1985.

232. Martin, *ibid.*

233. Diane Hamlin, "The Nature and Extent of Spouse Assault," *The Victim Advocate* (Alexandria, Va.: National District Attorneys Association, 1978), 3.

234. Bracey, note 69 *supra*, 151; Kumagai, note 113 *supra*.

235. "Private Violence," note 220 *supra*, 23.

236. *Ibid*, 18; Aromaa and Peltoniemi, note 115 *supra*; Teuvo Peltoniemi, "Family Violence: Police House Calls in Helsinki, Finland in 1977," *Victimology*, 5(1980), 213; Peggy Placier, "Victims of Victims: The Cycle of Abuse in a Violent Society," *The Dandelion* (April 1985), 3.

237. Linda MacLeod, "Wife Battering in Canada: The Vicious Circle," Paper presented at First World Congress on Victimology, Washington, D.C., 1980.

238. Salina Szechtman, "Wife Abuse: Women's Duties, Men's Rights," Paper presented at Third International Institute on Victimology, Lisbon, 1984; "Private Violence," note 220 *supra*, 23; Susanne K. Steinmetz, "The Battered Husband Syndrome," *Victimology*, 2(1977), 499.

239. Hamlin, note 233 *supra*, 4.

240. Don Dutton and Susan Lee Painter, "Traumatic Bonding: The Development of Emotional Attachments in Battered Women and Other Relationships of Intermittent Abuse," *Victimology*, 6(1981), 139; Don Dutton, Beverly Fehr, and Hope McEwan, "Severe Wife Battering as Deindividuated Violence," *Victimology*, 7(1982), 13; Cohn and Sugarman, note 231 *supra*, 203; Placier, note 236 *supra*; Mary Otto, "The Cycle of Abuse: From Victim to Victimizer," in Scherer and Shepard, note 15 *supra*, 172.

241. Viano, note 10 *supra*, 60.

242. Wilfred Masamura, "Wife Abuse and Other Forms of Aggression," *Victimology*, 4(1979), 46; Placier, note 236 *supra*.

243. L. E. Cohen and D. Cantor, "Residential Burglary in the U.S.: Lifestyle and Demographic Factors Associated with Probability of Victimization," *Journal of Research on Crime and Delinquency*, 18(1981), 113.

244. Conklin, note 208 *supra*.

245. Irvin Waller and Norman Okihiro, *Burglary: The Victim and the Public* (Toronto: University of Toronto Press, 1978); Paul J. Lavrakas, "On Households," in Lewis, note 17 *supra*, 67; T. Reppetto, *Residential Crime* (Cambridge: Ballinger, 1974); I. Waller, "Victim Research, Public Policy and Criminal Justice," in Viano, note 49 *supra*, 190; W. R. Paap, "Being Burglarized: An Account of Victimization," *Victimology*, 6(1981), 297.

246. Edwin Sutherland, *The Professional Thief* (Chicago: University of Chicago Press, 1937); Bruce Jackson, *A Thief's Primer* (New York: Macmillan, 1969).

247. James Brady, "Arson, Fiscal Crisis and Community Action," *Boston Observer*, 1(1981), 3; Elizabeth Lafferty, "Arson for Profit Sweeps Poor Urban Areas," *Pacific News Service* (December 1981), 1; Kevin Krajick, "The Arson Epidemic: Who Should Investigate?" *Police Magazine*, 2(1979), 4.

248. Conklin, note 208 *supra*,; Cohen and Cantor, note 243 *supra*.

249. Reiman, note 3 *supra*, 107.

250. Robert Goldstein, *Political Repression in America* (Cambridge: Schenkman, 1978).

251. David F. Greenberg (ed.), *Crime and Capitalism* (Palo Alto: Mayfield, 1981), 68; Donald R. Cressey, *Theft of the Nation: The Structure and Operations of Organized Crime* (Stanford: Hoover Institution Press, 1979); K. Musheno, "Victims of Organized Crime and the Process of Victimization," *Reports of the National Research Institute of Police Science*, 20(1979), 101.

252. Tony Platt, *The Child Savers* (Chicago: University of Chicago Press, 1969).

253. Gilbert Geis (ed.), *On White Collar Crime* (Beverly Hills, Calif.: Sage, 1978); Linda Martino, "Credit Card Fraud," *AAA World* (July 1984), 11; Gwynn Nettler, *Explaining Crime* (New York: McGraw-Hill, 1978).

254. Clinard and Yeager, note 21 *supra;* Donald R. Cressey, *Other People's Money* (New York: Free Press, 1953); Ellen Hochstedler, ed., *Corporations as Criminals* (Beverly Hills, Calif.: Sage, 1984).

255. Clinard and Yeager, note 21 *supra;* John W. Tomlin, "Victims of White Collar Crimes," in Schneider, note 16 *supra*, 274; Gilbert Geis, "Victimization Patterns in White Collar Crime," in Drapkin and Viano, note 46 *supra;* Marshall B. Clinard, *Corporate Ethics and Crime* (Beverly Hills, Calif.: Sage, 1983); McDonald, note 136 *supra*, 25; Schrager and Short, note 14 *supra*, 14; Marilyn Walsh and Donna Schram, "The Victim of White Collar Crime: Accusor or Accused?" in Shotland and Geis, note 14 *supra*, 32; Diane Vaughn, "Crime Between Organizations: Some Implications for Victimology," in Shotland and Geis, *ibid.*, 52; Neal Shover, "The Criminalization of Corporate Behavior: Federal Surface Coal Mining," in Shotland and Geis, *ibid.*, 98; Michael D. Maltz and Stephen M. Pollack, "Analyzing Suspected Collusion Among Bidders," in Shotland and Geis, *ibid.*, 142; Donn B. Parker, "Computer-Research White-Collar Crime," in Shotland and Geis, *ibid.*, 199; Mary V. McGuire and Herbert Edelhertz, "Consumer Abuse of Older Americans: Victimization and Remedial Action in Two Metropolitan Areas," in Shotland and Geis, *ibid.*, 266; Dwight C. Smith, "White-Collar, Organized Crime and the Business Establishment: Resolving a Crisis in Criminological Theory," in Wickman and Dailey, note 14 *supra*, 39; Harold C. Barnett, "The Production of Corporate Crime in Corporate Capitalism," in Wickman and Dailey, *ibid.*, 157; Snider, note 14 *supra*, 235; Harold Barnett, "Wealth, Crime and Capital Accumulation," *Contemporary Crises*, 3(1979), 171; Geis, note 253 *supra*; John Braithwaite, *Corporate Crime in the Pharmaceutical Industry* (London: Routledge and Kegan Paul, 1983); Graeme Newman, Jean C. Lester and Donald J. Articolo, "A Structural Analysis of Fraud," in Flynn and Conrad, note 33 *supra*, 151; Maurice Goldsmith, "The Thalidomide Affair," in Drapkin and Viano, note 86 *supra*, 205; Diane Vaughn and Giovanna Carlo, "Victims of Fraud: Victim-Responsiveness, Incidence and Reporting," in Viano, note 49 *supra*, 403; Diane Vaughan, "Victims of Fraud: Structural Barriers to Redress," Paper presented at Second International Symposium on Victimology, Boston, 1976; D. Vaughan and G. Carlo, "The Appliance Repairman: A Study of Victim Responsiveness to Fraud," *Journal of Research on Crime and Delinquency*, 12(1975), 153; Jane G. Schubert and Robert E. Krug, *Consumer Fraud: An Empirical Perspective* (Washington, D.C.: American Institute for Research, 1978); Morton Mintz, "At Any Cost: Corporate Greed, Women and the Dalkon Shield," *The Progressive* (November 1985), 20.

256. T. R. Young, "Corporate Crime: A Critique of the Clinard Report," *Contemporary Crises*, 5(1981), 323.

257. Clinard and Yeager, note 21 *supra*; I. Ross, "How Lawless Are Big Companies?" *Fortune*, December 1, 1980, 57; E. H. Sutherland, *White Collar Crime* (New York: Holt, Rinehart and Winston, 1961); Mark Green and John F. Berry, "White Collar Crime Is Big Business," *The Nation*, June 8, 1985, 698.

258. John E. Conklin, *Illegal But Not Criminal* (Englewood Cliffs, N.J.: Prentice-Hall, 1977).

259. Jonathan Kwitny, *Vicious Circles: Mafia in the Marketplace* (New York: Norton, 1979). Some, however, doubt its cohesiveness, and whether it really even qualifies as a distinct form of crime. See Dwight C. Smith, *The Mafia Mystique* (New York: Basic Books, 1975).

260. Marshall B. Clinard and Richard Quinney, *Criminal Behavior Systems: A Typology* (New York: Holt, Rinehart and Winston, 1967), 382.

261. Denny Pace and Jimmie Sykes, *Organized Crime* (Englewood Cliffs, N.J.: Prentice-Hall, 1983).

262. *Ibid.*

263. Cressey, note 251 *supra*.

264. Frank Pearce, *Crimes of the Powerful* (London: Pluto, 1976).

265. Silberman, note 38 *supra*, 132.

266. Cressey, note 38 *supra*.

267. Harold Lasswell and Jeremiah McKenna, *The Impact of Organized Crime on an Inner-City Community* (New York: Policy Sciences Center, n.d.).

268. Hembert Nelli, *The Business of Crime* (New York: Oxford University Press, 1976).

269. Clinard and Quinney, note 260 *supra*; Silberman, note 38 *supra*, 132.

270. Silberman, *ibid.*

271. Clinard and Quinney, note 269 *supra*,, 178.

272. *Ibid.*, Stephen Schafer, *The Political Criminal* (New York: Free Press, 1974); Julian Roebuck and Stanley C. Weeber, *Political Crime in the United States* (New York: Praeger, 1978).

273. Alan Wolfe, *The Seamy Side of Democracy: Repression in America* (New York: Longman, 1978); Roebuck and Weeber, *ibid;* Goldstein, note 250 *supra.*

274. Clinard and Quinney, note 269 *supra;* John Webster, "The Government as Terrorist and Torturer: The Citizen as Victim," Paper presented at Second International Symposium on Victimology, Boston, 1976; Ivan Jankovic, "Political Prisoners as Victims" Paper presented at Fifth International Symposium on Victimology, Zagreb, 1985.

275. Jack D. Douglas and John M. Johnson, *Official Deviance* (New York: Lippincott, 1977); Jethro Lieberman, *How the Government Breaks the Law* (Baltimore: Penguin, 1972); Theodore Becker and Vernon G. Murray (eds.), *Government Lawlessness in America* (New York: Oxford University Press, 1971); Robert Meier and Gilbert Geis, "The Abuse of Power as a Criminal Activity: Toward an Understanding of the Behavior and Methods of Control," in Geis, note 253 *supra,* 125; Charles Reasons, "Crime and the Abuse of Power: Offenses and Offenders Beyond the Reach of the Law," in Wickman and Dailey, note 14 *supra,* 59.

276. American Friends Service Committee, *The Police Threat to Political Liberty* (Philadelphia: Author, 1979); Rodney Stark, *Police Riots* (Belmont, Calif.: Wadsworth, 1972); Paul Takagi, "LEEA's Research Solicitation: Police Use of Deadly Force," *Crime and Social Justice* (Spring–Summer 1979), 51; William Waegel, "The Use of Lethal Force by Police: The Effect of Statutory Change," *Crime and Delinquency* (1984), 121; Gordon, note 24 *supra,* 125.

277. Parenti, note 10 *supra;* McNeely and Pope, note 176 *supra;* P. P. Hallie, "Justification and Rebellion," in N. Sanford and C. Comstock (eds.), *Sanctions for Evil* (Boston: Beacon Press, 1971), 257; Suzanne Gowan, et al., *Moving Toward A New Society* (Philadelphia: New Society Press, 1976).

278. Wolfe, note 273 *supra,* 21.

279. Noam Chomsky, "Watergate as Small Potatoes," *The Real Paper,* July 11, 1973.

280. Schur, note 52 *supra;* Leiser, note 56 *supra.*

281. Bedau, note 22 *supra;* Amnon Rubinstein, "The Victim's Consent in Criminal Law: An Essay on the Extent of the Decriminalizing Element of the Crime Concept," in E. M. Wise and G. O. Mueller (eds.), *Studies in Comparative Criminal Law* (Springfield, Ill.: Charles C. Thomas, 1975), 189.

282. Reiman, note 3 *supra.*

283. Rubinstein, note 70 *supra.*

284. Abraham Blumberg, *Criminal Justice* (New York: Franklin Watts, 1979), 46.

285. Reiman, note 3 *supra,* 101; Krisberg, note 34 *supra,* 62; Silberman,

note 38 *supra*, 53; Jay R. Williams and Martin Gold, "From Delinquent Behavior to Juvenile Delinquency," *Social Problems*, 20(1972), 209; Martin Gold, "Undetected Delinquent Behavior," *Journal of Research on Crime and Delinquency*, 3(1966); Nils Christie, et al., "A Study of Self-Reported Crime," in Christie, note 117 *supra*; William Chambliss, "Toward A Political Economy of Crime," *Theory and Society*, 2(1975), 166.

286. Wright, note 38 *supra*, 3.

287. Silberman, note 38 *supra*, 55.

288. Lawrence Zeitlin, "A Little Larceny Can Do a Lot for Employee Morale," *Psychology Today* (June 1971), 24.

289. Silberman, note 38 *supra*, 61.

290. Martin Gold and David Reimer, "Changing Patterns of Delinquent Behavior Among Americans 13 Through 16 Years Old: 1967–72," *Crime and Delinquency Literature*, 7(1975), 483.

291. Reiman, note 3 *supra*, 101.

292. Pearce, note 264 *supra*; Matthew Rothschild, "No Place for Scruples," *The Progressive* (November 1985), 26.

293. Reiman, note 3 *supra*,; Silberman, note 38 *supra*, 57.

294. Sutherland, note 257 *supra*.

295. Reiman, note 3 *supra*.

296. Yvette Delord-Raynal, "Victims of White Collar Crimes," in Schneider, note 16 *supra*, 257; Leiser, note 56 *supra*, 259.

297. McNeely and Pope, note 176 *supra*; Vine DeLoria and Clifford M. Lytle, *American Indians, American Justice* (Austin: University of Texas Press, 1983).

298. *Ibid.*; Warren T. Brookes, "Crime: Economic Scourge of the Ghetto," in Galaway and Hudson, note 105 *supra*, 92.

299. Greenberg, note 250 *supra*, 415.

300. William Julius Wilson, "The Urban Underclass," in Dunbar, note 24 *supra*, 80.

301. O. C. Stewart, "Questions Regarding American Indian Criminality," *Human Organization*, 23(1964), 63.

302. C. E. Reasons, "Crime and the Native American," in C. E. Reasons and E. Kykendall (eds.), *Crime, Race and Justice* (Santa Monica, Calif.: Goodyear, 1972).

303. Kumagai, note 113 *supra*; David Matza, *Delinquency and Drift* (New York: John Wiley, 1964); Richard Cloward and Lloyd Ohlin, *Delinquency and Opportunity* (New York: Free Press, 1960).

304. Patricia Miller and Mary Ellen Marsden, "Victimization, Norm Violation and Normative Integration," Paper presented at Second International Symposium on Victimology, Boston, 1976; Michael Hindelang, "Sex Differences in Criminal Activity," *Social Problems*, 27(1979), 143; H. Finestone, "The Delinquent and Society: The Shaw and McKay Tradition," in J. R. Short (ed.), *Delinquency, Crime and Society* (Chicago: University of Chicago Press, 1976); Harold Finestone, *Victims of Change: Juvenile Delinquents in American Society* (Westport, Conn.: Greenwood Press, 1976).

305. Vernetta D. Young, "Victims of Female Offenders," in Parsonage, note 92 *supra*, 72; Gabriella Rasko, "The Victim of the Female Killer," Paper presented at Second International Symposium on Victimology, Boston, 1976.

306. Cormier, note 213 *supra;* Truman Capote, *In Cold Blood* (New York: Signet, 1965); Norman Mailer, *The Executioner's Song* (New York: Ballantine Books, 1978); Jack Levin and James Alan Fox, *Mass Murder: America's Growing Menace* (New York: Plenum, 1985).

307. Amir, note 218 *supra*.

308. Martha R. Burt, "Justifying Personal Violence: A Comparison of Rapists and the General Public," *Victimology*, 8(1983), 131.

309. Brownmiller, note 218 *supra;* Schram, note 218 *supra;* Judith V. Becker and Gene G. Abel, "Men and the Victimization of Women," in Chapman and Gates, note 32 *supra*, 29.

310. "No Comment," *The Progressive* (September 1984), 13.

311. Marc Maden and David F. Wrench, "Significant Findings in Child Abuse Research," *Victimology*, 2(1977), 196.

312. Ryan, note 40 *supra*.

313. "Private Violence," note 220 *supra*, 21; Walker, note 63 *supra*, 215.

314. Sutherland, note 256 *supra;* Clinard and Yeager, note 21 *supra*.

315. Kidner, note 149 *supra*.

316. M. E. Wolfgang, R. M. Figlio and T. Sellin, *Delinquency in a Birth Cohort* (Chicago: University of Chicago Press, 1972).

317. Eduard Ziegenhagen, *Victims, Crime and Social Control* (New York: Praeger, 1977), 8.

318. Ford and Keitner, note 140 *supra;* L. Savitz, L. Rosen, and M. Lalli, "Delinquency and Gang Membership as Related to Victimization," *Victimology*, 5(1980), 152.

319. Robert Elias, *Victims of the System: Crime Victims and Compensation in American Politics and Criminal Justice* (New Brunswick, N.J.: Transaction Books, 1983), 99.

320. Leonard Buder, "Half of 1976 Murder Victims Had Police Records," *New York Times*, August 28, 1977, 9; M. E. Wolfgang, *Patterns in Criminal Homicide* (Philadelphia: University of Pennsylvania Press, 1958).

321. Frank Cannavale and William D. Falcon, *Witness Cooperation* (Lexington, Mass.: Lexington Books, 1976), 61.

322. J. H. Johnson, et al., "The Recidivist Victim: A Descriptive Study," *Criminal Justice Monograph*, 4(1973), 73.

323. Simon I. Singer, *Victims in a Subculture of Crime: An Analysis of the Social and Criminal Backgrounds of Surveyed Victims in the Birth Cohort Follow-Up* (Ann Arbor: University Microfilms International, 1980).

324. W. Nagel, "Crime Victim," *Tijkschrift voor Criminologie*, 24(1982), 310.

325. Hans von Hentig, "Remarks on the Interaction of Perpetrator and Victim," in Drapkin and Viano, note 86 *supra*, 45; Joachim Weber, "On the

Psychodiagnosis of the Offender-Victim Relationship," in Drapkin and Viano, note 50 *supra*, 155; Sung Tai Cho, "Criminality, Victim and Victimizer," in Drapkin and Viano, *ibid.*, 93; Sarah Ben-David, "Rapist-Victim Interaction During Rape," in Schneider, note 16 *supra*, 237; Richard Block, "Victim-Offender Dynamics in Violent Crime," *Journal of Criminal Law and Criminology*, 72(Summer 1981), 743; Stephen Schafer, *The Victim and His Criminal* (New York: Random House, 1968); Richard Block, "Victim and Offender in Violent Crime," Paper presented at Second International Symposium on Victimology, Boston, 1976; Romine R. Deming, "Advocating the Concept of the Victim-Offender Relationship," Paper presented at Second International Symposium on Victimology, Boston, 1976; E. Kube, "Crime Victim and Offender: How Does One Become a Victim?" *Kriminalistik*, 34(1980), 152; T. A. Mack, "A Victim-Role Typology of Rational-Economic Property Crime," *International Journal of Criminology and Penology*, 2(1974), 149; Deborah M. Galvin, "Concepts in Victimization and the Slave," in Viano, note 49 *supra*, 593; LeRoy G. Schultz, "The Victim-Offender Relationship," *St. Louis University Law Review*, 18(1967), 138; Allen Bartholemew, "On Offenders and Victims" Paper presented at Fifth International Symposium on Victimology, Zagreb, 1985.

326. Sally Engle Merry, *Urban Danger: Life in A Neighborhood of Strangers* (Philadelphia: Temple University Press, 1981), 7.

327. Vera Institute of Justice, *Felony Arrests: Their Prosecution and Disposition in New York City's Courts* (New York: Author, 1977), xiv.

328. Elias, note 86 *supra*; Karmen, note 92 *supra*, 70.

329. "The Curse of Violent Crime," note 148 *supra*, 22.

330. Task Force on Criminal Justice Research and Development Standards and Goals, *Research on Criminal Justice Problems: Victim Research* (Washington, D.C.: Rand, 1976), 48.

331. B. Mendelsohn, "Victimology," *Etudes Intl. de Psycho-Sociologie Criminelle* (July–September 1956), 105.

332. Hans Hentig, *The Criminal and His Victim* (New Haven: Yale University Press, 1948), 404.

333. Harry Elmer Barnes and Negley K. Teeters, *New Horizons in Criminology* (Englewood Cliffs, N.J.: Prentice-Hall, 1959), 595.

334. Ezzat A. Fattah, "Towards A Criminological Classification of Victims," *International Criminal Policy Review*, 209(1967), 162.

335. LeRoy Lamborn, "Toward A Victim Orientation in Criminal Theory," *Rutgers Law Review*, 22(1968), 733.

336. Schafer, note 325 *supra*.

337. Robert A. Silverman, "Victim Typologies: Overview, Critique and Reformulation," in Drapkin and Viano, note 86 *supra*, 55; Bosko Jakovljevic, "Types of Victims and a Concept of Victimology," Paper presented at Fifth International Symposium on Victimology, Zagreb, 1985.

338. Wesley G. Skogan and William R. Klecka, *The Fear of Crime* (Washington, D.C.: American Political Science Association, 1977), 32; C. H. D. Steinmetz, "An Approach to Victimological Risk Analysis: A Thought Model in the Prevention of 'Petty' Crime," *Just. Verkeningen*, 2(1980), 5; M. K. Block and G. J. Long, "Subjective Probability of Victimization and Crime," *Criminology,* 11(1973), 87; Neil S. Komesar, "A Theoretical and Empirical Study of Victims of Crime," *Journal of Legal Studies,* 4(1976), 301; LeRoy Lamborn, "The Vulnerability of the Victim," *Rutgers Law Review,* 22(1968), 757.

339. Small Business Administration, *Crimes Against Small Business* (Washington, D.C.: U.S. Government Printing Office, 1968).

340. Nettler, note 253 *supra.*

341. Benedict Alper, "Affluence as Victim," Paper presented at Second International Symposium on Victimology, Boston, 1976.

342. E. L. Quarantelli and Russell R. Dynes, "Organizations as Victims in American Mass Racial Disturbances: A Reexamination," in Drapkin and Viano, note 213 *supra,* 121; Russell R. Dynes and E. L. Quarantelli, "Organizations as Victims in Mass Civil Disturbances," in Drapkin and Viano, note 86 *supra,* 67.

343. E. O. Smigel and H. L. Ross, *Crimes Against Bureaucracy* (New York: Van Nostrand Reinhold, 1970); Alvar Nelson, "Public Agencies as Victims of Crime" Paper presented at Fifth International Symposium on Victimology, Zagreb, 1985.

344. Ezzat Fattah, "Some Recent Theoretical Developments in Victimology," *Victimology,* 4(1979), 198. Unlike for individuals, an organization's victimization has limited visibility, occurs over time, affects members unevenly, and may spread considerably beyond the organization itself. See Vaughan, in Geis and Shotland, note 14 *supra,* 87.

345. Walter Lacquer, *Terrorism* (Boston: Little, Brown, 1977); Hans Joachim Schneider, "Victims of Terrorism," in Schneider, note 16 *supra,* 298; V. V. Stanciu, "Political Terrorism and Its Victims," Paper presented at First World Congress on Victimology, Washington, D.C., 1980.

346. Edward S. Herman, *The Real Terror Network: Terrorism in Fact and Fiction* (Boston: South End Press, 1982).

347. A. Binder and P. Scharf, "The Violent Police-Citizen Encounter," *Annals* (November, 1980), 452; Krisberg, note 34 *supra,* 9, 11; Stark, note 276 *supra;* Ulrich Bauman and Klaus Sesser, "Police Officers as Victims," Paper presented at Second International Symposium on Victimology, Boston, 1976.

348. D. B. Lindsey, "Police as Victim," Paper presented at Annual Meeting of American Society of Criminology, San Francisco, 1980); David Lester, "The Police as Victims: Analysis of Murdered Police Officers," Paper presented at First World Congress on Victimology, Washington, D.C., 1980).

349. "The Curse of Violent Crime," note 148 *supra,* 24.

350. Ziegenhagen, note 317 *supra,* 5.

351. Fattah, note 17 *supra,* 15.

352. Klaus, note 223 *supra.*

353. Aromaa, note 115 *supra.*

354. A. Kaufman, "Recidivism Among Sex Assault Victims," *American Journal of Psychiatry,* 135(1978), 1103.

355. Ziegenhagen, note 317 *supra;* Richard F. Sparks, "Multiple Victimization: Evidence, Theory and Future Research," *Journal of Criminal Law and Criminology,* 72(Summer 1981), 762; Eduard Ziegenhagen, "The Recidivist Victim of Violent Crime," *Victimology,* 1(1976), 538; Hindelang, et al., note 215 *supra;* Karmen, note 92 *supra,* 76; T. H. Johnson, et al., *The Recidivist Victim: A Descriptive Study* (Houston: Institute for Contemporary Corrections and Behavioral Science, 1973).

356. Lester Thurow, "Equity Versus Efficiency in Law Enforcement," *Public Policy,* 18(1970), 454; Charles M. Gray, "The Assessment of Costs in Criminal Justice," in Galaway and Hudson, note 105 *supra,* 73.

357. Walsh and Schram, note 255 *supra,* 30.

358. von Hentig, note 325 *supra;* Henri Ellenberger, "Psychological Relationships Between the Criminal and the Victim," *Archives of Criminal Psychodymanics,* 1(1955), 385.

359. Viano, note 10 *supra;* M. Schmideberg, "Criminals and Their Victims," *International Journal of Offender Therapy and Comparative Criminology,* 24(1980), 128; Gordon, note 24 *supra,* 128; Jacqueline Scherer and Gary Shepard (eds.), *Victimization of the Weak: Contemporary Social Reactions* (Springfield, Ill.: Charles C Thomas, 1982).

360. McNeely and Pope, note 176 *supra.*

361. Klaus, note 223 *supra.*

362. Vahahn N. Dadrian, "The Victimization of the American Indian," *Victimology,* 1(1976), 517; McNeely and Pope, note 176 *supra.*

363. Viano, note 10 *supra.*

364. Donal MacNamara and Andrew Karmen, *Deviants: Victims or Victimizers?* (Beverly Hills, Calif.: Sage, 1983); Fattah, note 17 *supra;* S. Balkin, "Toward Victimization Research on the Mentally Retarded," *Victimology,* 6(1981), 331.

365. Mary C. Sengstock, "Predominance of the Culpable Victim Concept in Victimology," Paper presented at Annual Meeting of Midwest Sociological Society, Chicago, 1976.

366. Reiman, note 3 *supra,* 141.

367. Brookes, note 298 *supra;* Alvin F. Poussaint, "Black on Black Homicide: A Psychological and Political Perspective," *Victimology,* 8(1983), 161.

368. Klaus, note 223 *supra;* McNeely and Pope, note 176 *supra.* Marvin Wolfgang and Bernard Cohen, *Crime and Race: Conceptions and Misconceptions* (New York: American Jewish Committee, 1970), 40.

369. Reiman, note 3 *supra,* 141.

370. Conklin, note 76 *supra,* 26.

371. Reiman, note 3 *supra,* 141.

372. Platt, note 134 *supra,* 20.

373. *Ibid.*

374. *Ibid.*

375. Silberman, note 38 *supra,* 217.

376. Platt, note 134 *supra,* 21; J. Braithwaite and D. Biles, "On Being Unemployed and Being a Victim of Crime," *Australian Journal of Social Issues,* 14(1979), 192.

377. D. Stevens, "Dynamics of Victimization," *Journal of Social Work and Human Sexuality,* 1(1983), 29; Nwokocha K. U. Nkpa, "Female Victimization in Nigeria," in Schneider, note 16 *supra,* 279; Chapman and Gates, note 32 *supra;* Stanley R. Parcell and Eugene J. Kanin, "Male Sex Aggression: Survey of Victimized College Women," Paper presented at Second International Symposium on Victimology, Boston, 1976; E. Boulding, "Women and Social Violence," *Social Science Journal,* 30(1978), 801; Bruce Rounsaville, "Theories in Marital Violence: Evidence from a Study of Battered Women," *Victimology,* 3(1978), 11; M. A. Zahn, "The Female Victim," *Criminology,* 13(1975), 400; Hans Joachim Schneider, *Women as Victims of Crime* (Muenster: World Society of Victimology, 1984).

378. Klaus, note 223 *supra.*

379. Del Martin, "Battered Women: Scope of the Problem," in Galaway and Hudson, note 105 *supra,* 190.

380. Masamura, note 242 *supra;* Elizabeth Pleck, "Wife Beating in the 19th Century," *Victimology,* 4(1979), 60; R. E. Dobash and R. P. Dobash, "Wives: The 'Appropriate' Victims of Marital Violence," *Victimology,* 2(1977), 426.

381. Klaus, note 223 *supra.*

382. Kurt Weis and Sandra S. Borges, "Rape as a Crime Without Victims and Offenders? A Methodological Critique," in Viano, note 49 *supra,* 230; Julia R. Schwendinger and Herman Schwendinger, *Rape and Inequality* (Beverly Hills, Calif.: Sage, 1983); W. Wilson and S. F. Durrenburger, "Comparison of Rape and Attempted Rape Victims," *Psychological Reports,* 50(1982), 1; Miyazawa, note 113 *supra,* 295; S. Katz and M. A. Mazur, *Understanding the Rape Victim* (New York: John Wiley, 1979); Frank J. Javorek and Lou Anne Lyon, "Nice Girls Don't Get Raped, Or Do They," Paper presented at Second International Symposium on Victimology, Boston, 1976; Deanna R. Ness (ed.), *The Rape Victim* (Dubuque, Iowa: Kendall/Hunt, 1977).

383. C. E. Rinear and E. E. Rinear, "Sexual Assault Among Hospital Personnel," *Victimology,* 4(1979), 140; M. Lee, "Reactions of Nursing Staff to Physical Assault by a Patient," *Hospital and Community Psychiatry,* 34(1983), 44.

384. Hamlin, note 233 *supra,* 6.

385. D. Metzger, "It's Always the Woman Who Is Raped," *American Journal of Psychiatry,* 133(1976), 405.

386. Weis and Borges, note 382 *supra;* R. L. Terry, "Contextual Similarities in Subjective Probabilities of Rape and Other Events," *Journal of Social Psychology,* 113(1981), 293.

387. J. Pecar, "Women as Crime Victims," *Rev. Kriminal.,* 31(1980), 289; Nanci Koser Wilson, "Venerable Bedfellows: Women's Liberation and Women's Victimization," Paper presented at Third International Institute on Victimology, Lisbon, 1984.

388. Klaus, note 233 *supra;* Simon I. Singer, "The Seriousness of Crime and the Elderly Victim," Paper presented at Second International Symposium on Victimology, Boston, 1976; Richard Moran and Stephen Schafer, "Criminal Victimization of the Elderly in the City of Boston," Paper presented at Second International Symposium on Victimology, Boston, 1976; Andjelko Vujatovic, "Elderly People and Victimology" Paper presented at Fifth International Symposium on Victimology, Zagreb, 1985; Dianne Willocks, "The Construction of 'Social Victims': The Case of Old People" Paper presented at Fifth International Symposium on Victimology, Zagreb, 1985; Barbara Horum, "Cultural Stereotypes About the Elderly and Their Impact on Social Victimization" Paper presented at Fifth International Symposium on Victimology, Zagreb, 1985.

389. D. Jones, "Elderly Victimization: A Survey Report," *Royal Canadian Mounted Police Gazette*, 43(1981), 1; Jersey Liang and Mary C. Sengstock, *Criminal Victimization of the Elderly and Their Interaction with the Criminal Justice System: Summary of Findings* (Detroit: Wayne State University, 1980); N. Feinberg, *The Emotional and Behavioral Consequences of Violent Crime on Elderly Victims*, PhD Dissertation, University of Pittsburgh, 1977; F. F. Furstenberg, "Public Reaction to Crime in the Streets," *American Scholar*, 40(1971), 601; J. Goldsmith and S. S. Goldsmith (eds.), *Crime and the Elderly: Challenge and Response* (Lexington, Mass.: Lexington Books, 1977); F. L. Cook, "Criminal Victimization of the Elderly: A New National Problem," in Viano, note 49 *supra*, 130; F. L. Cook and T. D. Cook, "Evaluating the Rhetoric of Crisis: A Case Study of Criminal Victimization of the Elderly," *Social Service Review*, 50(1976), 632; Jordan Kosberg, "Victimization of the Elderly: Causation and Prevention," Paper presented at Third International Institute of Victimology, Lisbon, 1984; Susan Brown Eve, "Victimization of the Elderly in the U.S.: A Review of Theoretical and Research Literature," Paper presented at Third International Institute on Victimology, Boston, 1976; E. Rathbone-McCuan, "Elderly Victims of Family Violence and Neglect," *Social Casework*, 61(1980), 296; Marlene A. Young-Rifai, "Criminal Victimization of the Older Adult," Paper presented at Second International Symposium on Victimology, Boston, 1976; John C. Freeman, "Crimes Against the Elderly," Paper presented at Second International Symposium on Victimology, Boston, 1976; Norman Rushforth, et al., "Violent Death in a Metropolitan County," *Northeastern Journal of Medicine*, 297(1977), 531; Subcommittee on Housing and Consumer Interests, Select Committee on Aging, *In Search of Security: A National Perspective on Elderly Crime* (Washington, D.C.: U.S. Government Printing Office, 1977); Bureau of Justice Statistics, *Crime and the Elderly* (Washington, D.C.: U.S. Department of Justice, 1981).

390. "Private Violence," note 220 *supra*, 19.

391. J. F. Gubrium, "Victimization in Old Age," *Crime and Delinquency*, 20(1974), 245; J. Goldsmith and N. E. Tomas, "Crimes Against the Elderly: A Continuing National Crisis," *Aging*, 236(1974), 6; R. Forston, *Criminal Victimization of the Aged: The Houston Model Neighborhood Authority* (Austin: Texas Criminal Justice Council, 1974); C. E. Pope, "The Effects of Crime on the Elderly," *Police Chief*, 43(1976), 48.

392. W. Feyerherm and M. Hindelang, "On the Victimization of Juveniles: Some Preliminary Results," *Journal of Research on Crime and Delin-*

quency, 11(1974), 40; Mawby, note 110 *supra*; American Humane Association, *National Analysis of Official Child Neglect and Abuse Reporting: An Executive Summary* (Englewood, Colo.: Author, 1978); Alayne Yates, "The Eroticized Child," Paper presented at First World Congress on Victimology, Washington, D.C., 1980; John R. Hepburn and Daniel J. Monti, "Victimization, Fear of Crime and Adaptive Responses Among High School Students," in Parsonage, note 92 *supra*, 121; David Decker, Robert M. O'Brien, and David Schichor, "Patterns of Juvenile Victimization and Urban Structure," in Parsonage, *ibid.*, 88; Emilio C. Viano, "The Battered Child: A Review of Studies and Research in the Area of Child Abuse," in Drapkin and Viano, note 213 *supra*, 145; Susan Harlap and Israel Drapkin, "Child Injury in West Jerusalem," in Drapkin and Viano, *ibid.*, 165; LeRoy G. Schultz, "The Child as Sex Victim: Socio-Legal Perspectives," in Drapkin and Viano, *ibid.*, 177; J. E. Hall Williams, "The Neglect of Incest: A Criminologist's View," in Drapkin and Viano, *ibid.*, 191; Jean Cordier, "L'Enfant, Victime Privilegiee du Drame Passionnel," *Victimology*, 8(1983), 131; Charles L. McGehee, "Rethinking Child Abuse Theory," *Victimology*, 8(1983), 113; Charles McGehee, "Responses to Child Abuse in World Perspective," Paper presented at Third International Institute on Victimology, Lisbon, 1984; Reinhart Wolff, "Child Abuse and Neglect: Dynamics and Underlying Pattern," *Victimology*, 8(1983), 105; Joan M. McDermott, et al., "The Victimization of Children and Youth," *Victimology*, 6(1982), 162; Kee McFarlane, "Sexual Abuse of Children," in Parsonage, *ibid.*, 81; V. DeFrancis, "Protecting the Child Victim of Sex Crimes Committed by Adults," *Federal Probation*, 35(1971), 15.

393. Decker, O'Brien, and Schichor, *ibid.*, Savitz, Rosen, and Lalli, note 318 *supra*; Rushforth, note 389 *supra*; Akiyama, note 215 *supra*, 8.

394. "Private Violence," note 220 *supra*, 21.

395. C. E. Gentry and V. Bass Eaddy, "Treatment of Children in Spouse Abusive Families," *Victimology*, 5(1980), 240.

396. M. Nasjleti, "Suffering in Silence: The Male Incest Victim," *Child Welfare*, 59(1980), 269; Christine A. Courtois, "Studying and Counseling Women with Past Incest Experience," 5(1980), 322; Yates, note 392 *supra*; Valerie Julian and Cynthia Mohr, "Father-Daughter Incest: Profile of the Offender," *Victimology*, 4(1980), 348; J. J. Peters, "Children Who Are Victims of Sexual Assault and the Psychology of Offenders," *American Journal of Psychotherapy*, 30(1976), 398.

397. Agopian, note 211 *supra*.

398. H. C. Kempe, "Pediatric Implications of the Battered Baby Syndrome," *Archives of Disease in Childhood*, 46(1971), 28; D. Belhor, "Risk Factors in the Sexual Victimization of Children," *Child Abuse and Neglect*, 4(1980), 65.

399. Maden and Wrench, note 311 *supra*.

400. Clemens Bartollas, Stuart J. Miller, and Simon Dinitz, "Organizational Processing and Inmate Victimization in a Juvenile Training School," in Viano, note 49 *supra*, 569; Israel Drapkin, "The Prison Inmate as Victim," in Viano, *ibid.*, 560; Patricia R. Francis, "Offense Record as a Determinant of Victim-Victimizer Status within Institutions for Youth," in Viano, *ibid.*, 579; Simon Dinitz, Stuart J. Miller, and Clemens Bartollas, "Inmate Ex-

ploitation: A Study of the Juvenile Victim," in Drapkin and Viano, note 48 *supra*, 135; Stuart J. Miller, et al., "Games Inmates Play: Notes on Staff Victimization," in Drapkin and Viano, *ibid.*, 143; Clemens Bartollas, Stuart J. Miller, and Simon Dinitz, "Staff Exploitation of Inmates: The Paradox of Institutional Control," in Drapkin and Viano, *ibid.*, 157; John Jacobs, "Are These America's Political Prisoners?" *Washington Post*, January 8, 1978, 71; Ralph Charles C. Thomas, "The Forgotten Victim: Sexual Assaults in Penal Institutions," Paper presented at Second International Symposium on Victimology, Boston 1976; Israel Drapkin, "On Human Indifference: Violence, Suffering, Human Rights and the Prison Inmate," Paper presented at Second International Symposium on Victimology, Boston, 1976; L. H. Bowker, *Prison Victimization* (New York: Elsevier, 1980); Walter Moretz, "Separating the Sheep from the Goats: Reserving Prison for Those Who Really Need It," Paper presented at First World Congress on Victimology, Washington, D.C., 1980.

401. Bartollas, Miller, and Dinitz, *ibid.*

402. Silberman, note 38 *supra*, 263.

403. *Ibid.*, 528.

404. *Ibid.*, 514.

405. *Ibid.*, 515.

406. David Schichor, "The Wrongfully Accused and the Criminal Justice System," in Drapkin and Viano, note 86 *supra*, 121; Raymond L. Chambers, "When Is A Victim Not A Victim?" *Academy of Criminal Justice Sciences Newsletter* (September 1983), 14; Joseph Newman, "The Offender as the Victim," in Drapkin and Viano, *ibid.*, 113; Richard Moran and Stephen Zeidman, "Victims Without Criminals: Compensation to the Not Guilty," in Drapkin and Viano, note 16 *supra*; T. Chissione, "Defendant's Right to Reparation for Damage Caused by Detention Following a Verdict of Not Guilty," *Annuario del Instituto de Ciencias Penales y Criminologicas*, 5(1973), 23; Mark Starr, "Who Is the Real Victim?" *Newsweek*, May 20, 1985, 69; "Study Finds 25 Executed This Century Were Innocent," *Boston Globe*, November 17, 1985, 8; C. Huff, et al., "Victims of Justice: An Analysis of Wrongful Convictions" Paper presented at Fifth International Symposium on Victimology, Zagreb, 1985; Ayre Rattner and Gideon Fishman, "Wrongfully Convicted: A New Type of Victim" Paper presented at Fifth International Symposium on Victimology, Zagreb, 1985.

407. Tyndel, note 59 *supra*.

408. Fattah, note 17 *supra*, 23; Virginia Price, et al., "Social Characteristics of Adolescent Prostitution," *Victimology*, 9(1984), 211.

409. *Ibid.*

410. Sagarin and MacNamara, note 244 *supra*; Donal MacNamara and Lloyd McCorkle, "The Homosexual as Crime Victim," in Donal MacNamara and Lloyd McCorkle, *Crime, Criminals and Corrections* (New York: John Jay Press, 1982), 23.

411. Wolfgang, note 320 *supra*; M. A. Zahn and M. Bencivengo, "Violent Death: A Comparison Between Drug Users and Non-Drug Users," *Addictive Diseases: An International Journal*, 1(1974), 1; M. A. Zahn and M.

Bencivengo, "Murder in a Drug Using Population," in M. Reidel and T. Thornberry (eds.), *Crime and Delinquency: Dimensions of Deviance* (New York: Praeger, 1975); William E. Berg and Robert Johansen, "Assessing the Impact of Victimization: Acquisition of the Victim Role Among Elderly and Female Victims," in Parsonage, note 92 *supra*, 58.

412. Browning, note 82 *supra*, 29.

413. Fattah, note 17 *supra;* Ante Caric, "Some Social and Psychological Characteristics of Tourists as Victims and Tourist Criminality" Paper presented at Fifth International Symposium on Victimology, Zagreb, 1985; R. D. Francis, "The Foreign Born as Victims" Paper presented at Fifth International Symposium on Victimology, Zagreb, 1985.

414. Hepburn and Monti, note 392 *supra*.

415. Wolf Middendorff, "The Offender-Victim Relationship in Traffic Offenses," in Drapkin and Viano, note 48 *supra*, 187; Artur Solarz, "Driving Under the Influence of Drugs and Offender-Victim Relationships," in Drapkin and Viano, *ibid*, 181; Bruno Pannin, et al., Victimological Aspects of Involuntary Crimes, with Particular Reference to Road Accidents and Italian Law," *Victimology*, 8(1983), 53.

416. Leonard Bickman, "Bystander Intervention in Crime," in Viano, note 49 *supra*, 144; Ted L. Huston, et al., "Good Samaritans as Crime Victims," in Viano, note 49 *supra*, 518.

417. Klaus, note 223 *supra*.

418. *Ibid.*

419. Shirley Kuhle, "Domestic Violence in Rural America: Problems and Possible Solutions," Paper presented at First World Congress on Victimology, Washington, D.C., 1980.

420. Hepburn and Monti, note 392 *supra*.

421. National Institute of Education, *Violent Schools—Safe Schools: The Safe School Study Report to Congress* (Washington, D.C.: U.S. Department of HEW, 1978); Joan McDermott, *Criminal Victimization in Urban Schools* (Albany, N.Y.: Criminal Justice Research Center, 1978); Takahashi, et al., note 113 *supra*.

422. Richard Fabrikant, "The Distribution of Criminal Offenses in An Urban Environment: A Spatial Analysis of Criminal Spillovers and of Juvenile Offenders," *American Journal of Economy and Society*, 38(1979), 31; Edna Erez and Simon Hakim, "A Geo-Economic Approach to the Distribution of Crimes in Metropolitan Areas," in Parsonage, note 92 *supra*, 29.

423. B. L. Smith and C. R. Huff, "Crime in the Country: The Vulnerability and Victimization of Rural Citizens," *Journal of Criminal Justice*, 10(1982), 271; T. G. Eynon, "A Victim Survey in the Southern Fifteen Counties of Illinois," Paper presented at Annual Meeting of the American Society of Criminology, Tucson, 1976; Marlene Young, "Crime Victim Assistance: Programs and Issues in the U.S.," Paper presented at Fourth International Symposium on Victimology, Tokyo, 1982; Brent Smith, "Rural Victimization and Perceptions of Police Performance," *Victimology*, 9(1984), 159.

424. R. Ku, et al., *Victimization in Joliet and Peoria: A Baseline Survey* (Cambridge: ABT Associates, 1977); N.J. Beran and H.E. Allen, "Criminal

Victimization in Small Town USA," *International Journal of Criminology and Penology*, 2(1974), 391.

425. Dada Habibullah, *A Study of Selected Socio-Economic Variables Associated with Criminal Victimization in Rural Ohio* (Ann Arbor: University Microfilms International, 1979); Brent Smith, *Criminal Victimization in Rural Areas: An Analysis of Victimization Patterns and Reporting Trends* (Ann Arbor: University Microfilms International, 1980).

426. Skogan and Klecka, note 338 *supra*.

427. Robert Crosby and David Snyder, "Crime Victimization in the Black Community," in Drapkin and Viano, note 325 *supra*, 175; P. H. Kleinman, "Victimization and Perceptions of Crime in a Ghetto Community," *Criminology*, 11(1973), 307; Carl E. Pope, "Victimization Rates and Neighborhood Characteristics: Some Preliminary Findings," in Parsonage, note 92 *supra*, 48; C. Davies, "Crime, Police and Courts," *New Society*, 43(1978), 424; P. Harrison, "The Underside of Hackney: The Victims of Crime," *New Society*, 65(1983), 280; Richard A. Henry, "Urban Disturbances and Black Community Victimization," Paper presented at Second International Symposium on Victimology, Boston, 1976.

428. Peter B. Meyer, "Communities as Victims of Corporate Crimes," in Galaway and Hudson, note 105 *supra*, 33.

429. Don Wallace and Drew Humphries, "Urban Crime and Capitalist Accumulation: 1950–1971," in Greenberg, note 251 *supra*, 140.

430. Anthony Herbert, *International Traveler's Security Handbook* (New York: Hippocrene, 1984).

NOTES FOR CHAPTER 4

1. John Alan Stookey, "A Cost Theory of Victim Justice," in Burt Galaway and Joe Hudson (eds.), *Perspectives on Crime Victims* (St. Louis: Mosby, 1981), 80.

2. James Q. Wilson, *Thinking About Crime* (New York: Vintage, 1975), 50; Ernest Van den Haag, *Punishing Criminals* (New York: Basic Books, 1975); James Q. Wilson and Richard Hernstein, *Crime and Human Nature* (Cambridge, Mass.: Harvard University Press, 1985); Gregg Barak, "The Ominous Policies of Right-Wing Think Tanks: A Review of James Q. Wilson (ed.)., *Crime and Public Policy*," *Crime and Social Justice*, 23 (1985), 166.

3. Norval Morris and Gordon Hawkins, *The Honest Politician's Guide to Crime Control* (Chicago: University of Chicago Press, 1970), 47–50.

4. Stuart Scheingold, *The Politics of Law and Order: Street Crime and Public Policy* (New York: Longman, 1985), 138.

5. Robert P. Rhodes, *The Insoluble Problems of Crime* (New York: John Wiley, 1977), 3, 9.

6. Malcolm Feeley and Austin Sarat, *The Policy Dilemma: Federal Crime Policy and the LEAA, 1968–1978* (Minneapolis: University of Minnesota Press, 1980), 137, 148.

7. Barry Krisberg, *Crime and Privilege* (Englewood Cliffs, N.J.: Prentice-Hall, 1975), 18; Cyril Robinson, "Criminal Justice Research: Two Competing Futures," Crime and Social Justice, 23 (1985), 110; Elliott Currie, "Crime and the Conservatives: How Their Analysis Misses the Problem," *Dissent* (Fall 1985), 427; Samuel Walker, *Sense and Nonsense About Crime* (Monterrey, Calif.: Brooks/Cole, 1985), 222.

8. See Edwin Schur, *Our Criminal Society: The Social and Legal Sources of Crime in America* (Englewood Cliffs, N.J.: Prentice-Hall, 1969), 54.

9. See, for example, Michael Gottfredson, "On the Etiology of Criminal Victimization," *Journal of Criminal Law and Criminology*, 72 (1981), 714.

10. Wilson, note 2 *supra*.

11. Frank Browning, "Nobody's Soft on Crime Anymore: Rethinking America's Impossible Problem," *Mother Jones* (August 1982), 30.

12. Jeffrey A. Reiman, *The Rich Get Richer and the Poor Get Prison: Ideology, Class and Criminal Justice* (New York: John Wiley, 1979).

13. Rhodes, note 5 *supra*, 3.

14. Samuel Butler, *Erewhon* (New York: New American Library, 1960), 91.

15. "The Curse of Violent Crime," *Time*, March 23, 1981, 22.

16. For example, Harold Barnett, "Wealth, Crime and Capital Accumulation," *Contemporary Crises*, 3 (1979), 171.

17. Cesare Beccaria, *On Crimes and Punishments* (Indianapolis: Bobbs-Merrill, 1963).

18. Charles Silberman, *Criminal Violence, Criminal Justice* (New York: Vintage, 1978), 271, 344; Walker, note 7 *supra*, 92, 206.

19. *Ibid.*, 53.

20. *Ibid.*, 146.

21. See, for example, Frank Tannenbaum, *Crime and the Community* (Lexington, Mass.: Ginn, 1938).

22. Some wonder why we should be any more successful against official than against private crimes, especially if we ignore their common sources.

23. Silberman, note 18 *supra*, 270.

24. *Ibid.*, 149.

25. *Ibid.*, 352; "The Curse of Violent Crime," note 15 *supra*, 24.

26. Silberman, note 18 *supra*, 239; Walker, note 7 *supra*, 33, 207; Currie, note 7 *supra*, 436.

27. Edwin McDonnell, "House Panel on Violent Crime Finds Experts Are Short on Solutions," *New York Times*, January 15, 1978; David Rudovsky, "The Criminal Justice System and the Role of the Police," in David Kairys (ed.), *The Politics of Law: A Progressive Critique* (New York: Pantheon, 1982), 242; Don Wallace and Drew Humphries, "Urban Crime and Capital Accumulation, 1950–1971," in David F. Greenberg (ed.), *Crime and Capitalism* (Palo Alto, Calif.: Mayfield, 1981), 140.

28. Tannenbaum, note 21 *supra*, 19, 246; Walter C. Reckless, *The Crime Problems* (New York: Appleton-Century-Crofts, 1967), 508; Silberman, note

18 *supra*, 260; Jack P. Gibbs, *Crime, Punishment and Deterrence* (New York: Elsevier, 1975); Daniel Nagin, *General Deterrence: A Review of the Empirical Evidence* (Pittsburgh: Carnegie Mellon University Urban Systems Institute, 1975); Charles R. Tittle and Charles H. Logan, "Sanctions and Deviance: Evidence and Remaining Questions," *Law and Society Review*, 7 (1973), 372; Charles R. Tittle, "Deterrents or Labelling?" *Social Forces*, 53 (1975), 399.

29. Kurt Weis, "On Theory and Politics of Victimology and General Aspects of the Process of Victimization," in Edith Elizabeth Flynn and John P. Conrad (eds.), *The New and Old Criminology* (New York: Praeger, 1978), 182; Walker, note 7 *supra*, 74.

30. Silberman, note 18 *supra*, 328.

31. Elliott Currie, "Fighting Crime," *Working Papers* (July/August 1982), 17; Kurt Weis and Michael Milakovich, "Who's Afraid of Crime? Or: How to Finance a Decreasing Rate of Increase," in Sawyer F. Sylvester and Edward Sagarin (eds.), *Politics and Crime* (New York: Praeger, 1977), 34.

32. Terence Morris, *The Criminal Area* (London: Routledge and Kegan Paul, 1958).

33. Thomas Cronin, et al., *U.S. Against Crime in the Streets* (Bloomington: Indiana University Press, 1981).

34. Benedict Alper, "Affluence as Victim," Paper presented at Second International Symposium on Victimology, Boston, 1976.

35. Wilson, note 2 *supra*.

36. Morris and Hawkins, note 3 *supra*.

37. Roger Starr, "Crime: How It Destroys, What Can Be Done," *New York Times*, January 27, 1985, argues that improved public health has caused crime by preventing killers from dying before they have a chance to murder.

38. See Schur, note 8 *supra*.

39. Morris and Hawkins, note 3 *supra*.

40. Leonard Bickman, "Bystander Intervention in a Crime," in Emilio Viano (ed.), *Victims and Society* (Washington, D.C.: Visage Press, 1976), 144.

41. James Morris, *Victim Aftershock* (New York: Franklin Watts, 1983).

42. We can illustrate with a few examples: First, some suggest that we cannot cope with crime because we have not devoted enough resources. Yet, this falsely assumes that more resources will help the problem. [See Jack Douglas, "Crime and Justice in American Society," in Jack Douglas (ed.), *Crime and Justice in American Society* (Indianapolis: Bobbs-Merrill, 1971), 3.] In the last fifteen years our astronomical spending for law enforcement has not reduced crime; in fact, crime has risen. (See Feeley and Sarat, note 6 *supra*.) Recent federal and state cutbacks may better reflect the mounting "fiscal crisis of the state" [see James O'Connor, *The Fiscal Crisis of the State* (New York: St. Martins Press, 1973)] than deliberate efforts to shortchange crime control. We may have reached the practical and political limit of the government's ability to extract resources from the American public to soften our system's adverse effects, including crime [see Richard Quinney, *Class, State and Crime* (New York: Longman, 1980)].

Second, reshaping one's neighborhood environment has held great promise for controlling crime through architectual design [see Fred Heinzelmann, "Crime Prevention and the Physical Environment," in Dan A. Lewis (ed.), *Reactions to Crime* (Beverly Hills, Calif.: Sage, 1981), 87; Richard P. Taub, D. Garth Taylor and Jan D. Dunham, "Neighborhoods and Safety," in Lewis, *ibid.*, 103; Paul J. Brantingham and Patricia L. Brantingham (eds.), *Environmental Criminology* (Beverly Hills, Calif.: Sage, 1981); Oscar Newman, *Defensible Space* (New York: Macmillan, 1972); C. R. Jeffrey, *Crime Prevention Through Environmental Design* (Beverly Hills, Calif.: Sage, 1971); Keith D. Harries, *Crime and the Environment* (Springfield, Ill.: Charles C Thomas, 1980)]. Although "putting more eyes on the street" has contributed marginally to reducing crime, it has also diverted crime to neighborhoods with less resources for redesign and promoted an isolated, fortress mentality in some communities. And, as a security method, it falsely assumes that crime only occurs for lack of protection.

Third, some have suggested that we can prevent crime by requiring stricter third-party liability for crimes committed by offenders who were given access to their victims by other people who failed to provide adequate security, such as hospital and hotel owners, mental institutions and parole boards (see Morris, note 41 *supra.*, 36). Popularized recently by the Connie Francis rape case, this "solution" makes highly questionable predictions of dangerousness, falsely assumes that such mistakes produce considerable crime, jeopardizes individual rights, and unnecessarily bolsters the "security state" mentality [see Scheingold, note 4 *supra*, 121; Paul Takagi, "Garrison State in 'Democratic' Society," *Crime and Social Justice* (1974), 27], while again confusing the circumstances of crime with its sources.

Finally, some suggest that crime has been caused by our failure to control the media's influence on inducing victimization. Yet, for all we might validly criticize the media for portraying misconceptions about crime, criminals, and law enforcement, and for pandering to crime and violence in a way that undoubtedly socializes us to accept hardline crime policies and desensitizes us to the impact of violence, we have inconclusive evidence that it actually causes crime (see Schur, note 8 *supra*).

43. Scheingold, note 4 *supra*, 96, 156.

44. Philip J. Cook, "The Role of Firearms in Violent Crime," in Marvin E. Wolfgang and Neil Alan Weiner (eds.), *Criminal Violence* (Beverly Hills, Calif.: Sage, 1982), 236; Walker, note 7 *supra*, 151.

45. Charles D. Elder and Roger W. Cobb, *The Political Use of Symbols* (New York: Longman, 1983), 92; *Democratic Fact Book: Issues for 1982* (Washington, D.C.: Democrats for the 1980's, 1982), 175.

46. Ramsey Clark, *Crime in America* (New York: Pocket Books, 1971), 83.

47. Emilio Viano, "Violence, Victimization and Social Change: A Sociocultural and Public Policy Analysis," *Victimology*, 8 (1983), 55.

48. Clark, note 46 *supra*, 82; Conference on Alternative State and Local Policies, *The Issues of 1982* (Washington, D.C.: Author, 1982), 183.

49. Reiman, note 12 *supra*, 59.

50. Clark, note 46 *supra*, 84; Wesley G. Skogan and William R. Klecka, *The Fear of Crime* (Washington, D.C.: American Political Science Association, 1977), 2.

51. Norman B. Rushforth, et al., "Violent Death in a Metropolitan County," *Northeastern Journal of Medicine*, 297 (1977), 531.

52. James Gilsinan, *Doing Justice* (Englewood Cliffs, N.J.: Prentice-Hall, 1982), 215.

53. Franklin Zimring, *Firearms and Violence in American Life* (Washington, D.C. U.S. Government Printing Office, 1968).

54. Schur, note 8 *supra*, 15.

55. Overcriminalizing the laws generates significant secondary crime. Criminalizing certain drugs, for example, escalates their price dramatically, requiring users to resort to illegal sources of financing. Criminalizing prostitution embroils women unnecessarily in a broader atmosphere of extortion, robbery, and violence.

Discriminatory lawmaking and law enforcement for victimless crimes help generate a class of criminals caught in a cycle from which most find it impossible to escape [see Marvin Wolfgang and Franco Ferracuti, *Subculture of Violence* (London: Social Science Paperbacks, 1967)]. Vice crimes also provide the basis (by generating, for example, a market for the purchase and sale of illegal goods) for organized crime which otherwise might find their activities significantly curtailed. Enforcing vice crimes involves police officers unnecessarily in the underworld, tempting them into corruption and crime either to enforce the law or for personal gain [see Lois Forer, *The Death of the Law* (New York: McKay, 1975)]. It creates criminal situations, such as police posing as dealers, that would otherwise not exist. It increases the victimization of police officers attacked by bystanders, offenders, and fellow officers. It promotes nonenforcement of informers' crimes to win bigger cases. And it drains valuable resources away from preventing other, much more serious crimes [see Gary Marx, "Social Control and Victimization," *Victimology*, 8 (1983), 80]. Decriminalizing vice crimes, such as prostitution, drug use, gambling, pornography, and vagrancy could significantly reduce crime by eliminating some of the incentives the system creates for committing crime.

56. Martin Wright, *Making Good: Prisons, Punishment and Beyond* (New York: Humanities Press, 1982).

57. William A. Ryan, *Equality* (New York: Vintage, 1981), 172; David Rothman, *The Discovery of the Asylum* (Boston: Little, Brown, 1971); Michel Foucault, *Discipline and Punish: The Birth of the Prison* (New York: Pantheon, 1975).

58. Rudovsky, note 27 *supra*; Browning, note 11 *supra*, 29; Marvin Harris, *America Now* (New York: Simon and Schuster, 1981), 121; Walker, note 7 *supra*, 19; Currie, note 7 *supra*, 429.

59. Jonathan D. Casper, David Brereton and David Neal, *The Implementation of the California Determinate Sentencing Law: Executive Summary* (Washington, D.C.: National Institute of Justice, 1982), 45; Diane R. Gordon, "Towards Realistic Reform: A Commentary on Proposals for Change in New York City's Criminal Justice System" (Hackensack, N.J.: National Council on Crime and Delinquency, 1981), 16.

60. Scheingold, note 4 *supra*, 191; Silberman, note 18 *supra*.

61. *Ibid.*, 256; David S. Davis, "The Production of Crime Policies," *Crime and Social Justice* (1984), 121.

62. Currie, note 31 *supra*, 19; Reiman, note 12 *supra*; Yoel Yinon and Ilana Tennenbaum, "Employer's Attitudes Toward the Employment of Ex-Convicts in Israel," in Israel Drapkin and Emilio Viano (eds.), *Victimology: Society's Reaction to Victimization* (Lexington, Mass.: Lexington Books, 1974), 41.

63. Michael Lewis, *The Culture of Inequality* (New York: New American Library, 1978); Philip Zimbardo, "Pathology of Imprisonment" in *Crime, Criminals and the Courts* (New York: Harper and Row, 1978), 249.

64. *Ibid.*, 514; Walker, note 7 *supra*, 184.

65. George B. Vold, *Theoretical Criminology* (New York: Oxford University Press, 1958).

66. "A Curse of Violent Crime," note 15 *supra*, 29; Wilson and Hernstein, note 2 *supra*.

67. Edward C. Banfield, *The Unheavenly City* (Boston: Little, Brown, 1970).

68. For a critique, see Jeffrey A. Reiman, "Victims, Harm and Justice," in Israel Drapkin and Emilio Viano (eds.), *Victimology: Theoretical Issues* (Lexington, Mass.: Lexington Books, 1974), 77.

69. See descriptions in John E. Conklin, *The Impact of Crime* (New York: Macmillan, 1975), 67, 72; Silberman, note 18 *supra*, 73, 82.

70. Sarnoff A. Mednick, et al., "Biology and Violence," in Wolfgang and Weiner, note 44 *supra*, 21; Ernest B. Hack, "Behavioral Implications of the Human XYY Genotype," *Science*, 179 (January 12, 1973), 139; Richard S. Fox, "The XYY Offender: A Myth?" *Journal of Criminal Law, Criminology and Police Science*, 62 (1971), 34.

71. See discussion of Lombrosan theory in Schur, note 8 *supra*, 56; also Cesare Lombroso, *Crime: Its Causes and Remedies* (Boston: Little, Brown, 1913).

72. Louis Berman, *The Glands Regulating Personality* (Garden City, N.Y.: Garden City Pub., 1928); Ivo G. Cobb, *The Glands of Destiny* (London: Heinemann, 1927); John Heller, "Human Chromosome Abnormalities as Related to Physical and Mental Dysfunction," in Jack Bresler (ed.), *Genetics and Society* (Reading, Mass.: Addison Wesley, 1973), 57; Leon S. Minkler, "Chromosomes of Criminals," *Science*, 163 (1969), 1145.

73. Schur, note 8 *supra*, 55.

74. Seymour I. Halleck, *Psychiatry and the Dilemmas of Crime* (New York: Harper and Row, 1967); Edwin I. Megargee, "Psychological Determinants and Correlates of Criminal Violence," in Wolfgang and Weiner, note 44 *supra*, 81; Schur, note 8 *supra*, 61; John A. Humphrey and Stuart Palmer, "Stressful Life Events and Criminal Homicide Offender-Victim Relationships," *Victimology*, 8 (1983), 115; Stephen Wolf, "A Multi-Factor Model in Deviant Sexuality," Paper presented at Third International Institute on Victimology, Lisbon, 1984; Robert Burgess, "Social Importance as a Precipitant to and Consequence of Child Maltreatment," Paper presented at Third International Institute on Victimology, Lisbon, 1984; William Wilbanks, "Fatal Accidents, Suicide and Homicide: Are They Related?" Paper presented at

First World Congress on Victimology, Washington, D.C., 1980; Edward Gondolf, "Anger and Oppression in Men Who Batter," Paper presented at Third International Institute on Victimology, Lisbon, 1984; Linda Rouse, "Models, Self-Esteem and Locus of Control As Factors Contributing to Spouse Abuse," *Victimology*, 9 (1984), 130; Peggy Placier, "Victims of Victims: The Cycle of Abuse in A Violent Society," *The Dandelion* (April 1985), 3.

75. James Prescott, "Body Pleasure and the Origins of Violence," *The Futurist* (April 1975), 64; Oman Garrison, *The Tantra Yoga of Sex* (New York: Julian Press, 1983), 80.

76. Edwin H. Sutherland and Donald R. Cressey, *Principles of Criminology* (Philadelphia: J. P. Lippincott, 1966); "The Curse of Violent Crime," note 15 *supra*, 29; see Schur, note 8 *supra*, 82.

77. "The Curse of Violent Crime," note 15 *supra*, 20.

78. Cornelis L. J. Stokman and Patricia Heiber, "Incidents in Hospitalized Forensic Patients," *Victimology*, 5 (1980), 175.

79. Jack Levin and James Alan Fox, *Mass Murder: America's Growing Menace* (New York: Plenum, 1985).

80. Silberman, note 18 *supra*, 90; Currie, note 7 *supra*, 436.

81. Wesley G. Skogan, "The Fear of Crime and Its Behavioral Implications," in Ezzat A. Fattah (ed.), *Reorienting the Justice System: From Crime Policy to Victim Policy* (New York: Macmillan, 1985).

82. C. R. Jeffrey, *Biology and Crime* (Beverly Hills, Calif.: Sage, 1979); C. R. Jeffrey, *Crime Prevention Through Environmental Design* (Beverly Hills, Calif.: Sage, 1977); S. A. Mednick and K. O. Christiansen, *Biosocial Bases of Criminal Behavior* (New York: Gardner Publishers, 1977); Wilson and Hernstein, note 2 *supra*.

83. Conklin, note 69 *supra*, 38.

84. For example, in 44% of all murders both the victim and offender had been drinking (see M. E. Wolfgang and R. Strom, "The Relationship Between Alcohol and Criminal Homicide," *Quarterly Journal of Studies on Alcohol*, 17 (1956); K. Aromaa, *Alcohol Consumption and Victimization to Violence: Correlations in a National Sample* (Helsinki: Research Institute of Legal Policy, 1977); Val MacMurray, "The Effect and Nature of Alcohol Abuse in Cases of Child Neglect," *Victimology*, 4 (1979), 29; L. W. Gerson, "Alcohol-Related Acts of Violence: Who Was Drinking and Where the Acts Occurred," *Journal of Studies on Alcohol*, 39 (1978), 1294. Lenke Feher, "The Victimology of Alcoholism," *Victimology*, 8 (1983), 328; J. C. Ball, "The Impact of Heroin Addiction Upon Criminality," in Louis S. Harris (ed.), *Problems of Drug Dependence* (Washington, D.C.: U.S. National Institute of Drug Abuse, 1979).

85. "Private Violence," *Time*, September 5, 1983, 18.

86. Lonnie H. Athens, *Violent Criminal Acts and Actors: A Symbolic Interactionist Study* (Boston: Routledge and Kegan Paul, 1980).

87. William J. Chambliss, *Crime and the Legal Process* (New York: McGraw-Hill, 1969), 421.

88. Silberman, note 18 *supra*, 157.

89. Reiman, note 12 *supra*, 8; Scheingold, note 4 *supra*, 145.

90. Douglas, note 42 *supra*, 13.

91. Duncan Chappell and Jennifer James, "Victim Selection and Apprehension from the Rapist's Perspective," Paper presented at Second International Symposium on Victimology, Boston, 1976; Marvin Wolfgang, "Victim Precipitation in Victimology and Law" Paper presented at Fifth International Symposium on Victimology, Zagreb, 1985.

92. Weis, note 29 *supra*.

93. Gottfredson, note 9 *supra*.

94. Susan A. Salasin, "Services to Victims: Needs Assessment," in Susan Salasin (ed.), *Evaluating Victim Services* (Beverly Hills, Calif.: Sage, 1981), 21.

95. Hans von Hentig, *The Criminal and His Victim* (New Haven: Yale University Press, 1948), 303.

96. Henry Ellenberger, "Relations Psychologiques Entre Le Criminel et Sa Victime," *Revue Internationale de Criminologie et de Police Technique,* 2 (1954), 1.

97. Herman Mannheim, *Comparative Criminology* (Boston: Houghton Mifflin, 1965), 672.

98. Reckless, note 28 *supra*, 142.

99. LeRoy Schultz, "The Victim-Offender Relationship," *Crime and Delinquency,* 14 (1968), 135.

100. Stephen Schafer, *The Victim and His Criminal: A Study in Functional Responsibility* (New York: Random House, 1968), 144.

101. Viano, note 40 *supra*, 1.

102. William A. Parsonage, "Introduction," in William A. Parsonage (ed.), *Perspectives on Victimology* (Beverly Hills, Calif.: Sage, 1979), 10.

103. Charles McCaghy, Peggy Giordano and Trudy Henson, *Crime in American Society* (New York: Macmillan, 1980), 54.

104. Marvin E. Wolfgang, *Patterns in Criminal Homicide* (Philadelphia: University of Pennsylvania Press, 1958), 245.

105. Lynn A. Curtis, *Criminal Violence: National Patterns and Behavior* (Lexington, Mass.: Lexington Books, 1974).

106. Menachem Amir, *Patterns of Forcible Rape* (Chicago: University of Chicago Press, 1971), 275; Steve Nelson and Menachem Amir, "The Hitchhike Victim of Rape," in Israel Drapkin and Emilio Viano (eds.), *Victimology: Exploiters and the Exploited* (Lexington, Mass.: Lexington Books, 1974), 47; J. L. Gobert, "Victim Precipitation," *Columbia Law Review,* 77 (1977), 511; J. B. Best and H. S. Demmin, "Victim's Provocativeness and Victim's Attractiveness as Determinants of Blame in Rape," *Psychological Reports,* 51 (1982), 255; L. Clark and D. Lewis, *Rape: The Price of Coercive Sexuality* (Toronto: Women's Press, 1977); L. Paulsen, "Attribution of Fault to a Rape Victim as a Function of Locus of Control," *Journal of Social Psychology,* 107 (1979), 131. Michael Fooner, "Victim-Induced, Victim-Invited and Victim-Precipitated Criminality: Some Problems in Evaluation of Proposals for Victim Compensation," in Israel Drapkin and Emilio Viano (eds.), *Victimology* (Lexington, Mass.: Lexington Books, 1974), 231; Jeffrey, note 42 *supra*, 208.

108. Irwin Waller and Norman Okihiro, *Burglary: The Victim and the Public* (Toronto: University of Toronto Press, 1978), 5.

109. Charles McCaghy, Peggy Giordano and Trudy Henson, "Auto Theft: Offenders and Offense Characteristics," *Criminology*, 15 (1977), 369.

110. A. Normandeau, "Patterns in Robbery," *Criminologica*, 6 (1963), 2.

111. Curtis, note 105 *supra*.

112. Amir, note 106 *supra*; Menachem Amir, "Victim Precipitated Forcible Rape," *Journal of Criminal Law, Criminology and Police Science*, 58 (1967), 493.

113. Neville H. Avison, "Victims of Homicide," in Israel Drapkin and Emilio Viano (eds.), *Victimology: Violence and Its Victims* (Lexington, Mass.: Lexington Books, 1974), 58; Marvin E. Wolfgang, "Victim Precipitated Criminal Homicide," in Drapkin and Viano, note 107 *supra*, 79; J. Pecar, "Victims of Criminal Offenses and Formal Control," *Rev. Kriminalist. Kriminol.*, 30 (1979), 192; B. Holyst, "Factors Connected with Homicides and Their Importance in Investigations," *International Criminal Police Review*, 226 (1969), 78.

114. S. Kanekar and M. B. Kolsawalla, "Factors Affecting Responsibility Attributed to a Rape Victim," *Journal of Social Psychology*, 113 (1981), 285; LeRoy Lamborn, "The Culpability of the Victim," *Rutgers Law Review*, 22 (1968), 760; M. K. Block and G. J. Long, "Subjective Probability of Victimization and Crime Levels: An Econometric Approach," *Criminology*, 11 (1973), 87; Diane Vaughan and Giovanna Carlo, "Victims of Fraud: Victim Responsiveness, Incidence and Reporting," in Viano, note 40 *supra*, 403; E. Kube, "Crime Victim and Offender: How Does One Become a Victim?" *Kriminalistik*, 34 (1980), 152.

115. Michael J. Hindelang, "Victimization Surveying, Theory and Research," in Hans Joachim Schneider (ed.), *The Victim in International Perspective* (Berlin: Walter de Gruyter, 1982), 151.

116. Guglielmo Gulotta, "Victimization and Interpersonal Misunderstandings in Dyadic Systems," *Victimology*, 5 (1980), 110; Guglielmo Gulotta, "The Offender-Victim System," in Viano, note 40 *supra*, 50; Schafer, note 97 *supra*; L. Savitz, L. Rosen and M. Lalli, "Delinquency and Gang Membership as Related to Victimization," *Victimology*, 5 (1980), 152.

117. L. M. Graves and C. A. Lowe, "Salience and Assignment of Blame to Victims," *Psychological Reports*, 52 (1982), 835; Betty Grayson, *A Comparison of Criminal Perceptions of Potential Victims of Assault and a Movement Analysis Based on Labanalysis* (Ann Arbor: University Microfilms International, 1979).

118. Conklin, note 69 *supra*, 108.

119. Hindelang, note 115 *supra*.

120. Graves and Lowe, note 117 *supra*.

121. Viano, note 47 *supra*, 70.

122. Daniel S. Claster and Deborah S. David, "The Resisting Victim: Extending the Concept of Victim Responsibility," *Victimology*, 2 (1977), 109; Ezzat A. Fattah, "Victim Response to Intentional Victimization: A Neglected Aspect of Victim Research," *Crime and Delinquency*, 30 (1984), 75; Lynn A. Curtis, "Toward A Theory of Response to Rape: Some Methodological Considerations," in Viano, note 40 *supra*, 220.

123. Schafer, note 100 *supra*, 81; Pearl B. Cohen, "Resistance During Sexual Assaults: Avoiding Rape and Injury," *Victimology*, 9 (1984), 120.

124. Mary C. Sengstock, "Predominance of the Culpable Victim Concept in Victimology," Paper presented at Annual Meeting of the Midwest Sociological Society, St. Louis, 1976.

125. C. B. Csida and J. Csida, *Rape: How to Avoid It and What to Do About It If You Can't* (Chatsworth, Calif.: Books for Better Living, 1974).

126. J. R. Scroggs, "Penalties for Rape as a Function of Victim Provocativeness, Damage and Resistance," *Journal of Applied Social Psychology*, 6 (1974), 360.

127. Sengstock, note 124 *supra*, 19.

128. Best and Dimmin, note 106 *supra*.

129. Cathaleen Jones and Elliot Aronson, "Attribution of Fault to a Rape Victim as a Function of Respectability of the Victim," in Deanna R. Nass (ed.), *The Rape Victim* (Dubuque, Iowa: Kendall/Hunt, 1977), 27.

130. Hindelang, note 115 *supra*; D. Thissen and H. Wainer, "Toward the Measurement and Prediction of Victim Proneness," *Journal of Research on Crime and Delinquency*, 20 (1983), 243.

131. Richard A. Ball, "The Victimological Cycle," *Victimology*, 1 (1976), 379.

132. D. Biles, et al., "The Mental Health of the Victims of Crime," *International Journal of Offender Therapy and Comparative Criminology*, 23 (1976), 129; M. Herjanic and D. A. Meyer, "Psychiatric Illness in Homicide Victims," *American Journal of Psychiatry*, 133 (1976), 691; Betty Grayson and Morris Stein, "Attracting Assault: Victims' Nonverbal Cues," *Journal of Communications*, 31 (1981), 68.

133. J. M. Teutsch and C. K. Teutsch, "Victimology: An Effect of Consciousness, Interpersonal Dynamics and Human Physics," *International Journal of Criminology and Penology*, 2 (1974), 249; J. M. Teutsch and C. K. Teutsch, "Victimology: The Genetic Factor," Paper presented at First World Congress on Victimology, Washington, D.C., 1980; C. K. Teutsch and J. M. Teutsch, "The Dynamics of Victimization and Devictimization," Paper presented at Second International Symposium on Victimology, Boston, 1976.

134. Hans Goppinger, "The Victim as Seen by the Offender," Paper presented at Second International Symposium on Victimology, Boston, 1976.

135. Ezzat A. Fattah, "Some Recent Theoretical Developments in Victimology," *Victimology*, 4 (1979), 198.

136. Marilyn E. Walsh and Donna D. Schram, "The Victim of White-Collar Crime: Accusor or Accused?" in Gilbert Geis and Ezra Shotland (eds.), *White Collar Crime* (Beverly Hills, Calif.: Sage, 1980), 32.

137. Kurt Weis and Sandra Weis, "Victimology and the Justification of Rape," in Drapkin and Viano, note 106 *supra*, 6.

138. Fattah, note 135 *supra;* Weis and Weis, note 134 *supra*, 5; Joyce Williams, "Secondary Victimization: Confronting Public Attitudes About Rape," *Victimology*, 9 (1984), 66; Karen Gentemann, "Wife Beating: Attitudes of a Non-Clinical Population," *Victimology*, 9 (1984), 109; Jacqueline Scherer, "The Myth of Passion: Redefinition of Rape," in Jacqueline Scherer and Gary Shepard (eds.), *Victimization of the Weak* (Springfield, Ill.: Charles C Thomas, 1983), 153.

139. Curtis, note 105 *supra*.

140. Stanley Milgram, *Obedience to Authority* (New York: Harper and Row, 1974).

141. Ezzat A. Fattah, "Becoming a Victim: The Victimization Experience and Its Aftermath," *Victimology*, 6 (1981), 29.

142. Schafer, note 100 *supra*.

143. Amir, note 106 *supra*, 258.

144. Andrew Karmen, "Auto Theft: Beyond Victim Blaming," *Victimology*, 5 (1980), 161; A. Karmen, "Victim Facilitation: The Case of Automobile Theft," *Victimology*, 4 (1980), 361; Morton Bard, "Unblaming the Victim," *Social Policy* (Winter 1985), 43.

145. William A. Ryan, *Blaming the Victim* (New York: Vintage, 1976).

146. *Ibid.*

147. Clyde W. Franklin and Alice P. Franklin, "Victimology Revisited: A Critique and Suggestions for Future Directions," *Criminology*, 14 (1976), 177; Sengstock, note 124 *supra;* R. A. Silverman, "Victim Precipitation: An Examination of the Concept," in Drapkin and Viano, note 66 *supra*, 99.

148. Andrew Karmen, *Crime Victims* (Belmont, Calif.: Brooks/Cole, 1984), 101.

149. Karmen, *Ibid.*, 116; D. Caplovitz, *The Poor Pay More* (New York: Free Press, 1963).

150. See Karmen, *Ibid.*, 94 for extensive discussion of victim blaming and victim defending.

151. Sengstock, note 124 *supra;* Frank Carrington, *Victims* (New Rochelle, NY: Arlington House, 1975); Robert Rieff, *The Invisible Victim: The Criminal Justice System's Forgotten Responsibility* (New York: Basic Books, 1979); J. L. Barkas, *Victims* (New York: Schribners, 1978); President's Task Force on Victims of Crime, *Final Report* (Washington, D.C.: U.S. Government Printing Office, 1982).

152. Sheila Balkan, et al., *Crime and Deviance in America* (Belmont, Mass.: Wadsworth, 1980), 11.

153. Joseph Newman, "The Offender as Victim," in Israel Drapkin and Emilio Viano (eds.), *Victimology: Crimes, Victims and Justice* (Lexington, Mass.: Lexington Books, 1974), 113.

154. Russell R. Dynes and E. L. Quarantelli, "Organizations as Victims in Mass Civil Disturbances," in Drapkin and Viano, note 107 *supra*, 67; E.

L. Quarantelli and Russell R. Dynes, "Organizations as Victims in American Mass Racial Disturbances: A Reexamination," in Drapkin and Viano, note 113 *supra*, 121; Karmen, note 148 *supra*, 116.

155. Marx, note 55 *supra*.

156. Martha Burt, "Justifying Personal Violence: A Comparison of Rapists and the General Public," *Victimology*, 8 (1983), 131.

157. Reckless, note 28 *supra*, 137.

158. Weis and Weis, note 137 *supra*, 4; Peggy Placier, "Victims of Victims: The Cycle of Abuse in a Violent Society," *The Dandelion* (April 1985), 4.

159. Scheingold, note 4 *supra*, 159.

160. Gregg Barak, *In Defense of Whom? A Critique of Criminal Justice Reform* (Cincinnati: Anderson, 1980), 124; Alvin Gouldner, "The Sociologist as Partisan: Sociology and the Welfare State," in Jack Nelson (ed.), *The Relevance of Sociology* (New York: Harper and Row, 1970), 122.

161. Weis, note 29 *supra*, 195; Robinson, note 7 *supra*, 111.

162. Mary C. Sengstock, "Eclipse of the Individual Victim in Radical Victimology," Paper presented at the Annual Meeting of the American Society of Criminology, Tucson, 1976.

163. Marshall B. Clinard and Richard Quinney, *Criminal Behavior Systems: A Typology* (New York: Holt, Rinehart and Winston, 1967), 212.

164. Gary S. Becker, "Crime and Punishment: An Economic Approach," *Journal of Political Economy*, 76 (1968), 169; Jan Palmer, "Economic Analysis of the Deterrent Effect of Punishment: A Review," *Journal of Research on Crime and Delinquency*, 14 (1977), 4; Nicholas Elliott, "Economic Analysis of Crime and the Criminal Justice System," in John A. Gardiner (ed.), *Public Law and Public Policy* (New York: Praeger, 1977), 68.

165. Reiman, note 12 *supra*, 20.

166. Schur, note 8 *supra*, 125.

167. D. Schichor, D. L. Decker, and R. M. O'Brien, "The Relationship of Criminal Victimization, Police Per Capita, and Population Density in 26 Cities," *Journal of Criminal Justice*, 8 (1980), 309.

168. Reiman, note 12 *supra*, 25; See also, Giora Rahav and Shiva Jaamdar, "Development and Crime: A Cross-National Study," *Development and Change*, 13 (1982), 447.

169. David M. Gordon, "Class and the Economics of Crime," in William J. Chambliss and Milton Mankoff (eds.), *Whose Law? What Order?* (New York: John Wiley, 1976), 193; David Greenberg, *Crime and Class* (Palo Alto, Calif.: Mayfield, 1980).

170. Reiman, note 12 *supra*, 28.

171. B. F. Skinner, *Beyond Freedom and Dignity* (New York: Bantam Books, 1971), 70.

172. Ryan, note 145 *supra*.

173. Herbert Gans, *More Equality* (New York: Vintage, 1973); Lewis, note 63 *supra*; Philip Green, *The Pursuit of Inequality* (New York: Pantheon, 1981);

Lee Rainwater (ed.), *Social Problems and Public Policy: Inequality and Justice* (Chicago: Aldine, 1976); Scheingold, note 4 *supra*, 26; Schur, note 8 *supra*, 15; Ryan, note 57 *supra*.

174. Erik Olin Wright, *The Politics of Punishment* (New York: Harper and Row, 1973), 9, 21; Scheingold, note 4 *supra*, 149; Ryan, note 57 *supra*; Robert K. Merton, *Social Theory and Social Structure* (New York: Free Press, 1968); Richard A. Cloward and Lloyd Ohlin, *Delinquency and Opportunity* (New York: Free Press, 1960), 83.

175. "Private Violence," note 85 *supra*, 24.

176. Conklin, note 69 *supra*; D. Brown, "On Being Unemployed and Being a Victim of Crime: A Commentary," *Australian Journal of Social Issues*, 15 (1980), 223.

177. Currie, note 31 *supra*; Robert Bohm, "Beyond Employment: Toward a Radical Solution to the Crime Problem," *Crime and Social Justice* (1984), 213.

178. Barak, note 160 *supra*, 120.

179. Quinney, note 42 *supra*; Harris, note 58 *supra*, 125.

180. Silberman, note 18 *supra*, 147.

181. Schur, note 8 *supra*, 131; Harris, note 58 *supra*, 122; Joshua Cohen and Joel Rogers, *On Democracy* (New York: Penguin, 1983), 20.

182. Conklin, note 69 *supra*, 88; Wright, note 174 *supra*, 21; Amitai Etzioni, *Capital Corruption* (New York: Harcourt Brace Jovanovich, 1984).

183. Tony Platt, "Street Crime," in Tony Platt and Paul Takagi (eds.), *Crime and Social Justice* (Totowa, N.J.: Barnes and Noble, 1981), 21.

184. *Ibid.*, 27.

185. Ryan, note 145 *supra*; Jack Newfield and Paul Dubrul, *The Permanent Government* (New York: Pilgrim, 1982); Silberman, note 18 *supra*, 126.

186. Silberman, note 18 *supra*, 119; Ryan, note 145 *supra*.

187. See, for example, National Urban League, *Black Families in the 1974– 75 Depression* (Washington, D.C.: Author, 1975); Browning, note 11 *supra*, 31.

188. Silberman, note 18 *supra*, 118.

189. Platt, note 183 *supra*, 24.

190. Silberman, note 18 *supra*, 26.

191. Don C. Gibbons, *Changing the Lawbreaker* (Englewood Cliffs, N.J.: Prentice-Hall, 1965).

192. Silberman, note 18 *supra*, 142, 149, 151.

193. Tom Waits, "Romeo Is Bleeding," *Blue Valentine* (Los Angeles: Asylum, 1978).

194. Nathan Glazer, "When the Melting Pot Doesn't Melt," in Rainwater, note 173 *supra*, 251; Angela Davis, *Women, Race and Class* (New York: Vintage, 1981).

195. Jim Green and Allen Hunter, "Racism and Busing in Boston," in William Tabb and Larry Sawers (eds.), *Marxism and the Metropolis* (New York: Oxford University Press, 1978).

196. Silberman, note 18 *supra*, 107.

197. For example, blacks have lost economic ground since 1960. See *ibid.*, 224.

198. *Ibid.*, 182.

199. *Ibid.*

200. Jane Roberts Chapman, "The Economics of Women's Victimization," in Jane Roberts Chapman and Margaret Gates (eds.), *The Victimization of Women* (Beverly Hills, Calif.: Sage, 1978), 251; Karen Stollard, Barbara Ehrenreich, and Holly Sklar, *Poverty in the American Dream: Women and Children* (Boston: South End Press, 1984); Karmen, note 148 *supra*, 116; Weis and Weis, note 137 *supra*, 15; Placier, note 158 *supra*, 3.

201. Del Martin, "Battered Women: Society's Problem," in Chapman and Gates, *ibid.*, 111; Viano, note 47 *supra*, 67.

202. Julia R. Schwendinger and Herman Schwendinger, *Rape and Inequality* (Beverly Hills, Calif.: Sage, 1983); Chapman, note 200 *supra*; Susan Griffin, "Rape: The All-American Crime," *Ramparts*, 10 (September 1971), 26.

203. Richard Sennett and Jonathan Cobb, *The Hidden Injuries of Class* (New York: Vintage, 1972); T. R. Young, "Corporate Crime: A Critique of the Clinard Report," *Contemporary Crises*, 5 (1981), 323; Lillian Breslow Rubin, *Worlds of Pain: Life in the Working Class Family* (New York: Basic Books, 1976); Studs Terkel, *Working* (New York: Pantheon, 1971); Patricia Sexton and Brendon Sexton, *Blue Collars, Hard Hats* (New York: Random House, 1971); Walker, note 7 *supra*, 212, 223; Currie, note 7 *supra*, 436.

204. David F. Greenberg (ed.), *Crime and Capitalism* (Palo Alto, Calif.; Mayfield, 1981), 70–71; Silberman, note 18 *supra*, 129.

205. Silberman, note 18 *supra*, 50.

206. *Ibid.*, 127; Schur, note 8 *supra*, 182.

207. Bertram Gross, *Friendly Facism: The New Face of Power in America* (New York: M. Evans, 1980), 300.

208. Diane Vaughan, "Crime Between Organizations: Implications for Victimology," in Geis and Shotland, note 136 *supra*, 83.

209. Gilbert Geis, *White Collar Crime* (Lexington, Mass.: Lexington Books, 1978), 83.

210. Silberman, note 18 *supra*, 227.

211. *Ibid.*, 231.

212. John Braithwaite, *Inequality, Crime and Public Policy* (London: Routledge and Kegan Paul, 1979).

213. Schur, note 8 *supra*, 152.

214. For a defense of that structure, see Irving Kristol, *Two Cheers for Capitalism* (New York: Basic Books, 1978); Milton Friedman, *Capitalism and Freedom* (Chicago: University of Chicago Press, 1962); George Gilder, *Wealth and Poverty* (New York: Basic Books, 1978).

215. Ryan, note 57 *supra*; Green, note 173 *supra*; Lewis, note 63 *supra*. Briefly, structural theorists argue that corporate capitalism requires economic competition, by definition, even though increasing monopolization on the corporate level has reduced the number of competitors and changed the object of competition (from price to brand, for example). They say that corporate capitalism requires poverty and inequality because its model of economic growth and profits requires labor and resources to be extracted and rewarded at levels far below their value. It helps ensure this result by tolerating, if not creating, a perpetual level of unemployment and job competition that enhances insecurity, lowers wages, and discourages labor organization for all workers except a relative few unionized, but complicit, laborers. It perpetuates racism, sexism and other social divisions to help prevent organized opposition. The system's resources and income go mostly to upper-class owners and managers, much less so to most workers, and practically not at all to the marginally employed and the unemployed. The government welfare system, paid for primarily by the middle classes, far from correcting this imbalance, merely tempers its adversity, keeping discontent within manageable limits [see Frances Fox Piven and Richard O. Cloward, *Regulating the Poor: The Functions of Public Welfare* (New York: Pantheon, 1971)]. Critics argue that equitably sharing the society's resources would cripple this system and challenge the concentration of political and economic power upon which it rests. See Edward Greenberg, *Serving the Few: The Bias of Government Policy* (New York: John Wiley, 1974); Ralph Miliband, *The State in Capitalist Society* (New York: Basic Books, 1969); G. William Domhoff, *The Powers That Be* (New York: Vintage, 1978); Michael Parenti, *Democracy for the Few* (New York: St. Martins Press, 1980); Gross, note 206 *supra*; Frances Fox Piven and Richard O. Cloward, *The New Class War* (New York: Pantheon, 1982); Erich Fromm, *To Have or To Be?* (New York: Bantam Books, 1981); Mark Green, *Winning Back America* (New York: Bantam Books, 1982); Frank Ackerman, *Hazardous to Our Wealth* (Boston: South End Press, 1984); Robert Lekachman, *Greed It Not Enough* (New York: Pantheon, 1982).

216. Charles E. Reasons and Colin H. Goff, "Corporate Crime: A Cross-National Analysis," in Geis and Shotland, note 136 *supra*, 126; Murray Hausknecht, "Crime and the Culture of Business," *Dissent* (Fall 1985), 389; Morton Mintz, "At Any Cost: Corporate Greed, Women and the Dalkon Shield," *The Progressive* (November 1985), 20; Matthew Rothschild, "No Place for Scruples," *The Progressive* (November 1985), 26.

217. Marshall B. Clinard and Peter C. Yeager, *Corporate Crime* (New York: Free Press, 1980); Geis, note 209 *supra*.

218. Young, note 203 *supra*; David Warsh, "It's A Wonder Anyone Goes to Jail," *Boston Globe*, May 24, 1985, 68.

219. Clinard and Yeager, note 217 *supra*.

220. Greenberg, note 204 *supra*.

221. Edward Gross, "Organization Structure and Organizational Crime," in Geis and Shotland, note 136 *supra*, 52.

222. Laureen Snider, "Traditional and Corporate Theft: A Comparison of Sanctions," in Peter Wickman and Timothy Dailey (eds.), *White Collar and Economic Crime* (Lexington, Mass.: Lexington Books, 1982), 235.

223. Karmen, note 148 *supra*.

224. Christopher Lasch, *The Minimal Self: Psychic Survival in Troubled Times* (New York: Norton, 1984); Walli F. Leff and Marilyn G. Haft, *Time Without Work* (Boston: South End Press, 1984); Stanley Aronowitz, *False Promises: The Shaping of American Working Class Consciousness* (New York: McGraw-Hill, 1973); Theodore Roszak, *Person/Planet* (Garden City, N.Y.: Doubleday, 1979), 205; Richard Sennett, *The Fall of Public Man: On the Social Psychology of Capitalism* (New York: Vintage, 1976), 295; Terkel, note 203 *supra;* Del Martin, "The Economics of Wifebeating," Paper presented at Annual Meeting of American Sociological Association, New York, 1976; Barbara Garson, *All the Livelong Day: The Meaning and Demeaning of Routine Work* (New York: Penguin, 1975).

225. Geis, note 209 *supra*, 98; Christopher Lasch, *The Culture of Narcissism* (New York: Norton, 1979); Parenti, note 215 *supra.*

226. Platt, note 183 *supra,* 27.

227. Silberman, note 18 *supra,* 152.

228. Schur, note 8 *supra,* 121; Erich Fromm, *The Anatomy of Human Destructiveness* (New York: Fawcett, 1973); George Leonard, *The End of Sex* (New York: Bantam, 1983); Erich Fromm, *To Have or To Be?* (New York: Bantam, 1981).

229. Silberman, note 18 *supra,* 27.

230. Dee Brown, *Bury My Heart At Wounded Knee* (New York: Bantam Books, 1970); Vine DeLoria, *Custer Died for Your Sins* (New York: Macmillan, 1969).

231. Silberman, note 18 *supra,* 32.

232. Herbert Marcuse, *An Essay on Liberation* (Boston: Beacon Press, 1969), 75.

233. Scheingold, note 4 *supra,* 61.

234. Philip Slater, *Earthwalk* (New York: Bantam Books, 1974), 103.

235. Silberman, note 18 *supra,* 37.

236. Robert Justin Goldstein, *Political Repression in Modern America* (Cambridge: Schenkman, 1978); Alan Wolfe, *The Seamy Side of Democracy: Repression in America* (New York: Longman, 1978).

237. Marcuse, note 232 *supra,* 77.

238. Rodney Stark, *Police Riots* (Belmont, Calif.: Wadsworth, 1972).

239. Noam Chomsky and Edward S. Herman, *The Washington Connection and Third World Facism* (Boston: South End Press, 1979); William A. Williams, *Empire as a Way of Life* (New York: Oxford University Press, 1982).

240. Silberman, note 18 *supra,* 228.

241. Stuart A. Scheingold, *The Politics of Rights: Lawyers, Public Policy and Political Change* (New Haven: Yale University Press, 1974), 55; Charles W. Grau, "What Ever Happened to Politics?" in Piers Beirne and Richard Quinney (eds.), *Marxism and the Law* (New York: John Wiley, 1982), 196.

242. Davis, note 61 *supra,* 123; Jock Young, "Left Idealism: Reform and Beyond," in B. Fine, et al. (eds.), *Capitalism and the Rule of Law* (London: Hutchinson, 1979); Mark C. Kennedy, "Power and Victimization: The Political Relativity of Victims," Paper presented at Second International Symposium on Victimology, Boston, 1976.

243. Currie, note 31 *supra;* Charles E. Reasons, "Crime and the Abuse of Power: Offenses and Offenders Beyond the Reach of the Law," in Wickman and Dailey, note 222 *supra,* 59; Young, note 203 *supra.*

244. Schur, note 8 *supra,* 135.

245. Browning, note 11 *supra,* 31.

246. Forer, note 55 *supra.*

247. Although the Eastern bloc nations have a much lower crime rate than we do, with comparable economic development, they do not provide the model we seek. While they have minimized poverty, inequality, and economic competition, their totalitarian and bureaucratic governments and institutions produce social alienation and opposition that undoubtedly account for the crime that persists, including workplace and government corruption, black market racketeering, state crimes, and the theft of nationalized property (see Maria Los, "Crime and Economy in the Communist Countries," in Wickman and Dailey, note 222 *supra,* 121).

In the Western world, we have a few models, notably in Western Europe, that better approximate a political economy that reduces crime, yet they still have fatal flaws. Switzerland, for example, has a fairly low common crime rate, and a political democracy that tends toward decentralization and local control. It has strong government controls that lessen capitalism's adverse economic effects, thus substantially reducing poverty and inequality. Yet it also suffers strong economic competition, social isolation, and the other negative effects of corporate capitalism and large bureaucracy, which produces its high and increasing white-collar and corporate crime rate [see Marshall Clinard, *Cities With Little Crime* (New York: Cambridge University Press, 1978)].

248. James Q. Wilson, "Thinking About Crime" *Atlantic Monthly* (September 1983), 86, 88.

249. Harold C. Barnett, "The Production of Corporate Crime in Corporate Capitalism," in Wickman and Dailey, note 222 *supra,* 157.

Notes for Chapter 5

1. John Gilsinan, *Doing Justice* (Englewood Cliffs, N.J.: Prentice-Hall,, 1982), 216.

2. National Organization for Victim Assistance, *Campaign for Victim Rights* (Washington, D.C.: Author, n.d.), 3.

3. Patsy Klaus, "Victims of Crime," *Bureau of Justice Statistics Bulletin* (November 1981), 4.

4. M. J. Rizzo, "The Cost of Crime to Victims: An Empirical Analysis," *Journal of Legal Studies,* 8 (1979), 177.

5. S. D. Suarez and G. G. Gallup, "Chronic Immobility as a Response to Rape in Humans: A Theoretical Note," *Psychological Record,* 29 (1979), 315.

6. Michael R. Gottfredson and Michael J. Hindelang, "Bodily Injury in Personal Crime," in Wesley G. Skogan (ed.), *Sample Surveys of the Victims of Crime* (Cambridge: Ballinger, 1976), 65.

7. Mark Blumberg, "Injury to Victims of Personal Crimes: Nature and Extent," in William A. Parsonage (ed.), *Perspectives on Victimology* (Beverly Hills, Calif.: Sage, 1979), 133.

8. John Alan Stookey, "A Cost Theory of Victim Justice," in Burt Galaway and Joe Hudson (eds.), *Perspectives on Victims* (St Louis: Mosby, 1981), 88; Warren T. Brookes, "Crime: Economic Scourge of the Ghetto," in Galaway and Hudson, *ibid.*, 92.

9. Blumberg, note 7 *supra.*

10. Gottfredson and Hindelang, note 6 *supra.*

11. *Ibid.;* C. Swart and L. Berkowitz, "Effects of a Stimulus Associated with a Victim's Pain on Later Aggression," *Journal of Personality and Social Psychology,* 33 (1976), 623.

12. Mary C. Sengstock and Jersey Liang, *Responses of the Elderly to Criminal Victimization* (Detroit: Wayne State University, 1979).

13. Blumberg, note 7 *supra.*

14. M. Heller, S. Ehrlich and J. Lester, "Victim-Offender Relationships and Severity of Victim Injury," *Journal of Social Psychology,* 120 (1983), 229.

15. Gottfredson and Hindelang, note 6 *supra;* Richard Block, *Violent Crime: Environment, Interaction and Death* (Lexington, Mass.: Lexington Books, 1977).

16. S. I. Singer, "Homogeneous Victim-Offender Populations: A Review and Some Research Implications," *Journal of Criminal Law and Criminology,* 72 (Summer 1981), 779.

17. Eduard Ziegenhagen, *Victims of Violent Crime in New York City: An Exploratory Survey of Perceived Needs* (New York: Crime Victim's Consultation Project, 1974), 22.

18. Klaus, note 3 *supra.*

19. Joanna Shapland, "Victim Assistance and the Criminal Justice System: The Victim's Perspective," in Ezzat A. Fattah (ed.), *Reorienting the Justice System: From Crime Policy to Victim Policy* (New York: Macmillan, 1985), 285.

20. Ziegenhagen, note 18 *supra,* 22.

21. Shapland, note 19 *supra,* 4.

22. Klaus, note 3 *supra.*

23. Lucy Friedman, et al., *Victims and Helpers: Reactions to Crime* (New York: Victim Services Agency, 1982).

24. Joseph Sheley, *Understanding Crime* (Belmont, Calif.: Wadsworth, 1979), 37.

25. Frank Browning, "Nobody's Soft on Crime Anymore: Rethinking America's Impossible Problem," *Mother Jones* (August 1982), 30.

26. *Ibid.,* 29.

27. Gregg Barak, *In Defense of Whom? A Critique of Criminal Justice Reform* (Cincinnati: Anderson, 1980), 122.

28. Klaus, note 3 *supra.*

29. Thomas Cronin, et al., *U.S. Against Crime in the Streets* (Bloomington: Indiana University Press, 1981), 172.

30. James O'Connor, *The Fiscal Crisis of the State* (New York: St. Martins Press, 1973).

31. Stookey, note 8 *supra.*

32. David G. Peck, "Criminal Victimization of the Elderly: Some Implications for Care," *Journal of Humanics,* 6 (1978), 53.

33. Wesley G. Skogan, "The Fear of Crime and Its Behavioral Implications," in Fattah, note 19 *supra,* 201.

34. Wesley G. Skogan and Michael G. Maxfield, *Coping with Crime: Individual and Neighborhood Reactions* (Beverly Hills, Calif.: Sage, 1981).

35. *Ibid.*

36. John E. Conklin, *The Impact of Crime* (New York: Macmillan, 1975), 6: Herbert Denenberg, "Compensation for Victims of Crime: Justice for the Victim as Well as the Criminal," *Insurance Law Journal* (1979), 628; LeRoy Lamborn, "Remedies for the Victims of Crime," *Southern California Law Review* (1979), 43.

37. Robert Elias, *Victims of the System: Crime Victims and Compensation in American Politics and Criminal Justice* (New Brunswick, N.J.: Transaction Books, 1983).

38. Conklin, note 36 *supra,* 106.

39. Jeffrey A. Reiman, *The Rich Get Richer and the Poor Get Prison: Class, Ideology and Criminal Justice* (New York: John Wiley, 1979), 106.

40. Gwynn Nettler, *Explaining Crime* (New York: McGraw-Hill, 1978), 79.

41. Charles Silberman, *Criminal Violence, Criminal Justice* (New York: Vintage, 1978), 56.

42. Linda Martino, "Credit Card Fraud," *AAA World* (August 1984), 12.

43. Gilsinan, note 1 *supra,* 213.

44. *Ibid.,* 219.

45. Institute for the Study of Labor and Economic Crisis, *The Iron Fist and the Velvet Glove: An Analysis of U.S. Police* (San Francisco: Crime and Justice Associates, 1982).

46. *Ibid.*

47. According to Bureau of Labor Statistics. See "Careers 1984" *New York Times,* October 16, 1983, 52; George O'Toole, *The Private Sector: Private Spies, Rent A Cops and the Police Industrial Complex* (New York: Norton, 1978), xii.

48. Andrew Karmen, *Crime Victims* (Belmont, Calif.: Brooks/Cole, 1984), 12.

49. *Ibid.,* 15.

50. *Ibid.,* 14.

51. David F. Greenberg, *Crime and Capitalism* (Palo Alto, Calif.: Mayfield, 1981), 202; Reiman, note 39 *supra;* Conklin, note 36 *supra.*

52. Marshall B. Clinard and Peter C. Yeager, *Corporate Crime* (New York: Free Press, 1980).

53. "The Politics of Street Crime," *Crime and Social Justice* (Spring–Summer 1976), 1.

54. Reiman, note 39 *supra*, 82.

55. Frank Pearce, *Crimes of the Powerful* (London: Pluto Press, 1976), 78.

56. Philip Stern, *Rape of the Taxpayer* (New York: Vintage, 1976); Gwynn Nettler, *Explaining Crime* (New York: McGraw-Hill, 1978), 5; Joseph Sheley, *Understanding Crime* (Belmont, Calif.: Wadsworth, 1979), 37; Mark Green and John F. Berry, *The Challenge of Hidden Profits* (New York: William Morrow, 1985); Margaret Engel, "Fraud in Cataract Surgery: U.S. Puts Loss at $2 Billion," *International Herald Tribune*, July 20, 1985, 1.

57. Friedman, note 23 *supra*.

58. Shapland, note 19 *supra*, 288.

59. Paul J. Lavrakas, "On Households," in Dan A. Lewis (ed.), *Reactions to Crime* (Beverly Hills, Calif.: Sage, 1981), 68; Marvin Harris, *America Now* (New York: Touchstone, 1981), 116; R. LeJeune and N. Alex, "On Being Mugged: The Event and Its Aftermath," *Urban Life and Culture*, 2 (1973), 259; Silberman, note 41 *supra*, 25; Kai T. Erikson, *Everything In Its Path* (New York: Simon and Schuster, 1976).

60. Silberman, note 41 *supra*, 23.

61. Morton Bard and Dawn Sangrey, *The Crime Victims Book* (New York: Basic Books, 1979); Stookey, note 8 *supra*.

62. Conklin, note 36 *supra*.

63. Ronnie Janoff-Bulman and Irene Hanson Frieze, "A Theoretical Perspective for Understanding Reactions to Victimization," *Journal of Social Issues* 39 (1983), 1.

64. Silberman, note 41 *supra*, 24.

65. J. V. Beecher, G. G. Abel and L. J. Skinner, "The Impact of a Sexual Assault on the Victim's Sex Life," *Victimology*, 4 (1979), 229; A. W. Burgess and L. I. Holmstrom, "Rape: Sexual Disruption and Recovery," *American Journal of Orthopsychiatry*, 49 (1979), 648.

66. *Ibid.*

67. Kim Lane Scheppele and Pauline B. Burt, "Through Women's Eyes: Defining Danger in the Wake of Sexual Assault," *Journal of Social Issues*, 39 (1983), 63.

68. Cathaleen Jones and Eliot Aronson, "Attribution of Fault to a Rape Victim as a Function of Respectability of the Victim," in Deanna R. Nass (ed.), *The Rape Victim* (Dubuque, Iowa: Kendall/Hunt, 1977), 27; J. E. Krulewitz, "Sex Differences in Rape Attributions," Paper presented at Annual Meeting of Midwestern Psychological Association, Chicago, 1977; H. S. Field, "Attitudes Toward Rape: A Comparative Analysis of Police, Rapists, Crisis Counselors and Citizens," *Journal of Personality and Social Psychology*, 36 (1978), 156.

69. Stephanie Riger, "On Women," in Lewis, note 59 *supra*, 47; Julia Schwendinger and Herman Schwendinger, "Rape Victims and the False

Sense of Guilt," *Crime and Social Justice*, 13 (1980), 4; A. A. Libow, "An Exploratory Approach to Self-Blame and Self-Derogation by Rape Victims," *Journal of Orthopsychiatry*, 49 (1979), 670; G. Smale and H. Spickenhauer, "Need for Retribution and Guilt Feelings in Victims of Serious Aggressive and Property Offenses," *Journal of Criminology and Criminal Justice*, 19 (1977), 195.

70. Burgess and Holmstrom, note 65 *supra*.

71. Lenore Walker, "Psychological Impact of the Criminalization of Domestic Violence on Victims," Paper presented at Third International Institute on Victimology, Lisbon, 1984; Jon Conte, "The Effects of Sexual Abuse on Children: A Critique and Suggestions for Future Research," Paper presented at Third International Institute on Victimology, Lisbon, 1984; L. O. Ruch and S. Meyers Chandler, "The Crisis Impact of Sexual Assault on Three Victim Groups," *Journal of Social Service Review*, 5 (1982), 83.

72. R. K. Davies, "Incest: Some Neuropsychiatric Findings," *International Journal of Psychiatric Medicine*, 9 (1978), 117.

73. Roxane L. Silver, Cheryl Boon and Mary H. Stones, "Searching for Meaning in Misfortune: Making Sense of Incest," *Journal of Social Issues*, 39 (1983), 81.

74. Martha Burt and Bonnie Katz, "Rape, Robbery and Burglary: Responses to Actual and Feared Criminal Victimization, with Special Focus on Women and the Elderly," Paper presented at Third International Institute on Victimology, Lisbon, 1984; Lars Weisaeth, "Psychiatric Studies in Victimology in Norway: Main Findings and Recent Developments," Paper presented at Third International Institute on Victimology, Lisbon, 1984.

75. L. S. Perloff, "Perception of Vulnerability to Victimization," *Journal of Social Issues*, 39 (1983), 41.

76. C. Peterson and M. E. P. Seligman, "Learned Helplessness and Victimization," *Journal of Social Issues*, 39 (1983), 103; R. A. Feinberg, F. G. Miller, and R. F. Weiss, "Motivational Aspects of Learned Helplessness," *Journal of General Psychology*, 106 (1982), 273.

77. D. T. Miller and C. A. Porter, "Self-Blame in Victims of Violence," *Journal of Social Issues*, 39 (1983), 139; Trudy Mills, "Victimization and Self-Esteem: On Equating Husband Abuse and Wife Abuse," *Victimology*, 9 (1984), 254.

78. E. Tomorug-Miarka and T. Pirozynski, "Victimological Relations in Psycho-Involutive Maladjustment," Paper presented at Second International Symposium on Victimology, Boston, 1976; J. L. Krupnick and M. J. Horowitz, "Victims of Violence: Psychological Response, Treatment Implications," *Evaluation and Change* (Spring 1980); Janice Krupnick, "Brief Psychotherapy with Victims of Violent Crime," *Victimology*, 5 (1980), 347.

79. R. J. Bulman and C. B. Wortman, "Attributions of Blame and Coping in the 'Real World': Severe Accident Victims React to Their Lot," *Journal of Personality and Social Psychology*, 35 (1977), 351; Shelley E. Taylor, Joanne V. Wood, and Rosemary R. Lichtman, "It Could Be Worse: Selective Evaluation as a Response to Victimization," *Journal of Social Issues*, 39 (1983), 19.

80. Ellen S. Cohn and David B. Sugarman, "Marital Abuse: Abusing the One You Love," *Victimology*, 5 (1980), 203.

81. S. L. Halleck, "Vengeance and Victimization," *Victimology*, 5 (1980), 99; M. Wright, "Nobody Came: Criminal Justice and the Needs of Victims," *Howard Journal of Penology and Crime Prevention*, 16 (1977), 22.

82. C. R. Figley and D. H. Sprenkle, "Delayed Stress Response Syndrome: Family Therapy Indications," *Journal of Marriage and Family Counseling* (July 1978).

83. M. Symonds, "The Second Injury to Victims of Violent Crime," *Evaluation and Change* (Spring 1980).

84. Bard and Sangrey, note 61 *supra*.

85. Klaus, note 3 *supra*; E. Kahana, et al., "Perspectives of Aged on Victimization, 'Ageism,' and Their Problems in Urban Society," *Gerontologist*, 17 (1977), 121; D. L. Smith, "The Aftermath of Victimization: Fear and Suspicion," in Emilio Viano (ed.), *Victims and Society* (Washington, D.C.: Visage Press, 1976), 203; James Garofalo, "The Fear of Crime: Causes and Consequences," *Journal of Criminal Law and Criminology*, 72 (Summer 1981), 839; James Garofalo, *Public Opinion About Crime: The Attitudes of Victims and Nonvictims in Selected Cities* (Washington, D.C.: U.S. Department of Justice, 1977).

86. Conklin, note 36 *supra*, 8.

87. *Ibid.*; R. Lotz, "Public Anxiety About Crime," *Pacific Sociological Review*, 22 (1979), 241.

88. F. F. Furstenberg, "Fear of Crime and Its Effects on Citizen Behavior," in A. Biderman (ed.), *Crime and Justice: A Symposium* (New York: Nailburg, 192).

89. Wesley G. Skogan, "Public Policy and the Fear of Crime in Large American Cities," Paper presented at Annual Meeting of the Midwest Political Science Association, Chicago, 1979; Garofalo, note 81 *supra*; Skogan and Maxfield, note 34 *supra*, 228; Lewis, note 59 *supra*; James Garofalo and John Laub, "The Fear of Crime: Broadening Our Perspectives," *Victimology*, 3 (1978), 242; Jeffrey Henig and Michael G. Maxfield, "Reducing Fear of Crime: Strategies for Intervention," *Victimology*, 3 (1978), 297; Wesley Skogan, "The Impact of Victimization on Fear" Paper presented at Fifth International Symposium on Victimology, Zagreb, 1985; Allen E. Liska, "Victimization and Fear of Crime" Paper presented at Fifth International Symposium on Victimology, Zagreb, 1985.

90. M. J. Hindelang, M. R. Gottfredson and J. Garofalo, *Victims of Personal Crime: An Empirical Foundation for a Theory of Personal Victimization* (Cambridge: Ballinger, 1978); M. T. Gordon, et al., "Crime, Women and the Quality of Urban Life," *Signs*, 5 (1980), 133; J. Pecar, "The Fear of Crime," *Rev. Kriminalistik Criminol.*, 31 (1980), 30.

91. J. J. M. van Dijk, "Public Attitudes Toward Crime in the Netherlands," *Victimology*, 3 (1978), 265; J. Garofalo, "Victimization and the Fear of Crime," *Journal of Research on Crime and Delinquency*, 16 (1979), 80.

92. Skogan, note 33 *supra*.

93. Conklin, note 36 *supra*, 6.

94. van Dijk, note 91 *supra;* Robert J. Rubel, "Victimization and Fear in Public Schools: Survey of Activities," *Victimology,* 3 (1978), 339.

95. Riger, note 69 *supra;* Gordon, note 90 *supra;* V. H. Jaycox, "The Elderly's Fear of Crime: Rational or Irrational?" *Victimology,* 3 (1978), 329; Jean Giles-Sims, "A Multivariate Analysis of Perceived Likelihood of Victimization and Degree of Worry Among Older People," *Victimology,* 9 (1984), 222.

96. Fay Lomax Cook, "Crime and the Elderly: The Emergence of a Policy Issue," in Lewis, note 59 *supra,* 123; Raymond A. Eve and Susan Brown Eve, "The Effects of Powerlessness, Fear of Social Change and Social Integration on Fear of Crime Among the Elderly," *Victimology,* 9 (1984), 290.

97. J. H. Lundquist and J. M. Duke, "The Elderly Victim at Risk: Explaining the Fear-Victimization Paradox," *Criminology,* 20 (1981), 115; Skogan and Maxfield, note 34 *supra,* 27; S. Riger and M. T. Gordon, "Women's Fear of Crime: From Blaming to Restricting the Victim," *Victimology,* 3 (1978), 274.

98. Terry L. Baumer, "Research on Fear of Crime in the U.S.," *Victimology,* 3 (1978), 254.

99. Mark Stafford and Omer Galle, "Victimization Rates, Exposure to Risk, and Fear of Crime," *Criminology,* 22 (1984), 173.

100. Baumer, note 98 *supra.*

101. R. L. Shotland, et al., "Fear of Crime in Residential Communities," *Criminology,* 17 (1979), 34.

102. James Brooks, "The Fear of Crime in the U.S.," *Crime and Delinquency* (July 1974), 241; Silberman, note 41 *supra.*

103. M. Warr and M. Stafford, "Fear of Victimization: A Look at the Proximate Causes," *Social Forces,* 61 (1983), 1033.

104. Sally Engle Merry, *Urban Danger: Life in a Neighborhood of Strangers* (Philadelphia: Temple University Press, 1981).

105. R. W. Toseland, "Fear of Crime: Who Is Most Vulnerable?" *Journal of Criminal Justice,* 10 (1982), 199.

106. Merry, note 104 *supra,* 8; Conklin, note 36 *supra,* 30.

107. Wesley G. Skogan and William R. Klecka, *The Fear of Crime* (Washington, D.C.: American Political Science Association, 1977), 2.

108. Merry, note 104 *supra.*

109. Reiman, note 39 *supra.*

110. Merry, note 104 *supra,* 10–12.

111. William E. Berg and Robert Johnson, "Assessing the Impact of Victimization: Acquisition of the Victim Role Among Elderly and Female Victims," in Parsonage, note 7 *supra,* 58.

112. H. Erskine, "The Polls: Fear of Crime and Violence," *Public Opinion Quarterly,* 38 (1974), 797.

113. Riger, note 69 *supra,* 60; Lee H. Bowker, "The Criminal Victimization of Women," *Victimology,* 4 (1980), 371.

114. Margaret T. Gordon and Stephanie Riger, "The Fear of Rape Project," *Victimology,* 3 (1978), 346.

115. Riger, note 69 *supra,* 60.

116. Cook, note 96 *supra.*

117. U.S. Congress, House of Representatives Select Committee on Aging, *In Search of Security: A National Perspective on Elderly Crime Victimization* (Washington, D.C.: U.S. Government Printing Office, 1977).

118. L. Heath, M. T. Gordon and R. K. LeBailly, "What Newspapers Tell Us (And Don't Tell Us) About Rape," *The Newspaper Research Journal* (forthcoming).

119. A. H. Clarke and M. J. Lewis, "Fear of Crime Among the Elderly: An Exploratory Study," *British Journal of Criminology,* 22 (1982), 49.

120. David L. Decker, David Schichor, and Robert M. O'Brien, *Urban Structure and Victimization* (Lexington, Mass.: Lexington Books, 1982); M. Lalli and L. D. Savitz, "The Fear of Crime in the School Enterprise and Its Consequence," *Education and Urban Society,* 8 (1976), 401.

121. John R. Hepburn and Daniel J. Monti, "Victimization, Fear of Crime and Adaptive Responses Among High School Students," in Parsonage, note 7 *supra,* 121; G. Gallup, "Teenagers Fear School Violence," *St. Louis Post-Dispatch,* December 21, 1977, 5F.

122. E. S. Cohn, L. Kidder, and J. Harvey, "Crime Prevention vs. Victimization Prevention: The Psychology of Two Different Reactions," *Victimology,* 3 (1978), 285.

123. *Ibid.*

124. R. Lance Shotland and Lynne I. Goodstein, "The Role of Bystanders in Crime Control," *Journal of Social Issues,* 40 (1984), 9; Conklin, note 36 *supra,* 178, 248.

125. Lawrence E. Cummings, "Reaction to a Victimless Crime: An Assessment by Community Leaders, Control Agents, and the Offenders," in Viano, note 85 *supra,* 421.

126. Skogan and Klecka, note 107 *supra,* 2.

127. Henig and Maxfield, note 89 *supra,* 300.

128. Stuart A. Scheingold, *The Politics of Law and Order: Street Crime and Public Policy* (New York: Longman, 1984), 38; Howard A. Kurtz, "The Effects of Victimization on the Acceptance of Aggression and the Expectations of Assertive Traits in Children as Measured by the General Social Survey," *Victimology,* 9 (1984), 166.

129. Garofalo, note 84 *supra.*

130. *Ibid.*

131. *Ibid.*

132. Carl E. Pope and R. L. McNeely, "Race, Crime and Criminal Justice: An Overview," in R. L. McNeely and Carl E. Pope (eds.), *Race, Crime and Criminal Justice* (Beverly Hills, Calif.: Sage, 1981), 10; F. F. Furstenberg, "Public Reactions to Crime in the Streets," *American Scholar,* 40 (1971), 601.

133. David Lewis Smith, "The Aftermath of Victimization: Fear and Suspicion," in Viano, note 85 *supra,* 203.

134. J. McIntyre, "Public Attitudes Toward Crime and Law Enforcement," *Annals,* 374 (1967), 34; Brooks, note 102 *supra;* Conklin, note 36 *supra.*

135. Garofalo, note 85 *supra.*

136. Skogan and Maxfield, note 34 *supra.*

137. Garofalo, note 85 *supra.*

138. *Ibid.*

139. Wesley G. Skogan, "On Attitudes and Behaviors," in Lewis, note 59 *supra,* 19; Wesley G. Skogan, "Assessing the Behavioral Context of Victimization," *Journal of Criminal Law and Criminology,* 72 (Summer 1981), 727.

140. Gilbert Geis and Ivan Bunn, "Witches: the Nonesuch Victims," in Hans Joachim Schneider (ed.), *The Victim in International Perspective* (Berlin: Walter de Gruyter, 1982), 247; Kai Erikson, *The Wayward Puritans* (New York: John Wiley, 1966); Joseph Klaits, "Who's to Blame? An Examination of Witchcraft," in Jacqueline Scherer and Gary Shepard (eds.), *Victimization of the Weak* (Springfield, Ill.: Charles C Thomas, 1983), 31.

141. Irvin Waller and Norman Okihiro, *Burglary: The Victim and the Public* (Toronto: University of Toronto Press, 1978), 87.

142. *Ibid.*

143. Conklin, note 36 *supra,* 122.

144. Klaus P. Fink, "Ambivalence of Former Victims Toward Their Persecutors at the Petition for Indemnification," in Israel Drapkin and Emilio Viano (eds.), *Victimology: Crimes, Victims and Justice* (Lexington, Mass.: Lexington Books, 1974), 107.

145. Elias, note 37 *supra.*

146. Yona Cohn, "Crisis Intervention and the Victim of Robbery," in Israel Drapkin and Emilio Viano (eds.), *Victimology: Society's Reaction to Victimization* (Lexington, Mass.: Lexington Books, 1974), 19.

147. Scheingold, note 128 *supra,* 37.

148. Greenberg, note 51 *supra,* 9.

149. Michael D. Maltz, "Crime Statistics: A Historical Perspective," *Crime and Delinquency,* 23 (1977), 32.

150. Skogan, note 33 *supra.*

151. F. Dubow, *Reactions to Crime: A Critical Review of the Literature* (Washington, D.C.: U.S. Government Printing Office, 1979); Baumer, note 98 *supra.*

152. Skogan, note 139 *supra,* 31; C. Green, "Risks, Beliefs and Attitudes," in D. Center (ed.), *Fires and Human Behavior* (London: John Wiley, 1980), 277; Riger and Gordon, note 97 *supra,* 274; Furstenberg, note 132 *supra;* Skogan and Maxfield, note 34 *supra;* Conklin, note 36 *supra,* 111; M. T. Gordon and S. Riger, "Fear and Avoidance: A Link Between Attitudes and Behavior," *Victimology,* 4 (1979), 395.

153. Riger and Gordon, note 97 *supra.*

154. Garofalo, note 85 *supra.*

155. *Ibid.*

156. A. D. Biderman, et al., *Report on Victimization and Attitudes Toward Law Enforcement* (Washington, D.C.: U.S. Government Printing Office, 1967).

157. Eduard Ziegenhagen, "Toward a Theory of Victim-Criminal Justice Systems Interactions," in William F. McDonald (ed.), *Criminal Justice and the Victim* (Beverly Hills, Calif.: Sage, 1976), 269.

158. Skogan, note 33 *supra; J.* Garofalo, "The Fear of Crime: Causes and Consequences," in J. Dahman and J. Sasfy (eds.), *Victimology Research Conference Invited Papers* (MacLean, Va.: Mitre Corp., 1980).

159. Scheingold, note 128 *supra, 73;* Steven Balkin, "Victimization Rates, Safety and Fear of Crime," *Social Problems,* 26 (1979), 343.

160. Hindelang, Gottfredson and Garafalo, note 90 *supra.*

161. Scheingold, note 128 *supra,* 51.

162. Riger and Gordon, note 97 *supra;* Garofalo, note 85 *supra,* 81; S. Riger, M. T. Gordon, R. K. LeBailly, "Coping with Urban Crime: Women's Use of Precautionary Behaviors," *American Journal of Community Psychology,* 10 (1982), 369.

163. A. W. Burgess and L. L. Holmstrom, *Rape: Victims of Crisis* (Bowie, Md.: Brady, 1974).

164. Burgess and Holmstrom, note 65 *supra.*

165. Lenore E. Walker, "Treatment Alternatives for Battered Women," in Margaret Gates and Jane Roberts Chapman (eds.), *The Victimization of Women* (Beverly Hills, Calif.: Sage, 1978), 143; Lenore E. Walker, "Victimology and the Psychological Perspectives of Battered Women," *Victimology,* 8 (1983), 82.

166. Kathleen Ferrar, "Rationalizing Violence: How Battered Women Stay," *Victimology,* 8 (1983), 203.

167. S. Cleerhout, J. Elder, and C. Janes, "Problem Solving Skills of Rural Battered Women," *American Journal of Community Psychology,* 10 (1982), 605.

168. Walker, note 165 *supra;* Barbara Star, "Comparing Battered and Non-Battered Women," *Victimology,* 3 (1978), 32.

169. Lenore E. Walker, "Battered Women and Learned Helplessness," *Victimology,* 2 (1977), 532.

170. R. C. Summit, "The Child Sexual Abuse Accommodation Syndrome," *Child Abuse and Neglect,* 7 (1983), 177.

171. Hepburn and Monti, note 121 *supra.*

172. Conklin, note 36 *supra,* 109.

173. Richard D. Knutden, et al., *Victims and Witnesses: The Impact of Crime and Their Experience with the Criminal Justice System* (Milwaukee: Marquette University Victim/Witness Project: Center for Criminal Justice and Social Policy, 1976); Richard Block, "A Comparison of National Victim Surveys," Paper presented to Victims of Crime Conference, International Society of Criminology, Vancouver, 1983.

174. Knutden, et al., *ibid.*

175. Karmen, note 48 *supra*, 9.

176. Skogan and Maxfield, note 34 *supra;* Skogan, note 139 *supra.*

177. Lynn Curtis, "Toward A Theory of Response to Rape: A Methodological Critique," in Viano, note 85 *supra*, 220; Knutden, et al., note 173 *supra.*

178. Hepburn and Monti, note 121 *supra.*

179. J. DeFronzo, "Fear of Crime and Handgun Ownership," *Criminology*, 17 (1979), 331.

180. Lavrakas, note 59 *supra*, 69; Hans Joachim Schneider, "The Present Situation of Victimology in the World," in Hans Joachim Schneider (ed.), *The Victim in International Perspective* (Berlin: Walter de Gruyter, 1982), 11.

181. Conklin, note 36 *supra*, 108.

182. P. J. Lavrakas, *Factors Related to Citizen Involvement in Personal, Household and Neighborhood Anti-Crime Measures* (Evanston, Ill.; Center for Urban Affairs and Policy Research, 1980).

183. Skogan, note 33 *supra.*

184. Merry, note 104 *supra*, 225.

185. Ezzat Fattah, "Becoming A Victim: The Victimization Experience and Its Aftermath," 6 (1981), 29; Ziegenhagen, note 157 *supra*, 268; S. D. Rittenmeyer, "Of Battered Wifes, Self-Defense and Double Standards of Justice," *Journal of Criminal Justice*, 9 (1981), 389.

186. Seymour L. Halleck, "Vengeance and Victimization," *Victimology*, 5 (1980), 99.

187. Don Dutton and Susan Lee Painter, "Traumatic Bonding: The Development of Emotional Attachments in Battered Women and Other Relationships of Intermittent Abuse," *Victimology*, 6 (1981), 139; Dorothy Bracey, "The Juvenile Prostitute: Victim and Offender," *Victimology*, 8 (1983), 151; Fumie Kumagai, "Filial Violence in Japan," *Victimology*, 8 (1983), 173.

188. Ntozake Shange, "with no immediate cause," *Nappy Edges* (New York: Bantam Books, 1978).

189. Emilio Viano, "Violence, Victimization and Social Change: A Socio-Cultural and Public Policy Analysis," *Victimology*, 8 (1983), 67; D. L. Crochet, "Character and Prior Conduct of Victim in Support of a Plea of Self-Defense," *Louisiana Law Review*, 37 (1977), 1166; William F. McDonald, "Towards A Bicentennial Revolution in Criminal Justice: The Return of the Victim," *American Criminal Law Review*, 13 (1976), 664; Angela Davis, "Joanne Little—The Dialectics of Rape," *Ms. Magazine* (June 1975), 47.

190. Jayne Cortez, *Coagulations: New and Selected Poems* (New York: Thunder Mouth Press, 1984), 63.

191. Susan Salasin, "Services to Victims: Needs Assessment," in Susan Salasin (ed.), *Evaluating Victim Services* (Beverly Hills, Calif.: Sage, 1981), 21; R. Fields, "Victims of Terrorism: The Effects of Prolonged Stress," *Evaluation and Change* (Spring 1980); F. Ochberg, "Victims of Terrorism," *Journal* *of Clinical Psychiatry*, 41 (1980), 17; B. Bettleheim, *Surviving* (New York: Alfred Knopf, 1979); C. Figley, *Strangers at Home: Vietnam Veterans Since the War* (New York: Praeger, 1980); Frank Ochberg, "The Victim of Terrorism: Psychiatric Considerations," *Terrorism*, 1 (1978), 147.

192. Salasin, *ibid.*

193. "The Legacy of the Vietnam War," *Indochina Newsletter*, 18 (November/December 1982), 12.

194. Fattah, note 185 *supra.*

195. Ezzat A. Fattah, "Victims' Response to Confrontational Victimization: A Neglected Aspect of Victim Research," *Crime and Delinquency*, 30 (1984), 75.

196. Wesley G. Skogan and Richard Block, "Resistance and Injury in Non-Fatal Assaultive Violence," *Victimology*, 8 (1983), 215.

197. Joan McDermott, *Rape Victimization in 26 American Cities* (Washington, D.C.: U.S. Government Printing Office, 1979); Duncan Chappell and Jennifer James, "Victim Selection and Apprehension from the Rapist's Perspective: A Preliminary Investigation," Paper presented at Second International Symposium on Victimology, Boston, 1976.

198. Stephen Schafer, *The Victim and His Criminal: A Study in Functional Responsibility* (New York: Random House, 1968), 81.

199. Mary C. Sengstock, "Predominance of the Culpable Victim Concept in Victimology," Paper presented at Annual Meeting of Midwest Sociological Society, Chicago, 1976, 17.

200. Fattah, note 185 *supra.*

201. W. B. Sanders, *Rape and Women's Identity* (Beverly Hills, Calif.: Sage, 1980).

202. Sarah Ben-David, "Rapist-Victim Interaction During Rape," in Schneider, note 180 *supra, 237.*

203. Conklin, note 36 *supra,* 214; William F. McDonald, "Criminal Justice and the Victim: An Introduction," in McDonald, note 157 *supra,* 41; Leon Sheleff and David Schichor, "Victimological Aspects of Bystander Involvement," Paper presented at Second International Symposium on Victimology, Boston, 1976; L. Sheleff (Shaskolsky), "The Criminal Triad: Bystander, Victim and Criminal," *International Journal of Criminology and Penology,* 2 (1974), 15; R. I. Mawby, "Bystander Responses to the Victims of Crime: Is the Good Samaritan Alive and Well?" Paper presented to Third International Institute of Victimology, Lisbon, 1984; Carl H. D. Steinmetz, "Bystanders of Crime: Results from a National Survey," Paper presented at Third International Institute on Victimology, Lisbon, 1984.

204. James Ratcliffe, *The Good Samaritan and the Law* (Garden City, N.Y.: Doubleday, 1966).

205. Conklin, note 36 *supra,* 214.

206. L. F. Lowenstein, "Mugging: Crime of Greed and Vicious Hostility and Indifference," *Police Journal*, 53 (1980), 30; S. L. Gaertner and J. F. Dividio, "The Subtlety of White Racism, Arousal and Helping Behavior," *Journal of Personality and Social Psychology*, 35 (1977), 691; S. L. Gaertner, "The

Role of Racial Attitudes in Helping Behavior," *Journal of Social Psychology*, 97 (1975), 95; S. L. Gaertner, et al., "Race of Victim, Nonresponsive Bystanders and Helping Behavior," *Journal of Social Psychology*, 117 (1982), 69.

207. Sheleff, note 203 *supra;* Ted. L. Huston, et al., "Good Samaritan as Crime Victims," in Viano, note 85 *supra*, 518; Leon Sheleff-Shaskolsky, "The Innocent Bystander and Crime," *Federal Probation*, 34 (1970), 44; Gilbert Geis, et al., "Crime Victims as Seen By Intervening Bystanders," Paper presented at Second International Symposium on Victimology, Boston, 1976.

208. Lowenstein, note 206 *supra*.

209. Bibb Latane and John M. Darley, *The Unresponsive Bystander: Why Doesn't He Help?* (New York: Appleton Century Crofts, 1970); Harold Takooshian, "Looking Crime in the Eye, We Avert Our Gaze," *The New York Daily News*, December 28, 1980, 49; Raymond Haimes, "Some Reasons Why 'Helpless Bystanders' Just Don't React," *Newsday*, August 24, 1983, 56.

210. H. B. McKay and J. L. Lerner, "Sympathy and Suffering: Reactions to the Plight of an Innocent Victim," *Crime and Justice*, 4 (1977), 282; E. Bihm, et al., "Altruistic Responses Under Conditions of Anonymity," *Journal of Social Psychology*, 109 (1979), 25; P. Skolnick, "Helping as a Function of Time of Day, Location and Sex of Victim," *Journal of Social Psychology*, 102 (1977), 61; L. Zener-Solomon, et al., "The Effects of Bystander's Anonymity, Situational Ambiguity and Victim's Status of Helping," *Journal of Social Psychology*, 117 (1982), 285; S. Ungar, "The Effects of Effort and Stigma on Helping," *Journal of Social Psychology*, 107 (1979), 23; H. D. Schneider, "Are There Differences Between Helping and Helping?" *Archives of Psychology*, 131 (1978), 63; L. Wispe and J. Kiecolt, "Victim Attractiveness as a Function of Helping and Nonhelping," *Journal of Social Psychology*, 112 (1980), 67; W. A. Harrell and J. W. Goltz, "Effect of Victim's Need and Previous Accusation of Theft Upon Bystander's Reactions to Theft," *Journal of Social Psychology*, 112 (1980), 41; M. E. Valentine, "The Attenuating Influence of Gaze Upon the Bystander Intervention Effect," *Journal of Social Psychology*, 111 (1980), 197.

211. Latane and Darley, note 209 *supra*.

212. Leonard Bickman, "Bystander Involvement in a Crime," in Viano, note 85 *supra*, 144; U. Fullgrube, "The Problem of Refraining from Helping," *Kriminalistik*, 32 (1978), 160.

213. Huston, et al., note 207 *supra;* Ranald Hansen, "The Good Samaritan: A Psychological Profile," in Scherer and Shepard, note 140 *supra*, 190.

214. R. Goldman, et al., "Requests for Help and Prosocial Behavior," *Journal of Social Psychology*, 119 (1983), 55; D. W. Wilson, "Ambiguity and Helping Behavior," *Journal of Social Psychology*, 112 (1980), 155.

215. J. Kleinig, "Good Samaritanism," *Philosophy and Public Affairs*, 5 (1976), 382.

216. Scheingold, note 128 *supra*, 37, 84; S. Hall, et al., *Policing the Crisis: Mugging, the State and Law and Order* (London: Macmillan, 1978); Paul Takagi, "A Garrison State in a 'Democratic' Society," *Crime and Social Justice* (1974), 27.

217. Institute for the Study of Labor and Economic Crisis, note 45 *supra*.

218. *Ibid.*

219. Robert Elias, "The Symbolic Politics of Victim Compensation," *Victimology*, 8 (1983), 213; David R. Miers, "Compensation and Conceptions of Victims of Crime," *Victimology*, 8 (1983), 204.

220. LeJeune and Alex, note 59 *supra*, 283.

221. Conklin, note 36 *supra*, 50, 53.

222. *Ibid.*, 99; John Barron Mays, *Crime and the Social Structure* (London: Faber and Faber, 1963), 69; S. Riger and M. T. Gordon, "The Fear of Rape: A Study in Social Control," *Journal of Social Issues*, 37 (1981), 71; Dan A. Lewis, "Reactions to Crime Project," *Victimology*, 3 (1978), 345.

223. Schneider, note 180 *supra*; Richard Sennett, *The Fall of Public Man: On the Social Psychology of Capitalism* (New York: Vintage, 1976).

224. Cohn, Kidder, and Harvey, note 122 *supra*.

225. John A. Gardiner, "Wincanton: The Politics of Corruption," in President's Commission on Law Enforcement and the Administration of Justice, *Task Force Report: Organized Crime* (Washington, D.C.: U.S. Government Printing Office, 1967); Cummings, note 125 *supra*.

226. Lewis, note 222 *supra*.

227. Garofalo, note 85 *supra*, 20.

228. Merry, note 104 *supra*, 15; Conklin, note 36 *supra*, 64.

229. Merry, *ibid.*, 231.

230. *Ibid.*, 224.

231. Conklin, note 36 *supra*; Garofalo and Laub, note 89 *supra*; U.S. Congress, House of Representatives Select Committee on Aging, note 117 *supra* Fred Dubow and David Emmons, "The Community Hypothesis," in Lewis, note 59 *supra*, 167.

232. Shotland and Goodstein, note 124 *supra*, 16; Conklin, note 36 *supra*, 187.

233. James Brady, "Towards A Popular Justice in the U.S.: The Dialectics of Community Action," *Contemporary Crises*, 5 (1981), 159, 162.

234. Barry Krisberg, *Crime and Privilege* (Englewood Cliffs, N.J.: Prentice-Hall, 1975), 2.

235. Conklin, note 36 *supra*, 131.

236. Deborah M. Galvin, "Concepts in Victimization and the Slave," in Viano, note 85 *supra*, 593.

237. Knutden, et al., note 173 *supra*.

238. Paul J. Brantingham and Patricia L. Brantingham (eds.), *Environmental Criminology* (Beverly Hills, Calif.: Sage, 1981); Oscar Newman, *Defensible Space* (New York: Macmillan, 1972); Conklin, note 36 *supra*, 145.

239. Conklin, note 36 *supra*, 194.

240. Merry, note 104 *supra*, 232.

241. *Ibid.*, 239, 243.

242. Peter B. Meyer, "Communities as Victims of Corporate Crimes," in Galaway and Hudson, note 8 *supra*, 33.

NOTES FOR CHAPTER 6

1. As lawyer and New York University professor Graham Hughes argues, for example: "The notion that criminal procedures are biased toward the defendant is nonsense. Such a statement makes most members of the criminal defense bar rub their eyes in disbelief. In the plea-bargaining that has virtually replaced trials in many courts, the judge and prosecutor would more often seem hooked into a close alliance to deprive the defendant of his (sic) constitutional rights than the other way around." cited in Richard Higgins, "Help for the Victim," *Boston Globe*, January 11, 1981; Leslie Sebba, "Is the Criminal Process a Zero-Sum Game?" Paper presented at Fifth International Symposium on Victimology, Zagreb, 1985.

2. Ezzat A. Fattah, "Some Recent Theoretical Developments in Victimology," *Victimology*, 4(1979), 198.

3. John A. Stookey, "The Victim's Perspective on American Criminal Justice," in Joe Hudson and Burt Galaway (eds.), *Restitution in Criminal Justice* (Lexington, Mass.: Lexington Books, 1977).

4. Albert Reiss, *The Police and the Public* (New Haven: Yale University Press, 1971), 96.

5. Joanna Shapland, "Victims and the Criminal Justice System," in Ezzat A. Fattah (ed.), *Reorienting the Justice System: From Crime Policy to Victim Policy* (New York: Macmillan, 1985).

6. A. Schneider, "Evaluation of the Portland Neighborhood-Based Anti-Burglary Program," (Eugene: Oregon Research Institute, 1975).

7. Eduard Ziegenhagen, *Victims, Crime and Social Control* (New York: Praeger 1977), 99; Martin Gold, *Delinquent Behavior in an American City* (Belmont, Calif.: Brooks/Cole, 1970); Richard Lynch, "Improving the Treatment of Victims: Some Guides for Action," in William F. McDonald, *Criminal Justice and the Victim* (Beverly Hills, Calif.: Sage, 1976), 166.

8. B. L. Smith and C. R. Huff, "Crime in the Country: The Vulnerability and Victimization of Rural Citizens," *Journal of Criminal Justice*, 10(1982), 271.

9. Anne L. Schneider, et al., "The Role of Attitudes in the Decision to Report Crimes to the Police," in McDonald, note 7 *supra*, 89; Richard Block, "Why Notify the Police: The Victim's Decision to Notify the Police of an Assault," *Criminology*, 11(1974), 555; Richard O. Hawkins, "Who Called the Cops? Decisions to Report Criminal Victimization," *Law and Society Review*, 7(1973), 427; Michael J. O'Neil, *Calling the Cops: Responses of Witnesses to Criminal Incidents* (Ann Arbor: University Microfilms International, 1978); William F. McDonald, "Criminal Justice and the Victim: An Introduction," in McDonald, note 7 *supra*, 17; A. Emerson Smith and Dal Maness, "The Decision to Call the Police: Reactions to Burglary," in McDonald, note 7 *supra*, 79; Marlene A. Young Rifai, "The Older Crime Victim and the Criminal Justice System," Paper presented at Second International Symposium on Victimology, Boston, 1976; J. E. Eck and L. J. Riccio, "Relationship Between Reported Crime Rates and Victimization Survey Results: An Empirical and Analytical Study," *Journal of Criminal Justice*, 7(1979), 293; J. Pecar, "Unreported Conventional Crimes Against Individuals," *Revijaza Krimin-*

alistiko in Kriminologijo, 33(1982), 118; Robert F. Kidd and Ellen F. Chayet, "Why Do Victims Fail to Report? The Psychology of Criminal Victimization," *Journal of Social Issues*, 40(1984), 39; Leslie Sebba, "The Victim's Role in the Penal Process: The Need for a Theoretical Orientation," Paper presented at Second International Symposium on Victimology, Boston, 1976; Frank Furstenberg and Charles Wellford, "Calling the Police: The Evaluation of Police Service," *Law and Society Review*, 8(1972), 24; Ziegenhagen, note 7 *supra*; Robert Elias, *Victims of the System: Crime Victims and Compensation in American Politics and Criminal Justice* (New Brunswick, N.J.: Transaction Books, 1983); "Conclusions and Recommendations, International Study Institute on Victimology, Bellagio, Italy, July 1–12, 1975," *Victimology*, 1(1976), 130; Richard D. Knudten, et al., "The Victim in the Administration of Criminal Justice: Problems and Perceptions," in McDonald, note 7 *supra*, 115; Donald J. Hall, "The Role of the Victim in the Prosecution and Disposition of a Criminal Case," *Vanderbilt Law Review*, 28(1975), 932; Edith Flynn, "Report of the Discussion Sections," Second International Symposium on Victimology, Boston, 1976; Morton Bard and Dawn Sangrey, *The Crime Victims Book* (New York: Basic Books, 1979); R. LeJeune and N. Alex, "On Being Mugged: The Event and Its Aftermath," *Urban Life and Culture*, 2(1973), 259.

10. Elias, *ibid.*; Bellagio, *ibid.*; Schneider, *ibid.*; R. B. Ruback, et al., "An Archival Analysis of Victim Reporting," *Victimology*, 6(1981), 318; M. Mills, et al., "Victim Reporting and Recall Accuracy: A Field Laboratory Approach," Paper presented at the American Psychological Association Convention, Toronto, 1978; Gideon Fishman, "Patterns of Victimization and Notification," *British Journal of Criminology*, 19(1979), 146; Gideon Fishman, "Police, Law and Victimization: Differential Patterns and Attitudes," Paper presented at Second International Symposium on Victimology, Boston, 1976; Martin Greenberg and R. Barry Ruback, "A Model of Crime Victim Decisionmaking," Paper presented at Third International Institute on Victimology, Lisbon, 1984; R. Barry Ruback, et al., "Social Influence and Crime-Victim Decision Making," *Journal of Social Issues*, 40(1984), 51; Richard L. Dukes and Christine L. Mattley, "Predicting Rape Victim Reportage," *Sociology and Social Research*, 62(1977), 63; R. L. Dukes, "Rape Victims: Why Some Report and Others Don't," Paper presented at Annual Meeting of the American Society of Criminology, Tucson, 1976.

11. John Conklin, *The Impact of Crime* (New York: Macmillan, 1975).

12. Schneider, note 9 *supra*; Roger Hood and Richard Sparks, "Citizens' Attitudes and Police Practice in Reporting Offenses," in Israel Drapkin and Emilio Viano (ed.), *Victimology* (Lexington, Mass.: Lexington Books, 1974), 163.

13. Michael Hindelang and Michael Gottfredson, "The Victim's Decision Not to Invoke the Criminal Justice Process," in McDonald, note 7 *supra*, 57.

14. Linda Belden, "Why Women Do Not Report Sexual Assault," *Aegis* (September 1979), 38. J. J. Merchant, "Police Assistance to Rape Victims," *Police Chief*, 47(1980), 39.

15. Knudten, et al., note 9 *supra*, 115.

16. Block, note 9 *supra*; O'Neil, note 9 *supra*; Arturo Biblarz, et al., "To

Tell or Note to Tell: Differences Between Victims Who Report Crimes and Victims Who Do Not," *Victimology*, 9(1984), 153.

17. Knudten, note 9 *supra*; Eck and Riccio, note 9 *supra*.

18. Flynn, note *supra*.

19. Sharon Herzberger, "Identifying Cases of Child Abuse: A Social Psychological Phenomenon," Paper presented at Third International Institute on Victimology, Lisbon, 1984; Greenberg and Ruback, note 10 *supra*.

20. Greenberg and Ruback, note 10 *supra*.

21. Block, note 9 *supra*.

22. Fishman, note 12 *supra*; McDonald, note 9 *supra*; O'Neil, note 9 *supra*.

23. Schneider, note 9 *supra*; Wesley G. Skogan, "Citizen Reporting of Crime: Some National Panel Data," *Criminology*, 13(1976), 535.

24. Shapland, note 5 *supra*.

25. see Charles Silberman, *Criminal Violence, Criminal Justice* (New York: Vintage, 1978).

26. M. S. Greenberg and R. B. Ruback, "Decision-Making by Crime Victims: A Multimethod Approach," *Law and Society Review*, 17(1982), 47.

27. Lynda L. Holmstrom and Ann W. Burgess, "Delays in the Criminal Justice System: The Impact on the Rape Victim," Paper presented at Second International Symposium on Victimology, Boston, 1976.

28. M. McLeod, "Victim Noncooperation in the Prosecution of Domestic Assault," *Criminology*, 21(1983), 395.

29. Wesley G. Skogan and Michael G. Maxfield, *Coping with Crime* (Beverly Hills, Calif.: Sage, 1981).

30. Jeremy Travis, "The Crime Victim as Participant in Court Proceedings," Unpublished paper, Vera Institute of Justice, 1976.

31. Hall, note 9 *supra*.

32. President's Task Force on Victims of Crime, *Final Report* (Washington, D.C.: U.S. Government Printing Office, 1982).

33. A. S. Cutter, "Why the Good Citizen Avoids Testifying," *Annals*, 287(1953).

34. Travis, note 30 *supra*, 10.

35. Kristen M. Williams, "The Effects of Victim Characteristics on Judicial Decision Making," in McDonald, note 7 *supra*, 177.

36. Frank J. Cannavale, *Witness Cooperation* (Lexington, Mass.: Lexington Books, 1976).

37. *Ibid.*

38. Williams, note 35 *supra*, 208; American Bar Association, *Reducing Victim/Witness Intimidation: A Package* (Washington, D.C.: Author, 1979).

39. Cross-complainants are people who press charges against people who have pressed charges against them.

40. Shapland, note 5 *supra*.

41. Elias, note 9 *supra*, 94.

42. *Ibid*, 136.

43. *Ibid*.

44. Diane Vaughan and Giovanna Carlo, "Victims of Fraud: Victim Responsiveness, Incidence and Reporting," in Emilio Viano (ed.), *Victims and Society* (Washington, D.C.: Visage, 1976), 403.

45. Prosecutors often lack resources to seriously pursue these cases, and routinely inform victims that only a civil suit will suffice. Using that route almost invariably burdens victims with extra expenses, however, since their claims will usually be too great for small claims courts or too small for lawyers to take on contingency fees, and thus a lawyer must be hired to pursue a case that will quite likely fail anyway. See McDonald, note 9 *supra*, 25.

46. Vaughan and Carlo, note 44 *supra*.

47. William F. McDonald, "Towards a Bicentennial Revolution in Criminal Justice: The Return of the Victim," *The American Criminal Law Review*, 13(1976), 663.

48. William F. McDonald, "Notes on the Victim's Role in the Prosecutorial and Dispositional Stages of the American Criminal Justice Process," Paper presented at Second International Symposium on Victimology, Boston, 1976.

49. Shapland, note 5 *supra*.

50. Anthony Schembri, "The Victim and the Criminal Justice System," in Viano, note 44 *supra*, 348; P. Kobe, "The Victim's Position in Criminal Proceedings with Special Regard to the Adhesion Procedure," *Rev. Kriminalist. Kriminol.*, 28(1977), 3; Peter Burns, "Criminal Justice Responses to Crime Victims," Paper presented at Third International Institute on Victimology, Lisbon, 1984.

51. Herbert Maisch and Horst Schuler-Springorum, "Procedural Victimology and Its Contribution to Victimological Knowledge," in Israel Drapkin and Emilio Viano (eds.), *Victimology: Crimes, Victims and Justice* (Lexington, Mass.: Lexington Books, 1974), 13.

52. *Ibid*.

53. J. Fiselier, "Crime Victims and Administration of Criminal Justice," *Delikt Delinkwent*, 7(1977), 616.

54. McDonald, note 9 *supra*, 42.

55. S. A. M. Stolwijk, "The Victim in Criminal Proceedings," *Delikt Delinkwent*, 7(1977), 626.

56. M. Scheltema, "The Netherlands Ministry of Justice Research and Documentation Center Symposium on the Victim in Criminal Proceedings," *Justitiele Verkenningen*, 6(1982), 5.

57. Gilbert Geis, "Victims of Crimes of Violence and the Criminal Justice System," in Duncan Chappell and John Monahan (eds.), *Violence and Criminal Justice* (Lexington, Mass.: D. C. Heath, 1975), 61; William F. McDonald, "The Prosecutor's Domain," in William F. McDonald (ed.), *The Prosecutor* (Beverly Hills, Calif.: Sage, 1979), 15.

58. Jack Kress, "The Role of the Victim at Sentencing," Paper presented at Second International Symposium on Victimology, Boston, 1976, 5.

59. Stuart A. Scheingold, *The Politics of Law and Order: Street Crime and Public Policy* (New York: Longman, 1984), ch. 4–7; Hans Joachim Schneider, "The Present Situation of Victimology in the World," in Hans Joachim Schneider (ed.), *The Victim in International Perspective* (Berlin: Walter de Gruyter, 1982), 11; Flynn, note 9 *supra*.

60. P. F. Rothstein, "Statement" in *U.S. House Judiciary Subcommittee on Criminal Justice Hearings: Crime Victim Compensation* (Washington, D.C.: U.S. Government Printing Office, 1976), 12.

61. McDonald, note 47 *supra*, 650.

62. Scheingold, note 59 *supra*, 225; Jeffrey Reiman, *The Rich Get Richer and Poor Get Prison* (New York: John Wiley, 1979), 11; Doreen McBarnet, "Victim in the Witness Box: Confronting Victimology's Stereotype," *Contemporary Crises*, 7(1983), 296.

63. William A. Ryan, *Blaming the Victim* (New York: Vintage, 1976), 190; Peter K. Manning, "The Police: Mandate, Strategies, and Appearances," in Jack Douglas (ed.), *Crime and Justice in American Society* (Indianapolis, Ind.: Bobbs Merrill, 1971), 149.

64. Eleanor Chelimsky, "Serving Victims: Agency Incentives and Individual Needs," in Susan Salasin (ed.), *Evaluating Victim Services* (Beverly Hills, Calif.: Sage, 1981), 87; LeRoy Lamborn, "Remedies for the Victims of Crime," *Southern California Law Review* (1970), 43.

65. Fattah, note 2 *supra*.

66. Chelimsky, note 64 *supra*, 86.

67. *Ibid.*, 87.

68. Bard and Sangrey, note 9 *supra*.

69. William J. Chambliss and Robert B. Seidman, *Law, Order and Power* (Reading, Mass.: Addison Wesley, 1971), 477; Ziegenhagen, note 7 *supra*, 5, 6; Stookey, note 3 *supra*, 21; Harold Barnett, "Wealth, Crime and Capital Accumulation," *Contemporary Crises*, 3(1979), 171; Frank Pearce, *Crimes of the Powerful* (London: Pluto Press, 1976).

70. Jerome Skolnick, *Justice Without Trial: Law Enforcement in a Democratic Society* (New York: John Wiley, 1967).

71. David E. Aronson, et al., *Public Policy and Police Discretion: Processes of Decriminalization* (New York: Clark Boardman, 1984).

72. McDonald, note 47 *supra*, 665.

73. D. C. Bolin, "Police-Victim Interactions: Observations from the Police Foundation," *Evaluation and Change* (1980), 110.

74. Some argue that it may have more to do with promoting order and political repression. See Ryan, note 63 *supra*.

75. G. E. Galvan, "Crime Victims in the Criminal Justice System," *Law and Order*, 29(1981), 52.

76. William K. Muir, *Police: Streetcorner Politicians* (Chicago: University of Chicago Press, 1977), 38; William Kroes, *Society's Victim: The Policeman* (Springfield, Ill.: Charles C Thomas, 1980).

77. Scheingold, note 59 *supra*, 133.

78. F. Dill, "Victims, Police and Criminal Court Decisions: A Research Note on Witness Participation and Case Processing," *Victimology*, 6(1981), 345.

79. Bard and Sangrey, note 9 *supra*, 119.

80. LeJeune and Alex, note 9 *supra*, 277.

81. Andrew Karmen, *Crime Victims* (Belmont, Calif.: Wadsworth, 1984), 138.

82. Crime Victims Compensation Board, *1977–78 Annual Report* (Albany: State of New York, 1978).

83. Roger Parks, "Victims and Police Response," *Victimology*, 1(1976), 314.

84. Shapland, note 5 *supra*.

85. P. H. Ennis, "Criminal Victimization in the U.S.: A Report of a National Survey," in President's Commission on Law Enforcement and the Administration of Justice, *Field Surveys II* (Washington, D.C.: U.S. Government Printing Office, 1967), 49.

86. Shapland, note 5 *supra*.

87. P. E. Smith and R. O. Hawkins, "Victimization, Types of Citizen-Police Contacts, and Attitudes Toward the Police," *Law and Society Review*, 7(1973), 135.

88. The Institute for the Study of Labor and Economic Crisis, *The Iron Fist and the Velvet Glove: An Analysis of the U.S. Police* (San Francisco: Crime and Justice Associates, 1982), 13.

89. Karmen, note 81 *supra*, 165.

90. Ryan, note 63 *supra*.

91. LeJeune and Alex, note 9 *supra*, 277.

92. Joseph Goldstein, "Police Discretion Not to Invoke the Criminal Process: Low-Visibility Decisions in the Administration of Justice," in George F. Cole (ed.), *Criminal Justice: Law and Politics* (Belmont, Calif.: Duxbury Press, 1972), 59.

93. Reiman, note 62 *supra*.

94. Karmen, note 81 *supra*, 31.

95. Hall, note 9 *supra*.

96. Emilio Viano, "Violence, Victimization and Social Change: A Socio-Cultural and Public Policy Analysis," *Victimology*, 8(1983), 70; Teuvo Peltoniemi, "Family Violence: Police House Calls in Helsinki, Finland in 1977," *Victimology*, 5(1980), 213; Daniel J. Bell, "Ohio Urban, Suburban and Rural Police Dispositions of Domestic Disputes: A Multiyear Study," Paper presented at Third International Institute on Victimology, Lisbon, 1984; Commission on Victim Witness Assistance, *The Victim Advocate* (Washington, D.C.: National District Attorneys Association, 1977); Susan Maidment, "Civil vs. Criminal: The Use of Legal Remedies in Response to Domestic Violence in England and Wales," *Victimology*, 8(1983), 172; Nat Hentoff, "Help! Police?" *Village Voice*, September 3, 1985, 22.

97. F. Miller, *Prosecution: The Decision to Charge a Suspect with a Crime* (Boston: Little, Brown, 1969), 173.

98. Scheingold, note 59 *supra*, 123.

99. *Ibid.*, 124.

100. T. Sellin and M. Wolfgang, *The Measurement of Delinquency* (New York: John Wiley, 1964).

101. Hugh Barlow, "Crime Victims and the Sentencing Process," Paper presented at Second International Symposium on Victimology, Boston, 1976.

102. Barry Krisberg, *Crime and Privilege* (Englewood Cliffs, N.J.: Prentice-Hall, 1975), 74.

103. Reiman, note 62 *supra*, 102.

104. Jan J. M. van Dijk, "The Victims' Willingness to Report to the Police: A Function of Prosecution Policy?" in Schneider, note 59 *supra*, 327.

105. John Gardiner, "Wincanton: The Politics of Corruption," in Cole, note 92 *supra*, 101; Lawrence E. Cummings, "Reaction to a Victimless Crime: An Assessment by Community Leaders, Control Agents and the Offenders," in Viano, note 44 *supra*, 421.

106. McDonald, note 9 *supra*.

107. Ennis, note 85 *supra*.

108. Peter W. Greenwood, et al., *The Criminal Investigation Process* (Lexington, Mass.: D. C. Heath, 1977).

109. Karmen, note 81 *supra*, 134.

110. *Ibid.*

111. *Ibid.*

112. *Ibid.*, 135.

113. Hall, note 9 *supra*.

114. *Ibid.*

115. *Ibid.*

116. Michael Brown, *Working the Street: Police Discretion and the Dilemmas of Reform* (New York: Russell Sage, 1981).

117. Shapland, note 5 *supra*.

118. Elias, note 9 *supra*.

119. James L. Lacy, *National Standards Concerning the Prosecution Witness* (Washington, D.C.: Center for Prosecution Management, 1972), 129.

120. Elias, note 9 *supra*.

121. Hall, note 9 *supra*.

122. Karmen, note 81 *supra*, 151; Donald J. Newman, *Conviction: The Determination of Guilt or Innocence without Trial* (Boston: Little, Brown, 1966); Williams, note 35 *supra*; Martha Myers, *The Effects of Victim Characteristics on the Prosecution, Conviction and Sentencing of Criminal Defendants* (Ann Arbor: University Microfilms International, 1977); A. S. Goldstein, "Defining the Role of the Victim in Criminal Prosecution," *Mississippi Law Journal*, 82(1982), 516.

123. Williams, note 35 *supra*, 204; Elizabeth Anne Stanko, "Prosecutors' Screening Decisions: The Case of the New York County District Attorney's Office," *Law and Society Review*, 16(1982), 226; Notes, "Prosecutorial Discretion in the Initiation of Criminal Complaints," *Southern California Law Review*, 42(1969), 19.

124. Martha A. Myers and John Hagan, "Private and Public Trouble: Prosecutors and the Allocation of Court Resources," *Social Problems*, 26(1979), 439.

125. Stanko, note 123 *supra*, 230.

126. Commission on Victim Witness Assistance, note 96 *supra*.

127. Task Force on Criminal Justice Research and Development Standards and Goals, *Research on Criminal Justice Problems: Victim Research* (Washington, D.C.: Rand, 1976), 52.

128. *Ibid.*, 51–52.

129. McDonald, note 47 *supra*, 659–661.

130. McDonald, note 48 *supra*, 24; Stanley Z. Fisher, "The Victim's Role in Criminal Prosecutions in Ethiopia," Drapkin and Viano, note 51 *supra.*, 73.

131. A. Muller, "The Victim as Private Plaintiff," *Polizei*, 67(1976), 142.

132. McDonald, note 48 *supra*, 5.

133. *Ibid.*

134. Nils Christie, "Conflicts as Property," *British Journal of Criminology* 17(1978), 1; Ziegenhagen, note 7 *supra*, 76.

135. Hall, note 9 *supra*.

136. Ziegenhagen, note 7, *supra*, 76.

137. James Morris, *Victim Aftershock* (New York: Franklin Watts, 1983), 50.

138. *Ibid*, 51.

139. Lacy, note 119 *supra*, 129.

140. Morris, note 137 *supra*, 53.

141. McDonald, note 48 *supra*, 6.

142. J. M. Graecen, "Arbitration: A Tool for Criminal Cases?" *Barrister*, 2(1975), 10.

143. Karmen, note 81 *supra*, 66.

144. R. C. Davis and B. E. Smith, "Crimes Between Acquaintances: The Response of Criminal Courts," *Victimology*, 6(1981), 175.

145. "The Allocation of Prosecution: An Economic Analysis," *Michigan Law Review*, 74(1976), 586.

146. Vera Institute of Justice, *Felony Arrests: Their Prosecution and Disposition in New York City's Courts* (New York: Author, 1977), 135.

147. Hall, note 9 *supra*; Ziegenhagen, note 7 *supra*, 102; Isaac D. Balbus, *The Dialectics of Legal Repression* (New Brunswick, N.J.: Transaction, 1977); McDonald, note 9 *supra*, 47; Malcolm M. Feeley, *The Process Is the Punishment* (New York: Russell Sage, 1979), 273; Vera Institute of Justice, note 146 *supra*, 137; Karmen, note 81 *supra*, 153; Scheingold, note 62 *supra*, 155; Abraham Blumberg, *Criminal Justice* (New York: New Viewpoints, 1979), 194.

148. Vera Institute of Justice, note 146 *supra*.

149. Shapland, note 5 *supra*, 5; William Toomey, "Victim/Witness Intimidation," Paper presented at First World Congress on Victimology, Washington, D.C., 1980.

150. Michael Ash, "On Witnesses: A Radical Critique of Criminal Court Procedures," *Notre Dame Lawyer*, 48(1972), 395; Laura Banfield and C. David Anderson, "Continuances in the Cook County Criminal Courts," *University of Chicago Law Review*, 35(1968), 261.

151. Lacy, note 119, *supra*, 58.

152. *Ibid.*, 36.

153. Banfield and Anderson, note 150 *supra*, 276.

154. Ziegenhager, note 7 *supra*, 76.

155. McBarnet, note 62 *supra*, 295.

156. Barlow, note 101 *supra*.

157. James Eisenstein and Herbert Jacob, *Felony Justice* (Boston: Little, Brown, 1977), 35.

158. Williams, note 35 *supra*.

159. A. Alschuler, "The Prosecutor's Role in Plea Bargaining," *University of Chicago Law Review*, 36(1968), 50.

160. McDonald, note 57 *supra.*; McDonald, note 9 *supra*, 33; Samuel Walker, *Sense and Nonsense About Crime* (Monterrey, Calif.: Brooks/Cole, 1985), 22.

161. Alschuler, note 159 *supra*; George Cole, "The Decision to Prosecute," *Law and Society Review*, 4(1970), 331.

162. George Cole, *Politics and the Administration of Justice* (Beverly Hills, Calif.: Sage, 1973); Blumberg, note 147 *supra*.

163. Warren Burger, "The State of the Judiciary," Address to the Annual Meeting of the American Bar Association, Washington, D.C., 1970.

164. Abraham Blumberg, "The Practice of Law as a Confidence Game: Organizational Cooptation of a Profession," *Law and Society Review*, 1(1967), 15; A. Battle, "In Search of the Adversary System: The Cooperative Practices of Private Defense Attorneys," *Texas Law Review*, 50(1971), 60; Walker, note 160, *supra*, 126; B. A. Grossman, *The Prosecutor: An Inquiry into the Exercise of Discretion* (Toronto: University of Toronto Press, 1969); Cole, note 161 *supra*; Scheingold, note 62 *supra*, 155.

165. Gregg Barak, *In Defense of Whom? A Critique of Criminal Justice Reform* (Cincinnati: Anderson, 1980).

166. Feeley, note 147 *supra*, 282.

167. Silberman, note 25 *supra*, 412.

168. Feeley, note 147 *supra*, 270; Vera Institute of Justice, note 146 *supra*, 133.

169. Barlow, note 101 *supra*; Malcolm Feeley, "Two Models of the Criminal Justice System: An Organizational Perspective," *Law and Society Review*, 7(1973), 407; Feeley, note 147 *supra*.

170. Eisenstein and Jacob, note 157 *supra*.

171. Feeley, note 147 *supra*, 277.

172. Arthur Rosett and Donald R. Cressey, *Justice by Consent: Plea Bargains in the American Courthouse* (Philadelphia: J. B. Lippincott, 1976).

173. Robert Davis and Forrest Dill, "Comparative Study of Victim Participation in Criminal Court Decisionmaking," Unpublished paper, Vera Institute of Justice, 1978, 9; Karmen, note 81 *supra*, 169.

174. Ash, note 150 *supra*; Edward McCabe, "The Quality of Justice: Victims in the Criminal Justice System," in Jacqueline Scherer and Gary Shepard (eds.), *Victimization of the Weak* (Springfield, Ill.: Charles C Thomas, 1983), 117.

175. Morris, note 137 *supra*, 56.

176. McDonald, note 48 *supra*, 15, 17.

177. *Ibid.*, 15.

178. William F. McDonald, "The Victim's Role in the American Administration of Criminal Justice: Some Developments and Findings," in Schneider, note 10 *supra*, 397.

179. Cannavale, note 36 *supra*.

180. Travis, note 30 *supra*, 3.

181. Kirsten Williams, *The Role of the Victim in the Prosecution of Violent Crimes* (Washington, D.C.: Institute for Law and Social Research, 1978); Brian Forst, et al., *What Happens After Arrest? A Court Perspective of Police Operations in the District of Columbia* (Washington, D.C.: Institute for Law and Social Research, 1977).

182. W. A. Hamilton and C. R. Work, "The Prosecutor's Role in the Urban Court System: The Case for Management Consciousness," *Journal of Criminal Law and Criminology*, 64(1973), 183.

183. Cannavale, note 36 *supra*; Lacy, note 119 *supra*.

184. Ziegenhagen, note 7 *supra*, 93.

185. Davis and Dill, note 173 *supra*.

186. Elias, note 9 *supra*; Ziegenhagen, note 7 *supra*, 91.

187. Frederic L. DuBow and Theodore M. Becker, "Patterns of Victim Advocacy," in McDonald, note 7 *supra*, 150.

188. McBarnet, note 62 *supra*, 295.

189. Cannavale, note 36 *supra*, 72.

190. *Ibid.*, 84; J. Doomen, "Rape: Criminal Justice System Versus the Victim," *Delikt Delinkwent*, 7(1977), 636.

191. K. M. Williams, *The Prosecution of Sexual Assaults* (Washington, D.C.: Institute for Law and Social Research, 1978).

192. Davis and Smith, note 145 *supra*; D. M. McIntyre, "A Study of Judicial Dominance of the Charging Process," *Journal of Criminal Law, Criminology and Police Science*, 59(1968), 463.

193. McDonald, note 48 *supra,* 23; W. Boyd Littrell, *Bureaucratic Justice: Police, Prosecutors and Plea Bargaining* (Beverly Hills, Calif.: Sage, 1979), 68.

194. Cannavale, note 36 *supra,* 53.

195. Ziegenhagen, note 7 *supra,* 86.

196. Elias, note 9 *supra;* Shapland, note 5 *supra.*

197. Eduard Ziegenhagen, *Victims of Violent Crime in New York City: An Exploratory Survey of Perceived Needs* (New York: Crime Victim's Consultation Project, 1974), 34; Cannavale, note 36 *supra;* Shapland, note 5 *supra;* Greenwood, note 108 *supra.*

198. Joanna Shapland, "Victim Assistance and the Criminal Justice System: The Victim's Perspective," in Fattah, note 5 *supra.*

199. Ziegenhagen, note 87 *supra;* McDonald, note 48 *supra,* 14; Travis, note 30 *supra,* 11.

200. Shapland, note 5 *supra;* McBarnet, note 62 *supra,* 295.

201. John J. Cleary, "Coddling the Criminal Encourages Injustice," *USA Today,* April 19, 1984, 8A.

202. McBarnet, note 62 *supra,* 294.

203. Williams, note 35 *supra;* Karmen, note 81 *supra,* 156.

204. Shapland, note 198 *supra.*

205. Bard and Sangrey, note 9 *supra,* 104.

206. McDonald, note 47 *supra,* 664.

207. Cutter, note 33 *supra,* 108.

208. Williams, note 35 *supra,* 205.

209. Newman, note 122 *supra.*

210. James F. Gilsinan, *Doing Justice* (Englewood Cliffs, N.J.: Prentice-Hall, 1982), 217; Ziegenhagen, note 7 *supra,* 85.

211. Littrell, note 193 *supra,* 73.

212. Williams, note 181 *supra,* 43; Forst, note 181 *supra.*

213. David Landy and Elliott Aronson, "The Influence of the Characteristics of the Criminal and His Victim on the Decisions of Simulated Jurors," *Journal of Experimental Social Psychology,* 5(1969), 141; H. Simale and N. Ostrove, "Beautiful But Dangerous: Effects of Offender Attractiveness and the Nature of Crime on Juridic Judgment," *Journal of Personality and Social Psychology,* 31(1975), 410.

214. C. Jones and E. Aronson, "Attribution of Fault to a Rape Victim as a Function of the Respectability of the Victim," *Journal of Personality and Social Psychology,* 26(1974), 415.

215. Karmen, note 81 *supra,* 167; Guy Johnson, "The Negro and Crime," *Annals,* 217(1941), 93; Martha Myers, "Determinants of Conviction: The Prosecutorial Roles of the Victim and the Defendant," Paper presented at Second International Symposium on Victimology, Boston, 1976, 10.

216. Elias, note 9 *supra.*

217. Carol Bohmer, "Judicial Attitudes Towards Rape Victims," *Judicature,* 57(1974), 303.

218. David Rudovsky, "The Criminal Justice System and the Role of the Police" in David Kairys (ed.), *The Politics of Law: A Progressive Critique* (New York: Pantheon, 1982), 242.

219. Feeley, note 147 *supra,* 102.

220. *Ibid.,* 104.

221. Ziegenhagen, note 7 *supra,* 89.

222. McDonald, note 178 *supra.*

223. Feeley, note 147 *supra,* 103; McDonald, note 48 *supra,* 22.

224. Barlow, 101 *supra,* 139.

225. McDonald, note 47 *supra,* 658.

226. Bard and Sangrey, note 9 *supra,* 132.

227. Jones and Aronson, note 214 *supra.*

228. H. D. Schwind, "Victimology in Police and Judiciary Practice," *Kriminalistik,* 33(1979), 514.

229. Graecen, note 142 *supra;* Hall, note 9 *supra;* Nancy A. Gattuso Holman, "Criminal Sentencing and Victim Compensation Legislation: Where Is the Victim?" in Viano, note 44 *supra,* 363.

230. Deborah Denno and James A. Cramer, "The Effects of Victim Characteristics on Judicial Decision Making," in McDonald, note 7 *supra,* 222.

231. Myers, note 122 *supra.*

232. McDonald, note 178 *supra;* Joel Henderson and G. Thomas Gitchoff, "Victim Perceptions of Alternatives to Incarceration: An Exploratory Study," Paper presented at First World Congress on Victimology, Washington, D.C., 1980.

233. John P. J. Dussich, "The Victim Advocate: A Proposal for Comprehensive Victim Services," Paper presented at Second International Symposium on Victimology, Boston, 1976, 5.

234. M. E. Wolfgang, *Patterns in Criminal Homicide* (Philadelphia: University of Pennsylvania Press, 1958).

235. Viano, 96 *supra,* 70.

236. Dan Bein, "The Impact of the Victim's Behavior on the Severity of the Offender's Sentence," in Drapkin and Viano, note 51 *supra.*

237. Barlow, note 101 *supra,* 19.

238. McDonald, note 48 *supra,* 18.

239. H. Kalven and H. Zeisel, *The American Jury* (Chicago: University of Chicago Press, 1971).

240. L. Calhoun, et al., "The Effects of Victim Physical Attractiveness and Sex of Respondent on Social Reactions to Victims of Rape," *British Journal of Social Clinical Psychology,* 17(1978), 191.

241. Menachem Horowitz and Menachem Amir, "The Probation Officer, the Offender, and the Victim of the Criminal Offense," in Drapkin and Viano, note 51 *supra,* 95.

242. Krisberg, note 102 *supra,* 60.

243. Marvin Wolfgang and Marc Reidel, "Race, Judicial Discretion and the Death Penalty," *Annals,* (1973), 119; William J. Bowers and Glenn L. Pierce, "Arbitrariness and Discrimination Under Post-*Furman* Capital Statutes," *Crime and Delinquency,* 26(1980), 563.

244. Hall, note 9 *supra;* Horowitz and Amir, note 241 *supra.*

245. Hall, note 9 *supra;* Burt Galaway, "Victim Participation in the Corrective Process," Paper presented at Third International Institute on Victimology, Lisbon, 1984.

246. Feeley, note 147 *supra.*

247. *Ibid.,* 199.

248. *Ibid.,* 291.

249. *Ibid.,* 134.

250. Hall, note 9 *supra.*

251. Bard and Sangrey, note 9 *supra,* 108.

252. Laura Nader, "Alternatives to the American Judicial System," in Laura Nader (ed.), *No Access to Law* (New York: Academic Press, 1980), 3.

253. M. Knudten, et al., "Will Anyone Be Left to Testify? Disenchantment with the Criminal Justice System," Paper presented at the Annual Meeting of the American Sociological Association, San Francisco, 1975.

254. McDonald, note 9 *supra,* 28–29.

255. Richard Knudten, et al., *Victims and Witnesses: Impact of Crime and Their Experiences with the Criminal Justice System* (Milwaukee: Center for Criminal Justice and Social Policy, 1976); Knudten, note 9 *supra;* Elias, note 9 *supra;* Cannavale, note 36 *supra,* 54; Lynch, note 7 *supra;* American Bar Association, note 38 *supra;* National Organization for Victim Assistance, *Victim Rights and Services: A Legislative Directory* (Washington, D.C.: Author, 1983).

256. Fremont, California Police Department, *Proposal to Conduct a Program to Improve and Standardize Police Treatment of Victims and Witnesses* (Washington, D.C.: Police Foundation, 1974); Lacy, note 119 *supra,* 89.

257. McDonald, note 48 *supra,* 9.

258. Elias, note 9 *supra;* Knudten, note 255 *supra;* Cannavale, note 36 *supra,* 54; Knudten, note 9 *supra;* Lynch, note 7 *supra;* American Bar Association, note 38 *supra;* National Organization for Victim Assistance, note 255 *supra.*

259. Knudten, note 255 *supra,* 25.

260. Shapland, note 198 *supra.*

261. Karmen, note 81 *supra,* 145; Ash, note 150 *supra;* Shapland, note 198 *supra.*

262. Mary L. Keefe and Harry O'Reilly, "The Plight of the Rape Victim in New York City," in Viano, note 44 *supra,* 391.

263. Sacramento Police Department, *Seven Part Program to Improve the Manner in Which Crime Victims Are Handled by Police and Other Agencies of the Criminal Justice System and the Health Care Community* (Washington, D.C.:

Price Waterhouse, 1974); Ash, note 150 *supra;* Lacy, note 119 *supra,* 45; Elias, note 9 *supra;* Lynch, note 7 *supra.*

264. Knudten, note 255 *supra,* 86.

265. Elias, note 9 *supra.*

266. Travis, note 30 *supra;* Ziegenhagen, note 7 *supra,* viii; Silberman, note 25 *supra,* 269; Karmen, note 81 *supra,* 125.

267. Silberman, note 25 *supra,* 348, 351. Yet, the "funneling" may be less severe than often suggested. While law enforcement rarely apprehends criminals (partly because victims often do not report them), 69% of all those arrested and 95% of all those prosecuted are convicted. Also, while some avoid prison, many go to jail (52% of all those in jail), or have spent time in jail before trial (43% of all those in jail).

268. Elias, note 9 *supra,* 123.

269. *Ibid.*

270. Klaus P. Fink, "Ambivalence of Former Victims Toward Their Persecutors at the Petition for Indemnification," in Drapkin and Viano, note 51 *supra,* 107.

271. Cannavale, note 36 *supra,* 61; Louis Harris and Associates, *Study No. 2043* (New York: Author, 1970); Knudten, note 255 *supra;* Andreas Beurokens and Klaus Boers, "Attitudes of Victims and Nonvictims Towards Restitution, Crime and Punishment" Paper presented at Fifth International Symposium on Victimology, Zagreb, 1985.

272. Cannavale, note 36 *supra,* 61.

273. Knudten, note 255 *supra.*

274. Ziegenhagen, note 7 *supra;* John Hagan, "Victims Before the Law: A Study of Victim Involvement in the Criminal Justice Process," *Journal of Criminal Law and Criminology,* 73(1982), 328; Philip Ennis, "Crimes, Victims and the Police," *Transaction* (June 1967), 34.

275. Ziegenhagen, note 197 *supra,* 37–38.

276. Elias, note 9 *supra,* 124.

277. *Ibid.,* 125.

278. *Ibid.,* 126.

279. Cannavale, note 36 *supra,* 59, 61.

280. Elias, note 9 *supra,* 127.

281. *Ibid.,* 129; Knudten, note 255 *supra,* 100.

282. T. Bartell, *Citizen Perceptions of the Justice System* (Albuquerque, N.M.: Institute for Social Research and Development, 1975); James Garofalo, *Public Opinion About Crime: The Attitudes of Victims and Nonvictims in Selected Cities* (Washington, D.C.: U.S. Department of Justice, 1977).

283. Darlene Walker and Richard J. Richardson, *Public Attitudes Toward the Police* (Chapel Hill, N.C.: Institute for Research on Social Science, 1972), 11; Pecar, note 9 *supra.*

284. Fremont, California Police Department, note 256 *supra;* Sacramento Police Department, note 263 *supra;* Theodore Poister and James McDavid,

"Victims' Evaluation of Police Performance," *Journal of Criminal Law*, 6(1978), 133.

285. Shapland, note 198 *supra;* Smith and Hawkins, note 87 *supra,* 6; J. Goldsmith, "Victim Services and the Police," *Crime Prevention Review,* 5(1978), 1; Brent Smith, "Rural Victimization and Perceptions of Police Performance," *Victimology,* 9(1984), 159.

286. Jersey Liang and Mary C. Sengstock, *Criminal Victimization of the Elderly and Their Interaction with the Criminal Justice System: Summary of Findings* (Detroit: Wayne State University, 1980).

287. Frank Furstenberg, "Public Reaction to Crime in the Streets," in Cole, note 92 *supra,* 382; Walker and Richardson, note 287 *supra,* 11; Garofalo, note 282 *supra,* 28; Clark D. Ashworth and Shirley Feldman-Summers, "Perceptions of the Effectiveness of the Criminal Justice System: The Female Victim's Perspective," *Criminal Justice and Behavior,* 5(1978), 227; Daniel Kennedy and Robert Homant, "Battered Women's Evaluation of the Police Response," *Victimology,* 9(1984), 174.

288. D. B. Kennedy and R. J. Holman, "Attitudes of Abused Women Toward Male and Female Police Officers," *Criminal Justice and Behavior,* 10(1983), 391.

289. Cannavale, note 36 *supra,* 59.

290. Shapland, note 198 *supra.*

291. Cannavale, note 36 *supra,* 91.

292. Knudten, note 255 *supra.*

293. Geis, note 57 *supra,* 69; Dorothy Graber, "Evaluating Crime-Fighting Policies: The Public's Perspective," Paper presented at Annual Meeting of American Political Science Association, Washington, D.C., 1972.

294. Shapland, note 198 *supra.*

295. Ziegenhagen, note 7 *supra,* 34.

296. Knudten, note 9 *supra,* 121.

297. Knudten, note 253 *supra.*

298. Robert Crosby and David Snyder, "Crime Victimization in the Black Community," in Drapkin and Viano, note 12 *supra,* 175; Cannavale, note 36 *supra,* 60; Ashworth and Feldman-Summers, note 287 *supra.*

299. Ennis, note 274 *supra,* 41.

300. Elias, note 9 *supra,* 132.

301. Sacramento Police Department, note 263 *supra;* Cannavale note 36 *supra,* 60; Cincinnati Police Division, *Report on Why Victims Fail to Prosecute* (Cincinnati: Author, 1975), 16.

302. Ash, note 150 *supra.*

303. Knudten, note 253 *supra,* 218; Knudten, note 9 *supra,* 163; Samuel Walker, *Sense and Nonsense About Crime* (Monterrey, Calif.: Brooks/Cole, 1985), 144.

304. McDonald, note 9 *supra,* 21.

305. Dorie Klein and June Kress, "Any Woman's Blues: A Critical Over-

view of Women, Crime and the Criminal Justice System," in Tony Platt
and Paul Takagi (eds.), *Crime and Social Justice* (Totowa, N.J.: Barnes and
Noble, 1981), 152; Nadine Taub and Elizabeth M. Schneider, "Perspectives
on Women's Subordination and the Role of Law," in Kairys, note 218 *supra*,
117; Karen DeCrow, *Sexist Justice* (New York: Vintage, 1974); Julia R.
Schwendinger and Herman Schwendinger, *Rape and Inequality* (Beverly Hills,
Calif.: Sage, 1983); Susan Edwards, *Women on Trial* (Manchester: Manchester University Press, 1984); Judith V. Becker and Gene G. Abel, "Men and
the Victimization of Women," in Jane Roberts Chapman and Margaret Gates
(eds.), *The Victimization of Women* (Beverly Hills, Calif.: Sage, 1978), 29.

   306. Leslie Sebba and Sorel Cahan, "Sex Offenses: The Genuine and the
Doubted Victim," Israel Drapkin and Emilio Viano (eds.), *Victimology: Ex-
ploiters and the Exploited* (Lexington, Mass.: Lexington Books, 1975), 29; M.
D. Pagelow, *Blaming the Victim: Parallels in Crimes Against Women* (Chicago:
Society for the Study of Social Problems, 1977); M. A. Straus, "Sexual In-
equality, Cultural Norms and Wife-Beating," *Victimology*, 1(1976).

   307. Del Martin, "Battered Women: Society's Problem," in Chapman and
Gates, note 305 *supra*, 111; Lee H. Bowker, "The Criminal Victimization of
Women," *Victimology*, 4(1980), 371.

   308. C. S. Goldstein, *The Dilemma of the Rape Victim: A Descriptive Analysis* (Huntsville, Tex.: Institute of Contemporary Corrections and the Behavioral Sciences, 1976); Vesna Nikolic-Ristanovic, "The Status of Women
as Victims of Sexual Offenses in the Criminal Proceeding of Yugoslavia"
Paper presented at Fifth International Symposium on Victimology, Zagreb,
1985.

   309. Kurt Weis and Sandra Borges, "Rape as a Crime without Victims
and Offenders? A Methodological Critique," in Viano, note 44 *supra*, 320;
Kurt Weis and Sandra Weis, "Victimology and the Justification of Rape,"
in Drapkin and Viano, note 306 *supra*, 3.

   310. *Ibid.*

   311. Susan Edwards, "Sexuality, Sexual Offenses and Conceptions of
Victims in the Criminal Justice Process," *Victimology*, 8(1983), 113.

   312. Leslie Sebba, "The Requirement of Corroboration in Sex Offenses,"
in Drapkin and Viano, note 12 *supra*, 183; Lynda Lytle Holmstrom and Ann
Wolbert Burgess, *The Victim of Rape: Institutional Reactions* (New York: John
Wiley, 1978).

   313. Leigh Beimen, "Rape Reform Legislation in the United States: A
Look at Some Practical Effects," *Victimology*, 8(1983), 139.

   314. J. Sutherlin, "Indiana's Rape Shield Law: Conflict with the Con-
frontation Clause?" *Indiana Law Review*, 9(1976), 418; "Private Violence,"
Time, September 5, 1983, 29.

   315. Donna D. Schram, "Rape," in Chapman and Gates, note 305 *supra*,
75.

   316. Beinen, note 313 *supra*.

   317. Ann Wolbert Burgess and Lynda Lytle Holmstrom, "Rape: The
Victim and the Criminal Justice System," in Drapkin and Viano, note 51
supra, 21; Lynda Lytle Holmstrom and Ann Wolbert Burgess, "Rape: The

Victim Goes on Trial," in Drapkin and Viano, *ibid.*, 31; Mark Starr, "Who Is the Real Victim?" *Newsweek*, May 20, 1985, 69.

318. Belden, note 14 *supra*, 113; A. Medea and K. Thompson, *Against Rape* (New York: Farrar, Straus and Giroux, 1974).

319. Thomas W. McCahill, et al., *The Aftermath of Rape* (Lexington, Mass.: Lexington Books, 1979), 87; Deanna R. Nass, *The Rape Victim* (Dubuque, Iowa: Kendall/Hunt, 1977).

320. Keefe and O'Reilly, note 262 *supra*; Holmstrom and Burgess, note 312 *supra*.

321. Keefe and O'Reilly, note 262 *supra*, 16; Lynda Lytle Holmstrom and Ann Wolbert Burgess, "Rape: The Victim and the Criminal Justice System," *International Journal of Criminology and Penology*, 3(1975), 101.

322. P. M. Mazelan, "Stereotypes and Perceptions of the Victims of Rape," *Victimology*, 5(1980), 121.

323. McCahill, note 319 *supra*, 100, 110, 116.

324. *Ibid.*, 239.

325. *Ibid.*, 143.

326. Holmstrom and Burgess, note 312 *supra*.

327. Louis Waller, "Victims on Trial: Prosecutions for Rape," Paper presented at Second International Symposium on Victimology, Boston, 1976.

328. Holmstrom and Burgess, note 27 *supra*.

329. *Ibid.*

330. G. Kassebeum, "Criminal Procedure and Crimes Against Women: Efforts at Solutions in One American City," *Indian Journal of Criminology*, 11(1983), 3.

331. Holmstrom and Burgess, note 312 *supra*.

332. McCahill, note 319 *supra*, 186.

333. *Ibid.*

334. Task Force on Criminal Justice Research and Development Standards and Goals, note 127 *supra*, 58.

335. McCahill, note 319 *supra*, 189.

336. Holmstrom and Burgess, note 312 *supra*.

337. McCahill, note 319 *supra*.

338. Holmstrom and Burgess, note 312 *supra*; McDonald, note 9 *supra*; Ashworth and Feldman-Summers, note 287 *supra*.

339. McBarnet, note 62 *supra*, 293.

340. Lois Forer, *Criminals and Victims: A Trial Judge Reflects on Crime and Punishment* (New York: Norton, 1980), 290.

NOTES FOR CHAPTER 7

1. For other reviews of victim services, see Robert Elias, "Community Control, Criminal Justice and Victim Services," in Ezzat A. Fattah (ed.),

Reorienting the Justice System: From Crime Policy to Victim Policy (New York: Macmillan, 1985); J. Verin, "A Criminal Policy Based on Victimology and the Interests of Victims," *Revue de Science Criminelle et de Droit Penal Compare,* 4(1981), 895; John P. J. Dussich, "Evolving Services for Crime Victims," in Burt Galaway and Joe Hudson (eds.), *Perspectives on Crime Victims* (St. Louis: Mosby, 1981), 27; Anne Larson Schneider and Peter R. Schneider, "Victim Assistance Programs: An Overview," in Galaway and Hudson, *ibid.,* 364; Eduard A. Ziegenhagen and John Benyi, "Victim Interests, Victim Services and Social Control," in Galaway and Hudson, *ibid.,* 373; Frederic L. DuBow and Theodore M. Becker, "Patterns of Victim Advocacy," in William F. McDonald (ed.), *Criminal Justice and the Victim* (Beverly Hills, Calif.: Sage, 1976), 147; Ralph Glatfelter, "For the Victims of Crime: A New Approach," in Israel Drapkin and Emilio Viano (eds.), *Victimology: Society's Reaction to Victimization* (Lexington, Mass.: Lexington Books, 1974), 139; Mary Baluss, *Integrated Services for Victims of Crime: A County Based Approach* (Washington, D.C.: National Association of Counties Research Foundation, 1975); Gilbert Geis, "Application of Victimological Research to the Victim's Reintegration into Society," in Hans Joachim Schneider (ed.), *The Victim in International Perspective* (Berlin: Walter de Gruyter, 1982), 345; M. E. Baluss, "Services to Victims of Crimes: A Developing Opportunity," *Evaluation and Change* (1980), 94; Andrew Karmen, *Crime Victims* (Belmont, Calif.: Brooks/Cole, 1984); Susan Salasin (ed.), *Evaluating Victim Services* (Beverly Hills, Calif.: Sage, 1981); Morton Bard and Dawn Sangrey, *The Crime Victim's Book* (New York: Basic Books, 1979); M. Kneepkens, H. Moerland and H. Rodermond, "Assistance to Victims: A Survey," *Delikt Delink,* 7(1977), 58; H. Moerland, "What Are We Doing for Victims?" *Ned. T. Criminol.,* 18(1976), 97.

2. Charles Dean and Mary deBruyn-Kops, *The Crime and the Consequences of Rape* (Springfield, Ill.: Charles C Thomas, 1982); Karmen, note 1 supra, 142; Debra Whitcomb, Debra Day and Laura Studen, *Stop Rape Crisis Center, Baton Rouge, Louisiana: An Exemplary Project* (Washington, D.C.: U.S. Department of Justice, 1979); Steve Chesney and Carol Schneider, "Crime Victim Crisis Centers: The Minnesota Experience," in Galaway and Hudson, note 1 supra, 391; Yona Cohn, "Crisis Intervention and the Victim of Robbery," in Drapkin and Viano, note 1 supra, 17; John Hollister Stein, "Victim Crisis Intervention: An Evaluation Proposal," in Salasin, note 1 supra, 98; Shirley Oberg and Ellen Pence, "Responding to Battered Women," in Galaway and Hudson, note 1 supra, 385; Jayne Thomas Rich, "Background Notes on Community Based Services for Rape Victims," in Galaway and Hudson, note 1 supra, 391; Ziegenhagen and Benyi, note 1 supra, 377; Elizabethann O'Sullivan, "What Has Happened to Rape Crisis Centers: A Look at Their Structures, Members and Funding," *Victimology,* 3(1978), 45; Ken S. Menzies, "The Road to Independence: The Role of A Refuge," *Victimology,* 3(1978), 141; J. H. Pfouts and C. Renz, "The Future of Wife Abuse Programs," *Social Work,* 26(1981), 451; L. Ledray and M. J. Chaignot, "Services to Sexual Assault Victims in Hennepin County," *Evaluation and Change* (1980), 131; J. Cherbot and M. Mermoz, "S.O.S. Battered Women," *Victimology,* 8(1983), 270; G. Erquay and R. Weiler, *Services to Victims and Witnesses of Crime in Canada* (Ottawa: Ministry of Solicitor General of Canada, 1981); P. Divasto, et al., "Caring for Rape Victims: Its Impact on Providers," *Journal of Community Health,* 5(1980), 204; Ginny NiCarthy Crowe, "Beyond Shelters: Abused Women's Network," Paper presented at First World Congress on Victimology, Washington, D.C., 1980; Sybille Kappell and Erika Leuteritz, "Wife Battering in the Federal Republic of Germany," *Victimology,* 5(1980), 225; K. A. Holmes, "Services for Victims of Rape: A Dualistic Practice Model," *Social Casework,* 62(1981), 30; Donna Miller, "Innovative Program Development for Battered Women and Their Families," *Victimology,* 5(1980), 335; Deborah Matystik, "Reduce Fear of Elderly Victimization," Paper presented at First World Congress on Victimology, Washington, D.C., 1980; L. J. Center, "Victim Assistance to the Elderly," *Victimology,* 5(1980), 374; J. Grayson and G. Smith, "Marital Violence and Help-Seeking Patterns in a Micropolitan Community," *Victimology,* 6(1981), 1; L. Van Eekelen, "Background and Operation of a Refuge for Battered Women," *Panopticon,* 1(1980), 406; Eleanor Chelimsky, "Serving Victims: Agency Incentives and Individual Needs," in Salasin, note 1 *supra,* 73; Barbara H. Hafer, "Rape is a Four-Letter Word," in Emilio Viano (ed.), *Victims and Society* (Washington, D.C.: Visage Press, 1976), 502; Rusty Gagnon, "The Pomona Project: An Effective Model for Community-Wide Child Abuse Intervention and Prevention," Paper presented at First World Congress on Victimology, Washington, D.C., 1980; G. Abarbanel, "Helping Victims of Rape," *Social Work,* 21(1976), 478.

3. Rich, note 2 *supra,* 392.

4. Menachem Amir and Delila Amir, "Rape Crisis Centers: An Arena for Ideological Conflicts," *Victimology,* 4(1979), 247; Karmen, note 1 *supra,* 142; S. L. McCombie, et al., "Development of a Medical Center Rape Crisis Intervention Program," *American Journal of Psychiatry,* 133(1976), 418; LeRoy Schultz, "Victim-Helpers as Hostages to Ideology: The Case for Adult-Minor Interaction," Paper presented at First World Congress on Victimology, Washington, D.C., 1980; Jacqueline Campbell and Janice Humphries, *Nursing Care of Victims of Family Violence* (Reston, Va.: Reston, 1984); "Private Violence," *Time,* September 5, 1983, 29; C. Constantino, "Intervention with Battered Women: The Lawyer-Social Worker Team," *Social Work,* 26(1981), 456; W. F. Enos and J. C. Beyer, "Treatment of Rape Victims," *Journal of Forensic Science,* 22(1977), 3; John G. Higgins, "Social Services for Abused Wives," *Social Casework,* 59(1978), 266; M. A. Schneider and S. M. Cordner, "Role Responsibility Versus Role Confusion: Implications for the Care of the Rape Victim," *Australian and New Zealand Journal of Criminology,* 13(1980), 103; Durrenda Nash Ojanuga, "Medical Care for Victims of Road Accidents in Nigeria," *Victimology,* 5(1980), 391.

5. "Private Violence," *ibid.,* 29; R. F. Rich and S. Stenzel, "Mental Health Services for Victims: Policy Paradigms," *Evaluation and Change* (1980), 47; M. Bard and D. Sangrey, "Things Fall Apart: Victims in Crisis," *Evaluation and Change* (1980), 28; M. Tysoe, "Self Help for Incest Victims," *New Society,* 58(1981), 199; Frank Ochberg and Richard Spates, "Services Integration for Victims of Personal Violence," in Salasin, note 1 *supra,* 113; Thomas J. Kiresuk and Sander Lund, "Knowledge Transfer for Victim Services," in Salasin, *ibid.,* 39; M. Symonds, "Victims of Violence: Psychological Effects and Aftereffects," *American Journal of Psychoanalysis,* 35(1975), 19; Susan Salasin, "Services to Victims: Needs Assessment," in Salasin, *ibid.,* 21; Robert

Rich, "Evaluating Victims of Rape: Their Needs and a New Treatment Approach," in Salasin, note 1 *supra*, 358; Karmen, note 1 *supra*, 240; Christine A. Courtois, "Studying and Counseling Women with Past Incest Experience," *Victimology*, 5(1980), 322; Lenore E. Walker, "Treatment Alternatives for Battered Women," in Jane Roberts Chapman and Margaret Gates (eds.), *The Victimization of Women* (Beverly Hills, Calif.: Sage, 1978), 143; Del Martin, "Battered Women: Society's Problem," in Chapman and Gates, *ibid.*, 111; Janice Krupnick, "Brief Psychotherapy with Victims of Violent Crime," *Victimology*, 5(1980), 347; E. J. Knittle and S. J. Tuana, "Group Therapy as Primary Treatment for Adolescent Victims of Intrafamilial Sexual Abuse," *Clinical Social Work Journal*, 8(1980), 236; C. E. Gentry and V. Bass Eaddy, "Treatment of Children in Spouse Abusive Families," *Victimology*, 5(1980), 240; D. Scott and L. Hewitt, "Short Term Adjustment to Rape and the Utilization of a Sexual Assault Counselling Service," *Australia and New Zealand Journal of Criminology*, 16(1983), 93; H. I. Evans, "Psychotherapy for the Rape Victim: Some Treatment Models," *Hospital and Community Psychiatry*, 29(1979), 309; M. Tsai and N. N. Wagner, "Therapy Groups for Women Sexually Molested as Children," *Archives of Sexual Behavior*, 7(1978), 417; D. B. Wexler, "Victimology and Mental Health Law: An Agenda," *Virginia Law Review*, 66(1980), 681; B. D. Forman, "Psychotherapy with Rape Victims," *Psychotherapy: Theory, Research, Practice*, 17(1980), 304; R. E. Mitchell and C. A. Hodson, "Coping with Domestic Violence: Social Support and Psychological Health Among Battered Women," *American Journal of Community Psychiatry*, 11(1983), 629; D. C. Silverman, "Sharing the Crisis of Rape: Counseling the Mates and Families of Victims," *American Journal of Orthopsychiatry*, 48(1978), 166; R. Wolff, "Systematic Desensitization and Negative Practices to Alter the Aftereffects of a Rape Attempt," *Journal of Behavioral Therapy and Experimental Psychiatry* (1977), 423; Lois G. Veronen, Dean Kilpatrick, and Patricia Resick, "Treating Fear and Anxiety in Rape Victims," in William H. Parsonage (ed.), *Perspectives on Victimology* (Beverly Hills, Calif.: Sage, 1979), 148; H. M. Hughes, "Advocacy for Children of Domestic Violence: Helping the Battered Women with Non-Sexist Childraising," *Victimology*, 6(1981), 262; Joyce N. Thomas, "Multidisciplinary and Multimodal Treatment of Child Victims of Sexual Abuse," Paper presented at First World Congress on Victimology, Washington, D.C., 1980; S. Sutherland Fox, "Families in Crisis: Reflections on the Children and Families of the Offender and the Offended," *International Journal of Offender Therapy and Comparative Criminology*, 25(1981), 254; Charles E. Gentry, "A Family Systems/Social Systems Approach to Family Violence," Paper presented at First World Congress on Victimology, Washington, D.C., 1980; L. M. McCarty, "Investigation of Incest: Opportunity to Motivate Families to Seek Help," *Child Welfare*, 60(1981), 679; Catherine Smith, "Beyond Medical and Police Mandates: Community Response to Victims," Paper presented at Third International Institute on Victimology, Lisbon, 1984; T. Myers and S. Gilbert, "Wifebeater's Group Through a Women's Center: Why and How," *Victimology*, 8(1983), 238; June Siegel, "Working with Intrafamilial Child Sexual Victimization: A Role Training Model," Paper presented at First World Congress on Victimology, Washington, D.C., 1980; Robert Towell, "Treatment of Child Abuse in a Family Practice Clinic," in Viano, note 2 *supra*, 511; Concetta Stallone Adleman, "Psychological Intervention into the Crisis of Rape," in Viano, *ibid.*, 493; Dan Coates and Tina Winston, "Counteracting the Deviance of Depression: Peer Support Groups for Victims," 39(1983), 169; J. L. Krupnick and M. J. Horowitz, "Victims of Violence: Psychological Response, Treatment Implications," *Evaluation and Change* (1980); Donna Miller, "Innovative Program for Battered Women and Their Families," *Victimology*, 5(1980), 335; Fae A. Deaton and Dan A. Sandlin, "Sexual Victimology Within the Home: A Treatment Approach," *Victimology*, 5(1980), 311; David W. Lloyd, "Multi-Agency Collaboration and Coordination," Paper presented at First World Congress on Victimology, Washington, D.C., 1980; A. W. Burgess and L. L. Holmstrom, "Coping Behavior of the Rape Victim," *American Journal of Psychiatry*, 133(1976), 413; Christine A. Courtois, "The Incest Experience Aftermath," *Victimology*, 4(1980), 337; Sharon Hymer, "The Self in Victimization: Conflict and Development Perspectives," *Victimology*, 9(1984), 142.

6. Schneider and Schneider, note 1 *supra;* Z. T. Stelmachers, "Evaluation of Victims Services: Is Enough Being Done?" *Evaluation and Change* (1980), 127. W. G. Doerner, et al., "Correspondence Between Crime Victim Needs and Available Public Services," *Social Service Review*, 50(1976), 482; Lorene Hemphill Stone, "Shelters for Battered Women: A Temporary Escape from Danger or the First Step Toward Divorce?" *Victimology*, 9(1984), 284.

7. David M. Friedman, "A Program to Service Crime Victims," in Viano, note 2 *supra*, 48.

8. Barbara Dulberg, "Social and Psychological Barriers Inhibiting the Use of Crime Victims Compensation Board," M.A. Thesis, John Jay College of Criminal Justice, 1978; Cinda Gault, "Perceptions of the Victims About the Helpers and the Helping System," Paper presented at First World Congress on Victimology, Washington, D.C., 1980.

9. Rich, note 5 *supra*.

10. Amir and Amir, note 4 *supra,* 247; Pfouts and Renz, note 2 *supra;* Catherine Begnoche Smith, et al., "Defining a Social Problem and Its Solution: The Case of Services to Victims of Sexual Assault," *Victimology*, 9(1984), 234.

11. Friedman, note 7 *supra;* Schneider and Schneider, note 1 *supra;* H. M. Hughes and S. J. Barad, "Changing the Psychological Functioning of Children in a Battered Women's Shelter: A Pilot Study," *Victimology*, 7(1982), 60.

12. For an extensive bibliography, see Robert Elias, *Victims of the System: Crime Victims and Compensation in American Politics and Criminal Justice* (New Brunswick, N.J.: Transaction Books, 1983); Also, Karmen, note 1 *supra*, 206; Alan T. Harland, "Victim Compensation: Programs and Issues," in Galaway and Hudson, note 1 *supra*, 412; LeRoy L. Lamborn, "Victim Compensation Programs: An Overview," in Galaway and Hudson, note 1 *supra*, 418; D. Carrow, *Crime Victim Compensation: Program Model* (Washington, D.C.: U.S. Department of Justice, 1980); David Miers, *Responses to Victimization: A Comparative Study of Compensation for Criminal Violence in Great Britain and Ontario* (Abingdon, Oxon: Professional Books, 1978); European Committee on Crime Problems, *Compensation of Victims of Crime* (Strassburg, Austria:

Author, 1978); Daniel McGillis and Patricia Smith, *Compensating Victims of Crime: An Analysis of American Programs* (Washington, D.C.: U.S. Department of Justice, 1983); Sven Thorjaldson and Mark Karsknik, "On Recovering Compensation Funds from Offenders," *Victimology*, 5(1980), 20; Edwin T. Fujii, "On the Compensation of Victims of Torts," *Victimology*, 5(1980), 42; David Miers, "Victim Compensation as a Labelling Process," *Victimology*, 5(1980), 3; David Miers, "The Provision of Compensation for Victims of Violent Crime in Continental Europe," Paper presented at Third International Institute on Victimology, Lisbon, 1984; Joanna Shapland, "The Victim in the Criminal Justice System," *Home Office Research Bulletin* 14(1982), 21; Joanna Shapland, "Victim Assistance and the Criminal Justice System: The Victim's Perspective," in Ezzat A. Fattah (ed.), *Reorienting the Justice System: From Crime Policy to Victim Policy* (New York: Macmillan, 1985); Allan Grossman, "Victim Compensation in Child Abuse Cases: Problems in Practical Application," *Victimology*, 5(1980), 57; Randall A. Schmidt, "Crime Victim Compensation Legislation: A Comparative Study," *Victimology*, 5(1980), 401; Peter Burns, "A Comparative Overview of the Criminal Injuries Compensation Schemes," *Victimology*, 8(1983), 102; A. T. Harland, "Compensating the Victims of Crime," *Criminal Law Bulletin*, 14(1978), 203; LeRoy Lamborn, "Reparations for Victims of Crime: Developments and Directions," *Victimology*, 4(1979), 214; A. R. Bloembergen, "The Aggressive Crimes Compensation Fund Revisited," *Delikt Delinkwent*, 4(1974), 325; Abdul W. M. Borafia, "Compensation to Victims of Crime," Paper presented at Second International Symposium on Victimology, Boston, 1976; Burt Galaway, "Differences in Victim Compensation and Restitution," *Social Work*, 24(1979), 57; P. Sallman, "Victim Compensation in Australia: the Victorian Experience," *International Journal of Criminology and Penology*, 6(1978), 203; H. S. Dijk, "Fund for Compensation of Victims of Violent Crimes," *Process*, 55(1976), 191; G. Schulz-Luke and M. Wolf, *Acts of Violence and Compensation of Victims: Commentary on the Law Concerning Compensation of Victims of Violence* (Berlin: Walter de Gruyter, 1977); David Miers, "Compensation and Conceptions of Victims of Crimes," *Victimology*, 8(1983), 204; Jean Marc Bertrand, "L'Indemnisation des Victimes Criminels au Quebec," *Victimology*, 8(1983), 225; Leslie Sebba, "Victimological Aspects of the German Reparations Agreements with the Jewish People," in Schneider, note 1 *supra*, 381; C. L. Tomeny, "Compensation Under the Warsaw Convention for Victims of Hijackings and Terrorists Attacks," *Brooklyn Journal of International Law*, 3(1976), 31.

13. Alan T. Harland, "Monetary Remedies for the Victims of Crime: Assessing the Role of the Criminal Courts," *UCLA Law Review*, 30(1982), 52; Elias, note 12 *supra*, 39; Randy Barnett and John Hagel (eds.), *Assessing the Criminal: Restitution, Retribution and the Legal Process* (Cambridge: Ballinger, 1977); Joe Hudson and Burt Galaway (eds.), *Restitution in Criminal Justice* (Lexington, Mass.: Lexington Books, 1977); Burt Galaway and Joe Hudson (eds.), *Offender Restitution in Theory and Action* (Lexington, Mass.: Lexington Books, 1978); Robert Gottesman and Lynn Mountz, *Restitution: Legal Analysis* (Reno, Nev.: National Council of Juvenile and Family Court Judges, 1979); Burt Galaway and Joe Hudson (eds.), *Victims, Offenders and Restitutive Sanctions* (Lexington, Mass.: Lexington Books, 1979); Alan T. Harland,

Restitution to Victims of Personal and Household Crimes (Washington, D.C.: U.S. Department of Justice, 1981); M. Harris, *Sentencing to Community Service* (Washington, D.C.: American Bar Association, 1979); Peter Burns, "Criminal Justice Responses to Crime Victim Needs," Paper presented at Third International Institute on Victimology, Lisbon, 1984; Joe Hudson and Burt Galaway, *Victims, Offenders and Alternative Sanctions* (Lexington, Mass.: Lexington Books, 1980); Martin Wright, *Making Good: Prisons, Punishment and Beyond* (New York: Humanities Press, 1982); Dorothy McKnight, "The Victim-Offender Reconciliation Project," in Galaway and Hudson, note 1 *supra*, 292; B. Read, *Offenders' Restitution Programs in Georgia* (Atlanta: Department of Corrections, 1977); Burt Galaway, "The Use of Restitution," in Galaway and Hudson, note 1 *supra*, 277; Romine R. Deming, "Correctional Restitution: A Strategy for Correctional Conflict Management," in Galaway and Hudson, note 1 *supra*, 285; Alan T. Harland, "One Hundred Years of Restitution: An International Review and Prospectus for Research," *Victimology*, 8(1983), 190; Julie Vennard, "Compensation to the Offender: The Victim's Perspective," *Victimology*, 3(1978), 154; L. Siegal, "Court Ordered Victim Restitution: An Overview of Theory and Action," *New England Journal of Prison Law*, 5(1979), 135; T. L. Van Der Veen, "Compensation: Decisions of the Dutch Courts Concerning Restitution for Non-Material Damage in Traffic Cases," *Verkeersrecht*, 27(1979); Burt Galaway, "Preliminary Experiences of an Urban Victim Offender Reconciliation Project" Paper presented at Fifth International Symposium on Victimology, Zagreb, 1985.

14. G. Wardlaw, "The Human Rights of Victims in the Criminal Justice System," *Australian and New Zealand Journal of Criminology*, 12(1979), 145; Karmen, note 1 *supra*, 192; Elias, note 12 *supra*, 20; Joan Covey, "Alternatives to a Compensation Plan for Victims of Physical Violence," *Dickinson Law Review*, 69(1965); Rubin Castillo, et al., "The Use of Civil Liability to Aid Crime Victims," *Journal of Criminal Law and Criminology*, 70(1979), 57; Gerhard O. W. Mueller and H. H. A. Cooper, "Civil Alternatives for Victims of Crimes," Unpublished paper, New York University, 1973; P. Kobe, "The Victim's Position in Criminal Proceedings with Special Regard to the 'Adhesion Procedure'," *Rev. Kriminalist. Kriminol.*, 28(1977), 3; Peter Kobe, "The Victim in Judicial Procedure," Paper presented at Second International Symposium on Victimology, Boston, 1976; Joyce Hes, "From Victim of Sexual Violence to Claimant in a Civil Law Case" Paper presented at Fifth International Symposium on Victimology, Zagreb, 1985.

15. Mueller and Cooper, *ibid.*; Karmen, note 1 *supra*, 202; James E. Starrs, "A Modest Proposal to Insure Justice for Victims of Crime," *Minnesota Law Review*, 50(1965), 285; Minocher Sethna, "Compensation of Victims of Offences," in Drapkin and Viano, note 1 *supra*, 168; Fred E. Inbau, Comment on the Proposal," *Journal of Public Law*, 8(1959), 201.

16. Herbert Denenberg, "Compensation for Victims of Crime: Justice for the Victim as Well as the Criminal," *Insurance Law Journal* (1970), 628.

17. Karmen, note 1 *supra*, 203.

18. Notes, "Use of Record of Criminal Conviction in Subsequent Civil Action Arising from Same Facts as the Prosecution," *Michigan Law Review*, 64(1966), 708.

19. Diane Vaughan and Giovanna Carlo, "Victims of Fraud: Victim Responsiveness, Incidence and Reporting," in Viano, note 2 *supra*, 403; John Powers, "Murder Victim's Family Files Claim Against City," *Boston Globe*, February 16, 1986, 1.

20. Karmen, note 1 *supra*, 193; H. L. Nelson, "Victims' Suits Against Government Entities and Officials for Reckless Release," *American University Law Review*, 29(1980), 595.

21. David Fogel, et al., "Restitution in Criminal Justice: A Minnesota Experiment," *Criminal Law Bulletin*, 8(1973), 681; M. S. Serrill, "Minnesota Restitution Center," *Corrections Magazine*, 1(1975), 13.

22. Harland, note 13 *supra*; A. Carufel, "Victims' Satisfaction with Compensation: Effects of Initial Disadvantages and Third Party Intervention," *Journal of Applied Social Psychology*, 45(1981), 445.

23. see Karmen, note 13 *supra*.

24. McKnight, note 13 *supra*; Vennard, note 13 *supra*; Karmen, note 13 *supra*, 188; Schneider and Schneider, note 1 *supra*, 367; Bill Read, "How Restitution Works in Georgia," *Judicature*, 60(1977), 322; Joe Hudson, "Undoing the Wrong," *Social Work*, 19(1974), 313; S. Chesney, "Restitution in the Minnesota Probation Services: The Victims' Perspective," Paper presented at Second International Symposium on Victimology, Boston, 1976; S. Chesney, *Assessing Restitution in the Minnesota Probation Services* (St. Paul: Minnesota Governor's Commission, 1976); R. O. Steggerda, *Victim Restitution: An Assessment of the Restitution in Probation Experiment Operated by the Fifth Judicial District Department of Court Services* (Des Moines: Polk County Department of Program Evaluation, 1975); T. Balivet, *Connecticut: Recommendations for Improving the Use of Restitution as a Dispositional Alternative* (Washington, D.C.: American University Institute for Studies in Justice, 1975); Nancy A. Gattuso Holman, "Criminal Sentencing and Victim Compensation Legislation: Where is the Victim?" in Viano, note 2 *supra*, 363.

25. R. W. Hodgin, "The Criminal Injuries Compensation Board: The First Ten Years," *Home Office Research Bulletin* (1977), 34.

26. Robert Elias, "Alienating the Victim: Compensation and Victim Attitudes," *Journal of Social Issues*, 40(1984), 103.

27. Robert Elias, "The Symbolic Politics of Victim Compensation," *Victimology*, 8(1983), 213; Joanna Shapland, "Victim-Witness Services and the Needs of the Victim," *Victimology*, 8(1983), 233.

28. W. G. Doerner, et al., "An Analysis of Victim Compensation Programs as a Time-Series Experiment," *Victimology*, 1(1976), 295; W. G. Doerner, "A Quasi-Experimental Analysis of Selected Victim Compensation Programs," *Canadian Journal of Criminology*, 20(1978), 239; S. S. Silverman and W. G. Doerner, "The Effect of Victim Compensation Programs Upon Conviction Rates," *Sociological Symposium*, 25(1979), 40.

29. W. G. Doerner, "An Examination of the Alleged Latent Effects of Victim Compensation Programs Upon Crime Reporting," *Lambda Alpha Epsilon Journal*, 41(1978), 71; W. G. Doerner and S. Lab, "Impact of Crime Compensation Upon Victim Attitudes Toward the Criminal Justice System," *Victimology*, 5(1980), 61.

30. Elias, note 26 *supra*.

31. James Brooks, "Who Gets What? An Analysis of Five Model Proposals for Criminal Injury Compensation Legislation," *State Government* (1974), 18; James Brooks, "How Well Are Criminal Injury Compensation Boards Performing?" *Crime and Delinquency*, 21(1975), 50; James Brooks, "Compensating Victims of Crime: The Recommendations of Program Administrators," *Law and Society Review*, 7(1973), 445; David Bental, "Selected Problems in Public Compensation to Victims of Crime," *Issues in Criminology*, 3(1968), 217; Michael Fooner, "Victim-Induced, Victim-Invited and Victim Precipitated Criminality: Some Problems in Evaluation of Proposals for Victim Compensation," in Israel Drapkin and Emilio Viano (eds.), *Victimology* (Lexington, Mass.: Lexington Books, 1974), 231; Duncan Chappell and L. Paul Sutton, "Evaluating the Effectiveness of Programs to Compensate the Victims of Crime," in Israel Drapkin and Emilio Viano (eds.), *Victimology: Theoretical Issues* (Lexington, Mass.: Lexington Books, 1974), 213; Eduard Ziegenhagen, "Toward a Theory of Victim-Criminal Justice System Interactions," in McDonald, note 1 *supra*, 261; Jacqueline Vaughn and Richard Hofrichter, "Program Visibility in State Victim Compensation Programs," *Victimology*, 5(1980), 30; Evelyn Younger, "Commendable Words: A Critical Evaluation of California's Victim Compensation Law," *Journal of Beverly Hills Bar Association*, 7(1973), 12; Sylvia Fogelman, "Compensation to Victims of Violence," M. S. W. Thesis, University of Southern California, 1971; Willard Shank, "Aid to Victims of Crime in California," *Southern California Law Review*, 43(1970), 85; William Doerner, "The Diffusion of Victim Compensation Laws in the U.S.," *Victimology*, 4(1979), 119; Herbert Edelhertz and Gilbert Geis, *Public Compensation to Victims of Crime* (New York: Praeger, 1974); Gilbert Geis and Dorothy Zeitz, "California's Program of Compensation to Crime Victims," *Legal Aid Briefcase*, 25(1966), 66; George E. Redja and Emil Meuer, "An Analysis of State Criminal Compensation Plans," *Journal of Risk and Insurance* (1975), 599; Samuel Vitali, "A Year's Experience with the Massachusetts Compensation of Victims of Violent Crime Law, 1968–69," *Suffolk University Law Review*, 40(1970), 175; Gilbert Geis, "Crime Victims and Victim Compensation Programs," in McDonald, note 1 *supra*, 237; Gilbert Geis, "Experimental Design and the Law: A Prospectus for Research on Victim Compensation in California," *California Western Law Review*, 2(1966), 85; W. T. Westling, "Some Aspects of Judicial Determination of Compensation Payable to Victims of Crime," *Australian Law Journal*, 48(1974), 428; Gilbert Geis, et al., "Public Compensation of Victims of Crime: A Survey of the New York Experience," *Criminal Law Bulletin*, 9(1973), 9; Richard Knudten, et al., *Victims and Witnesses: Impact of Crime and Their Experiences with the Criminal Justice System* (Milwaukee: Center for Criminal Justice and Social Policy, 1975).

32. Martin Symonds, "The Second Injury to Victims," *Evaluation and Change*, 7(1980), 36; Karmen, note 1 *supra*, 139; Mary L. Keefe and Henry T. O'Reilly, "The Plight of the Rape Victim in New York City," in Viano, note 2 *supra*, 391; Concetta Adleman, "Teaching Police Officers Techniques of Crisis Intervention with Victims of Rape," *Journal of Police Administration*, 7(1979), 45; R. Nelson, "Establishing Rapport with Victims Is the Key to Effective Rape Investigations," *Police Chief*, 48(1981), 60; Emilio Viano, "Violence, Victimization and Social Change: A Socio-Cultural and Public Policy Analysis," *Victimology*, 8(1983), 54; J. J. Merchant, "Police Assistance to Rape Victims," *Police Chief*, 47(1980), 39; Z. Abel and K. Broderick, "Victimization and the Fear of Crime Among the Urban Aged," *Police Chief*, 47(1980), 34; M. Alpert and S. Schecter, "Sensitizing Workers to the Needs of Victims: Common Worker and Victim Responses," *Victimology*, 4(1974), 385; "Private Violence," note 4 *supra*, 29; Bard and Sangrey, note 1 *supra;* Fremont Police Department, *Proposal to Conduct Program to Improve and Standardize Police Treatment of Victims and Witnesses* (Washington, D.C.: Police Foundation, 1974); Harry O'Reilly, "Victim-Witness Services: The Police Perspective," in Emilio Viano (ed.), *Victim/Witness Programs: Human Services in the 1980's* (Alexandria, Va.: National Victim/Witness Resource Center, 1980).

33. Theodore Becker, *Victims and Their Lawyer: A Study of Victim Advocacy* (Ann Arbor: University Microfilms International, 1980); Dubow and Becker, note 1 *supra;* William F. McDonald, "Criminal Justice and the Victim: An Introduction," in McDonald, note 1 *supra,* 34; "A Spokesman for Victims: Past and Future," *Law Enforcement Journal*, 5(1975), 4; Leo Callahan, "The Victim Advocate: Programmed Police Response for the Crime Victim," *Police Chief*, 42(1975), 50; Emilio Viano, "Victim/Witness Services: A Review of the Model," (Washington, D.C.: U.S. Department of Justice, 1978); "Crime Victims Advocate Urged," *Trial*, 12(1976), 52; David Hirshel, "Providing Rape Victims with Assistance at Court: The Erie County Volunteer Supportive Advocate Court Assistance Program," *Victimology*, 3(1978), 149; Commission on Victim Witness Assistance, *Final Report* (Washington, D.C.: National District Attorneys Association, 1977); Viano, note 32 *supra;* John Dussich, *The Victim Ombudsman* (Tallahassee, Fla.: Governor's Council on Criminal Justice, 1972); John Dussich, "The Victim Ombudsman Revisited," Paper presented at Second International Symposium on Victimology, Boston, 1976; Friedman, note 7 *supra;* American Judicature Society, "Changing the Treatment of Victims," *Citizens Forum on the Courts*, 1(Winter 1985), 1.

34. Karmen, note 1 *supra*, 146; Robert Rosenblum and Carol Blew, *Victim/Witness Assistance* (Washington, D.C.: U.S. Government Printing Office, 1979); James L. Lacy, *National Standards Concerning the Prosecution Witness* (Washington, D.C.: Center for Prosecution Management, 1972); Richard P. Lynch, "Improving the Treatment of Victims: Some Guides for Action," in McDonald, note 1 *supra,* 165; William F. McDonald, "Towards A Bicentennial Revolution in Criminal Justice: The Return of the Victim," *The American Criminal Law Review*, 13(1976), 649; Anna T. Laszlo, "Intake Screening as a Concept in Victim Assistance: A Prosecutorial Model," Paper presented at Second International Symposium on Victimology, Boston, 1976; Joseph Mueller, "Aid to Victims of Crime in St. Louis," *Victimology*, 1(1976), 457; Georgia Cuddeback, *An Evaluation of the Victim/Witness Advocate Program for Victims and Witnesses of Criminal Acts* (Ann Arbor: University Microfilms International, 1978); John Blackmore, "Paying the Price of Crime," *Police Magazine*, 2(1979), 54; National Association of Victims Support Schemes, *Second Annual Report* (London: Author, 1982); Commission on Victim Witness Assistance, note 33 *supra;* A. Alcabes and J. A. Jones, "Juvenile Victim Assistance Programs: A Proposal," *Crime and Delinquency*, 26(1980), 202; D. Mandel, "Victims and Witnesses: San Mateo County's Cooperative Solution," *Crime Prevention Review,* 5(1978), 10; A. A. Cain and M. Kravitz, *Victim Witness Assistance* (Washington, D.C.: U.S. Department of Justice, 1978); J. Bernat de Celis, "The Experience of a Consultation Center for Witnesses and Victims Attached to the Paris Court," *Revue de Science Criminelle et de Droit Penal Compare* (1981), 695; Schneider and Schneider, note 1 *supra;* David A. Lowenberg, "An Integrated Victim Services Model," in Galaway and Hudson, note 1 *supra,* 404; John Dussich, "Victim Service Models and Their Efficacy," in Viano, note 2 *supra,* 473; Ziegenhagen and Benyi, note 1 *supra,* 373; James Ahrens, et al., *Law Enforcement and Victim Services* (Washington, D.C.: Aurora Associates, 1980); Lucy Friedman, et al., *Victims and Helpers: Reactions to Crime* (New York: Victims Service Agency, 1982); Helen Reeves, "Victim Support Schemes: The U.K. Model," Paper presented at Third International Institute on Victimology, Lisbon, 1984; Viano, note 32 *supra;* Eduard Ziegenhagen, *Victims, Crime and Social Control* (New York: Praeger, 1977); Baluss, note 1 *supra;* John Dussich, "The Victim Ombudsman: A Proposal," in Drapkin and Viano, note 1 *supra,* 11; Leonard Bickman, "Research and Evaluation: Cook County State's Attorney Victim Witness Assistance Project," *Victimology,* 1(1976), 454; Ann Newton, "Aid to the Victim: Victim Aid Programs," *Crime and Delinquency Literature,* 8(1976), 368; David Bolin, "The Pima County Victim/Witness Program: Analyzing Its Successes," *Evaluation and Change,* 7(1980), 120; James Reilly, "Victim/Witness Services in Prosecutor's Offices," *Prosecutor* (October 1981), 8.

35. James Morris, *Victim Aftershock* (New York: Franklin Watts, 1983); Frank Carrington, "Victim Rights Legislation: A Wave of the Future?" in Galaway and Hudson, note 1 *supra,* 306; National Organization for Victim Assistance, *Victim Rights and Services: A Legislative Directory* (Washington, D.C.: Author, 1983); S. Cohn, "Protecting Child Rape Victims from the Public and Press after *Globe Newspaper* and *Cox Broadcasting," George Washington Law Review,* 53(1983), 269; J. P. Busch, "Victim Rights in Stolen Property in California," *California Law Review,* 64(1976), 1018; Robert Grayson, "Criminal Justice vs. Victim Justice: A Need to Balance the Scales," *The Justice Reporter,* 1(1981), 1; Paul Hudson, "A Bill of Rights for Crime Victims," *Victimology,* 5(1980), 428; Ziegenhagen and Benyi, note 1 *supra,* 377; William F. McDonald, "Expanding the Victim's Role in the Disposition Decision: Reform in Search of a Rationale," in Galaway and Hudson, note 13 *supra,* 101; William F. McDonald, "Notes on the Victim's Role in the Prosecution and Disposition Stages of the American Criminal Process," Paper presented at Second International Symposium on Victimology, Boston, 1976; Randy Barnett and John Hagel, "Assessing the Criminal: Restitution, Retribution and the Legal Process," in Barnett and Hagel, note 13 *supra,* 1; American Bar Association Committee on Victims, *Reducing Victim/Witness Intimidation: A Package* (Washington, D.C.: Author, 1979); Anne Heinz and Wayne Kerstetter, "Pretrial Settlement Conference: Evaluation of a Reform in Plea Bargaining," *Law and Society Review,* 13(1979), 349; President's Task Force on Victims of Crime, *Final Report* (Washington, D.C.: U.S. Government Printing Office, 1982); David Reifen, "Court Procedures in Israel to Protect Child-Victims of Sexual Assaults," in Israel Drapkin and Emilio Viano (eds.), *Victimology: Crimes, Victims and Justice* (Lexington, Mass.: Lexington Books, 1974), 67; Nat Hentoff, "Help! Police?" *Village Voice,* September 3, 1985, 22; Ralph Marino, "Victim Witness Intimidation A Crime," *The Pennysaver*, July 17, 1985, 15; Lou Hulsman, "The Right of the Victim Not to Be Subjected to the Dynamics of Criminal Justice," Paper presented at Fifth International Symposium on Victimology, Zagreb, 1985; Sevine Erc- man, "The Right to Privacy and the Status of the Victim Before Criminal Proceedings," Paper presented at Fifth International Symposium on Vic- timology, Zagreb, 1985; Mirjan Damaska, "Some Remarks on the Status of the Victim in Continental and Other Criminal Jurisdictions," Paper pre- sented at Fifth International Symposium on Victimology, Zagreb, 1985.

36. Anne Strick, *Injustice for All* (New York: Penguin, 1977).

37. John W. Palmer, "The Night Prosecutor: Columbus Finds Extraju- dicial Solutions to Interpersonal Disputes," in Galaway and Hudson, note 1 *supra*, 262; Leon Sheleff, "The Impact of Victimology on Criminal Law," Paper presented at Second International Symposium on Victimology, Bos- ton, 1976; Paul Keve, "Therapeutic Uses of Restitution," in Galaway and Hudson, note 13 *supra*, 59; Irvin Waller, "Caring About Crime Victims," *Perception* (January/February 1983), 18; T. M. Schalken, "The Legal Position of the Aggrieved Party in the Dutch System of Penal Proceedings," *Delikt Delinkwent* 10(1980), 266; Dubow and Becker, note 1 *supra*; Dorothy Mc- Knight, "The Victim-Offender Reconciliation Project," in Galaway and Hudson, note 1 *supra*, 292.

38. Keefe and O'Reilly, note 32 *supra*.

39. Schneider and Schneider, note 1 *supra*, 366; Lois P. Kraft, et al., "An Evaluation of the Victim-Witness Advocate Program of Pima County," (Tucson: Office of Pima County Attorney, 1977); Heinz and Kerstetter, note 35 *supra*; Ziegenhagen and Benyi, note 1 *supra*; Ziegenhagen, note 34 *supra*; Frank Cannavale, *Witness Cooperation* (Lexington, Mass.: D. C. Heath, 1975); Mary Knudten, et al., *Crime Victims and Witnesses as Victims of the Admin- istration of Justice* (Milwaukee: Center for Criminal Justice and Social Policy, 1975); Vera Institute of Justice, "The Brooklyn Victim-Witness Assistance Project" (New York: Author, 1974).

40. Lois Kraft, et al., *An Evaluation of the Victim-Witness Advocate Program of Pima County* (Tucson: Office of Pima County Attorney, 1979); Knudten, *ibid.*; L. G. Brewster, "Cost Effectiveness in Victim-Witness Advocate Pro- grams: A Case Study," *Journal of Criminal Justice*, 8(1980), 97.

41. Karmen, note 1 *supra*, 146.

42. Dubow and Becker, note 1 *supra*.

43. *Ibid.*

44. Karmen, note 1 *supra*, 151.

45. Ziegenhagen and Benyi, note 1 *supra*.

46. Elias, note 12 *supra*; Shapland, note 12 *supra*.

47. Edwin M. Schur, "The Case for Abolition," in Schur and Bedau, note 22 *supra*, 3; Edwin M. Schur, *Our Criminal Society: The Social and Legal Sources of Crime in America* (Englewood Cliffs, N.J.: Prentice-Hall, 1969), 291; Sawyer F. Sylvester, "Iatrogenics, Law and Decriminalization," in Sawyer F. Sylvester and Edward Sagarin (eds.), *Politics and Crime* (New York: Prae- ger, 1972), 1; Joseph J. Fitzpatrick, "Cultural Differences, Not Criminal Of-

fenses: A Redefinition of Types of Social Behavior," in Sylvester and Sagarin, *ibid.*, 119; Edwin M. Schur, "The Trend Toward Decriminalization: Some Sociological Observations," in Sylvester and Sagarin, *ibid.*, 108; David J. Pittman, "Decriminalization of the Public Drunkenness Offense: An International Overview," in Sylvester and Sagarin, *ibid.*, 127; Francine Watman, "Sex Offenses Against Children and Minors: Victimological Implications for Decriminalization," in Sylvester and Sagarin, *ibid.*, 137; Mary D. Howard and John R. Howard, "Toward A Theory of Decriminalization," in Sylvester and Sagarin, *ibid.*, 148; Robert C. Bourchowitz, "Victimless Crimes: A Proposal to Free the Courts," *Judicature*, 57(1973), 69; Edith Flynn, "Report of the Discussion Sections of the Second International Symposium on Victimology," *Victimology*, 2(1977), 32; Norval Morris and Gordon Hawkins, *The Honest Politician's Guide to Crime Control* (Chicago: University of Chicago Press, 1970); Jeffrey Reiman, *The Rich Get Richer and the Poor Get Prison* (New York: John Wiley, 1979); Mary S. Knudten and Richard D. Knudten, "Decriminalization and the Victim," in Edith Elisabeth Flynn and John Conrad (eds.), *The New and the Old Criminology* (New York: Praeger, 1978), 200.

48. Patrick B. McGuigan and Randall R. Rader (eds.), *Criminal Justice Reform* (Chicago: Regnery, 1983); John Braithwaite and Gilbert Geis, "On Theory and Action for Corporate Crime Control," in Gilbert Geis (ed.), *On White Collar Crime* (Lexington, Mass.: Lexington Books, 1982), 189; Harold C. Barnett, "The Production of Corporate Crime in Corporate Capitalism," in Peter Wickman and Timothy Dailey (eds.), *White Collar and Economic Crime* (Lexington, Mass.: Lexington Books, 1982), 157.

49. Jocelynne A. Scutt, "To Love, Honour and Rape with Impunity: Wife as Victim of Rape and Criminal Law," in Schneider, note 1 *supra*, 423; Viano, note 32 *supra*; Francine Watman, "Sex Offenses Against Children and Minors: Some Proposals for Legal Reform," in Drapkin and Viano, note 31 *supra*, 235; Leigh Beinen, "Rape Reform Legislation in the United States: A Look at Some Practical Effects," *Victimology*, 8(1983), 1391; P. Edqvist and S. Wennberg, "Recent Legislation and Research on Victims in Sweden," *Victimology*, 8(1983), 310; Paul Hudson, "A Bill of Rights for Crime Victims," *Victimology*, 5(1980), 428; R. G. Fox and C. O'Hare, "Criminal Bankruptcy," *Monash University Law Review*, 4(1978), 181; Cohn, note 35 *supra*; Z. Separovic, "The Victim and Society: Some New Problems Posed by the Advancement of Medicine," *Rev. Kriminalist. Kriminol.*, 27(1976), 235; F. R. Scarpitti and E. C. Scarpitti, "Victims of Rape," *Society*, 14(1977), 29; A. Normandeau, "For A Canadian and International Charter of Rights for Crime Victims," *Canadian Journal of Criminology*, 25(1983), 463; A. Normandeau, "Toward a League for Victim's Rights and Liberties," *Canadian Journal of Criminology*, 24(1981), 87; Ann R. Bristow, "*State v. Marks*: An Analysis of Expert Testimony on Rape Trauma Syndrome," *Victimology*, 9(1984), 273.

50. Karmen, note 1 *supra*, 230; Margaret Hyde, *The Rights of Victims* (New York: Franklin Watts, 1983); James Reilly, "Victim Rights Legislation," *Prosecutor* (October 1981), 18.

51. Karmen, note 1 *supra*, 19, 24, 115; Vicki Rose, "Rape as a Social Problem: A By-Product of the Feminist Movement," *Social Problems*, 25(1977), 75; Kappell and Leuteritz, note 2 *supra*; Viano, note 32 *supra*; Normandeau, note 49 *supra;* Thelma Rutherford, "Abuses on the Elderly and What the Gray Panthers Are Trying to Do About Them," Paper presented at First World Congress on Victimology, Washington, D.C., 1980.

52. William Kornblum and Vernon Boggs, "New Alternatives for Fighting Crime," *Social Policy* (Winter 1984), 25. Brent Smith and Eileen Cullen, "Victims Organize for Legislative Change," *Citizen Participation* (Summer 1985), 20.

53. Seymour Halleck, "Vengeance and Victimization," *Victimology,* 5(1980), 99.

54. Beinen, note 49 *supra;* Frans Willem Winkel, "Changing Misconceptions About Rape Through Informational Campaigns," *Victimology,* 9(1984), 262.

55. Tom Campbell, *The Left and Rights* (Boston: Routledge and Kegan Paul, 1983); Robert Lefcourt, "Lawyers for the Poor Can't Win," in Robert Lefcourt (ed.), *Law Against the People* (New York: Vintage, 1971), 123; Samuel Walker, *Sense and Nonsense About Crime* (Monterrey, Calif.: Brooks/Cole, 1985), 145.

56. Ellen S. Cohn, et al., "Crime Prevention vs. Victimization Prevention: The Psychology of Two Different Reactions," *Victimology,* 3(1978), 285; Jeffrey Henig and Michael G. Maxfield, "Reducing Fear of Crime: Strategies for Intervention," *Victimology,* 3(1978), 297; Michael Castleman, *Crime Free* (New York: Simon and Schuster, 1984); Robert Elias, "Citizen Participation in Criminal Justice: A Critique," *Citizen Participation* (July/August 1982), 6; Stephanie Riger, et al., "Women's Fear of Crime: From Blaming to Restricting the Victim," *Victimology,* 3(1973), 274; H. D. Schwind, "Victimology in Police and Judiciary Practice," *Kriminalistik,* 33(1979), 514; C. H. D. Steinmetz, "An Approach to Victimological Risk Analysis. A Thought Model in the Prevention of Petty Crime," *Just. Verkenningen,* 2(1980), 5; L. H. Kidder, et al., "Rights Consciousness and Victimization Prevention: Personal Defense and Assertiveness Training," *Journal of Social Issues,* 39(1983), 153; Michael Castleman, "Crime Free," *Social Policy* (Spring 1984), 4; Judith Burns, "A SAFE Place for Children," *Victimology,* 9(1984), 23.

57. Mark Levine, "Cambridge's Answer to Crime," *Social Policy* (Summer 1982), 52.

58. Robert C. Trojanowicz and Samuel L. Dixon, *Criminal Justice and the Community* (Englewood Cliffs, N.J.: Prentice-Hall, 1976); Robert C. Trojanowicz, et al., *Community Based Crime Prevention* (Pacific Palisades, Calif.: Goodyear, 1975); John Hylton, "The Growth of Punishment: Imprisonment and Community Corrections in Canada," *Crime and Social Justice* (1981), 18; Andrew Scull, "Community Corrections: Panacea, Progress or Pretence?" in Richard L. Abel (ed.), *The Politics of Informal Justice: The American Experience* (New York: Academic Press, 1982), 99; Gerald Suttles, *The Social Condition of Communities* (Chicago: University of Chicago Press, 1972).

59. Edward J. Pesce, et al., "Crime Prevention Through Environmental Design," in Galaway and Hudson, note 1 *supra,* 347; Paul J. Brantingham and Patricia L. Brantingham (eds.), *Environmental Criminology* (Beverly Hills, Calif.: Sage, 1981); Oscar Newman, *Defensible Space* (New York: Macmillan,

1972); C. R. Jeffrey, *Crime Prevention Through Environmental Design* (Beverly Hills, Calif.: Sage, 1971).

60. Karmen, note 1 *supra*, 257; Dubow and Becker, note 1 *supra*; Chicago Department of Planning, City and Community Development, "The Cabrini-Green High Impact Program," *Victimology*, 3(1978), 334; Robert J. Zion, "Reducing Crime and Fear of Crime in Downtown Cleveland," *Victimology*, 3(1978), 341; Lynn Curtis, "Victimization and Its Concentration: Crime Prevention and Public Housing in the United States," in Schneider, note 1 *supra*, 441; Donald Perlgut, "Manageable Space: Proposals for Crime Prevention in Subsidized Housing," in Schneider, *ibid.*, 453; Betsy Lindsay, "The Community Crime Prevention Program," in Schneider, *ibid.*, 472; Irvin Waller, "What Reduces Residential Burglary: Action and Research in Seattle and Toronto," in Schneider, *ibid.*, 479; Patricia Mayhew and Ronald V. G. Clarke, "Crime Prevention and Public Housing in England," in Schneider, *ibid.*, 493; Institute for the Study of Labor and Economic Crisis, *The Iron Fist and the Velvet Glove: An Analysis of U.S. Police* (San Francisco: Crime and Justice Associates, 1982); Charles Silberman, *Criminal Violence, Criminal Justice* (New York: Vintage, 1978), 575; Leonard Bickman, "Bystander Intervention in a Crime," in Viano, note 2 *supra*, 144; S. Balkin and P. Houlden, "Reducing Fear of Crime Through Occupational Presence," *Criminal Justice and Behavior*, 10(1983), 13; Carol Shapiro and Lorraine Gutierrez, "Crime Victims Services," *Social Policy* (Summer 1982), 50; George J. Washnis, *Citizen Involvement in Crime Prevention* (Lexington, Mass.: Lexington Books, 1976; Anthony Sorrentino, *Organizing Against Crime* (New York: Human Sciences Press, 1977); Castleman, note 56 *supra*, Elias, note 56 *supra*; Kornblum and Boggs, note 52 *supra*; Abel, note 58 *supra*; Thomas J. Cook and Frank P. Scioli, "Public Participation in the Criminal Justice System: Volunteers in Police, Court and Correctional Agencies," in John A. Gardiner and Michael A. Mulkey (eds.), *Crime and Criminal Justice* (Lexington, Mass.: Lexington Books, 1975), 107; Laura Nader (ed.), *No Access to Law: Alternatives to the American Judicial System* (New York: Academic Press, 1980); Roman Tomasic and Malcolm Feeley (eds.), *Neighborhood Justice* (New York: Longman, 1982); Philip Parnell, "Community Justice Versus Crime Control," in R. L. McNeely and Carl E. Pope (eds.), *Race, Crime and Criminal Justice* (Beverly Hills, Calif.: Sage, 1981), 147; Fred Heinzelmann, "Crime Prevention and the Physical Environment," in Dan A. Lewis (ed.), *Reactions to Crime* (Beverly Hills, Calif.: Sage, 1981), 87; Richard Taub, et al., "Neighborhoods and Safety," in Lewis, *ibid.*, 103; Marlys McPherson and Glenn Silloway, "Planning to Prevent Crime," in Lewis, *ibid.*, 167; Fred DuBow and David Emmons, "The Community Hypothesis," in Lewis, *ibid.*, 167; Janice A. Beecher, et al., "The Politics of Police Responses to Urban Crime," in Lewis, *ibid.*, 183; Elliott Currie, "Fighting Crime," *Working Papers* (July/August 1982), 16; Frank Browning, "Nobody's Soft on Crime Anymore: Rethinking America's Impossible Dream," *Mother Jones* (August 1982), 26; Charles Ohaeri, "Community Responsibility and the Victim in Nigerian Society," in Viano, note 2 *supra*, 440; Sandra Baxter and Richard Bennett, "Crime Control vs. Crime Prevention," *Citizen Participation* (Summer 1985), 3.

61. McGuigan and Rader, note 48 *supra*.

62. Stuart A. Scheingold, *The Politics of Law and Order: Street Crime and Public Policy* (New York: Longman, 1983); Silberman, note 60 *supra*.

63. Hans Joachim Schneider, "The Present Situation of Victimology in the World," in Schneider, note 1 *supra*, 11.

64. Ironically, this may increase other victimization due to accidents, most of which occur in the home.

65. Cohn, et al., note 56 *supra*.

66. Kanti Kotecha and James Walker, "Vigilantism and the American Police," in Joe Rosenbaum and Peter Sederberg (ed.), *Vigilante Politics* (Philadelphia: University of Pennsylvania Press, 1976), 158.

67. Washnis, note 60 *supra*; Castleman, note 56 *supra*.

68. Elias, note 56 *supra*; Institute for the Study of Labor and Economic Crisis, note 60 *supra*; Werner Elmstadt, "Citizen Patrols: Prevention or Control?" *Crime and Social Justice* (1984), 200; Andrew Karmen, "Citizen Participation in Crime Prevention: Some Reservations," *Citizen Participation* (Summer 1985), 4.

69. Knudten and Knudten, note 47 *supra*, 201; Schneider, note 63 *supra*, 33; Jerold Auerbach, *Justice Without Law? Resolving Disputes Without Lawyers* (New York: Oxford University Press, 1983); Martin D. Schwartz, "Punishment or Treatment? Criminalization and Decriminalization in the Law of Father-Daughter Incest," Paper presented at First World Congress on Victimology, Washington, D.C., 1980.

70. L. F. Felstiner and Lynne Williams, "Community Mediation in Dorchester, Massachusetts," in Tomasic and Feeley, note 60 *supra*, 111; Martin Wright, "The Impact of Victim/Offender Mediation on the Assumptions and Proceedings of Criminal Justice: Impact on the Victim," Paper presented at Third International Institute on Victimology, Lisbon, 1984.

71. Robert Davis, et al., *Mediation and Arbitration as Alternatives to Criminal Prosecution in Felony Arrest Cases: An Evaluation of the Brooklyn Dispute Resolution Center* (New York: Vera Institute of Justice, 1980); Richard Danzig, "Toward the Creation of a Complementary Decentralized System of Criminal Justice," in Tomasic and Feeley, note 60 *supra*, 2.

72. Daniel McGillis, *Neighborhood Justice Centers* (Washington, D.C.: U.S. Government Printing Office, 1981); Ziegenhagen and Benyi, note 1 *supra*, 378.

73. McDonald, note 33 *supra*, 30.

74. James Brady, "Toward a Popular Justice in the U.S.: The Dialectics of Community Action," *Contemporary Crises*, 5(1981), 155.

75. Brady, *ibid.*, Kornblum and Boggs, note 56 *supra*; Institute for the Study of Labor and Economic Crisis, note 60 *supra*; Richard Quinney, *Class, State and Crime* (New York: Longman, 1980); Jonathan Garlock, "The Knights of Labor Courts: A Case Study of Popular Justice," in Abel, note 58 *supra*, 17; Christine Harrington, "Delegalization Reform Movements: A Historical Analysis," in Abel, *ibid.*, 35; Paul Wahrhaftig, "An Overview of Community-Oriented Citizen Dispute Resolution Programs in the U.S.," in Abel, *ibid.*, 75; Mark H. Lazerson, "In the Halls of Justice, the Only Justice Is in the Halls," in Abel, *ibid.*, 119; Robert Hofrichter, "Neighborhood Justice and the Social Control Problems of American Capitalism: A Perspective," in Abel, *ibid.*, 207; Boaventura de Sousa Santos, "Law and Community: The Changing Nature of State Power in Late Capitalism," in Abel, *ibid.*, 249; Richard Abel, "The Contradictions of Informal Justice," in Abel, *ibid.*, 267; Raymond Michalowski, "Crime Control in the 1980's: A Progressive Agenda," *Crime and Social Justice* (1983), 13; Ronald L. Boostrom and Joel Henderson, "Community Action and Crime Prevention: Some Unresolved Issues," *Crime and Social Justice* (1983), 24; Nader, note 60 *supra;* Tomasic and Feeley, note 60 *supra;* Dennis R. Longmire, "A Popular Justice System: A Radical Alternative to the Traditional Criminal Justice System," *Contemporary Crises*, 5(1981), 15; James Brady, "Sorting Out the Exile's Confusion: Or Dialogue on Popular Justice," *Contemporary Crises*, 5(1981), 31; Harold Pepinsky, "Communist Anarchism as an Alternative to the Rule of Criminal Law," *Contemporary Crises*, 2(1978), 315; Larry L. Tifft, "The Coming Redefinitions of Crime: An Anarchist Perspective," *Social Problems*, 26(1979), 392; Elias, note 56 *supra;* Robert Elias, "Victims and Crime Prevention: A Basis for Social Change?" *Citizen Participation* (Summer 1985), 22; Mark Levine, "Crimewatch in Cambridgeport: A Community Reconstruction," *Citizen Participation* (Summer 1985), 12; Lynn A. Curtis and Betsy Lindsay, "Going Beyond What Is Fashionable: The Inner City and Community Crime Prevention," *Citizen Participation* (Summer 1985), 6; Cyril Robinson, "Criminal Justice Research: Two Competing Futures," *Crime and Social Justice*, 23(1985), 121.

76. Massachusetts Public Research Interest Group, *The Plight of the People's Court* (Boston: Author, 1982); John Weiss, "Justice Without Lawyers: Transforming Small Claims Courts," *Working Papers* (Fall 1974), 45.

77. Philip Schrag, *Counsel for the Deceived* (New York: Pantheon Books, 1975).

78. Danzig, note 71 *supra;* Davis, et al., note 71 *supra.*

79. David Friedrichs, "Crime, Deviance and Criminal Justice: In Search of a Radical Humanist Perspective," *Humanity and Society*, 6(1982), 200; Larry Tifft and Dennis Sullivan, *The Struggle to Be Human: Crime, Criminology and Anarchism* (Mt. Pleasant, Mich.: Cienfuegos Press, 1980).

80. James P. Brady, "A Season of Startling Alliance: Chinese Law and Justice in the New Order," in Piers Beirne and Richard Quinney (eds.), *Marxism and Law* (New York: John Wiley, 1982), 343; Boaventura de Sousa Santos, "Popular Justice, Dual Power and Socialist Strategy," in Beirne and Quinney, *ibid.*, 364; Boaventura de Sousa Santos, "Law and Revolution in Portugal: The Experiences of Popular Justice after the 25th of April 1974," in Richard Abel (ed.), *The Politics of Informal Justice: Comparative Studies* (New York: Academic Press, 1982), 251; Barbara Isaacman and Allen Isaacman, "A Socialist Legal System in the Making: Mozambique Before and After Independence," in Abel, *ibid.*, 281; Jack Spence, "Institutionalizing Neighborhood Courts: Two Chilean Experiences," in Abel, *ibid.*, 215; Sally Engle Merry, "The Social Organization of Mediation in Nonindustrial Societies: Implications for Informal Community Justice in America," in Abel, *ibid.*, 17; R. Cantor, "Law without Lawyers: Cuba's Popular Tribunals," *Juris*

Doctor, 4(1974), 74; Steven Spitzer, "The Dialectics of Formal and Informal Control," in Abel, note 58 *supra,* 167; Jack Spence, *Search for Justice: Neighborhood Courts in Allende's Chile* (Boulder, Colo.: Westview Press, 1979); Luis Salas, "The Role of the Judicial System and Law," in Luis Salas, *Social Control and Deviance in Cuba* (New York: Praeger, 1979); Vilma Nunez de Escorcia, "Justice and the Control of Crime in the Sandinista Popular Revolution," *Crime and Social Justice,* 23(1985), 5; Max Azicri, "Crime, Penal Law and the Cuban Revolutionary Process," *Crime and Social Justice,* 23(1985), 51.

81. Aglaia Tsitsoura, "The Role of the Victim in the Framework of Crime Policy: International Aspects," *Victimology,* 8(1983), 47.

82. LeRoy Lamborn, "Toward A United Nations Declaration of Crime, Abuses of Power, and the Rights of Victims," Paper presented to the Ninth International Congress on Criminology, Vienna, 1983; Irvin Waller, "Declaration on the Protection and Assistance of Victims of Crime," Paper prepared for the Committee on the Code of Conduct for the Protection and Assistance of Victims, World Society of Victimology, 1983; LeRoy Lamborn, "The Proposed United Nations Declaration on Justice and Assistance for Victims," Paper presented at International Meeting on Criminality and Development, San Jose, 1984; Normandeau, note 49 *supra;* LeRoy Lamborn, "Vers une Declaration de Nations Unies sur la criminalite, les abus de pouvoir et les droits de victimes," *Annales de Droit de Liege,* 2(1984), 205; "Special Issue: Towards A United Nations Declaration on Justice and Assistance for Victims," *World Society of Victimology Newsletter,* 3(1983–84); LeRoy Lamborn, "The Proposed United Nations Declaration on Justice and Assistance for Victims of Crimes or Other Acts Involving the Abuse of Power: Defining 'Abuse of Power' " Paper presented at Fifth International Symposium on Victimology, Zagreb, 1985.

83. Stanley Johnston, "If You Want Peace, Prepare for Law: People as Victims of Their Own Political Bigotry," Paper presented at International Institute of Victimology, Bellagio, 1975; Stanley Johnston, "Instituting Criminal Justice in the Global Village," in Viano, note 46 *supra,* 325; Stanley Johnston, "Toward a Supra-National Criminology: The Right and Duty of Victims of National Government to Seek Defense Through World Law," in Drapkin and Viano, note 42 *supra,* 37.

84. Robert Elias, "Transcending Our Social Reality of Victimization: Toward A New Victimology of Human Rights," *Victimology,* 9(1985); Luisella de Cataldo Neuberger, "An Appraisal of Victimological Perspectives in International Law," Paper presented at Third International Institute on Victimology, Lisbon, 1984.

85. W. Clifford, "Official Policies to Help the Victims of Crime in Europe," *Justice of the Peace,* 148(1984), 42.

86. James Garofalo and John McDermott, "National Victim Compensation: Its Costs and Coverage," *Law and Policy Quarterly,* 1(1979), 439; David T. Austern, "Crime Victim Compensation Programs: The Issue of Costs," *Victimology,* 5(1980), 61; Roger Meiners, *Victim Compensation: Economic, Legal and Political Aspects* (Lexington, Mass.: D. C. Heath, 1978); James Garofalo and L. Paul Sutton, *Compensating Victims of Violent Crime: Potential Costs and*

Coverage of a National Program (Albany, N.Y.: Criminal Justice Research Center, 1977); Edward D. Jones, "A Cost Analysis of Federal Victim Compensation," in Wesley G. Skogan (ed.), *Sample Surveys of Victims of Crime* (Cambridge: Ballinger, 1976); Barbara McClure, "Crime: Compensation for Victims," (Washington, D.C.: Library of Congress, 1979); Reilly, note 34 *supra;* Deborah M. Carrow, *Crime Victim Compensation: Program Model* (Washington, D.C.: U.S. Government Printing Office, 1980); Roger Meiners, "Public Compensation of the Victims of Crime: How Much Would It Cost?" in Barnett and Hagel, note 13 *supra,* 309.

87. Joseph Maggadino, "Crime, Victim Compensation, and the Supply of Offenses," *Public Policy*, 54(1976), 437; Lester Thurow, "Equity Versus Efficiency in Law Enforcement," *Public Policy*, 18(1970), 454.

88. Elias, note 27 *supra;* McDonald, note 33 *supra,* 31.

89. Friedman, note 7 *supra;* Rich, note 5 *supra.*

90. Miers, note 12 *supra;* Shapland, note 12 *supra.*

91. Jacquelien Soetenhorst, "Concern for Victims of Sexual Violence: Lever for Change?" Paper presented at Third International Institute on Victimology, Lisbon, 1984.

92. Miers, note 12 *supra;* Shapland, note 12 *supra;* Elias, note 1 *supra;* McDonald, note 33 *supra.*

93. Dubow and Becker, note 1 *supra;* Rona Fields, "Research on Victims: Problems and Issues," in Salasin, note 1 *supra,* 56.

94. Randy Barnett, "Restitution: A New Paradigm in Criminal Justice," in Galaway and Hudson, note 1 *supra,* 245.

95. Dubow and Becker, note 1 *supra;* Tomar Mason, "The Objectification and Use of Children as Weapons in Both Custody and Child Sex Abuse Legislation," Paper presented at Fifth International Symposium on Victimology, Zagreb, 1985.

96. For suggestions that we may "maintain" poverty and crime because it performs certain functions, see Herbert Gans, *More Equality* (New York: Vintage, 1973); William Ryan, *Blaming the Victim* (New York: Vintage, 1976); Reiman, note 47 *supra.*

97. Chelimsky, note 2 *supra.*

98. Miers, note 12 *supra;* Shapland, note 12 *supra.*

99. Elias, note 26 *supra.*

100. Ziegenhagen and Benyi, note 1 *supra;* Meiners, note 86 *supra;* Herbert Edelhertz and Gilbert Geis, *Public Compensation to Victims of Crime* (New York: Praeger, 1974).

101. Duncan Chappell, "Providing for the Victims of Crime: Political Placebos or Progressive Programmes?" *Adelaide Law Review*, 4(1972), 294; David Friedrichs, "Victimology: A Consideration of the Radical Critique," *Crime and Delinquency* (April 1983), 288; William Macauley, "Victim Compensation: Cure or Placebo," in Jacqueline Scherer and Gary Shepard (eds.), *Victimization of the Weak* (Springfield, Ill.: Charles C Thomas, 1983), 136; Lee Bridges and Liz Fekete, "Victims, the 'Urban Jungle,' and the New Racism," *Race and Class*, 27(1985), 46, 49–51, 53, 57.

102. Elias, note 27 *supra;* Chappell, *ibid.*

103. Ziegenhagen and Benyi, note 1 *supra;* Ziegenhagen, note 34 *supra.*

104. Elias, note 1 *supra.*

105. O'Sullivan, note 2 *supra.*

NOTES FOR CHAPTER 8

1. We will use the term "oppression" here to imply violations that surpass "repression." While "repression" commonly connotes violations of political and civil rights, "oppression" encompasses the complete array of internationally recognized human rights, including economic, social, and cultural rights, as well as political and civil rights.

2. The materials cited in this chapter show a poor American human rights record both at home and abroad. Yet we do not pretend to conclusively evaluate the American performance, nor are we unaware of serious violations in most other nations. Instead, we examine oppression and human rights, using the American example, mainly to show their relationship to criminal victimization and victimology. We can make no final judgments based on the general, critical view we provide here. It should suggest only that we cannot necessarily assume the legitimacy of state actions, including its definition and treatment of victims.

Also, rather than introducing oppression and human rights as a subject "separate" from victimology, this chapter suggests the richness, advantages, and imperative of practicing a broader "victimology of human rights." We cannot develop a full theory of that new victimology here, but instead will only suggest its possible directions.

3. Beniamin Mendelsohn, "Victimology and Contemporary Society's Trends," in Emilio Viano (ed.), *Victims and Society* (Washington, D.C.: Visage Press, 1976), 7.

4. Walter Lacquer and Barry Rubin (eds.), *The Human Rights Reader* (New York: New American Library, 1979), 59.

5. *Ibid.,* 75, 85.

6. Kenneth Minogue, "The History of the Idea of Human Rights," in Lacquer and Rubin, note 4 *supra,* 11.

7. Richard B. Lillich and Frank C. Newman, *International Human Rights* (Boston: Little, Brown, 1979), 1.

8. *Ibid,* 4.

9. Kurt Weis and Sandra Weis, "Victimology and the Justification of Rape," in Israel Drapkin and Emilio Viano (eds.), *Victimology: Exploiters and the Exploited* (Lexington, Mass.: Lexington Books, 1974), 3.

10. Lillich and Newman, note 7 *supra,* 11.

11. Richard A. Falk, "Ideological Patterns in the United States Human Rights Debate: 1945–1978," in Natalie Kaufman Hevener (ed.), *The Dynamics of Human Rights in U.S. Foreign Policy* (New Brunswick, N.J.: Transaction Books, 1981), 29.

12. Robert Drinan, "Human Rights and the Reagan Administration," *America*, March 5, 1983, 165.

13. Bruno Bitker, "The United States and International Codification of Human Rights: A Case of Split Personality," in Hevener, note 11 *supra*, 77.

14. Richard Falk, "The Algiers Declaration of the Rights of People and the Struggle for Human Rights," in Richard Falk, *Human Rights and State Sovereignty* (New York: Holmes and Meier, 1981), 185.

15. Official restrictions on sending foreign aid to repressive allies hardly stops them from receiving assistance. The legislation itself has many loopholes: It might prevent military aid, yet continue economic aid, with no way of preventing it from being used for military purposes. Aid will also still go to repressive regimes if they claim they must handle an emergency. The legislation also relies on State Department reports about violations that consistently, and sometimes grossly, understate oppression. In those few cases where some aid has been cut off, the United States promotes other sources, including aid from the World Bank, from our allies (often indirectly from us), and from our multinational banks and corporations. Some wonder whether a nation might not receive *more* aid with a poor human rights record than with a good one, given past experience. See, for example, Isabel Letelier and Michael Moffitt, "How American Banks Keep the Chilean Junta Going," in Mark Green and Robert Massie, *The Big Business Reader: Essays on Corporate America* (New York: Pilgrim Press, 1980), 413.

16. Leonard Levy, *Against the Law* (New York: Harper, 1976).

17. Alice Walker, *The Color Purple* (New York: Harcourt Brace Jovanovich, 1982).

18. E. L. Doctorow, *The Book of Daniel* (New York: Bantam, 1979).

19. Manlio Argueta, *One Day of Life* (New York: Vintage, 1983).

20. James Baldwin, *Nobody Knows My Name* (Garden City, N.Y.: Doubleday, 1961).

21. Marge Piercy, *Woman on the Edge of Time* (New York: Fawcett, 1981).

22. Eduardo Galeano, *Days and Nights of Love and War* (New York: Monthly Review Press, 1983).

23. Gabriel Garcia Marquez, *One Hundred Years of Solitude* (New York: Avon, 1970).

24. Ariel Dorfman, *Widows* (New York: Pantheon, 1983).

25. Jay Cantor, *The Death of Che Guevara* (New York: Vintage, 1977).

26. Carlos Fuentes, *The Death of Artemio Cruz* (New York: Farrar and Straus, 1964).

27. Carolyn Forche, "The Colonel," in Carolyn Forche, *The Country Between Us* (New York: Harper and Row, 1981), 16.

28. Michael Parenti, *Democracy for the Few* (New York: St. Martins Press, 1983); Edward S. Greenberg, *Serving the Few: Corporate Capitalism and the Bias of Government Policy* (New York: John Wiley, 1974).

29. Cosmas Desmond, *Persecution East and West* (New York: Penguin, 1983).

30. Milton Mayer, "The Trouble with the ACLU," *The Progressive* (February 1980), 48; Minogue, note 6 *supra*; Micahel J. Kennedy, "The Civilliberties Lie," in Robert Lefcourt (ed.), *Law Against the People* (New York: Vintage, 1971), 140.

31. Stuart A. Scheingold, *The Politics of Rights* (New Haven: Yale University Press, 1974).

32. John Salzberg, "Monitoring Human Rights Information: How Good Is the Information?" in Peter G. Brown and Douglas MacLean (eds.), *Human Rights and U.S. Foreign Policy* (Lexington, Mass.: Lexington Books, 1979), 173; Nigel S. Rodley, "Monitoring Human Rights Violations in the 1980's," Jorge I. Dominguez, et al., *Enhancing Global Human Rights* (New York: McGraw-Hill, 1979), 117.

33. See, for example, Raymond D. Gastil, *Freedom in the World* (Boston: G. K. Hall, 1983).

34. Jorge Dominguez, "Assessing Human Rights Conditions," in Dominguez, note 32 *supra*, 21.

35. Laurie S. Wiseberg and Harry M. Scoble, "Monitoring Human Rights Violations: The Role of Nongovernmental Organizations," in Donald P. Kommers and Gilburt D. Loescher (eds.), *Human Rights and American Foreign Policy* (Notre Dame, Ind.: University of Notre Dame Press, 1979), 179.

36. William Ryan, *Blaming the Victim* (New York: Vintage, 1976).

37. Weis and Weis, note 9 *supra*, 5.

38. Christian Bay, *Strategies for Political Emancipation* (Notre Dame, Ind.: University of Notre Dame Press, 1981); Bertram Gross, *Friendly Facism* (New York: M. Evans, 1980); Parenti, note 28 *supra*.

39. Noam Chomsky, "Foreign Policy and the Intelligentsia," in Noam Chomsky, *Human Rights and American Foreign Policy* (Nottingham: Spokesman Books, 1978); David Rockwell, "The Education of the Capitalist Lawyer: The Law School," in Lefcourt, note 30 *supra*, 90; Florynce Kennedy, "The Whorehouse Theory of Law," in Lefcourt, *ibid.*, 81; Richard Quinney, "Knowledge and Power," in Richard Quinney, *A Critique of Legal Order* (Boston: Little, Brown, 1974), 17; Alan Wolfe, "Public Ideological Repression," in Alan Wolfe, *The Seamy Side of Democracy: Repression in America* (New York: Longman, 1978), 131; Duncan Kennedy, *Legal Education and the Reproduction of Hierarchy* (Cambridge: Afar, 1983); Philip Meranto, et al. (eds.), *Guarding the Ivory Tower: Repression and Rebellion in Higher Education* (Denver: Lucha Pub., 1985).

40. Noam Chomsky and Edward Herman, *The Washington Connection and Third World Facism* (Boston: South End Press, 1979).

41. Frank Brodhead and Edward Herman, *Demonstration Elections: U.S. Staged Elections in the Dominican Republic, Vietnam and El Salvador* (Boston: South End Press, 1984).

42. Edward Herman, *The Real Terror Network: Terrorism in Fact and Propaganda* (Boston: South End Press, 1982).

43. For the most general treatments, see Robert Justin Goldstein, *Political Repression in Modern America* (Cambridge: Schenkman, 1978); William Ryan, *Equality* (New York: Vintage, 1981); Wolfe, note 39 *supra;* Howard Zinn, *A People's History of the United States* (New York: Harper and Row, 1980); Claude M. Lightfoot, *Human Rights U.S. Style* (New York: International Publishers, 1977); Parenti, note 28 *supra;* Greenberg, note 28 *supra;* Susanne Gowan, et al., *Moving Toward a New Society* (Philadelphia: New Society Press, 1976); Chomsky and Herman, note 40 *supra;* Jeffrey Reiman, *The Rich Get Richer and the Poor Get Prison: Class, Ideology and Criminal Justice* (New York: John Wiley, 1979); Bay, note 38 *supra;* Gross, note 38 *supra;* Ralph Miliband, *The State in Capitalist Society* (New York: Harper and Row, 1969); Holly Sklar, *Trilateralism* (Boston: South End Press, 1980); Penny Lernoux, *Cry of the People* (Garden City, N.Y.: Doubleday, 1980); Frances Moore Lappe and Joseph Collins, *Aid as Obstacle* (San Francisco: Institute for Food and Development Policy, 1982); Gerald Mische and Patricia Mische, *Toward A Human World Order* (New York: Paulist Press, 1983).

44. Leslie W. Dunbar (ed.), *Minority Report: What Has Happened to Blacks, Hispanics, American Indians and Other Minorities in the 1980's* (New York: Pantheon, 1984).

45. Nadine Taub and Elizabeth Schneider, "Perspectives on Women's Subordination and the Role of Law," in David Kairys (ed.), *The Politics of Law: A Progressive Critique* (New York: Pantheon, 1982), 117; Angela Davis, "The Myth of the Black Rapist," *Women, Race and Class* (New York: Vintage, 1981), 172; Jacqueline Dowd Hall, "The Mind That Burns Each Body: Women, Rape and Racial Violence," in Ann Snitow, et al. (eds.), *Powers of Desire: The Politics of Sexuality* (New York: Monthly Review Press, 1983), 183. Rand E. Rosenblatt, "Legal Entitlement and Welfare Benefits," in Kairys, *ibid.,* 262; W. Haywood Burns, "Race Discrimination Law and Race in America," in Kairys, *ibid.,* 89; Karl E. Klare, "Critical Theory and Labor Relations Law," in Kairys, *ibid.,* 65; Alan D. Freeman, "Antidiscrimination Law: A Critical Review," in Kairys, *ibid.,* 9; William J. Chambliss and Robert B. Seidman, "Prosecution: Law, Order and Power," in Richard Quinney (ed.), *Criminal Justice in America: A Critical Understanding* (Boston: Little, Brown, 1974), 235; Stanley Aronowitz, "Law, the Breakdown of Order, and Revolution," in Quinney, *ibid.,* 394; Robert Lefcourt, "Law Against the People," in Quinney, *ibid.,* 253; Jeff Gerth, "The Americanization of 1984," in Quinney, *ibid.,* 213; Harvey A. Silvergate, "The 1970's: A Decade of Repression?" in Quinney, *ibid.,* 127; Alan Wolfe, "Political Repression and the Liberal Democratic State," in Quinney, *ibid.,* 49; Haywood Burns, "Racism and American Law," in Quinney, *ibid.,* 263; Goldstein, note 43 *supra;* Kenneth Cloke, "The Economic Basis of Law and State," in Lefcourt, note 30 *supra,* 65; Ann Garfinkle, et al., "Women's Servitude Under Law," in Lefcourt, *ibid.,* 105; Robert Lefcourt, "Lawyers for the Poor Can't Win," in Lefcourt, note 30 *supra.,* 123; Jacqueline Sherer and Gary Shepard (ed.), *Victimization of the Weak: Contemporary Social Reactions* (Springfield, Ill.: Charles C Thomas, 1982); Barry Krisberg, *Crime and Privilege* (Englewood Cliffs, N.J.: Prentice-Hall, 1975); Gregg Barak, *In Defense of Whom? A Critique of Criminal Justice Reform* (Cincinnati: Anderson, 1980); Erik Olin Wright, *The Politics of Punishment* (New York: Harper and Row, 1973); Isaac D. Balbus, *The Dialectics of Legal Repres-*

sion (New Brunswick, N.J.: Transaction Books, 1973); American Friends Service Committee, *Struggle for Justice* (New York: Hill and Wang, 1971); Ian Taylor, et al., *Critical Criminology* (Boston: Routledge and Kegan Paul, 1975); Ian Taylor, et al., *The New Criminology* (New York: Harper and Row, 1973); Pat Carlen and Mike Collison (eds.), *Radical Issues in Criminology* (Totowa, N.J.: Barnes and Noble, 1980); Isidore Silver (ed.), *The Crime-Control Establishment* (Englewood Cliffs, N.J.: Prentice-Hall, 1974); Edwin M. Schur, *Our Criminal Society: The Social and Legal Sources of Crime in America* (Englewood Cliffs, N.J.: Prentice Hall, 1969); Jane Roberts Chapman and Margaret Gates (eds.), *The Victimization of Women* (Beverly Hills, Calif.: Sage, 1978); Julia R. Schwendinger and Herman Schwendinger, *Rape and Inequality* (Beverly Hills, Calif.: Sage, 1983); Institute for the Study of Labor and Economic Crisis, *The Iron Fist and the Velvet Glove: An Analysis of U.S. Police* (San Francisco: Crime and Justice Associates, 1982); Karen DeCrow, *Sexist Justice* (New York: Vintage, 1974); Frank Pearce, *Crimes of the Powerful* (London: Pluto Press, 1976); Lennox S. Hinds, *Illusions of Justice: Human Rights Violations in the United States* (Iowa City: University of Iowa, 1978); James A. Inciardi, *Radical Criminology* (Beverly Hills, Calif.: Sage, 1980); James P. Brady, "Towards A Popular Justice in the U.S.: The Dialectics of Community Action," *Contemporary Crises*, 5(1981), 155; David S. Davis, "The Production of Crime Policies," *Crime and Social Justice* (1984), 121; William J. Chambliss, "Toward A Political Economy of Crime," *Theory and Society* 2(1975), 149; David M. Gordon, "Capitalism, Class and Crime in America," *Crime and Delinquency* (April 1973), 163; Joseph Scimecca, "The Implications of the Sociology of C. Wright Mills for Modern Criminology," *International Journal of Criminology and Penology*, 3(1975), 145; Gary T. Marx, "Social Control and Victimization," *Victimology*, 8(1983), 80; Herman Schwendinger and Julia Schwendinger, "Defenders of Order or Guardians of Human Rights?" in Taylor, *ibid.*, 113; John R. Hepburn, "Social Control and the Legal Order: Legitimated Repression in a Capitalist State," *Contemporary Crises*, 1(1977), 77; Richard Quinney, "Who Is the Victim?" *Criminology*, 10(1972), 314; William J. Chambliss and Milton Mankoff (eds.), *Whose Law? What Order?* (New York: John Wiley, 1976); David F. Greenberg, *Crime and Capitalism* (Palo Alto, Calif.: Mayfield, 1981); William Chambliss and Robert Seidman, *Law, Order and Power* (Reading, Mass.: Addison Wesley, 1971); Raymond Michalowski and Edward Bohlander, "Repression and Criminal Justice in Capitalist America," *Sociological Inquiry*, 46(1982), 95; Tony Platt and Paul Takagi (eds.), *Crime and Social Justice* (Totowa, N.J.: Barnes and Noble, 1981); Stewart Hall, et al., *Policing the Crisis: Mugging, the State, and Law and Order* (London: Macmillan, 1978); Jack D. Douglas (ed.), *Crime and Justice in American Society* (Indianapolis, Ind.: Bobbs Merrill, 1971); John Braithwaite, *Inequality, Crime and Public Policy* (London: Routledge and Kegan Paul, 1979); Howard Zinn, *Justice?* (Boston: Beacon Press, 1976); Norman Dorsen, *Our Endangered Rights* (New York: Pantheon, 1984).

46. Theodore Becker and Vernon G. Murray (eds.), *Government Lawlessness in America* (New York: Oxford University Press, 1971); Jack D. Douglas and John M. Johnson (eds.), *Official Deviance* (New York: J.B. Lippincott, 1977); Julian Roebuck and Stanley C. Weeber, *Political Crime in the United States* (New York: Praeger, 1979; Paul Chevigny, "Police Power," in Quinney, note 45 *supra,* 200; Jethro Lieberman, *How the Government Breaks the Law* (Baltimore: Penguin, 1973); Jonathan Caspar, *Politics of Civil Liberties* (New York: Harper and Row, 1970).

47. David Wise, *The American Police State* (New York: Random House, 1976); David Wise, *The Politics of Lying: Government Deception, Secrecy and Power* (New York: Vintage, 1973); Frank J. Donner, *The Age of Surveillance: The Aims and Methods of America's Political Intelligence System* (New York: Vintage, 1980); American Friends Service Committee, *The Police Threat to Political Liberty* (Philadelphia: Author, 1979); Nelson Blackstock, *COINTEL-PRO: The FBI's Secret War on Political Freedom* (New York: Vintage, 1975); Thomas Emerson, *The System of Freedom of Expression* (New York: Vintage, 1970); Chomsky and Herman, note 40 *supra;* Herman, note 42 *supra;* Richard Quinney, *Class, State and Crime* (New York: Longman, 1980); Goldstein, note 43 *supra;* Wolfe, note 39 *supra;* Gross, note 38 *supra;* Miliband, note 43 *supra;* Roebuck and Weeber, note 46 *supra;* Reiman, note 43 *supra;* Morton Halperin, et al., *The Lawless State: The Crisis of the U.S. Intelligence Agencies* (New York: Penguin, 1976); Richard Criley, "The Cult of the Informer Revisited: Antiterrorism Policy in the U.S.," *Crime and Social Justice* (1984), 183; James Bamford, *The Puzzle Palace: Inside the National Security Agency, America's Most Secret Intelligence Organization* (New York: Penguin, 1983); Rona Fields, "Research on Victims," in Susan Salasin (ed.), *Evaluating Victim Services* (Beverly Hills, Calif.: Sage, 1981), 56; Mark Tushnet, "Corporations and Free Speech," in Kairys, note 45 *supra,* 253; David Kairys, "Freedom of Speech," in Kairys, *ibid.,* 140; Gilbert Geis, "The NAM in the Schools," in Gilbert Geis, *On White Collar Crime* (Lexington, Mass.: Lexington Books, 1982); Martin Shapiro, *Freedom of Speech* (Berkeley: University of California Press, 1971).

48. Schwendinger and Schwendinger, note 45 *supra;* Jeffrey Schrank, *Snap, Crackle and Popular Culture: The Illusion of Free Choice in America* (New York: Dell, 1977).

49. Levy, note 16 *supra;* Israel Drapkin and Emilio Viano, "Institutional Victimization," in Drapkin and Viano, note 9 *supra,* 133; Balbus, note 45 *supra;* Quinney, note 39 *supra;* Krisberg, note 45 *supra;* Wright, note 45 *supra;* American Friends Service Committee, note 47 *supra;* Zinn, note 45 *supra;* Marvin Frankel, *Criminal Sentences* (New York: Hill and Wang, 1972); Patricia Francis, "Offense Record as a Determinant of Victim-Victimizer Status Within Institutions for Youth," in Viano, note 3 *supra,* 579; Israel Drapkin, "The Prison Inmate as Victim," in Viano, note 3 *supra,* 560; Walter J. Moretz, "Separating the Sheep from the Goats: Reserving Prison for Those Who Really Need It," Paper presented at First World Congress on Victimology, Washington, D.C., 1980; G. K. Harris, "Anomalous Jurisdiction: Pre-Indictment Relief for Victims of Unlawful Searches and Seizures," *Columbia Law Review,* 80(1980), 597. John Tomlin, "DWI Defendants: Victims and Beneficiaries of a Court System," Paper presented at First World Congress on Victimology, Washington, D.C., 1980.

50. Stephen Schafer, *The Political Criminal* (New York: Free Press, 1974); Theodore Becker (ed.), *Political Trials* (Indianapolis, Ind.: Bobbs Merrill, 1971); Arthur Dobrin, et al., *Convictions: Political Prisoners, Their Stories* (Maryknoll, NY: Orbis, 1981); Austin Turk, *Political Criminality* (Beverly Hills, Calif.: Sage,

1982); Edward Sagarin and Robert Kelly, "The Brewster Effect: Political Trials and the Self-Defeating Prophesy," in Sawyer Sylvester and Edward Sagarin (eds.), *Politics and Crime* (New York: Praeger, 1973), 98; Roebuck and Weeber, note 46 *supra;* Goldstein, note 43 *supra;* David Sternberg, "The New Radical-Criminal Trials," in Quinney, note 45 *supra,* 274; Ward Sinclair and John Jacobs, "Are These America's Political Prisoners?" *The Washington Post,* January 8, 1978, 71; John Webster, "The Government as Terrorist and Torturer: The Citizen as Victim," Paper presented at Second International Symposium on Victimology, Boston, 1976; Mary Timothy, *Jury Woman: The Story of the Trial of Angela Davis* (San Francisco: Glade Pub., 1975); Eric Mann, *Comrade George* (New York: Harper and Row, 1974); Jessica Mitford, *The Trial of Dr. Spock* (New York: Alfred Knopf, 1969); Jim Messerschmidt, *The Trial of Leonard Peltier* (Boston: South End Press, 1983).

51. Charles Silberman, *Criminal Violence, Criminal Justice* (New York: Vintage, 1978); Roebuck and Weeber, note 46 *supra;* Dave O'Brien, "Private Courage," *The Boston Phoenix,* August 27, 1985, 1; J. Slater, "Condemned to Die for Science: The Tuskegee Study," *Ebony* (November 1972); "Convicts as Guinea Pigs," *Time,* March 19, 1973; "Experiments Behind Bars: Doctors, Drug Companies and Prisoners," *Atlantic* (May 1973); Carl Rogers, "Clockwork Orange in California," *Christian Century,* October 31, 1973; "Sterilization: Newest Threat to Poor," *Ebony* (October 1973); Richard Babcock, "Sterilization: Coercing Consent," *The Nation,* January 12, 1974; Richard Rubinstein, *The Cunning of History: The Holocaust and the American Future* (New York: Harper and Row, 1975), 53; Albert Reiss, *The Police and the Public* (New Haven: Yale University Press, 1971), 142; Paul Takagi, "LEAA's Research Solicitation: Police Use of Deadly Force," *Crime and Social Justice* (Spring/Summer 1979), 51; William Waegel, "The Use of Lethal Force by Police: The Effect of Statutory Change," *Crime and Delinquency* (January 1984), 121; Diana Gordon, "Equal Protection, Unequal Justice," in Dunbar, note 44 *supra,* 118; Thomas Szasz, *The Manufacture of Madness* (New York: Harper and Row, 1970); Jessica Mitford, *Kind and Usual Punishment* (New York: Alfred Knopf, 1973); Karl Menninger, *The Crime of Punishment* (New York: Viking Press, 1968).

52. Hugh Davis Graham and Ted Robert Gurr, *Violence in America* (New York: New American Library, 1969); Wolfe, note 39 *supra;* Roebuck and Weeber, note 46 *supra;* Chevigny, note 46 *supra;* American Friends Service Committee, note 45 *supra;* Quinney, note 39 *supra;* Goldstein, note 43 *supra;* Institute for the Study of Labor and Economic Crisis, note 45 *supra;* Zinn, note 45 *supra;* Marx, note 45 *supra;* Jennifer James, "The Prostitute as Victim," in Chapman and Gates, note 45 *supra,* 175; M. A. Jennings, "The Victim as Criminal: A Consideration of California's Prostitution Law," *California Law Review,* 64(1976), 1235; Edward Sagarin and Donal E. J. MacNamara, "The Homosexual as a Crime Victim," in Drapkin and Viano, note 9 *supra,* 73; Donal MacNamara and Andrew Karmen, *Deviants: Victims or Victimizers?* (Beverly Hills, Calif.: Sage, 1983); Frank Donner, *Legacy of Haymarket: Police Repression in America* (New York: Vintage, 1985); Malcolm Bell, *The Turkey Shoot: Tracking the Attica Coverup* (New York: Grove Press, 1985).

53. Rodney Stark, *Police Riots* (Belmont, Calif.: Wadsworth, 1972); Graham and Gurr, *ibid.*

54. Zinn, note 45 supra; Dee Brown, *Bury My Heart at Wounded Knee* (New York: Bantam, 1972); Dick Gregory, *Nigger* (New York: Pocket Books, 1964); Dick Gregory, *No More Lies: Myth and Reality of American History* (New York: Harper and Row, 1971); DeLoria, note 19 *supra;* Steve Talbot, *Roots of Oppression: The American Indian Quest* (New York: International Publishers, 1982); Roland Taylor, *Cesar Chavez and The Farmworkers* (Boston: Beacon Press, 1976); Rex Weyler, *Blood of the Land: The Government and Corporate War Against the American Indian Movement* (New York: Vintage, 1983); Ward Churchill, ed., *Marxism and Native Americans* (Boston: South End Press, 1984).

55. Hugo Bedau, "Human Rights and Foreign Assistance Programs," in Brown and MacLean, note 32 *supra,* 29.

56. Richard Estes, *The Social Progress of Nations* (New York: Praeger, 1985).

57. Richard Falk, *This Endangered Planet* (New York: Vintage, 1972); Maurice Goldsmith, "The Thalidomide Affair," in Israel Drapkin and Emilio Viano (eds.), *Victimology* (Lexington, Mass.: Lexington Books, 1974), 205; Gilbert Geis and Thomas Clay, "Criminal Enforcement of California's Occupational Carcinogens Control Act," in Geis, note 47 *supra,* 103; Neal Shover, "The Criminalization of Corporate Behavior: Federal Surface Coal Mining," in Gilbert Geis and Ezra Shotland (eds.), *White Collar Crime* (Beverly Hills, Calif.: Sage, 1980), 98; Reiman, note 43 *supra;* Greenberg, note 28 *supra;* Roebuck and Weeber, note 46 *supra;* Gowan, note 43 *supra;* Green and Massie, note 15; Andrew Baum, "Coping with Victimization by Technological Disaster," *Journal of Social Issues,* 39(1983), 117; Z. Separovic, "The Victim and Society: Some New Problems Posed by the Advancement of Medicine," *Rev. Kriminalist. Kriminol.,* 27(1976), 235; Morton Mintz, "At Any Cost: Corporate Greed, Women and the Dalkon Shield," *The Progressive* (November 1985), 20; Sarah Ben-David, "Victimization by Medicine" Paper presented at Fifth International Symposium on Victimology, Zagreb, 1985; Rozsa Halasi, "Risks Due to Chemicals and Decision-Making in Science and Society" Paper presented at Fifth International Symposium on Victimology, Zagreb, 1985; Ana Rojnik-Lovrin, "The Noxious Medical Arrangement: Electro-Convulsive Therapy on Psychiatric Patients" Paper presented at Fifth International Symposium on Victimology, Zagreb, 1985; Otto Triffterer, "Victimological Aspects of Environmental Criminal Law" Paper presented at Fifth International Symposium on Victimology, Zagreb, 1985.

58. Richard Parker, *The Myth of the Middle Class* (New York: Harper and Row, 1972); Joshua Cohen and Joel Rogers, *On Democracy* (New York: Penguin, 1983); Bob Howard and John Logue (eds.), *American Class Society in Numbers* (Kent, Ohio: Kent Popular Press, 1981).

59. Chester Hartman (ed.), *America's Housing Crisis* (Boston: Routledge and Kegan Paul, 1983); Physicians' Taskforce, *Hunger in America: The Growing Epidemic* (Middletown, Conn.: Wesleyan University Press, 1985); David Gil and Eva Gil (eds.), *Toward Social and Economic Justice* (Cambridge: Schenkman, 1985); "Poverty Amidst Affluence: The Poor Get Poorer," *The Boston Globe Magazine,* December 15, 1985, 12; Lee Rainwater (ed.), *Social Problems and Public Policy: Inequality and Justice* (Chicago: Aldine, 1976); Green and Massie, note 15; Roebuck and Weeber, note 46 *supra;* Barrington Moore, *Reflections on the Causes of Human Misery* (Boston: Beacon Press, 1972); Schwendinger and Schwendinger, note 43 *supra.*

60. R. L. McNeely and Carl E. Pope (eds.), *Race, Crime and Criminal Justice* (Beverly Hills, Calif.: Sage, 1981); Gregory, note 54 *supra;* Manning Marable, *From the Grassroots* (Boston: South End Press, 1980); Manning Marable, *How Capitalism Underdeveloped Black America* (Boston: South End Press, 1983); Claude Brown, *Manchild in the Promised Land;* Hinds, note 43 *supra;* Ryan, note 36 *supra;* Lightfoot, note 43 *supra;* Brown, note 54 *supra* Zinn, note 43 *supra;* Parenti, note 28 *supra;* Emilio Viano, "Victimization of the Immigrant," Paper presented at Second International Symposium on Victimology, Lisbon, 1976; Kurt Weis and Sandra Borges, "Rape as a Crime Without Victims and Offenders? A Methodological Critique," in Viano, note 3 *supra;* Schwendinger and Schwendinger, note 45 *supra;* Bernard D. Headley, "Black-on-Black Crime: The Myth and the Reality," *Crime and Social Justice* (1983), 50; Robert A. Evans and Alice Frazer Evans, *Human Rights* (Maryknoll, N.Y.: Orbis, 1983); Elise Boulding, "Women and Social Violence," *Social Science Journal,* 30(1978), 801; Katherine Saltzman, "Women and Victimization" in Chapman and Gates, note 43 *supra,* 269; Jane Roberts Chapman, "The Economics of Sexual Harassment: Women's Victimization," in Chapman and Gates, note 43 *supra,* 251; Laura Evans, "Sexual Harassment: Women's Hidden Occupational Hazard," in Chapman and Gates, note 43 *supra,* 203; Julia Graham Lear, "Women's Health: The Side Effects of Sex Bias," in Chapman and Gates, note 43 *supra,* 225; Michael Garrity, "The U.S. Colonial Empire is as Close as the Nearest Reservation," in Holly Sklar (ed.), *Trilateralism* (Boston: South End Press, 1980), 238; DeLoria, note 19 *supra;* Seymour Leventman, "The Victimization of Vietnam Veterans in American Society," Paper presented at Second International Symposium on Victimology, Boston, 1976; Susan Salasin, "Services to Victims: Needs Assessment," in Salasin, note 47 *supra,* 21; Claude Brown, *Manchild in the Promised Land* (New York: New American Library, 1971); DeWitt Dykes, "American Blacks as Perpetual Victims," in Jacqueline Scherer and Gary Shepard (eds.), *Victimization of the Weak* (Springfield, Ill.: Charles C Thomas, 1983); Karen Stallard, et al., *Poverty in the American Dream* (Boston: South End Press, 1983); Angela Davis, *Women, Race and Class* (New York: Vintage, 1981).

61. Peter B. Meyer, "Communities as Victims of Corporate Crimes," in Burt Galaway and Joe Hudson (eds.), *Perspectives on Crime Victims* (St. Louis: Mosby, 1981), 33; Bay, note 38 *supra;* Green, note 43 *supra;* David Hapgood, *The Screwing of the Average Man* (New York: Bantam Books, 1974); Ronald Kramer, "Corporate Crime: An Organizational Perspective," in Peter Wickham and Timothy Dailey (eds.), *White Collar and Economic Crime* (Lexington, Mass.: Lexington Books, 1982), 75; Greenberg, note 28 *supra;* Parenti, note 28 *supra;* Leon Sheleff, "International White Collar Crime," in Wickham and Dailey, *ibid,* 39; Knowlton Johnson, "Consumer Protection: Responsiveness of Consumer Agents to Victims of Fraud," *Victimology,* 5(1980), 225; Reiman, note 43 *supra;* Roebuck and Weeber, note 46 *supra;* Ryan, note 36 *supra;* Gowan, note 43 *supra;* Gross, note 38 *supra;* Reiman, note 43 *supra;* Quinney, note 47 *supra;* Diane Vaughan and Giovanna Carlo, "Victims of Fraud: Victim Responsiveness, Incidence and Reporting," in Viano, note 3 *supra;* Diane Vaughan, "Crime Between Organizations: Implications for

Victimology," in Geis and Shotland, note 57 *supra*, 77; Peter Schrag, *Councel for the Deceived* (New York: Pantheon, 1976).

62. Robert Johansen, *The National Interest and the Human Interest* (Princeton: Princeton University Press, 1980); Michael T. Klare and Cynthia Arnson, *Supplying Repression* (Washington, D.C.: Institute for Policy Studies, 1981); Chomsky and Herman, note 40 *supra;* Herman, note 42 *supra;* Alan Wolfe, "Exporting Repression," in Wolfe, note 39 *supra*, 148; L. L. Cripps, *Human Rights in a United States Colony* (Cambridge: Schenkman, 1982); Halperin, note 47 *supra;* Amnesty International, *Political Killings by Governments* (London: Author, 1983); Amnesty International, *Torture in the 1980's* (London: Amnesty International, 1984); Sandy Vogelgesang, *American Dream, Global Nightmare* (New York: Norton, 1980); Central America Information Office, *El Salvador: Background to the Crisis* (Cambridge: Author, 1982); Lars Schoultz, *Human Rights and U.S. Policy toward Latin America* (Princeton: Princeton University Press, 1981); World Council of Churches, *Militarism and Human Rights* (Geneva: Author, 1982); World Council of Churches, *El Salvador: One Year of Repression* (Geneva: World Council of Churches, 1981); Martin Weinstein, "The United States, the Organization of American States, and Political Repression in the Western Hemisphere," in Hevener, note 11 *supra*, 215; Marcus Raskin and Ann Wilcox, "The United States, International War, and the Preservation of Human Rights: The Control of Arms," in Hevener, note 11 *supra*, 135; Jan Frappier, "Above the Law: Violations of International Law by the U.S. Government from Truman to Reagan," *Crime and Social Justice* (1984), 1; Francis A. Boyle, "International Lawlessness in the Caribbean Basin," *Crime and Social Justice* (1984), 37; Mische and Mische, note 43 *supra;* Lernoux, note 43 *supra;* Gowan, note 43 *supra;* Desmond, note 29 *supra;* Gross, note 38 *supra;* Jerome A. Cohen, "Arms Sales and Human Rights: The Case of South Korea," in Brown and MacLean, note 32 *supra*, 255; Richard W. Cottam, "Arms Sales and Human Rights: The Case of Iran," in Brown and MacLean, note 32 *supra*, 281; Richard P. Claude, "Human Rights in the Philippines and U.S. Responsibility," in Brown and MacLean, note 32 *supra*, 229; Jenny Pearce, *Under the Eagle* (Boston: South End Press, 1982); Mansour Farhang, *U.S. Imperialism* (Boston: South End Press, 1982); Institute for the Study of Labor and Economic Crisis, note 43 *supra;* Martin Diskin (ed.), *Trouble in Our Backyard* (New York: Pantheon, 1984); Yoshikazu Sakamoto and Richard Falk, "World Demilitarized: A Basic Human Need," *Alternatives*, 5(1980), 1; Philip Alston, "Peace as a Human Right," *Bulletin of Peace Proposals*, 12(1981), 319; Bruce Russett, "Disarmament, Human Rights and Basic Human Needs," *Bulletin of Peace Proposals*, 10(1979), 275; Jan Knippers Black, "Brazil: Myths and Realities on Human Rights and Wrongs," in Peter Schwab and Adamantia Pollis (eds.), *Toward A Human Rights Framework* (New York: Praeger, 1982), 71; Kenneth E. Payne, "Human Rights, Genocide and Ethnocide: The Case of the Philippines' National Minorities," in Schwab and Pollis, *ibid.*, 151; Cynthia Brown, ed., *With Friends Like These: The America's Watch Report on Human Rights and U.S. Policy in Latin America* (New York: Pantheon, 1985); Noam Chomsky, *Turning the Tide* (Boston: South End Press, 1985); Roger Burbach and Patricia Flynn (eds.), *The Politics of Intervention: The U.S. in Central America*

(New York: Monthly Review Press, 1984); Marlene Dixon (ed.), *On Trial: Reagan's War Against Nicaragua* (San Francisco: Synthesis Pub., 1985); Reed Brody, *Contra Terror in Nicaragua* (Boston, South End Press, 1985).

63. Fouad Ajami, *Human Rights and World Order Politics* (New York: World Policy Institute, 1978); Joseph Elder, "Social Justice and Political Equality: Land Tenure Policies and Rural Development in South Asia," in Paula Newberg (ed.), *The Politics of Human Rights* (New York: New York University Press, 1980); Sidney Weintraub, "Human Rights and Basic Needs in U.S. Foreign Aid Policy," in Newberg, *ibid.*, 217; Peter Weiss, "The United States and Recognition of New Human Rights," in Hevener, note 11 *supra,* 123; Bay, note 38 *supra;* Henry Shue, *Basic Rights* (Princeton: Princeton University Press, 1980); Teresa Hayter, *The Creation of World Poverty* (London: Pluto Press, 1981); Richard Barnet and Ronald Muller, *Global Reach* (New York: Simon and Schuster, 1974); Charles Beitz, *Political Theory and International Relations* (Princeton: Princeton University Press, 1979); Charlotte Waterlow, *Superpowers and Victims* (Englewood Cliffs, N.J.: Prentice-Hall, 1974); Richard Falk, *A Study of Future Worlds* (New York: Free Press, 1975); Richard Falk and Samuel Kim, *An Approach to World Order Studies and the World System* (New York: Institute for World Order, 1982); Elias Carranza, "Development and Victimization" Paper presented at Fifth International Symposium on Victimology, Zagreb, 1985.

64. Richard Barnet, "Human Rights Implications of Corporate Food Policies," in Newberg, note 63 *supra,* 143; Roger Burbach and Patricia Flynn, *Agribusiness in the Americas* (New York: Monthly Review Press, 1980); Cheryl Christenson, *The Right to Food: How to Guarantee* (New York: World Policy Institute, 1978); Susan George, *How the Other Half Dies* (Montclair, N.J.: Allenheld and Osmun, 1977); Susan George, *Feeding the Few: Corporate Control of Food* (Washington, D.C.: Institute for Policy Studies, 1979); Arthur Simon, *Bread for the World* (New York: Paulist Press, 1975); Jack Nelson, *Hunger for Justice* (Maryknoll, NY: Orbis Books, 1980); James McGinnis, *Bread and Justice* (New York: Paulist Press, 1979; Frances Moore Lappe and Joseph Collins, *World Hunger: Ten Myths* (San Francisco: Institute for Food and Development Policy, 1979).

65. Richard Fagen (ed.), *Capitalism and the State in U.S.-Latin American Relations* (Stanford: Stanford University Press, 1979); Barnet and Muller, note 63 *supra;* Alexandro Portes, "Why Illegal Migration: A Human Rights Perspective," in Abdul Said (ed.), *Human Rights* (New York: Praeger, 1980), 79.

66. John Bodley, *Victims of Progress* (Palo Alto, Calif.: Mayfield, 1982); Shelton Davis, *Victims of the Miracle* (Cambridge: Cambridge University Press, 1977); Gowan, note 43 supra; Fagen, note 65 *supra;* Norman Girvan, *Corporate Imperialism* (New York: Monthly Review Press, 1976); Rajni Kothari, *Footsteps into the Future* (New York: Free Press, 1974); Richard Falk, note 57 *supra;* Sklar, note 60 *supra.*

67. Maurice Odle, *Multinational Banks and Underdevelopment* (New York: Pergamon, 1981); Michael Moffitt, *The World's Money* (New York: Touchstone Books, 1983); Gowan, note 43 *supra;* McGinnis, note 64 *supra;* Penny Lernoux, *In Banks We Trust* (Garden City, NY: Doubleday, 1984); Martin

Honeywell, *The Power Brokers: The IMF and Latin America* (London: Latin American Bureau, 1983); Cynthia Payer, *The Debt Trap* (New York: Monthly Review Press, 1984).

68. Robert G. Wirsing, "The United States and the International Protection of Minorities," in Hevener, note 11 *supra*, 157; C. Clyde Ferguson, "The United States, the United Nations and the Struggle Against Racial Apartheid," in Hevener, note 11 *supra*, 203; Lernoux, note 43 *supra*; Lisa Leghorn and Katherine Parker, *Women's Worth* (Boston: Routledge and Kegan Paul, 1981); Diane Russell and Nicole Van den Ven, *Crimes Against Women* (Palo Alto, Calif.: Frog in the Well Pub., 1984).

69. Herbert Schiller, *Mass Communications and American Empire* (New York: Kelley, 1969); Herbert Schiller, *Communication and Cultural Domination* (White Plains, NY: M.E. Sharpe, 1976); Wolfe, note 39 *supra*; Brian Wren, *Education for Justice* (Maryknoll, N.Y.: Orbis, 1977).

70. Elliott Abrams, "Human Rights and the Reagan Administration: Another View," *America*, June 4, 1983, 433; Jeanne Kirkpatrick, "Dictatorships and Double Standards," *Commentary* (November 1979), 34.

71. Gene Sharp, *Social Power and Political Freedom* (Boston: Porter Sargent, 1980).

72. Stanley Johnston, "If You Want Peace, Prepare for Law: People as Victims of Their Own Political Bigotry," Paper presented at International Institute of Victimology, Bellagio, 1975.

73. Ryan, note 36 *supra*.

74. Kirkpatrick, note 70 *supra*.

75. Falk, note 57 *supra*; Sakamoto and Falk, note 62 *supra*.

76. Duncan Kennedy, note 39 *supra*; Florynce Kennedy, note 39 *supra*; Rockwell, note 39 *supra*; Jerold Auerbach, *Unequal Justice* (New York: Oxford University Press, 1976); Taub and Schneider, note 45 *supra*; Alan Freeman, "Legitimizing Racial Discrimination Through Antidiscrimination Law: A Critical Review of Supreme Court Doctrine," in Piers Beirne and Richard Quinney (eds.), *Marxism and Law* (New York: John Wiley, 1982), 210; Lefcourt, note 30 *supra*; Burns, note 45 *supra*; Freeman, note 45 *supra*; Rosenblatt, note 45 *supra*; DeCrow, note 43 *supra*; Rubinstein, note 51 *supra*, 27, 82.

77. Seymour Melman, *Pentagon Capitalism* (New York: McGraw-Hill, 1970).

78. Chomsky and Herman, note 40 *supra*.

79. James Petras and Morris Morley, *The United States and Chile* (New York: Monthly Review Press, 1975); Klare and Arnson, note 62 *supra*.

80. Robert Elias, "The Political Economy of Homelessness," *Society* (forthcoming 1986).

81. Elie Wiesel, *Night* (New York: Avon, 1969).

82. Jacobo Timmerman, *Prisoner Without A Name, Cell Without A Number* (New York: Vintage, 1981).

83. Richard Wright, *Black Boy* (New York: Harper and Row, 1945).

84. Carolina M. de Jesus, *Child of the Dark* (New York: New American Library, 1964).

85. Brown, note 60 *supra.*

86. Gregory, note 54 *supra.*

87. Maya Angelou, *I Know Why the Caged Bird Sings* (New York: Bantam Books, 1969).

88. Paule Marshall, *The Chosen Place, The Timeless People* (New York: Vintage, 1969).

89. Toni Morrison, *The Bluest Eye* (New York: Washington Square Press, 1970).

90. See, for example, Stanley Aronowitz, *False Promises* (New York: McGraw-Hill, 1973); Richard Sennett and Jonathan Cobb, *The Hidden Injuries of Class* (New York: Vintage, 1972); Michael Parenti, *Power and the Powerless* (New York: St. Martins Press, 1978); Studs Terkel, *Working* (New York: Avon, 1974); Herbert Gans, *More Equality* (New York: Vintage, 1973); Christopher Jencks, *Inequality* (New York: Basic Books, 1973).

91. Yael Danieli, "Countertransference in the Treatment and Study of Nazi Holocaust Survivors and Their Children," *Victimology,* 5(1980), 355; Fields, note 47 *supra,* 56; Klaus Fink, "Ambivalence of Former Victims toward Their Persecutors at the Petition for Indemnification," in Israel Drapkin and Emilio Viano (eds.), *Victimology: Crimes, Victims and Justice* (Lexington, Mass.: Lexington Books, 1974), 107; D. M. Berger, "The Survivor Syndrome: A Problem of Nosology and Treatment," *American Journal of Psychotherapy* 31(1977), 238; L. Eitinger, "Jewish Concentration Camp Survivors in Norway," *Israel Ann. Psychiat. Disc.,* 13(1975), 321; J. Segal, et al., "Universal Consequences of Captivity: Stress Reactions Among Divergent Populations of Prisoners of War and Their Families," *Evaluation and Change* (1980), 84; M. Symonds, "Acute Responses of Victims to Terror," *Evaluation and Change* (1980), 39; J. Shanon, "Psychogenic Pruritus in Concentration Camp Survivors," *Dynamic Psychiatry,* 12(1979), 232; Jack Porter, "The Impact of the Holocaust on Children and Survivors," Paper presented at Second International Symposium on Victimology, Boston, 1976; T. Radil-Weiss, "Men in Extreme Conditions," *Psychiatry,* 46(1983), 259; M. Rosenbloom, "Implications of the Holocaust for Social Work," *Social Casework,* 64(1983), 205.

92. Barrington Moore, *Injustice: The Social Bases of Obedience and Revolt* (White Plains, NY: M.E. Sharpe, 1978); Jack Porter, "Social and Psychological Obstacles to Resistance During Genocide," Paper presented at Second International Symposium on Victimology, Boston, 1976; Rubinstein, note 51 *supra,* 69; Thomas Adler and Jehudit Stern, "The Psychopathology and Psychodynamics of Youth and Children in Holocaust Survivors," in Israel Drapkin and Emilio Viano (eds.), *Victimology: Society's Reaction to Victimization* (Lexington, Mass.: Lexington Books, 1974), 69; Judith Kestenberg and Milton Kestenberg, "Psychoanalyses of Children of Survivors from the Nazi Persecution: The Continuing Struggle of Survivor Parents," 5(1980), 355; R. Krell, "Family Therapy with Children of Concentration Camp Survivors," *American Journal of Psychotherapy,* 36(1982), 513; P. A. Rosenthal and S. Rosenthal, "Holocaust Effect in the Third Generation: Child of An-

other Time," *American Journal of Psychotherapy*, 34(1980), 572; H. A. Barocas and C. B. Barocas, "Wounds of the Fathers: The Next Generation of Holocaust Victims," *International Review of Psychoanalysis*, 6(1979), 331; Erich Fromm, *Escape from Freedom* (New York: Avon, 1970); Stanley Milgram, *Obedience to Authority* (New York: Harper and Row, 1974); Jean Francois Revel, *The Totalitarian Temptation* (New York: Penguin, 1978).

93. Lillich and Newman, note 7 *supra.*

94. Telford Taylor, *Courts of Terror* (New York: Vintage, 1975).

95. A. H. Robertson, *Human Rights in Europe* (London: Heinemann, 1975).

96. John Barton, "The Likely Effects of the New American Convention on Human Rights," in Newberg, note 63 *supra*, 249.

97. David Forsythe, *Human Rights and World Politics* (Lincoln: University of Nebraska Press, 1983); Joyce, note 62 *supra.*

98. Lillich and Newman, note 7 *supra.*

99. Thomas Buergenthal, "Domestic Jurisdiction, Intervention, and Human Rights: The International Law Perspective," in Brown and MacLean, note 32 *supra*, 111; Richard Lillich, "The Contribution of the U.S. to the Promotion and Protection of International Human Rights," in Hevener, note 11 *supra*, 291.

100. Stanley Johnston, "Toward a Supra-National Criminology: The Right and Duty of Victims of National Government to Seek Defense Through World Law," in Israel Drapkin and Emilio Viano (eds.), *Victimology: Theoretical Issues* (Lexington, Mass.: Lexington Books, 1974), 37.

101. David Weissbrodt, "The Influence of Interest Groups on the Development of U.S. Human Rights Policies," in Hevener, note 11 *supra*, 229; Lernoux, note 43 *supra*; Forsythe, note 97 *supra*; Schoultz, note 62 *supra*; Ved Nanda, et al., "NGO Strategies" in *Global Human Rights* (Boulder, Colo.: Westview Press, 1981), 213; Wiseberg and Scoble, note 35 *supra.*

102. Martin Carnoy and Derek Shearer, *Economic Democracy* (White Plains, NY: M.E. Sharpe, 1980); Philip Green, *Retrieving Democracy* (Totowa, N.J.: Rowman and Allenheld, 1985); David Morris and Karl Hess, *Neighborhood Power* (Boston: Beacon Press, 1975); Harry Boyte, *The Backyard Revolution* (Philadelphia: Temple University Press, 1980); Joshua Cohen and Joel Rogers, *On Democracy* (New York: Penguin, 1983); Stephen Wineman, *The Politics of Human Services* (Boston: South End Press, 1984).

103. James Brady, "Towards a Popular Justice in the U.S.: The Dialectics of Community Action," *Contemporary Crises*, 5(1981), 155.

104. Gowan, note 43 *supra.*

105. Lester Brown, *Building a Sustainable Society* (New York: Norton, 1981).

106. Johansen, note 62 *supra*; Falk, note 63 *supra*; Barbara Wien (ed.), *Peace and World Order Studies* (New York: World Policy Institute, 1984).

107. Kothari, note 66 *supra.*

108. Denis Goulet, *Survival with Integrity* (Colombo: Marga Institute, 1981).

109. See described in Dominguez, note 34 *supra.*

110. Chadwick Alger, "Foreign Policies of U.S. Publics," *International*

Studies Quarterly, 21(1977), 277; Richard Falk, et al. (eds.), *Toward a Just World Order* (Boulder, Colo.: Westview Press, 1982); Louis Beres and Harry Targ, "Constructing Alternative World Futures," (Cambridge: Schenkman, 1977); Samuel Kim, *The Quest for a Just World Order* (Boulder, Colo.: Westview Press, 1984).

111. Erich Fromm, *To Have or To Be?* (New York: Bantam Books, 1981).

112. Johan Galtung, *The True Worlds* (New York: Free Press, 1981); Guy Gran, *Development by People* (New York: Praeger, 1983).

113. Hazel Henderson, "Citizen Movements for Greater Global Equity," *International Social Science Journal*, 28(1976), 773.

114. Bay, note 38 *supra.*

115. Lernoux, note 43 *supra;* Mische and Mische, note 43 *supra.*

116. Mische and Mische, *ibid.*

117. McGinnis, note 64 *supra.*

118. See, for example, Henri Weber, *Nicaragua: The Sandinist Revolution* (London: Verso, 1981); George Black, *Triumph of the People: The Sandinista Revolution in Nicaragua* (London: Zed Press, 1980); EPICA Task Force, *Nicaragua: A People's Revolution* (Washington, D.C.: Author, 1980); Joseph Collins, *What Difference Could A Revolution Make?* (San Francisco: Institute for Food and Development Policy, 1982).

119. Lillich and Newman, note 7 *supra*, 753.

120. Johnston, note 100 *supra.*

121. Robert Elias, "NonGovernmental Organizations and Human Rights: A Losing Battle?" (unpublished paper, 1984).

122. Schoultz, note 62 *supra.*

123. Desmond, note 29 *supra.*

124. Falk, note 14 *supra.*

125. Brady, note 103 *supra*, 185.

126. Robert Elias, "Transcending Our Social Reality of Victimization," *Victimology*, 10(1985), 1.

127. Robert Elias, "The Political Victim: Toward A Critical Victimology," (unpublished paper, 1984).

128. John Rawls, *A Theory of Justice* (Cambridge: Harvard University Press, 1971), 7.

NOTES FOR CHAPTER 9

1. Eduard Ziegenhagen, *Victims, Crime and Social Control* (New York: Praeger, 1977); Eduard Ziegenhagen, "Controlling Crime by Regulating Victim Behavior: Two Alternative Models," in Hans Joachim Schneider (ed.), *The Victim in International Perspective* (Berlin: Walter de Gruyter, 1982), 335.

2. Andrew Karmen, *Crime Victims* (Belmont, Calif.: Brooks/Cole, 1984), 221.

3. Lynn Curtis, "Victims, Policy and the Dangers of a Conservative Mentality," Paper presented at Second International Symposium on Victimology, Boston, 1976; Lynn Curtis, "The Conservative New Criminology," *Society*, 14(1977), 3; Samuel Walker, *Sense and Nonsense About Crime* (Belmont, Calif.: Brooks/Cole, 1985), 137; Elliott Currie, "Crime and the Conservatives," *Dissent* (Fall 1985), 427.

4. LeRoy Lamborn, "Toward a United Nations Declaration on Crime, Abuses of Power, and the Rights of Victims," Paper presented to the Ninth International Congress on Criminology, Vienna, 1983; LeRoy Lamborn, "The Proposed United Nations Declaration on Justice and Assistance for Victims," Paper presented at International Meeting on Criminality and Development, San Jose, 1984; LeRoy Lamborn, "Vers une Declaration des Nations Unies sur la criminalite, les abus de pouvoir et les droits des victimes," *Annales de Droit de Liege*, 2(1984), 205; Irvin Waller, "Declaration on the Protection and Assistance of Victims of Crime," Paper prepared for the Committee on the Code of Conduct for the Protection and Assistance of Victims, World Society of Victimology, 1983; "Special Issue: Towards A United Nations Declaration on Justice and Assistance for Victims," *World Society of Victimology Newsletter*, 3(1983–84), 1.

5. Emilio Viano, "Violence, Victimization and Social Change: A Socio-Cultural and Public Policy Analysis," *Victimology*, 8(1983), 54; Hans Joachim Schneider, "The Present Situation of Victimology in the World," in Schneider, note 1 *supra*, 11; Beniamin Mendelsohn, "Victimology and Contemporary Society's Trends," in Emilio Viano (ed.), *Victims and Society* (Washington, D.C.: Visage Press, 1976), 7; Zvonimir P. Separovic, "Victimology: A New Approach in the Social Sciences," in Israel Drapkin and Emilio Viano (eds.), *Victimology: Theoretical Issues* (Lexington, Mass.: Lexington Books, 1974), 15; Stanley Johnston, "Institutionalizing Criminal Justice in the Global Village," in Viano, *ibid.*; Kurt Weis and Sandra Weis, "Victimology and the Justification of Rape," in Israel Drapkin and Emilio Viano (eds.), *Victimology: Exploiters and the Exploited* (Lexington, Mass.: Lexington Books, 1975), 3.

6. Viano, *ibid.*, 59.

7. Erich Fromm, *Escape from Freedom* (New York: Avon, 1970).

8. Stuart A. Scheingold, *The Politics of Law and Order: Street Crime and Public Policy* (New York: Longman, 1984).

9. David Friedrichs, "The Problem of Reconciling Divergent Perspectives on Urban Crime: Personal Experience, Social Ideology and Scholarly Research," *Qualitative Sociology*, 4(1981), 217.

10. Quoted in Stanley Hoffman, *Duties Beyond Borders* (Syracuse: Syracuse University Press, 1980).

11. Robert Elias, "A Political Strategy for Victims," unpublished paper, 1984.

12. David Miers, "Victim Compensation as a Labelling Process," *Victimology*, 5(1980), 3.

13. Robert Elias, *Victims of the System: Crime Victims and Compensation in*

American Politics and Criminal Justice (New Brunswick, N.J.: Transaction Books, 1983).

14. Duncan Chappell, "Providing for the Victims of Crime: Political Placebos or Progressive Programs?" *Adelaide Law Review*, 4(1972), 294.

15. Frances Fox Piven and Richard O. Cloward, *Regulating the Poor: The Functions of Public Welfare* (New York: Vintage, 1971); W. G. Doerner, "The Diffusion of Victim Compensation Laws in the United States," *Victimology* 4(1979), 119; Blacks mention crime, in political polls, as one of the most serious social problems even more than whites, suggesting that programs aimed toward lower class discontent may have stressed the right target. See Diana R. Gordon, "Equal Protection, Unequal Justice," in Leslie Dunbar (ed.), *Minority Report: What Has Happened to Blacks, Hispanics, American Indians and Other Minorities in the 1980's* (New York: Pantheon, 1984), 118.

16. Elias, note 13 *supra*.

17. Viano, note 5 *supra*.

18. Martha Burt, "A Conceptual Framework for Victimological Research," *Victimology*, 8(1983), 261.

19. See, for example, Richard Abel (ed.), *The Politics of Informal Justice: The American Experience* (New York: Academic Press, 1982); Richard Abel (ed.), *The Politics of Informal Justice: Comparative Studies* (New York: Academic Press, 1982); Philip Parnell, "Community Justice versus Crime Control," in R. L. McNeely and Carl E. Pope (eds.), *Race, Crime and Criminal Justice* (Beverly Hills, Calif.: Sage, 1981), 147; Institute for the Study of Labor and Economic Crisis, *The Iron Fist and the Velvet Glove: An Analysis of U.S. Police* (San Francisco: Crime and Justice Associates, 1982); Sally Engle Merry, *Urban Danger: Life in a Neighborhood of Strangers* (Philadelphia: Temple University Press, 1981); James Brady, "Towards A Popular Justice in the U.S.: The Dialectics of Community Action," *Contemporary Crises*, 5(1981), 155; Elliott Currie, "Fighting Crime," *Working Papers* (July/August 1982), 16; Frank Browning, "Nobody's Soft on Crime Anymore: Rethinking America's Impossible Problem," *Mother Jones* (August 1982), 26; Bernard A. Headley, " 'Black on Black' Crime: The Myth and the Reality," *Crime and Social Justice*, (1984), 50; Raymond Michalowski, "Crime Control in the 1980's: A Progressive Agenda," *Crime and Social Justice*, (1983), 24; Robert Elias, "Citizen Participation in Criminal Justice: A Critique," *Citizen Participation*, 3(1982), 6; Herman Schwendinger and Julia Schwendinger, "Defenders of Order or Guardians of Human Rights?" in Ian Taylor, et al. (eds.), *Critical Criminology* (London: Routledge and Kegan Paul, 1975), 113; Larry Tifft, "The Coming Redefinition of Crime," *Social Problems*, 26(1979), 392; Dennis Longmire, "A Popular Justice System: A Radical Alternative to the Traditional Criminal Justice System," *Contemporary Crises*, 5(1981), 15; Michael Castleman, "Crime Free," *Social Policy* (Spring 1984), 4; William Kornblum and Vernon Boggs, "New Alternatives for Fighting Crime," *Social Policy* (Winter 1984), 24; Roman Tomasic and Malcolm Feeley (eds.), *Neighborhood Justice* (New York: Longman, 1982); Ziegenhagen, note 1 *supra*; Charles Silberman, *Criminal Violence, Criminal Justice* (New York: Vintage, 1978), 575; Scheingold, note 8 *supra*, 205; Fred DuBow and David Emmons, "The Community Hypothesis," in Dan A. Lewis (ed.), *Reactions to Crime* (Beverly Hills,

Calif.: Sage, 1981), 167; Jeffrey A. Reiman, *The Rich Get Richer and the Poor Get Prison* (New York: John Wiley, 1979); Nils Christie, "Conflicts as Property," *British Journal of Criminology*, 17(1978), 1; David F. Greenberg (ed.), *Crime and Capitalism* (Palo Alto, Calif.: Mayfield, 1981); David Friedrichs, "Crime, Deviance and Criminal Justice: In Search of a Radical Humanist Perspective," *Humanity and Society*, 6(1982), 200; Larry Tifft and Dennis Sullivan, *The Struggle to Be Human: Crime, Criminology and Anarchism* (Orkney: Cienfuegos Press, 1980); Michael Yeager, "Community Redress Against Corporate Offenders," *Crime and Social Justice* (1984), 223; Gary T. Marx and Dane Arthur, "Community Self-Defense," *Society*, 13(March 1976), 38; Luis Salas, "The Role of the Judicial System and Law" in Luis Salas, *Social Control and Deviance in Cuba* (New York: Praeger, 1979); Werner Einstadter, "Citizen Patrols: Prevention or Control?" *Crime and Social Justice* (1984), 200; James P. Brady, "A Season of Startling Alliance: Chinese Law and Justice in the New Order," *International Journal of the Sociology of Law*, 9(1981), 41; Tony Platt and Paul Takagi (eds.), *Crime and Social Justice* (Totowa, NJ: Barnes and Noble, 1981); Laura Nader (ed.), *No Access to Law: Alternatives to the American Judicial System* (New York: Academic Press, 1980); Jack Spence, *Search for Justice: Neighborhood Courts in Allende's Chile* (Boulder, Colo.: Westview Press, 1979); Robert Elias, "Progressive and Crime," *Social Policy* (Winter 1983), 37.

20.   See, for example, Martin Carnoy and Derek Shearer, *Economic Democracy* (Armonk, N.Y.: M.E. Sharpe, 1980); Michael Harrington, *Decade of Decision* (New York: Simon and Schuster, 1980); David Morris, *Self-Reliant Cities* (San Francisco: Sierra Club, 1980); David Morris and Karl Hess, *Neighborhood Power* (Boston: Beacon Press, 1975); Barry Bluestone and Bennett Harrison, *The Deindustrialization of America* (New York: McGraw-Hill, 1982); Mark Green, *Winning Back America* (New York: Bantam, 1982); Martin Carnoy, Derek Shearer, and Russell Rumberger, *The New Social Contract* (New York: Harper and Row, 1983); Gar Alperovitz and Jeff Faux, *Rebuilding America* (New York: Pantheon, 1984); William Ryan, *Equality* (New York: Vintage, 1981); Suzanne Gordon, et al., *Moving Toward A New Society* (Philadelphia: New Society Press, 1976); Samuel Bowles, et al., *Beyond the Wasteland* (New York: Doubleday, 1984); Eric Olin Wright, "Capitalism's Futures," *Socialist Review*, 68(1983), 77.

21.   See, for example, Guy Gran, *Development By People: Citizen Construction of a Just World* (New York: Praeger, 1983); Robert Johansen, *The National Interest and the Human Interest* (Princeton: Princeton University Press, 1980); Richard Falk, *A Study of Future Worlds* (New York: Free Press, 1975); Johan Galtung, *The True Worlds* (New York: Free Press, 1981); Rajni Kothari, *Footsteps into the Future* (New York: Free Press, 1974); Gene Sharp, *Social Power and Political Freedom* (Boston: Porter Sargent, 1980); Christian Bay, *Strategies for Political Emancipation* (Notre Dame, Ind.: University of Notre Dame Press, 1981); Hazel Henderson, *Creating Alternative Futures* (New York: Putnam, 1978); Ervin Laszlo, *A Strategy for the Future* (New York: Braziller, 1974); Saul Mendlovitz (ed.), *On the Creation of a Just World Order* (New York: Free Press, 1975); Erich Fromm, *To Have or To Be?* (New York: Bantam, 1981); Aurelio Peccei, *The Human Quality* (New York: Pergamon, 1977; James Ogilvy, *Many Dimensional Man* (New York: Harper, 1977); Theodore Roszak,

Person/Planet (Garden City, N.Y.: Doubleday, 1979); James B. McGinnis, *Bread and Justice* (New York: Paulist Press, 1979); Richard Sennett, *The Fall of Public Man* (New York: Vintage, 1977); Philip Slater, *Earthwalk* (New York: Bantam, 1978); Cosmas Desmond, *Persecution East and West* (New York: Penguin, 1983); Gerald Mische and Patricia Mische, *Toward A Human World Order* (New York: Paulist Press, 1982); Harry C. Boyte, *The Backyard Movement* (Philadelphia: Temple University Press, 1980); Richard Falk, et al. (eds.), *Toward A Just World Order* (Boulder, Colo.: Westview Press, 1982); Samuel S. Kim, *The Quest for a Just World Order* (Boulder, Colo.: Westview Press, 1984); Warren Wagar, *Building the City of Man* (New York: Grossman, 1971); Chadwick Alger, "The Role of People in the Future Global Order," *Alternatives*, 4(1978), 233; Richard Falk, et al., *International Law and A Just World Order* (Boulder, Colo.: Westview Press, 1985); Richard Falk, et al., *The United Nations and A Just World Order* (Boulder, Colo.: Westview Press, 1985); Institute for Defense and Disarmament Studies, *The Peace Resource Book* (Cambridge: Ballinger Books, 1985).

22. Paul Wachtel, *The Poverty of Affluence* (New York: Free Press, 1983).

23. C. Wright Mills, *Power, Politics and People* (New York: Oxford University Press, 1963).

24. Robert Elias, "Transcending Our Social Reality of Victimization," *Victimology*, 9(1985), 3; Robert Elias, "A 'New' Victimology: The Dialectics of Criminology and Human Rights," unpublished paper, 1984; David Friedrichs, "Crime Victimization: Positive and Problematic Dimensions of the Radical Criminological Perspective," Paper presented at First World Congress on Victimology, Washington, D.C., 1980; David Friedrichs, "Victimology: A Consideration of the Radical Critique," *Crime and Delinquency* (April 1983), 283.

25. Howard Becker, "Whose Side Are We On?" *Social Problems*, 14(1967), 239.

26. Bertold Brecht, *Galileo: A Play* (New York: Grove Press, 1966), 123–124.

27. Bertram Russell, *Political Ideals* (London: Unwin, 1963).

28. For more views of how political science could contribute much more to this endeavor, see Theodore Roszak (ed.), *The Dissenting Academy* (New York: Pantheon, 1969); Marvin Surkin and Alan Wolfe (eds.), *An End to Political Science* (New York: Basic Books, 1970); David Ricci, *The Tragedy of Political Science* (New Haven: Yale University Press, 1984); George Beam and Dick Simpson, *Political Action* (Chicago: Swallow Press, 1984); Philip Green and Sanford Levinson (eds.), *Power and Community: Dissenting Essays in Political Science* (New York: Vintage, 1970); Michael Parenti, "The State of the Discipline: Everyone's Favorite Controversy," *PS* (Spring 1984), 172; Roy Preiswerk, "Could We Study International Relations As If People Mattered?" in Richard Falk, et al. (eds.), *Toward A Just World Order* (Boulder, Colo.: Westview Press, 1982), 175; Ernest Wilson, "Why Political Scientists Don't Study Black Politics, But Historians and Sociologists Do," *PS* (Summer 1985), 600.

Name Index

Subject Index